ARRL's

Even More Wire Antenna Classics

Volume 3

More Than 40 Antenna Designs For Any Application!

Compiled by
Steve Ford, WB8IMY

Production
Jodi Morin, KA1JPA

Cover Design
Sue Fagan, KB1OKW

Published by
ARRL
100 YEARS

Copyright © 2014 by
The American Radio Relay League, Inc.

Copyright secured under the
Pan-American Convention

International Copyright secured

All rights reserved. No part of this work
may be reproduced in any form except
by written permission of the publisher. All
rights of translation are reserved.

Printed in the USA

Quedan reservados todos los derechos

ISBN: 978-1-62595-014-7

First Edition
Second Printing

Foreword

Although amateurs are enchanted by the sight of towers and massive beam antennas, the truth is that most hams use wire antennas for everyday operating. Wire antennas are not only inexpensive, they are relatively easy to build, depending on the design.

In this book you'll find a number of useful wire antenna designs that were published in *QST* magazine over a 11 year span between 2002 and 2013. Among these designs you'll find clever multiband antennas, efficient single band antennas, portable antennas and even "stealth" antennas for those of us who must enjoy our avocation under homeowner restrictions. Each design has been carefully reviewed by the *QST* editorial staff and a number of volunteer engineers. If a design was subsequently corrected or modified after it was published, that change has been incorporated into the article.

For more information about antennas in general, refer to the latest edition of the *ARRL Antenna Book*. You can purchase it online at the ARRL Store at **www.arrl.org/shop**.

David Sumner, K1ZZ
ARRL Chief Executive Officer
February 2014

Contents

Portable

1   **A Near End-Fed Antenna for Low Power 20 Meter Operation**
Herman Birkner, W2FRH

3   **The Quick and Easy Balloon Assisted Low Band Loop Antenna**
Jim DeLoach, WU0I

6   **Zip Cord Antennas and Feed Lines For Portable Applications**
William A. Parmley, KR8L

9   **The Tee Pee V 20 and 40 Meter Antenna**
Robert Giuliano, KB8RCO

12   **A Portable Inverted V Antenna**
Joseph R. Littlepage, WE5Y

Directional

17   **A Four Wire Steerable V Beam for 10 through 40 Meters**
Sam Moore, NX5Z

21   **Inverted V Wire Yagi with Switchable Pattern Rotation for 14 MHz**
Dr Ing Klaus Solbach, DK3BA

Multiband

25   **A Fan Dipole for 80 through 6 Meters**
Richard P. Clem, W0IS

27   **A Pneumatically Switched Multiband Antenna**
Craig Bishop, WB2EPQ

30   **An All Band HF Dipole Antenna**
Jim Weit, KI8BV

35   **A No Compromise Off-Center Fed Dipole for Four Bands**
Rick Littlefield, K1BQT

Multiband (continued)

38   **Six Band Loaded Dipole Antenna**
Albert C. Buxton, W8NX

41   **An All-Band Attic Antenna**
Kai Siwiak, KE4PT

46   **A Wire Antenna Combination for DX**
Tony Estep, KT0NY

49   **The Horizontal Loop — An Effective Multipurpose Antenna**
Scott M. Harwood, Sr, K4VWK

52   **The Horizontal EWE Antenna**
Floyd Koontz, WA2WVL

54   **The Fan Dipole as a Wideband and Multiband Antenna Element**
Joel Hallas, W1ZR

57   **Modernizing the V Antenna**
John S. Raydo, K0IZ

62   **The Classic Multiband Dipole**
Steve Ford, WB8IMY

63   **A 3-Band No Trap Dipole for 40, 15 and 6 Meters**
Charles W. Pearce, K3YWY

65   **The "C Pole" — A Ground Independent Vertical Antenna**
Brian Cake, KF2YN

68   **A 10/17 Meter Hanging Loop Antenna**
Sam F. Kennedy, KT4QW

72   **Designing a Shortened Antenna**
Luiz Duarte Lopes, CT1EOJ

77   **A Dipole Curtain for 15 and 10 Meters**
Mike Loukides, W1JQ

82   **Two Bands from One Dipole**
Marc Tarplee, N4UFP

84   **Build a Parallel-Wire Dipole**
Joe Deaton Jr, N4EWS

86   **A Balanced, Everyday Approach to All-Band Bliss**
Kirk Kleinschmidt, NT0Z

Multiband (continued)

- **90**   **The N4GG Array**
  Hal Kennedy, N4GG

- **95**   **Taming the Trap Dipole**
  Dave Benson, K1SWL

- **98**   **A "One-Masted Sloop" for 40, 20, 15 and 10 Meters**
  Richard C. Rogers, KI8GX

- **101**   **K8SYL's 75 and 10-Meter Dipole**
  Sylvia Hutchinson, K8SYL

- **104**   **Delta Loop Collinear Antennas**
  James K Boomer, W9UJ

- **107**   **Moving Yet Another Band Lower with that HF Loop**
  Dave Robertson, KE5QWP

- **110**   **The Shared Apex Loop Array**
  Mark Bauman, KB7GF

- **115**   **Nested Full Wave Delta Loops for 20 and 10 Meters**
  Don McMinds, K7DM

Single Band

- **119**   **A Simple Broadband 80 Meter Dipole**
  George Prince Jr, N6DNA

- **122**   **Shortened End-Fed Half-Wave Antenna for 80 Meters**
  Michael J. Polia, AB1AW

- **125**   **A Portable Twin-Lead 20-Meter Dipole**
  Rich Wadsworth, KF6QKI

- **127**   **A Horizontal Loop for 80-Meter DX**
  John S. Belrose, VE2CV

- **133**   **A Wideband Dipole for 75 and 80 Meters**
  Ted Armstrong, WA6RNC

- **136**   **160 Meter Inverted Delta Loop**
  C.T. Kluttz Jr, W4TMR

- **138**   **A Quad Loop Revisited**
  Floyd Koontz, WA2WVL

- **140**   **A Suspended Quarter Wave 40 Meter Wire Vertical Monopole**
  Robert Glorioso, W1IS

Stealth (Low Visibility)

143 Surprising Results with a Low, Hidden Wire Antenna
Bruce Pontius, NØADL

148 One Stealthy Delta
Steve Ford, WB8IMY

Resources

A Near End-Fed Antenna for Low Power 20 Meter Operation

This simple antenna may be what you need for your next radio camping expedition.

Herman J. Birkner, W2FRH

On past vacations and camping trips I have had a lot of fun working portable low power (QRP), especially on 20 meter CW. Most of the time I have used the half wave center fed dipole described by Rich Wadsworth, KF6QKI.[1] It is made entirely from 300 Ω TV twinlead, needs no antenna tuner, is easy to backpack and has been very effective. But in some locations it has been hard to find two supports for it, and it seemed not to work as well when used with only one support as a sloper. Because of this, I looked into the possibility of using an end-fed wire that would work well with just one support.

Trial and Error, and Error...

At first I tried a quarter wave wire with an equally long counterpoise but I could seldom get the SWR below 3:1 without using an antenna tuner. A half wave wire can be end fed with an antenna tuner along with an RF ground or a counterpoise, or even with a quarter wave matching section, but each of these solutions required carrying more stuff than I would like. This led to a search of recent articles on the topic and I found some very helpful ideas.

Les Moxon, G6XN, described a way to end feed a wire about

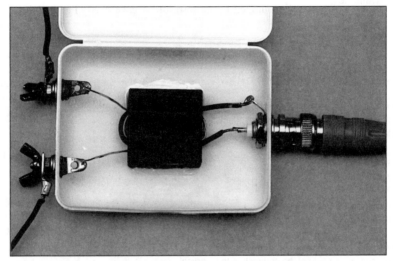

Figure 1 — RF transformer with 4:1 turns ratio on binocular core.

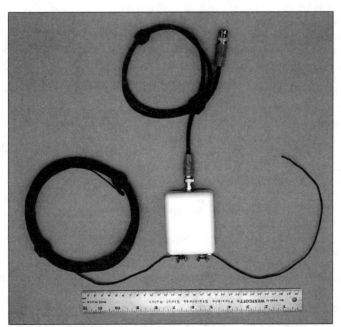

Figure 2 — Complete antenna with RF transformer, 27.5 foot radiator, 1 foot counterpoise and 3 feet of RG-58 feed line.

a half wave long by using a short counterpoise, a loading coil, a series capacitor and a matching transformer.[2] Steve Yates, AA5TB, did the same with a 64:1 RF transformer that had a variable capacitor across the high impedance side, similar to a system proposed by Tom Rauch, W8JI.[3,4] Rauch also devised a version that didn't need a tuner by using a 60:1 transformer and an RF ground. But what I found most attractive is the antenna suggested by Ron Skelton, W6WO.[5] He fed a half wave wire just 10% from one end at which point the impedance was about 800 Ω, matching it to 50 Ω by means of a 16:1 transformer wound on a rather large binocular core. W6WO's idea seemed to be one of the simpler solutions to the end-feed problem, so I thought I might try scaling it down for QRP.

A Solution at Hand

I bought a small binocular ferrite core, an Amidon BN43 7051, wound a primary with one turn of #18 AWG wire and a secondary with four turns of #26 AWG, both plastic coated. It easily fit into a 3.5 × 2.5 × 1 inch plastic box (see Figure 1). With a known resistance connected across the secondary winding, measurements using an MFJ-259B antenna analyzer confirmed a resistance transformation of 16:1 across the 20 meter band. So the transmitter would see about 50 Ω at the

[1]Notes appear on page 2.

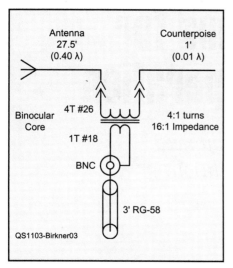

Figure 3 — Schematic diagram of the antenna. The binocular core is available from www.amidoncorp.com.

antenna feed point. Trials with different lengths of antenna wire, counterpoise and feed line revealed several successful combinations.

One that worked especially well was 27.5 feet (0.40 wavelengths) of antenna wire, just 1 foot (0.01 wavelengths) of counterpoise and 3 feet of RG-58/U feed line, as shown in Figures 2 and 3. This arrangement had a relatively flat SWR across the 20 meter band, ranging from 1.1:1 to 1.5:1. This held true with the antenna in a horizontal position, at a 30° slope and as an inverted L, fed from the top or fed from the bottom.

To test the transformer's efficiency I enclosed it in a thermally insulated container with small holes for the leads and feed line. A steady 10 minute application of 5 W of RF at 14.175 MHz caused no rise in its temperature, so losses seemed to be low.

Encouraged by these results I gave it a try in the field, actually my backyard, just several feet above sea level. The antenna was strung as an inverted L and fed from the bottom with the flat top at a height of 12 feet. My first call with 5 W on 20 meter CW raised a W7 at a distance of 2400 miles — not bad for a sunspot null — and the antenna has continued to work very well since then.

There are a number of potential drawbacks to this antenna system. The 16:1 transformer, if wound as described, has an inductive reactance of 25 Ω across the 20 meter band. Theoretically, this could make it difficult to obtain a satisfactory SWR, but this proved not to be the case. It remained less than 1.5:1 from 14.00 to 14.35 MHz.

The coax feed line presents another possible problem. A change in its length also changes the SWR, so if you need a feed line length other than 3 feet it will be necessary to experiment with different lengths of antenna wire and counterpoise, but that is not hard to do. In fact, it proved to be much easier than trying to trim a standard dipole to an optimal length. Also, no attempt has been made to suppress common mode currents. The amount of radiation arising from unbalanced current in this short a feed line is likely to be quite small. [Alternately, a few turns of the coax on an FT-240-43 toroid core should remove the common mode currents. — *Ed.*]

Along with the time-tested KF6QKI dipole, this antenna has proved to be a useful addition to my portable QRP gear. I hope you also find it helpful.

Notes

[1] R. Wadsworth, KF6QKI, "A Portable Twin-lead 20 Meter Dipole," *QST*, Feb 2002, pp 36-37.
[2] L. Moxon, G6XN, "Ground Planes, Radial Systems and Asymmetric Dipoles," *ARRL Antenna Compendium*, Volume 3, pp 19-27.
[3] S. Yates, **www.aa5tb.com**.
[4] T. Rauch, **www.w8ji.com**.
[5] R. Skelton, W6WO, "Exploring Near End-Fed Wire Antennas," *QEX*, Mar/Apr 2009, pp 33-34.

ARRL member Herman J. Birkner, W2FRH, is a retired gastroenterologist and currently serves as a volunteer in his local community medical clinic and as a math and science mentor in his middle school.

He received his Novice call, WN2EIH, in 1951, followed thereafter by W2MNE and then DL4HK during an Army tour. He upgraded to Amateur Extra in 2001.

Herman's major Amateur Radio interests are antennas, homebrew QRP and CW on the satellites, especially VO-52. He also makes some time for sailing and has a commercial pilot certificate. You can reach Herman at 1537 Caribbean Dr, Sarasota, FL 34231 or at **hbirkner@gmail.com**.

Hamspeak

- **300 Ω twin lead** — Type of transmission line used for almost all TV receive antennas before the advent of coaxial cable. Twin lead was a balanced line with two conductors separated by a plastic web of about ½ inch width. Some amateurs used this line for antenna connections.
- **Antenna tuner** — Device that sits between an antenna and a transmission line, or a transmission line and a radio, and transforms the impedance to match the radio or line.
- **Binocular core** — Dual ferrite core structure often used in RF transformers.
- **Counterpoise** — Artificial ground system raised above earth ground and typically used as one side of the connection to a vertical monopole antenna.
- **CW** — Abbreviation for *continuous wave;* another name for *Morse code* telegraphy by radio. Also, International Morse code telegraphy emissions having designators with A, C, H, J or R as the first symbol; 1 as the second symbol; A or B as the third symbol, and emissions J2A and J2B.
- **Dipole** — An antenna often, but not always, center fed with two halves along the same line. Usually refers to an antenna with a length equal to half an electrical wavelength. Often a reference antenna and also used as an element of multielement arrays.
- **Inverted L** — Common name for a ¼ wave vertical monopole antenna with too short a support for the full required height. The antenna is bent to horizontal at the highest point to provide the required length, giving it the appearance of an inverted letter L.
- **Loading coil** — An inductor inserted into an antenna to make it electrically longer.
- **QRP** — Strictly speaking, operating shorthand for "I am sending with low power." In common use, refers to low power, typically under 5 W output, operation viewed as a special challenge by many amateurs.
- **RG-58/U coaxial cable** — Coaxial cable type with typically 50 Ω (some variants at 52 or 53 Ω) characteristic impedance and 0.195 inch outer diameter. Compatible with a PL-259 coaxial plug with the use of a sizing adapter.
- **Sloper** — Common name for a sloping dipole or top fed monopole. The sloping configuration provides some directivity away from the direction of the support.
- **SWR** — Standing wave ratio. Measure of how well a load, such as an antenna, is matched to the design impedance of a transmission line. An SWR of 1:1 indicates a perfect match. Coaxial cables, depending on length, type and frequency, can often work efficiently with an SWR of 3:1, sometimes higher. Solid state transmitters frequently require an SWR of 2:1 or less for proper operation.
- **Toroid core** — Circular donut shaped structure made from metal oxides in a ceramic material. Used as the basis for inductors that have the property that they are self-shielding in that the magnetic fields stay within the core.

The Quick and Easy Balloon Assisted Low Band Loop Antenna

My Field Day club has been flying a balloon lifted 80 meter full wave loop antenna for years, and this year we decided to add a second balloon-lifted antenna for 40 meters.[1] We wanted that same great full wave loop performance to help get our low power (QRP) signal out, but we needed a much easier and quicker deployment. The answer we found is a new type of balloon lifted antenna. We call it the *balloon assisted* antenna.

In a balloon assisted antenna, part of the antenna is lifted with helium, but part of the antenna is suspended between masts or trees in the manner of a conventional dipole. In this design, the loop is arranged as a triangle, with a horizontal leg at the bottom secured to masts or trees, and the apex tip lifted by the balloon. The mast or tree tethers spread the loop, eliminating the need for tricky antenna spreading mechanisms in the balloon lifted portion of the antenna. Since the weight of the transmission line and lower section of the antenna is held by masts, only a single, smaller balloon is necessary. The result is a much simpler to deploy balloon lifted antenna.

[1]Notes appear on page 5.

Try this simple, easy-to-deploy "balloon assisted" full wave loop antenna for your next ARRL Field Day or other contest operation, and enjoy great low band performance!

Jim DeLoach, WU0I

Above — Svend, KF6EMB (left), author Jim, WU0I (center) and Jon, KF6WPR, ex-G0XAS, right, tying balloon to the antenna apex during ARRL Field Day 2008, in the Rancho San Antonio Open Space Preserve, near Los Altos Hills, California.

Loops are the ideal antenna for ARRL Field Day operation on the lower HF bands. They can be horizontally polarized so they receive less noise — an important characteristic on 40 and 80 meters. They also don't need a messy ground plane system. Loops are easy to match and provide a broad, bidirectional pattern. They can perform well on multiple bands if using a balanced antenna tuner and open wire or window transmission line. Since loops are broadband and thus easy to tune, the SWR and radiation pattern of a balloon lifted loop tends to remain consistent as the antenna's shape and orientation shift in the wind.

The main disadvantage of this balloon assisted antenna over my previous design is that the height of the antenna base is limited to the height of the masts or trees available.[2] Fortunately, low loops perform reasonably well. A loop can be a quarter wavelength above the ground at the base, or even less, and still give excellent performance — easily outperforming most other simple antenna types at these heights. A quarter wavelength at 40 meters is only about 33 feet, a height easily achieved at most Field Day sites. A quarter wavelength height at 80 meters (about

66 feet) may be achievable at some locations.

Making it Happen

Just how easy is this antenna to build? Turns out not all that much more difficult than a dipole. In this article, I will show you how to build and deploy a balloon assisted full wave loop antenna so that you too can have a big signal for your next Field Day or other contest operation!

Construction

The balloon assisted full wave loop design is shown in Figure 1. The full wave loop is arranged as an equilateral triangle with the lower horizontal leg made of 14 or 16 gauge wire, and the two side legs made of one unbroken piece of 22 gauge wire. The antenna is fed with window transmission line in the middle of the lower leg to achieve horizontal polarization. The light wire is secured to the heavy wire just after the end insulators, and a single helium balloon lifts the upper section to form the triangle.

The overall length of a full wave loop is given by Circumference (feet) = 1005/Frequency (MHz), with one-sixth of this length in each of the two pieces of heavy wire used for the lower section, and two-thirds of this length in the light wire used for the upper section.[3] Cut three pieces of wire to the lengths shown in Table 1 for the desired operating frequency.[4]

Strip ¾ inches from each end of the heavy wires and lightly tin. Gently fold the light wire in half to identify the apex position, being careful not to kink or bend the wire. Shrink a piece of shrink wrap at this halfway point. This shrink wrap identifies the antenna's apex position. Strip about 1.5 inches from each end of the light wire, fold the stripped portion back on itself once, twist tightly and lightly tin.

Secure each heavy wire to an end insulator, as shown in Figure 2. About 3 inches of heavy wire will be sticking up from each end insulator. Connect these heavy wires to each end of the light wire using one section cut from a double-row terminal block. Secure the other end of each heavy wire to the center insulator, as shown in Figure 3.

Cut about 7 inches of the center insulation away from the end of the window transmission line, leaving the insulation around each conductor intact. Strip about ¾ inches of insulation off each conductor, and tin if the line uses stranded wire. Bend the transmission line around the middle of the center insulator where the center insulation is present, and cable tie the line to the insulator using two medium sized cable ties, as shown in Figure 3. Bend the transmission line conductors and the ends of the heavy wire around toward each other on each side, and secure using a section cut from a double-row terminal block. Your balloon-assisted loop antenna is now complete and ready to launch!

Deployment

The loop launches easily by first attaching the lower tether line to the antenna's apex as shown in Figure 4. Make sure this line will be long enough to reach the ground. Now raise the loop's bottom section as you would any dipole, leaving the top section drooping (toward upwind) and the lower tether line accessible from the ground. Make sure there is no torsion on the ropes that would cause the bottom section to twist.

Prepare the upper tether line as shown in Figure 4, then inflate the balloon. Have one person tightly hold the lip of the balloon over the tank nozzle while a second person carefully holds the tank steady and gently opens the valve. Have a third person judge the size of the balloon and warn the inflator when it is time to stop. We used a 5½ foot balloon and inflated it to about 5 feet, but a 4 foot diameter would have been plenty of

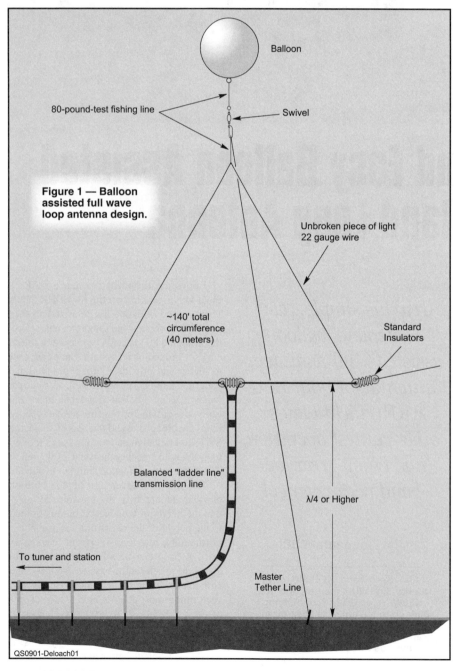

Figure 1 — Balloon assisted full wave loop antenna design.

Table 1

Required Wire Lengths for 40 and 75 Meter Full Wave Loops

Design Frequency (MHz)	7.15	3.75
Overall circumference	140' 7"	268' 0"
Length of heavy pieces of wire (2 needed)*	24' 9"	46' 0"
Length of light piece of wire**	93' 11"	178' 11"

*Includes 8" for the mechanical connection at the end insulator plus 8" for the mechanical connection to the center insulator.
**Includes 1½" for splicing on each end.

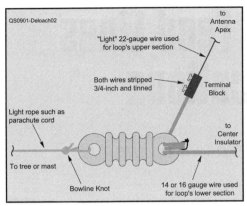

Figure 2 — End insulator detail.

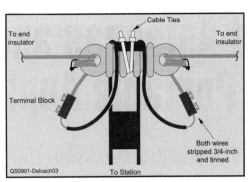

Figure 3 — Center insulator detail.

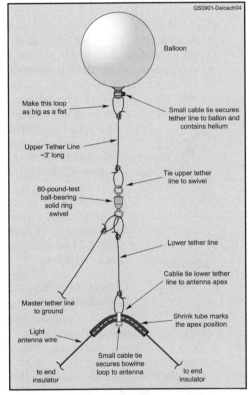

Figure 4 — Balloon tethering system.

lift for a 40 meter loop (for an 80 meter loop inflate to about 5 feet). Secure the balloon to the upper tether line using the technique described in Figure 4 and tie the other end to the swivel. Secure the master tether line to the bottom end of the swivel. Use bowline knots throughout.[5]

When you are ready to launch the balloon, tie the lower tether line to the swivel on the same side as the master tether line. Slowly unreel the master tether line, standing slightly upwind of the loop's bottom section, and allow the balloon to lift the loop's upper section. Make sure the upper section wire is not tangled on debris and is not kinked or tangled as it rises. Once the antenna is fully raised and a triangle has formed, leave a little slack in the master tether line and tie it to a solid object slightly upwind of the antenna.

That's it. Your balloon assisted loop is ready! We found at our last Field Day that the balloon assisted antenna went up much more quickly than our 80 meter, full wave loop, primarily because spreading the 80 meter loop's diamond is time consuming.

Figure 5 shows an intriguing alternative tethering arrangement for this antenna. Since the balloon is easily raised and lowered, the antenna's apex could be tethered to a tree or mast during the day for a cloud warmer (near vertical incidence skywave or NVIS) configuration optimal for local and regional coverage, then the balloon could be tied on and lifted at night for optimum long range coverage.

Performance

While working 40 meter CW, if I called them, they came back the first time. That's what we need in our antennas for our QRP Field Day station — an antenna that helps make up for our power disadvantage in heavy interference (QRM). Jon, W6PI (ex-G4OSX), reported that "The loop had the performance to overcome the limitations of QRP. On phone I could work what I could hear, and the broad tuning made it easy to operate."

This antenna performed better then any conventional wire 40 meter antenna we have ever deployed, and operating with it was just plain fun! So try this simple, easy-to-deploy balloon assisted, full wave loop antenna for your next ARRL Field Day, and experience for yourself what it's like to have a big low-band signal!

Notes
[1]The ESL Amateur Radio Club of Sunnyvale California and the West Valley Amateur Radio Association of San Jose.
[2]J. DeLoach, WU0I, "Balloon-Lifted Full-Wave Loop Antennas," *QST*, Jul 2007, pp 31 34. See this article for additional details about FAA regulations, balloon inflation, tethering systems, balanced transmission line distribution and static build-up.
[3]R.D. Straw, Editor, *The ARRL Antenna Book*, ARRL, 21st Edition. Available from your ARRL dealer or the ARRL Bookstore, ARRL order no. 9876. Telephone 860-594-0355 or toll-free in the US 888-277-5289; **www.arrl.org/shop/**; **pubsales@arrl.org**.
[4]The author's balloon Web site, **www.deloach.net/balloons**, provides a spreadsheet for calculating wire dimensions, gives balloon safety tips, lists sources for materials and provides references to additional balloon antenna Web sites.
[5]See R. Collins, WX3A, "The Knots of Ham Radio," *QST*, Jun 2006, pp 57-58, or **www.tollesburysc.co.uk/Knots/Bowline.htm** for an illustrated example of the bowline knot.

Jim DeLoach, WU0I, formerly HB9BSV, EI2VHD, EL2GA and VK6WUI, was first licensed in 1976 and is an ARRL member. He is a Principal Engineering Manager with Qualcomm Inc, working on GPS and other location technologies for wireless devices. Jim loves to construct high-performance temporary contest stations, including balloon lifted antennas, with his friends from his local ham club. Jim lives in Los Altos, California, and can be reached at **jim@deloach.net**.

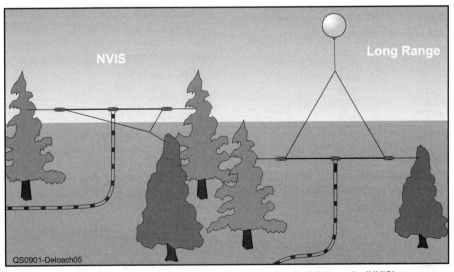

Figure 5 — Alternative tethering arrangements to provide for high angle (NVIS) coverage.

Zip Cord Antennas and Feed Lines For Portable Applications

Don't let lack of real transmission line keep you off the air!

William A. Parmley, KR8L

Because of my interest in portable low power operation on the HF bands (often referred to as *HFpacking*), I decided to look into the possibility of constructing lightweight, portable antennas and feed lines using commonly available "zip cord."[1] This is a subject that was explored previously in a *QST* article that questioned the usefulness of zip cord as a feed line for the higher HF bands.[2]

Although my results are in general agreement with the earlier tests, I believe I can show that with the proper selection of material and careful deployment, feed line losses can be minimized on the higher HF bands, making zip cord dipole and feed line combinations satisfactory performers. This is especially true for portable, low-power operations in which some compromise may be acceptable in the interest of saving weight and bulk. Other potential uses for this type of antenna and feed line combination might include ARRL Field Day or a "stealth" situation in which the operator needed an easily stowed antenna that could be erected quickly whenever she wanted to operate. Of course, this would also make an ideal addition to an emergency operations *Go Kit*.

My plan was to use zip cord as a half-wavelength feed line so that the dipole's impedance would be repeated at the transmitter end of the feed line. The impedance terminating a feed line is repeated every half wavelength. Please see any edition of *The ARRL Antenna Book* for more discussion.[3] Because of this, the characteristic impedance of the feed line would be of secondary importance. Also, because the resulting feed line would be relatively short, losses would be minimized. This meant that I would not be able to erect the dipole at "optimum" height, but since the goal of this project was to create light weight, compact, pocket sized antennas and feed lines that could be used in the field with temporary supports, antenna height was not a primary consideration.

After testing a couple of different samples I settled on RadioShack No. 278-1385, #22 speaker wire as a likely candidate. This wire is sold in 100 foot rolls and has a clear insulating jacket. All electrical property measurements were made using an Autek Research Model VA1 Vector RX Antenna Analyst. Formulas and physical property information were taken from *The ARRL Antenna Book*, *The ARRL Electronics Data Book*[4] and the *VA1 Instruction Manual*. I made an effort to characterize the wire as completely as possible, as discussed below.

Characteristic Impedance

This is a property that I could not measure directly with the VA1, although I was able to make some calculations and educated guesses.

To begin I measured the center-to-center distance (S) between the conductors of RadioShack No. 278-1385 speaker wire as 0.082 inches, and found the conductor diameter (d) of #22 wire listed in *The ARRL Electronics Data Book* as 0.0253 inch. For parallel conductors with air dielectric the characteristic impedance is given by:

$$Z = 276 \times \log(2S/d)$$

or

$$Z = 276 \times \log(2 \times 0.082 / 0.0253) = 224 \ \Omega$$

Again, this is for an air dielectric. The plastic insulation on the wire should reduce the characteristic impedance by some amount, and although I didn't have a way to measure this effect I did come up with a way to estimate it. Here's where the "educated guess" part comes in.

First I did a similar calculation for nominal 300 Ω twin lead, yielding a result of about 400 Ω, meaning that the polyethylene insulation must reduce the calculated

Table 1
Measured Velocity Factor

Frequency (MHz)	Velocity Factor (VF)
3.31	0.68
6.75	0.69
13.67	0.70
27.77	0.71

Table 2
Calculated Attenuation of Zip Cord Compared to Small Coax, dB/100 feet

Frequency (MHz)	RS 278-1385	RG-174	RG-58
3.31	0.97	2.7	0.8
6.75	1.48	3.3	1.2
13.67	2.39	4.0	1.6
27.77	3.41	5.3	2.4

[1]Notes appear on page 8.

value by a factor of about 0.75. *The ARRL Antenna Book* says that for an insulated line, the characteristic impedance can be calculated by multiplying the "in air" value by the inverse square root of the dielectric constant for the particular insulation being used. For polyethylene the dielectric constant is 2.3, so the adjustment factor should be about 0.65. However, with typical 300 Ω line the insulator is very thin so that the field between the conductors is only partially in the insulation and partially in air. It seemed reasonable that the adjustment factor (0.75 in this case) would fall somewhere between pure insulation (0.65) and pure air (1.0).

The type of insulation used on the RadioShack speaker wire isn't specified, but I made the assumption that it is polyethylene or a similar material (this seemed safe since many plastics have a similar dielectric constant of about 2.3). In addition, since the insulation between the conductors of the speaker wire is thicker (perpendicular to the plane containing the two wires) than the insulation for 300 Ω twin lead, it seemed reasonable that it must have a greater influence on the characteristic impedance since more of the field between the conductors will pass through the insulation and less through the air. Based on all of this I assumed that the adjustment factor for the characteristic impedance would probably be closer to 0.65 than to 0.75, so the characteristic impedance for this line might be:

Z = 224 × 0.65 = 145.6, or about 150 Ω.

Again, this value is not particularly important, but keep it in mind and we will use it later to estimate line loss.

Velocity Factor

The velocity factor (VF) of the line was measured using the VA1. The technique involves shorting the end of the line, then sweeping the instrument over a range of frequencies to find the lowest impedance at several points. The lowest frequency will be the frequency at which the line is a half wavelength, the next will be two half wavelengths, etc. The velocity factor can then be calculated by the ratio of the physical line length to the value of a half wavelength in vacuum at the particular frequency (given by the formula L = 492/f, where L is in feet and f is in MHz). The results for my roll of No. 278-1385 speaker wire near four amateur bands are shown in Table 1.

Since I planned to build my antennas mostly for the 20 meter band and above, I chose to use 0.70 as the velocity factor of this line. (I could just as well have said that I picked 0.70 because it is a round number or because it is approximately the average of the four readings. I think these results are

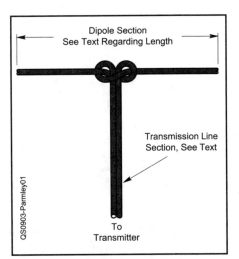

Figure 1 — The center of the antenna section can be secured with an electrician's (or underwriter's) knot as shown.

amazingly consistent considering the use of a consumer grade handheld instrument. There is only a 4% variation in measured velocity factor over a frequency range of about an order of magnitude.)

Attenuation

The attenuation or line loss was also measured using the VA1. For this calculation the series of minimum impedance measurements taken during the frequency sweep (see Velocity Factor, above) were applied to the following formula from the *VA1 Instruction Manual*:

Loss = 8.69 × Z_{MIN}/Z_0, where Z_0 is the characteristic impedance of the line.

The calculated loss is given in Table 2. Values for RG-174 and RG-58 (as read from the log-log graph in *The ARRL Antenna Book*) are listed for comparison.

Now, let's think again about how I planned to use this feed line (a single half wavelength between transceiver and antenna). As the frequency increases so does the loss, but the length of a half wavelength of feed line decreases. As a result, the feed line loss remains less than 1 dB as we go up in frequency. In fact, the loss of a half wavelength line decreases from about 1 dB at 80 meters to about 0.5 dB at 10 meters.

If the estimate of a 150 Ω characteristic impedance is correct, then the SWR on the line will be about 3:1, which introduces at most an additional 0.7 dB of loss (as read from the graph of mismatched line loss in *The ARRL Antenna Book*). Total feed line loss would then be about 1.5 dB, and certainly less than 2 dB. As you can see from the table, the line is slightly more lossy than RG-58. It is closer in size and flexibility to RG-174 and is much less susceptible to damage from bending and rough handling than is coaxial cable, an important consideration given the intended use. It might be reasonable to make the feed line a full wavelength long on the higher bands in order to increase the antenna height. Whether the increase in height would offset the increase in feed line loss probably depends on the individual installation.

Construction

Having characterized the wire as completely as possible I next wanted to check my calculations by building and testing some examples. First I calculated the antenna length using the formula L_A = 234/f and then calculated the feed line length using the formula L_F = (VF) × 492/f. I used the quarter wavelength formula for the dipole since the wire was going to be "unzipped" to form the two halves of the antenna and applied the standard 5% reduction in length for "end effects." I used the half wavelength formula for the feed line multiplied by the measured velocity factor. A single piece of speaker wire of length L = L_F + L_A + X was then cut, where X had a couple of feet added to the length for margin of error. The feed line length (L_F) was measured and marked, and the remainder of the wire, including the extra length, was unzipped to make the dipole section. An electricians' knot (see Figure 1) was tied at the junction of the dipole and the feed line.

At the transmitter end of the feed line I unzipped the wire a couple of inches and attached a banana plug to one side and an alligator clip to the other. The banana plug fits perfectly in the center conductor of a transceiver's SO-239 coax connector, while the alligator clip makes a convenient way to attach to the transceiver's ground connection (as shown in Figure 2). I completely ignored the issue of feeding a balanced load with an unbalanced source here, but if you think about it, this is not an uncommon practice for simple wire antennas, and hams have been doing this kind of thing for ages. We're just more accustomed to seeing this where the feed line (coax) meets the antenna (dipole) than where the transceiver meets the feed line. For low power (QRP) applications I have not found this arrangement to be a problem. For those who are concerned about this, a few turns of the transceiver end of the feed line can be wound through an appropriate toroidal core to make a 1:1 transmission line transformer. I did test the transformer configuration briefly and found no difference in performance, feed point impedance or SWR.

For the initial setup of the dipole I measured and marked the calculated antenna length on each leg and folded the wire back on itself at this point and taped it in place. Later I found that a spring compression cord

Figure 2 — Rear of radio showing banana plug and clip lead connections.

Figure 3 — Self contained station using a zip cord antenna and feed line.

stop of the type found on drawstrings on jackets and other items of clothing worked much better than tape, especially when the length of the dipole legs needed to be adjusted. These should be available in most fabric stores. In addition to shortening the dipole while leaving the option of lengthening it without subsequent splicing and soldering, I found that this technique created a convenient attachment loop at the end of the wire. Finally, I tied a piece of light nylon line to the loop on each end of the dipole (no other insulator was used) and proceeded with deployment and testing.

Deployment and Testing

After building antennas and feed lines for 30, 20 and 17 meters, the initial testing was done by installing the antennas in an inverted V configuration with the apex at about 20 feet. This was done using either a telescoping fishing pole, or by tossing a line over a tree branch and pulling the dipole up with that. The ends of the dipole were brought down to 6 to 8 feet off the ground and tied off with nylon line that was then tied to tent stakes. The dipole was pruned to resonance using the VA1 by changing the fold point at the end. The extra wire was left in place and was not trimmed off. The 20 meter and 17 meter antennas were also tested as indoor dipoles by attaching the apex to a ceiling lamp and taping the ends to the walls with masking tape. In this configuration they were easily tuned to resonance.

In practice I found that once the antenna was tuned to resonance it was possible to adjust and optimize the feed point impedance by changing both the horizontal and vertical angles between the two legs. In my particular outdoor installation the best match was found with the dipole legs arranged at a horizontal (azimuthal) angle of between 90 and 120°. For indoor applications the feed point impedance was found to be adjustable by changing the amount of droop in the legs, proximity to walls or floors, and the angle between the legs. As should always be done with parallel wire feeders, I made an effort to keep the feed line clear of other objects and equidistant from both legs of the dipole to the maximum extent practicable.

Conclusion

I have used these antennas and feed lines for SSB, CW and PSK31 at QRP power levels in indoor, backyard and backpack portable situations. Figure 3 shows a self contained portable station. Portability is excellent, deployment is simple and on-air performance seems to be very good. As noted in the original article by K1TD, some zip cord may be significantly more lossy than the type that I used, so it is important to make measurements before committing to a particular type. (One sample I tested, an example of #24 speaker wire, was at least as lossy as the wire that Jerry used.) If you want to try building your own zip cord antennas and feed lines I suggest spending some time with *The ARRL Antenna Book*, particularly the chapters on transmission lines and Smith charts. This will enhance not only your understanding but also your enjoyment of this project.

Notes
[1] Information about HFpacking is available on the Internet at **hfpack.com**.
[2] J. Hall, K1TD, "Zip Cord Antennas — Do They Work?" *QST*, Mar 1979, pp 31-32. This was reprinted in C. Hutchinson, K8CH, Editor, *More Wire Antenna Classics Volume 2*. Available from your ARRL dealer or the ARRL Bookstore, ARRL order no. 7709. Telephone 860-594-0355, or toll-free in the US 888-277-5289; **www.arrl.org/shop**; **pubsales@arrl.org**.
[3] R. D. Straw, Editor, *The ARRL Antenna Book*, 21st Edition. Available from your ARRL dealer or the ARRL Bookstore, ARRL order no. 9876. Telephone 860-594-0355, or toll-free in the US 888-277-5289; **www.arrl.org/shop**; **pubsales@arrl.org**.
[4] *The ARRL Electronics Data Book* is out of

Photos by the author.

*Bill Parmley, KR8L, was first licensed in high school, then dropped out of Amateur Radio while in college and the military. He was licensed again in 1979 and upgraded to Amateur Extra in 1981. He is an ARRL member. His interests range from QRP on 160 meters to meteor scatter on 222 MHz and from CW to digital voice. Bill has a Master's degree in physics from Michigan State University. He served as a nuclear submarine officer in the US Navy, and has worked as a nuclear engineer for several electric utilities, and as a safety engineer, project manager and program manager for the US Department of Energy. Bill and his wife Anne, KA8TER, are now retired and enjoy living on the small southern Illinois farm where he grew up. You can read more about his Amateur Radio interests and activities at **kr8l.us**, and you can contact him at 1123 Country Club Rd, Metropolis, IL 62960 or at **kr8l@kr8l.us**.*

The Tee Pee V 20 and 40 Meter Antenna

This simple to prepare and erect dual-band HF antenna is great for Field Day or emergency use.

Robert Giuliano, KB8RCO

The Need

Our local radio group enjoys setting up portable stations for special events and public service outings. Typically, we have no problem locating a couple of trees or other antenna supports. On one occasion, we found ourselves in a field with no available supports. Fortunately we had brought a Mosley ground mounted, trapped vertical and we were on the air as usual. This incident led to a discussion about antennas for portable work. We decided to find a simple, self-supporting, but effective antenna that could be put up about anywhere and be carried easily.

The Idea

During a local hamfest, I saw many telescoping fiberglass poles advertised as antenna supports. An Internet search turned up a 22 foot telescoping pole with a ⅝ inch diameter tip that looked sturdy.[1] A couple of e-mails and phone calls (researching and ordering) later, the 22 foot pole was on its way.

I strapped the pole to a support on my deck, hooked a pulley at the top for swapping antennas during experimenting, strung a dipole as an inverted V, trimmed it to 14.1 MHz and gave it a try. Simple, portable and practical — this pole can do the job.

[1]Notes appear on page 11.

The Tee Pee V concept came from Robert, N8RGF, as he looked up at our inverted V and asked, "Why do we need four guys *and* the dipole wires?" The next comment was something about parallel dipoles with a common feed point and whether that concept would work for two inverted Vs. Can we combine the concepts and get two band operation from one pole using the antenna as the guys?

The Development

To me that sounded like a challenge, and I was determined to check the concept with

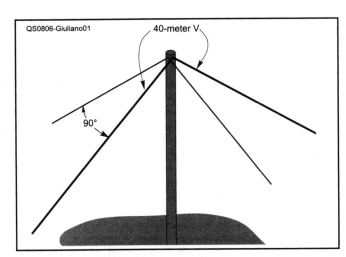

Figure 1 — Isometric view of the antenna configuration.

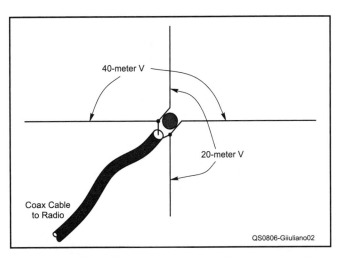

Figure 2 — Details of the feed point connection arrangements.

Table 1

SWR Bandwidth of the Tee Pee V on 40 and 20 Meters

Band (meters)	Frequency Range (MHz)	Maximum SWR
40	7.0- 7.30	1.9:1
20	14.0-14.35	1.4:1

some antenna modeling. The development process would be:

- Rough model to determine if the concept was feasible.
- Build a prototype based on the model results.
- Verify the prototype for match and hopefully put it on the air.

The Modeling

I remembered reading about *EZNEC* as an antenna modeling application.[2] I hoped that *EZNEC* could be used to verify the concept and provide starting dimensions for the antenna. I had heard good things about it and decided to give it a try.

EZNEC was able to provide all that I needed to know about two antenna aspects of the Tee Pee V. I first determined the modeled SWR bandwidth of the antenna made from 16 gauge wire. The results are shown in Table 1. Because the two antennas are perpendicular to each other, the coupling that often causes problems with multiband parallel wire dipoles is minimized, and *EZNEC* predicts that operation on each band is much as a separate inverted V.

An isometric view of the antenna is shown in Figure 1, while the details of the connections are shown in Figure 2. The origin of the name should be clear from the figure. I didn't use a balun at the feed point. If you experience the effects of common mode currents on the outside of the coax (I had none) you may want to add a balun. A choke as simple as half a dozen turns of coax, about 8 inches in diameter, might be all you need.

Real Ground Model

The predicted performance over typical ground is shown in the azimuth patterns for both bands in Figures 3 and 4. As seen, the patterns are just what would be expected of any relatively low inverted V, largely omnidirectional. The other information I wanted from modeling the Tee Pee V was the approximate wire lengths, and of course, some indication that the antenna would work. The wire lengths were needed to determine how much wire and how much rope would be required. It would also provide the "clear area" needed for antenna erection.

Sizing the Antenna

The antenna model determined the element lengths to be approximately 17 feet for 20 meters and 33 feet for 40 meters. The total wire required would thus be about 100 feet. A little geometry was used to keep the angle with respect to the pole at 56.75°.[3] This allows each guy stake to be the same distance from the pole and makes setup easy.

The distance the stakes need to be from the pole was calculated by multiplying the height by the tangent of the included angle (56.75°) and that came out to be about 33.5 feet. The 56.75° angle of each wire to the pole results in the angle between the antenna wires of 113.5°, nicely larger than the design goal for inverted Vs of being greater than 90° according to most dipole documentation I've read.[3]

The Materials

What is needed for the Tee Pee V? I already had the pole, but that is the first item needed. Next was an antenna to coax connector. I used the good old reliable Budwig HQ-1 dipole center insulator (available at radio dealers) because of its light weight and small size. Their HQ-2 end insulators are a good choice to go between the element ends and the support ropes. Any lightweight connection arrangement will do, even direct connection of the wires to the coax.

Next was wire. For my concept proveout, I purchased cheap 16 gauge speaker wire (largest diameter where I shopped) made from stranded copper, one side tinned. Last, I added some antenna rope to extend the additional distance to reach the ground and I was ready to build. Again, geometry was used to determine the exact length at 40.1 feet. Subtract the length of wire and the rest is rope. You will need enough extra rope to tie around the stake and any needed antenna wire trimming.

Build the Prototype

I cut the 50 feet of two conductor wire into a 17 foot section and a 33 ft section. Then, I separated the cord into 2 single wires, one for each leg. The next step was to attach the wire to the center insulator such that the legs are arranged with the proper lengths 180° from each other.

In an effort to make an easy connection to the rope, and with enough wire to trim the antenna for a good match, I measured 1.5 feet from the tip of each wire, slit the wire, bunched it out into a loop with part of the wire on each side, and soldered the wire into a ring. The extra 1.5 feet can be trimmed to get the desired match.

Next was a Saturday morning trip to the field with an MFJ analyzer and the makings for the Tee Pee V. With a helper to hold the pole, I trimmed the 20 meter antenna

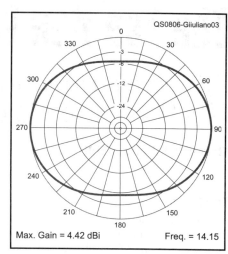

Figure 3 — Azimuth plot of 20 meter Tee Pee V at elevation angle of 35°.

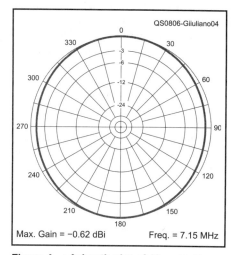

Figure 4 — Azimuth plot of 40 meter Tee Pee V at elevation angle of 35°.

first. I trimmed and trimmed and just before reaching the solder loop, I got the match I was looking for. My guess of 1.5 feet was cutting things too close — only 1.5 inches remained.

Next was the 40 meter section. This time I cut off less than a foot to achieve a good match. Wow, close call, but 50 feet and the 17/33 foot split worked out fine.

On the Air

A couple of checks back and forth between bands with the analyzer and the antenna measured at the predicted flat SWR across both bands. Next I connected my Yaesu FT-100D transceiver to the antenna and gave it a try. I check into a local net on 40 meters and received a good signal report (59) and I confirmed 40 was working.

Now for the 20 meter side. I usually ask the Maritime Mobile Net operator, but the Coast Guard net had just started. I made a quick swing through the band to find a contact and got a 59 report from Georgia.

This made me feel the antenna was usable. No DX, but this is the bottom of the sunspot cycle. The FT-100D without the tuner fed the antenna with 100 W (no roll back in power) and the meter showed low SWR.

The Mosley vertical was also set up, so we checked it against that. Swapping the antennas back and forth, the signals were pretty close. Overall, I'd say the antenna is capable.

Repeatable?

Another Saturday trip to a different spot in the park would determine if everything will stay in tune.

I picked a spot for the pole and stepped off 11 paces (about 33 feet) in each direction where I pounded in a tent stake for each of the support ropes and wires. I tied slip knots around the stakes (adding rope slide stops would make this even easier), and raised the pole. The pole stayed up with the loose guy ropes and I was able to step out to adjust the ropes for a touch more tension to keep everything straight. Wow — this antenna can go up with one person.

Conclusion

The Tee Pee V is a simple dual band antenna that can be setup by a single person and will get you a decent signal on the design bands. Best of all, if you trim it properly, it doesn't need a tuner. I have set up this antenna in many locations now, and it appears to give a good consistent SWR reading in each location.

I hope you build and experiment with the Tee Pee V and I hope it fills a need in your antenna pack. You never know when you will need this type of antenna for field work.

I'd like to thank Robert Laundra, N8RGF, for the inspiration and his direction that resulted in this antenna.

Notes
[1] **www.tmastco.com**.
[2] Several versions of *EZNEC* antenna modeling software are available from developer Roy Lewallen, W7EL, at **www.eznec.com**.
[3] For a discussion and example of using geometry and trigonometry to determine antenna dimensions, see **www.arrl.org/files/qst-binaries**.

Robert Giuliano, KB8RCO, is an engineer for an automotive supplier that tests electrohydraulic brake systems. He was first licensed in January 1994 as a Technician Plus and currently holds an Amateur Extra class license. Robert is a member of the KC8KGA special event radio group, which was the inspiration behind this project and article. You may contact him at 1069 Arboretum Ct, Saline, MI 48176 or at **kb8rco@yahoo.com**.

A Portable Inverted V Antenna

A portable antenna that is great for ARRL Field Day, offers directional control and may be useful where fixed antennas are not allowed.

By Joseph R. Littlepage, WE5Y

If necessity is the mother of invention then restrictive covenants must be the mother of desperate measures. I recently moved into a new neighborhood and found that the covenants made it difficult for me to erect or install any type of ham radio antenna structure. If you are faced with a similar situation or simply have need for a portable antenna that you can erect quickly and easily, this may be what you need.

The problem I faced is common to many living in newer subdivisions and is quite restrictive of Amateur Radio operations. I was determined, however, to find a way to get back on the air. My challenge was to develop a portable antenna system that would be easy and quick to erect and enable me to work a reasonable amount of DX without being obvious to the neighbors. In addition, I needed to determine a low enough power level to avoid TVI and other potential interference that could draw attention to my Amateur Radio activity. QRP and a good antenna proved to be the answer!

The Inverted V

I tried end-fed long wires, difficult-to-support dipoles and finally decided to try an inverted V cut for 17 meters. But how could I support it without a sky hook? That's when I hit upon the idea of using a lightweight telescopic pushup pole for a support mast. To serve as the base support for the pushup mast, I purchased a portable antenna tripod.

Table 1

Wire Half-Element Lengths, Portable Inverted V Antenna

Band (Meters)	Design Frequency (MHz)	Length
20	14.175	16' 6 1/8"
17	18.1	12' 11 1/8"
15	21.175	11' 5/8"
12	24.94	9' 4 5/8"
10	28.4	8' 2 7/8"

I spread the tripod legs to about 40 inches apart and locked them in place. This combination is my sky hook!

The top of the antenna should bring together the feed line and two wire elements angled at least 90° apart. Each of the wire elements is cut for a $1/4\ \lambda$ on the desired band. I chose to try the 17 meter band and cut each element for 18.1 MHz using the formula 234/f, with f the frequency in MHz for each quarter wave as shown in Table 1 for compromise CW and phone operation. You may wish to change the design frequency to suit your operational preferences. Final measurement and trimming was accomplished after the finished antenna was erected on site using an MFJ-259B antenna analyzer.

The next step was to devise a spreader assembly to hold the lower ends of the wire elements apart and keep the spread angle near 90° without resorting to ground anchor points. I wanted to be able to rotate the antenna using the "Armstrong" method to maximize its efficiency in selected directions. The solution was to use two 10 foot lightweight telescoping fiberglass fishing poles held end-to-end. A simple support arm assembly made of two 12 inch lengths of 1/2 inch thin-wall PVC pipe joined to a 3/4 inch PVC X connector. This holds the spreaders in a horizontal position and enables them to ride up and down on the main support mast. The free ends of the wire elements are attached to the eyelets on the outer ends of the two spreader poles that are extended to full length

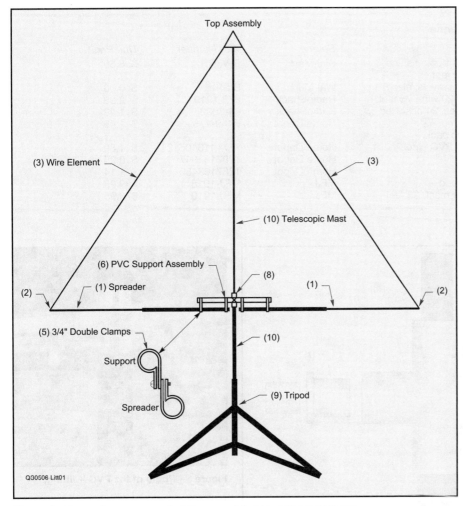

Figure 1—General arrangement of the completed inverted V antenna.

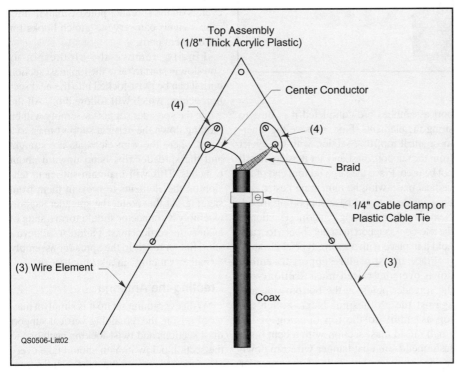

Figure 2—Details of the top assembly.

as shown in Figure 1. Table 2 provides the bill of materials and sources for all the antenna's components.

Top Piece Assembly

A top fitting is required to bring the elements and transmission line together and to fix them to the top of the support. I constructed this assembly using a triangular piece of $1/8$ inch thick clear acrylic plastic or similar dielectric material. Its dimensions are not critical. Drill holes to accommodate a top hanger, two solder lugs, a nylon cable clamp for holding the coax and a hole in each lower corner to support the antenna wire. Neither the construction method nor the dimensions are critical.

Solder one end of an element wire and the center conductor of the coax to one solder lug and secure that to the top piece. Route the free end of that element half down through the lower hole on its side of the top piece. Solder the other element wire and the coax braid to the other solder lug and secure to the top piece in a like manner. Route that element half's free end through the other lower hole. Secure the coax to the top piece using a small nylon cable clamp as a strain relief. A small cable tie can be used instead if you carefully drill a hole on either side of the coax to route it through. The details are shown in Figures 2 and 3.

Spreader Support Assembly

A $3/4$ inch PVC X connector with $3/4$ to $1/2$ inch bushings pressed into opposite side holes is used to hold the two 12 inch long support arms as shown in Figures 4 and 5. The support arms are cut from thin wall $1/2$ inch PVC pipe, used in preference to regular schedule 40 pipe to reduce weight.

Figure 3—Photo of the top assembly.

Table 2
Materials List for Portable Inverted V Antenna

Item	Quantity	Description	Source	Part Number	Unit Price
1	2	B'n'M Black Widow crappie fishing pole, 3 sections, 10 feet.	Wal-Mart	BW3RR	$ 8.50
2	Package	Black interlock snap swivels, size 5.	Wal-Mart	BISS-5	$ 0.50
3	Roll	Insulated stranded #20 wire, 75 feet.	RadioShack	278-1219	$ 2.99
4	Pack	Crimp-on ring tongues, 24 assorted.	RadioShack	64-3030	$ 1.49
5	Pack	One-hole plastic clamp, 3/4" PP-1575UVB, six in pack.	Home Depot	E449-176	$ 1.49
6	10 feet	Silver line (thin wall) PVC pipe, 1/2"	Home Depot	717141340512	$ 1.80
7	2	PVC bushings, 3/4" × 1/2"	Home Depot	1287162647	$ 0.25
8	1	PVC "X" fitting, 3/4"	Home Depot	1287162483	$ 1.14
9	1	Portable antenna tripod.	MFJ	MFJ-1918	$39.95
10	1	Telescoping antenna mast, 33 feet.	MFJ	MFJ-1910	$79.95

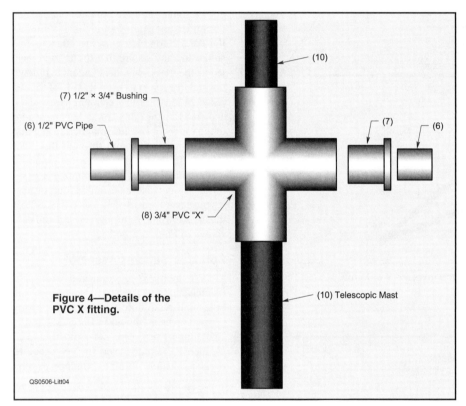

Figure 4—Details of the PVC X fitting.

Figure 5—Photo of the PVC X fitting.

Press the bushings into opposite holes of the X piece until they are firmly seated. Then firmly press a 12 inch support arm into each bushing. Cement all joints using PVC cement. The two remaining holes will allow the spreader assembly to ride up and down the vertical mast. A slight raised lip molded inside these holes should be dressed down flush with the inside surface using a round file. To each support arm install two sets of back-to-back cable clamps. One end of each set is firmly attached around the support arm and the other end of each set around a fishing pole spreader. The outer clamp sets should be placed very near the end of each 12 inch PVC support arm, as detailed in Figure 6.

Stringing the Elements

When the top piece and the spreader support assemblies are completed it is time to string the elements. First, remove the innermost small top mast section with the eyelet from the support mast and set it aside. It will not be used. Place the large bottom end of the vertical mast, with the remaining nested sections inside, into the base supporting tripod. Next, raise the remaining centermost section of the telescopic support mast out about a foot and hold it in place with a spring-type clothespin.

Place the spreader support assembly down over the raised mast section with the spreader poles on the bottom side and against the clothespin. Next, attach the top assembly to the top opening of the small raised mast section with a bent hook fashioned from coat hanger wire run down inside the mast. The ends of the spreader poles can now be fully extended and twist locked in position. The free end of each wire element is then attached to the tip end eyelets on the spreader poles. Small fishing snap swivels can serve as attach hooks for the element ends.

Finally, remove the clothespin as you slowly start to raise the top mast section until it can be twist-locked into the next section below, which will follow it up. All the while the spreader support assembly will be moving down the vertical support mast to a point where the wire elements are straight and the spreader tips bend upward about 6 inches. This will maintain sufficient tension on the elements to prevent them from sagging. At this point, the spreader support assembly X connector should form a snug fit against the vertical mast. Failure to achieve a snug fit can result in the spreader assembly "weather vaneing" in a strong breeze.

Erecting the Antenna

With everything set up it is simply a matter of raising the remaining vertical support mast sections and twist-locking each one to the section below it. You should take every precaution to prevent the mast sections from loosening and falling back down. This can

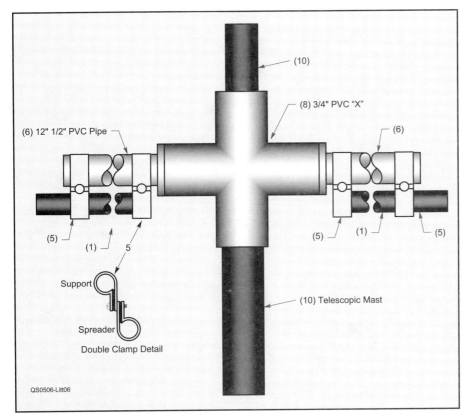

Figure 6—Details of the spreader attachment method.

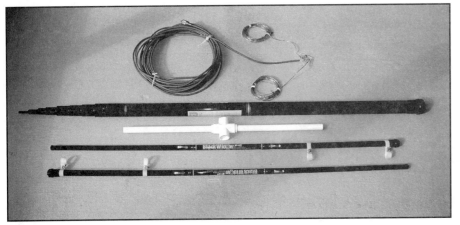

Figure 7—The completed antenna broken down for storage or travel.

of the QSOs were with pedestrian mobile stations.

The real test came a few weeks later when I worked ON6WA in Belgium and GI3DZE in Ireland using the same setup and power. I have received many good signal reports from the stations I have worked. When not in use, the antenna system can be broken down for storage or transport as shown in Figure 7.

For the 20 meter phone band, you can simply substitute a 1 inch PVC X connector with 1 inch to $1/2$ inch bushings and assemble the support arms as described above. This modification allows the entire spreader assembly to ride farther down the vertical support mast and thereby maintain the spreader tension on the longer 20 meter wire elements. As an alternative, you can add a 3 foot 6 inch long drop-down extension wire to the lower end of each 17 meter element and retune the antenna accordingly. Placing a small fishing weight on the free end of each extension wire will help to keep it vertical. For the 10, 12 and 15 meter bands the wire elements will be shorter than the 17 meter wire that I cut. To compensate for this, simply add a length of monofilament fishing line to each element to enable it to reach the spreader ends. This will ensure that the 90° element spread is maintained as well as tension on the wire elements.

Conclusion

The result is a strong, lightweight, rotatable portable antenna system that can be easily constructed of inexpensive and readily available materials. In addition, you can elevate the apex of the V to any convenient height to clear an obstruction such as the edge of a roof or lower it to avoid neighborhood scrutiny. This antenna project has gotten me back on the air and could be the answer to some of your problems. The prospects for ARRL Field Day, emergency operations or backpacking to some remote site are limited only by your imagination.

*Joe Littlepage, WE5Y, was first licensed in 1969 as WB5AAI. He upgraded to Advanced Class in 1975 and more recently to Amateur Extra in 2002. He holds a degree in physics and is retired from the USAF. Joe is an active member of the Mississippi Coast Amateur Radio Association (MCARA) and serves as editor of the club newsletter. He enjoys QRP, kit building, homebrewing, building wire antennas and solar power experimentation. Joe can be reached at **jlextra@netzero.net**.*

result in fracturing the lower ends of the sections as they hit the bottom of the support tripod tube. Although the fiberglass sections are strong, they are thin and very brittle and will chip or crack when overstressed. Simply placing a couple of inches of cushioning material inside the bottom end of the tripod tube will prevent damage. The coax cable can be attached to the mast as it goes up. The final height depends on how many sections your support mast has. The pushup pole that I use has 11 sections. I use all but the smallest top section (with the small eyelet tip) since it is too weak to support the antenna assembly without bending over.

Results

My first contacts were on 17 meter SSB running 5 W with an ICOM IC-703 powered by a 33 Ah gel-cell battery. A Connecticut station gave me a Q5 report during our 25 minute QSO. Two days later I worked Costa Rica, Guatemala, Colorado, New Mexico and Wisconsin with the same setup. Two

A Four Wire Steerable V Beam for 10 through 40 Meters

Sam Moore, NX5Z

This simple to build system provides bidirectional gain switchable between four azimuths.

Ever wished you could work multiple bands and have antenna gain in different directions without the bother, upkeep and expense of a rotator and Yagi? Tired of expensive ice storm damage? Here's one answer.

Enter the V Beam

A simple arrangement of four wires can be used to accomplish this task. A version of this antenna was described in *QST* and is included in *ARRL's Wire Antenna Classics*.[1,2] That version had wires 584 feet long. In this version, each wire is only 106 feet long. Many DX stations have had great success with this type of antenna.

An unterminated V beam gain pattern is bidirectional with two main gain lobes 180° apart if the leg lengths are at least a wavelength long. In Figure 1, a long wire antenna at the left is shown to have a gain pattern of four major lobes. Another long wire antenna positioned 45° from the first is also shown. If these are combined to form a V, it has the gain pattern as shown to the right in Figure 1.

In this design, four 106 foot wires are spaced at 45°. The length of the wire is not as important as that they all be the same length. I installed my V beam with the apex and relay control box at a height of 40 feet with the wire ends 10 feet off the ground in a sloping V configuration. This V beam's gain approximates that of a three element Yagi on 10, 12, 15 and 17 meters and is within a few dB on 20 meters. The antenna provides useful operation on 30 and 40 meters, with essentially an omnidirectional pattern on 40. The beam direction is controlled by simply switching two switches in the station.

Make It Fit Your Space

This antenna may also be built with wire lengths as short as 60 feet to more easily fit on a city lot. There will be a small decrease in gain. The V beam gain increases with the length of the wires. The longer the wires, the greater the gain. As the wire lengthens, however, the beamwidth narrows. The gains and beamwidths of 106 and 60 foot versions are shown in Table 1, based on *EZNEC* analysis.[3] As a reference, the typical two element Yagi has 6 to 7 dBi gain while a three element Yagi can be expected to have a 7.5 to 8.1 dBi gain, depending on design, especially boom length.

The azimuth pattern looking down on a V beam is shown in Figure 2. If the height of the V beam is less than ½ wavelength, the gain pattern will distort and make the antenna more omnidirectional.

To reduce the gain lobe to the rear of the V beam you can terminate the wire ends with

[1]Notes appear on page 20.

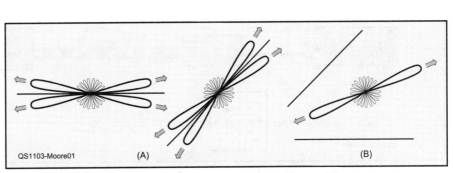

Figure 1 — The azimuth patterns of two long wire antennas are shown at (A). If the two are combined in phase to form a V, the resulting pattern is shown at (B).

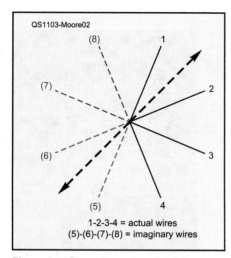

Figure 2 — The selectable azimuth looking down on the V beam. The arrow shows directions of maximum radiation with wires 1 and 2 connected.

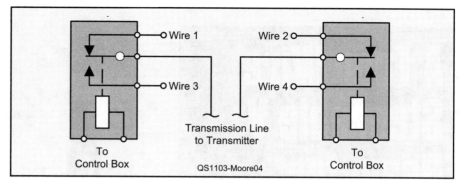

Figure 4 — Schematic diagram of the relay box used to remotely select the V beam wires.

a resistor. I opted to leave mine unterminated so I'd have gain in both directions. If terminated, the antenna would need eight wires instead of four to have gain in all directions.

Since this antenna may be used for multiband operation, the gain waveform changes somewhat depending on the frequency of operation. The higher the frequency, the greater the gain, since the frequency to wire length ratio changes. For example, if your V beam is 1 wavelength long at 20 meters, it is 2 wavelengths long at 10 meters, thus causing greater gain and narrower beamwidth as shown in Table 1. While essentially bidirectional on the upper bands, there is a 1 to 2 dB front to back ratio, with the maximum signal to the open end of the V. The beamwidth shown in Table 1 is of the front beam, with the rear beam generally somewhat narrower. A horizontal, rather than sloping, V beam will be more symmetrical.

The block diagram of the V beam system is shown in Figure 3. The antenna tuner must be able to accept balanced transmission line and a built in or external 4:1 balun is necessary. I made a homebrew air core external 4:1 balun using 1 inch PVC pipe and used a small automatic antenna tuner.

Controls and Indicators

The LED switch box supplies power to the relays in the antenna relay box at the center of the V beam via a three wire cable. I used three wire electrical zip cord for mine, but smaller wires would have worked.

The relay box schematic is shown in Figure 4. Only two switches are needed to power relays 1 and 2. Relay 1 switches between wire 1 and 3 and relay 2 switches between wire 2 and 4. Note that wire 4 is used in combination with wire 1 instead of (imaginary) wire 5. This obtuse angle yields the about same gain and waveform as wire 4 to 5 would have offered, without having to string another wire. Figure 5 shows an assembled relay box in a power entry PVC cover.

The schematic in Figure 6 shows the relay power switches and the 17 LED connections. LED and relay common connections go to a 12 V return. A top view of the LEDs is shown in Figure 7. The LED switch box illuminated LEDs indicate the direction of greatest gain. Note LED 1 is always on,

Table 1

Gain and Beamwidth of the V Beam on Each Band

Frequency (MHz)	Gain (dBi) at 106'	3 dB Beamwidth (°) at 106'	Gain (dBi) at 60'	3 dB Beamwidth (°) at 60'
7.15	1.9*	Omnidirectional	2.4*	Omnidirectional
10.12	3.6	133	3.7*	Omnidirectional
14.15	6.7	71	4.1	137
18.11	8.5	42	4.1	136
21.2	9.1	33	6.0	63
24.93	9.7	28	6.1	61
28.3	10.7	23	7.3	40

*Essentially omnidirectional with maximum gain nearly perpendicular to the wire bisector.

Figure 3 — The block diagram of the V beam system. The antenna tuner must be able to accept balanced transmission line and a built-in or external 4:1 balun is necessary.

Figure 5 — Relay box assembled in a power entry PVC cover.

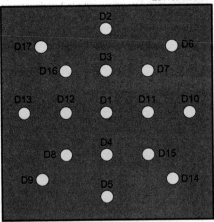

Figure 7 — Top view of the indicator panel showing LED placement.

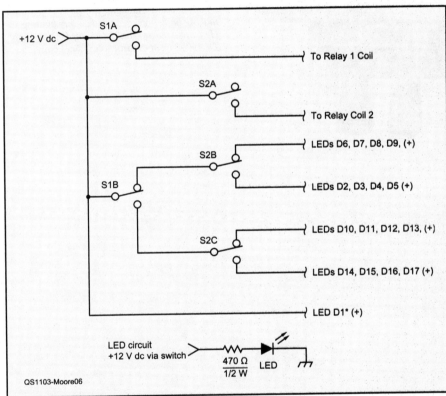

Figure 6 — Schematic diagram of the relay power switches and the 17 LEDs used as direction indicators.

since it's used in all directions. The other 4 LEDs in a particular row, in a bingo board pattern, are connected and supplied with +12 V dc via switch 1 or 2, depending on wires chosen. Since I could not readily find a 3 pole switch for S2, I used two closely spaced DPDT switches and switch them at the same time. A view of an energized LED switchbox is shown in Figure 8.

My total cost was under $50, not counting the balun and balanced transmission line. For my four wires, I used electric fence wire, which accepted solder surprisingly well. You can buy a ¼ mile roll of electric fence wire for only $14 at agricultural supply stores. You may also have a few necessary parts in your junk box.

On Air Results

My autotuner tuned the V beam on all bands from 10 through 80 meters. It was the first weekend of March and a DX contest was in full swing with the best 15 meter openings I've heard in years. Using the V beam on 15 meters, I worked into to Brazil, Argentina, Surinam, the Dominican Republic and many others. On 20 meters, where it was much more crowded, I contacted Switzerland and Spain before the band closed for the evening.

The V beam also has minor lobes, but is definitely directional. Sometimes I would point the V beam off a station to diminish interference. This resulted in the DX station being stronger in proportion to the others, creating a better contact opportunity. There are four direction choices and it is great to be able to flip two switches and direct your signal to different parts of the globe very quickly. No rotor can move this quickly. Ready to build yours?

Hamspeak

- **Beamwidth** — Angular range over which a receiving antenna will accept signals, or a transmitting antenna will transmit signals. Typically stated as the angular range over which power is no less than 0.5 (–3 dB) from the maximum value within the beam.
- *EZNEC* — Antenna modeling software that provides a user friendly interface to the powerful *Numerical Electromagnetic Code* (*NEC*) calculating engine. Several versions of *EZNEC* antenna modeling software are available from developer Roy Lewallen, W7EL, at www.eznec.com.
- **LED, light emitting diode** — Semiconductor device from which light is emitted when current flows. These were originally used in place of incandescent bulbs as indicator lights. They now can be used in place of larger light bulbs and form the basis of some display screens. See hyperphysics.phy-astr.gsu.edu/hbase/electronic/leds.html.
- **Yagi** — Multielement beam antenna based on straight rod or wire elements approximately a half wavelength in length. Generally only one element is connected to the transmission line. The other elements are *parasitically* coupled by the fields from the driven element.

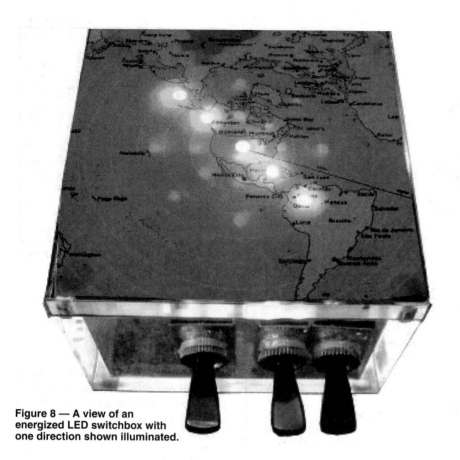

Figure 8 — A view of an energized LED switchbox with one direction shown illuminated.

Notes
[1]L. Colvin, DL4ZC, "Multiple V Beams," *QST*, Aug 1956, pp 28-29.
[2]*ARRL's Wire Antenna Classics*. Available from your ARRL dealer or the ARRL Bookstore, ARRL order no. 7075. Telephone 860-594-0355, or toll-free in the US 888-277-5289; **www.arrl.org/shop**; **pubsales@arrl.org**.
[3]Several versions of *EZNEC* antenna modeling software are available from developer Roy Lewallen, W7EL, at **www.eznec.com**.

ARRL member and Amateur Extra class operator Sam Moore, NX5Z, has a Master's degree in electronics, as well as PhDs in biblical studies and Christian counseling. He spent 24 years as an electronics technician and engineer at Texas Instruments. After he got his license over 30 years ago, ham radio got him interested in returning to college in electronics. He works in the Radio Support Group at the Texas Youth Commission, in a juvenile prison, plays guitar in church and is a retired pastor. Sam enjoys building antennas, low power operation, making homebrew gear and county hunting. He can be reached at 22 Cundiff Dr, Sherman, TX 75092 or at **drsammoore@aol.com**.

Inverted V Wire Yagi with Switchable Pattern Rotation for 14 MHz

A two element rotary beam antenna without moving parts.

Ashraf Abuelhaija and Klaus Solbach, DK3BA

Yagi or quad, beam antennas are well established antenna types for improved directivity and gain compared to a single dipole antenna.[1] Using an electromechanical rotator, these antennas can be turned toward the desired direction in ±180° of azimuth. Due to the considerable inertia involved in most practical beam antennas, however, rotation is fairly slow. This makes it difficult under typical short wave propagation conditions, for example, to switch between two different directions while listening to an ongoing conversation, or to find the direction of a station that makes short transmissions.

An alternative is offered by phased array antennas, in which the beam can be rotated by the switching of feed networks. With different phase excitations of the elements of the array, different beam patterns can be provided. The popular *four square* array of four vertical ground mounted monopole antennas with about quarter wave spacing and that provide four beam directions with 90° separation in azimuth is an example of such a system.[2]

A comparable alternative with horizontal polarization has not been available, to the knowledge of the authors. A phased array of four horizontal dipoles arranged in a square is not a good idea because of the orientation and coupling of the dipoles arranged under an angle of 90°. Also, this array would require four poles to carry the dipoles high above the ground.

A simpler configuration was found that requires only one support pole and that uses inverted V wire dipoles to create a two element Yagi antenna that can be remotely switched in its beam direction in steps of 60° in azimuth. The result is shown in Figure 1.

The Inverted V Wire Yagi

This two element inverted V based wire Yagi requires four wires of exactly the same length, each sloping from the top of a support pole or tower. Each is oriented with the same 30° elevation angle (mea-

[1]Notes appear on page 24.

Figure 1 — Inverted V wire switched beam array antenna on the roof platform. The dipole wires have been colored for better visibility.

sured from the horizontal) and spaced 60° and 120° apart in azimuth. Two wires are combined to form the driven element and the other two wires are combined to form a director element. Each pair combines two wires at an angle of 120° and both pairs are separated by an angle of 60°. Simulations were performed using *EZNEC5+* and the azimuth and elevation patterns are shown in Figures 2 and 3, respectively.

The combination of wires #2 and #4 driven by the RF source while the combination of wires #1 and #5 is center loaded by a series capacitance to electrically shorten the element to form a director. Mutual coupling between the two dipoles is strong in this configuration due to the short distance between the elements. Thus, we can adjust the phase, and also the amplitude to some extent, of the parasitic element current by choosing a frequency slightly above or below the half-wavelength resonance in combination with the choice of a series reactance load.

Our design employs a wire length of about 0.26 wavelengths and a series capacitor load to create a director element. The design and the realized radiation patterns look similar to the inverted V wire Yagi described by VE7CA in *The ARRL Antenna Book*.[3] Our antenna, however, uses equal length wires and reactive loading and wires radially extending from the apex while the referenced design uses parallel wires with reflector and driven elements of different length.

We tested the theoretical design by building a model for 1 GHz and measuring the reflection coefficient and the radiation patterns in our anechoic chamber. Results were quite satisfactory and this allowed us to proceed in building a full size version for 14 MHz.

Peak gain and the elevation angle of the peak critically depend on the height over ground. In the simulation, a height of 40 feet was assumed as an example. The pattern shows a half-power beamwidth in azimuth of about 65°, broad sidelobes and a relatively low front to back ratio between 10 and 15 dB, depending on elevation angle.

Although this certainly is not the perfect pattern of a two element Yagi, the antenna concept is useful since it can be extended into an antenna design with switch selectable beam directions.

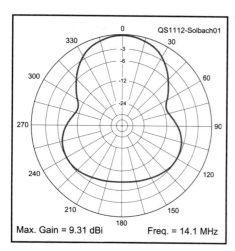

Figure 2 — *EZNEC5+* azimuth pattern of the two element inverted V wire Yagi at a height of 40 feet over typical ground (conductivity 0.005 S/M, relative dielectric constant 13). Wires 2 and 4 are driven, wires 1 and 5 form the director.

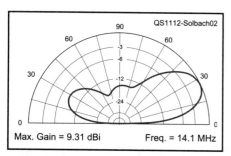

Figure 3 — Elevation pattern under the same conditions as in Figure 2.

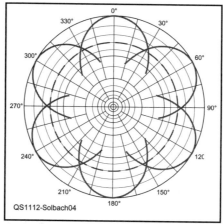

Figure 4 — Six wire arrangement of the switched beam array.

Figure 5 — Sketch of principal patterns created by six selections of wires for the two element inverted V wire Yagi array.

Hamspeak

dBi — Decibels with a reference to an ideal isotrpic antenna. A way of indicating antenna gain in comparison to an antenna with uniform radiation in all directions.

EZNEC — Antenna modeling software that provides a user friendly interface to the powerful Numerical Electromagnetic Code (NEC) calculating engine. Several versions of *EZNEC* antenna modeling software are available from developer Roy Lewallen, W7EL, at www.eznec.com.

Inverted V — Common name for a center fed dipole antenna in which the center is supported at a higher point than the ends, giving the appearance of an inverted letter V. Such antennas operate in a manner similar to a horizontal dipole at a height about ⅔ as high.

Monopole — Single vertical antenna element, typically a quarter or more wavelengths long. Often used as a transmit and receive antenna, singly or in combination with other similar antennas.

Quad — Multielement directional antenna array in which the elements are made of square, rectangular or round loops approximately 1 wavelength in circumference.

Transceiver — Radio transmitter and receiver combined in one unit. In many cases some circuitry is shared between the two functions.

Yagi — The name of a multielement narrowband directive antenna array using multiple parallel dipole type elements. It is more properly called a Yagi-Uda array, named after its inventors.

The Switched Beam Antenna

Our switched beam antenna is comprised of six wires spaced equally by 60° in azimuth as shown in Figure 4. Using remotely activated switches, we select one pair of wires for the driven inverted V dipole and one pair for the director inverted V dipole. The four selected wires represent the two operating elements, with the two unused wires sitting exactly on the symmetry axis of the driven and the parasitic dipoles. Thus there is no net mutual coupling to the unused wires and they are virtually invisible to the operating elements. We can cyclically interchange the selection of wires to create six different combinations which produce six different patterns rotated in azimuth by steps of 60°. See Figure 5.

It is seen that the six beam positions cover the 360° azimuth range and that the beam cross-over level is slightly above –3 dB; thus, while scanning the antenna around, the worst case pointing loss for any direction is less than 3 dB.

The switching in and out of dipole wires has to be accomplished at the center of the array where the wires are fastened and electrically connected and from where the six wires stretch out radially. Figure 6 shows one of six routing configurations for the connection of two wires to the coaxial feed for the driven dipole and two wires to the reactive load for the director dipole.

For this switch unit we use electromechanical relay switches of SPDT type (Takamisawa SY-12W-K) and DPDT type (Omron G5V-2) arranged on a circular 12 cm diameter circuit board (Rogers RO4003, 0.5 mm thickness) with 50 Ω microstrip lines connecting the wires, relay terminals, capacitor, coaxial cable and the five wire control lines as shown in Figure 7. The relays are conventional miniature sealed signal relays with low capacitance (about 1 pF) between contacts and voltage handling of several hundred volts and load current up to 1 A. Power handling has been tested with 100 W of carrier power in short transmit periods, but high duty-cycle power handling and higher peak power have not been tested.

The six dipole wires are electrically connected and mechanically fixed to the board by eyes at the periphery while the RF coaxial cable and the five wire control cable thread through openings in the middle. With the switch unit and dipole wires in place at the top of our tower, the control cable and the coaxial cable run downward from the board — the RF transmission line with a cable choke balun just below the board. At the other end of the cables, the relays are actuated by a rotary switch with six positions controlling a digital encoding and interface circuit as shown in Figure 8.

Our antenna is mounted on a 23 foot mast placed centrally on the roof platform of our building (see Figure 1): The tower also carries a microwave dish antenna below the top. Other VHF, UHF and microwave antennas also are present on the platform and a three element Yagi is placed at a distance of 40 feet from the tower. The switch unit is mounted on a short PVC tube just above the top of the metal tower and an inverted plastic salad bowl is used as a top cover to protect the unit from rain (see Figure 9).

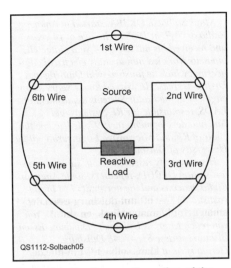

Figure 6 — Routing configuration of the switch unit for a beam pointing to 90° azimuth.

Figure 8 — Relay digital control unit with rotary switch.

Figure 9 — Switch unit with dipole wires and weather protection cover placed on top of the supporting mast.

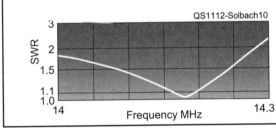

Figure 10 — *EZNEC* SWR plot of the two element Yagi.

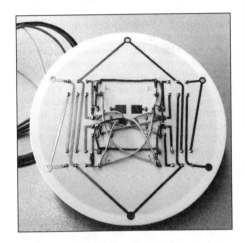

Figure 7 — Switch unit with eight relays to switch six dipole wires at their periphery. At the top is a view of the wiring side showing the use of microstrip lines for the RF connections. At the bottom is the relay side.

To keep the weight low, we used thin insulated copper stranded wire of 0.42 mm diameter [approximately #26 AWG—*Ed.*] for the dipole arms (expected conductor loss of about 1 dB) and supported the open ends at an equal height of 14 feet by ½ inch PVC pipes which were fastened to the railings of the platform. Some wires had to be extended by Nylon string to reach their supports.

From simulation with *EZNEC5+*, an optimum wire length of 18.4 feet was calculated with the director loaded by 120 pF. The model assumed an infinite conducting ground and projected a maximum gain of 7.44 dBi under 45° elevation.

Since the roof of our 13 story concrete building is about 165 feet above ground, the ground plane assumption is much too pessimistic as it applies to the far-field pattern and we can expect higher gain at lower elevation angles. The antenna feed-point impedance was as predicted, after we cut the dipole wires by about a foot to adjust the resonant frequency (Figure 10). Within a bandwidth of about 200 kHz, the SWR is below 2:1 and the pattern has acceptable variation in gain and beam shape over the range.

Operating Experience

The antenna was operated using an FT-101 transceiver from our University club station, DLØUD. While we observed the signal strength indicator we rotated the pattern by turning the switch through all six positions within a few seconds or fast toggling between two positions in order to find the maximum indication for CW stations in the 20 meter band. Although the antenna patterns indicate only a moderate front-to-back ratio, a clear maximum position was found in most cases and also a clear minimum position at the opposite beam direction. Correspondence of antenna beam direction and theoretical azimuth could also be verified in most cases.

DIRECTIONAL 23

We compared the switched beam antenna to our rotatable three element Yagi by quickly switching between the two antennas. This tended to be frustrating because often the rotatable beam took more time to move to the optimum direction than the duration of transmission of the observed amateur station. Unfortunately, the comparison can give only a very rough indication of the actual antenna gain, since we are not sure about the gain of the rotatable Yagi.

The rotatable beam is operated under inferior conditions compared to our switched beam antenna as it is situated 40 feet west of the tower at the edge of our roof platform only 10 feet above the platform level. Including additional cable loss, this should reduce the gain by about 2 dB. Nevertheless, comparisons using signals from the Eastern Hemisphere tended to give one-half up to one S-meter unit advantage for the switched antenna while signals from the Western Hemisphere tended to give equal signal strength with both antennas. The difference may be explained by the mutual coupling and diffraction effects when the Yagi radiation has to pass through the switched beam and vice versa. As a rough estimate of the gain from these results, we conclude that the switched beam antenna would come close within a few dB of the traditional Yagi if both were in the same position.

Conclusion

The six wire switched beam antenna has been found to be a useful antenna for shortwave operation due to its inertialess beam rotation and simple construction based on the inverted V design. A four wire version has also been investigated but this presents only four beam directions while an eight wire version promises more interesting features with eight beam directions based on six wires selection to create a three element Yagi array rotatable through eight directions. The presented concept could be expanded to multiple bands operation be using wires with traps and multiple capacitors.

Additional construction details are provided on the QST-in-Depth website.[4]

Notes
[1] R. D. Straw, Editor, *The ARRL Antenna Book*, 22nd Edition, Chapters 11 and 12. Available from your ARRL dealer or the ARRL Bookstore, ARRL order no. 9876. Tel 860-594-0355, or toll-free in the US 888-277-5289; **www.arrl.org/shop; pubsales@arrl.org**.
[2] See Note 1, "A "Four Square Array," p 8-27.
[3] See Note 1, "40-Meter Wire Yagis," p 15-18.
[4] **www.arrl.org/qst-in-depth**

Klaus Solbach, DK3BA, started in Amateur Radio as SWL in 1965 at the age of 14 years, and received his full license 4 years later. His amateur work led him to study electrical engineering, which he finished with Dipl-Ing and Dr-Ing degrees. He worked for 17 years as an engineer at the Radar Systems department of EADS, responsible for RF Systems and Antenna development. In 1997, he became the chair of RF and Microwave Engineering at the University of Duisburg.

His university research group supports contest station DF0UD, repeaters, some Amateur Radio beacons and the university FM broadcast station (see **hft.uni-duisburg-essen.de/ amateurfunk/amateurfunk_en.shtml**). You can reach Klaus at University Duisburg-Essen, Bismarckstrasse 81, 47048 Duisburg, Germany or at **klaus.solbach@uni-due.de**.

Coauthor Ashraf Abuelhaija is from Jordan. He received the BSc in Communications and Electronics Engineering in 2002 at the Applied Science University in Amman, Jordan and worked 6 months as a Laboratory Technician and Supervisor at the Department of Electronics and Computer Engineering at the same university. He came to Germany to receive his MSc in Electrical and Electronics Engineering (Communication Engineering) at Duisburg-Essen University.

This article is based on his Master's thesis, "Development of a Novel Switched Beam Antenna for Communications," selected from the Amateur Radio projects offered by the department and through this had his first ham radio experience.

A Fan Dipole for 80 through 6 Meters

The parallel or fan dipole can be effective if you keep a few facts in mind.

Richard P. Clem, WØIS

While variations on the design have appeared many times in *QST* over the years, many newer hams (and more than a few old timers) are unaware of the simple antenna design shown in Figure 1, variously referred to as fan, fanned or parallel dipoles.[1] This antenna requires neither tuner nor switching for operation on multiple bands, and requires only a single coaxial feed line.

The mechanical details of this antenna are not critical. It can be adapted to a variety of configurations to take advantage of existing support structures, or to operate on different bands. The configuration shown in Figure 1 has been in use at WØIS for a number of years, and provides good results on 80, 40, 20, 15, 10 and 6 meters, and a sufficiently acceptable SWR on 30 and 17 meters to allow for occasional ventures onto those bands.

Antenna Concept

This antenna consists of four dipoles, all sharing the same coaxial feed line. These dipoles are cut for the approximate centers of 80, 40, 20 and 10 meters. Essentially, the signal from the transmitter "sees" only the antenna that is resonant, since the antennas for the other bands present a high impedance.[2] The 40 meter element is ³⁄₂ wavelengths on 15 meters, and ⁷⁄₂ wavelengths on 6 meters, so the antenna is also resonant on those bands. I have the antenna installed in inverted V fashion, with the center supported by a mast made of schedule 80 PVC pipe secured to the house and extending a few feet above the top support. The eight half dipole legs run to convenient points on the house and trees.

Most of the previous *QST* references to similar antennas show the elements running parallel to one another and in close proximity. For example, ON4UF shows construction with 300 Ω ribbon cable, and W9DOS shows the use of four conductor rotator cable. One comment I've heard from users of similar antennas is that if the elements are tightly coupled, while the completed antenna uses less real estate, there is a great deal of interaction between adjacent elements. Such an antenna requires a great deal of careful trimming to achieve resonance on all bands.

[1]Notes appear on page 26.

Table 1
Final Element (Half Dipole) Lengths for Each Band

Band (Meters)	Length (Feet)
80	66
40	32.5
20	16.5
10	8.25

The WØIS Version

At WØIS, the eight wires are run in all directions, each spaced approximately 45° from the next element. This provides a certain amount of mechanical stability to the PVC mast. More importantly, this has greatly reduced interaction between the various elements.[3] Each side of each dipole was simply cut according to the familiar formula

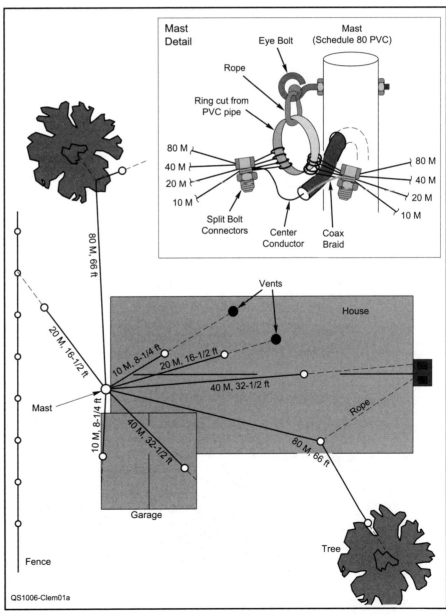

Figure 1 — Aerial view of WØIS fan dipole. The inset shows detail of center connections.

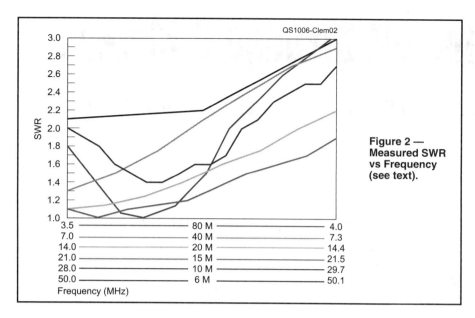

Figure 2 — Measured SWR vs Frequency (see text).

$L = 234/f$, where L is the length in feet, and f is the frequency in MHz.

The only tuning that was necessary in my case was lengthening the 80 meter dipole by about 4 feet on each side. On all other bands, there was an acceptable SWR across the entire band.

I believe that the reason I had to lengthen the 80 meter elements had nothing to do with the fact that the other elements were present. As can be seen from Figure 1, I needed to zigzag the 80 meter dipole somewhat, and this probably accounted for the fact that they needed to be longer than the value derived from the formula. The final lengths for each element (that is, the length of one half of each dipole) are shown in Table 1.

The final SWR curves are shown in Figure 2. My intention was to tune the antenna for optimum SWR in the middle of each band. As installed, the SWR actually favors the bottom of the band. Since I operate mostly CW, I actually preferred this result, and didn't do any further tuning. For those who will do most of their operating higher in the band, it might be advisable to shorten the elements for the higher bands for optimum SWR. Note that my old SWR meter is optimistic above 2:1.

Surprisingly, even though no effort was made to make this antenna function on 30 or 17 meters, the SWR on those bands is also marginally acceptable (approximately 3:1). I suspect this is because those frequencies are close enough to being an odd multiple of 3.5 MHz. In my antenna, the SWR is unacceptably high on 12 meters.

The same design could be used on different bands simply by removing elements or adding elements of different length. This is a very versatile design, and is the ultimate in operating convenience — to change bands, absolutely no tuning or switching is required.

Building Your Own

The construction details are not critical. I used some available #18 AWG stranded copper wire. While a balun could be used, and is generally recommended, I did not use one. Instead, I cut a small piece of PVC pipe to use as the center insulator. All of the elements are secured to this center insulator merely by twisting a loop around the insulator. The coax is connected to the elements with a split bolt connector a few inches away from the center insulator.[4] The center conductor of the coax is connected to the four elements running in one direction, and the shield of the coax is connected to the four elements running in the other direction. [It is a good idea to put sealer on the exposed braid. — Ed.] The split bolt connector compresses the five wires together. This connection is not soldered, and has continued to work well for several years. The coax should run initially upward from this point, to prevent water from entering the coax. I used type RG-8X coax; however, any 50 Ω coax can be used with type depending on tolerable loss and power level.

The various elements are secured to convenient points on or near the house, such as the gutters, the chimney, vent pipes, a fence, and trees. The ends are secured with rope, either tied directly to the antenna wire, or to insulators made from rings formed by cutting PVC pipe.

A Few Additional Notes

Many of the early *QST* references to an antenna of this type contain an editor's note pointing out that such an antenna has absolutely no harmonic suppression capabilities. If a 7 MHz signal is generating a harmonic on 14 MHz, then the 14 MHz signal will have an efficient radiator at its disposal. One should be aware of this possibility; however, if a modern rig complies with FCC spectral purity requirements, it shouldn't be necessary to rely on the antenna for additional attenuation.

An antenna of this type is infinitely adaptable. For example, the design could be adapted by those needing a "stealth" antenna by hiding the coax and using materials such as thin gauge wire and monofilament line. I frequently use a similar antenna for low power operation while camping. I use a piece of coax terminated with a PL-259 UHF plug on one end and two alligator clips on the other end. To erect an antenna, I merely measure sections of wire for the bands I'm interested in (often using an 8 foot picnic table as a convenient measuring stick), and then erect them in trees or whatever other supports are available, using string, or simply draping them over branches.[5] In the center, I attach one alligator clip to one set of wires, and the other alligator clip to the other set of wires. The result is a dipole that can be erected in minutes.

This type of antenna is one of the simplest ways to construct a multiband antenna. It does requires a fair amount of wire in the air. However, the fact that the placement of the elements is not critical makes it very adaptable to most real estate.

Notes

[1] For example: H. Berg, W3KPO, "Multiband Operation with Paralleled Dipoles," *QST*, Jul 1956, pp 42-43; J. Grebenkemper, KA3BLO, "Multiband Trap and Parallel HF Dipoles—A Comparison," *QST*, May 1985, pp 26-31; S. Wysocki, W9DOS, "Using Four-Conductor Rotator Cable in Paralleled Dipole Antennas (Hints and Kinks)," *QST*, Sep 1958, p 50; L. Richard, ON4UF, "Parallel Dipoles of 300-Ohm Ribbon," *QST*, Mar 1957, p 14.

[2] See discussion in H. Berg, W3KPO, "Multiband Operation with Paralleled Dipoles," *QST*, Jul 1956, pp 42-43.

[3] Grebenkemper (Note 1) does show some interaction between elements at a 45° angle, but less than for parallel radiators. In my experience, this lesser interaction is not so severe as to require adjustment of the element lengths.

[4] Halex Company part number 32403B or equivalent.

[5] Having insulated antenna wire actually touch the trees is acceptable at low power levels. At higher power levels, however, care should be taken, since it might be possible for such an arrangement to actually set fire to the tree.

ARRL member Richard Clem, WØIS, was originally licensed in 1974 as WNØMEB, and later as WBØMEB. He holds an Amateur Extra class license and has held his current call sign since 1977. He is an attorney and ARRL Volunteer Counsel. The antenna described in this article was recently used to win ARRL Triple Play award #215, which included working all states on PSK-31 with 5 W. You can reach Richard at 1616 N Victoria St, St Paul, MN 55117 or at **w0is@arrl.net**.

A Pneumatically Switched Multiband Antenna

This creative design uses pneumatically activated switches to increase or decrease the electrical length of an antenna.

Gary S. Kath, N2OT, and Craig Bishop, WB2EPQ

For a number of years we have been experimenting with wire antennas trying to come up with that ideal multiband antenna that is fed with a single length of coaxial cable. Some two band 80 and 40 meter dipole antennas we tried and rejected were:

- *Multiband antenna using paralleled dipoles.* One approach is to cut a dipole for each band and connect the feed points of the two dipoles in parallel and to a single feed line as shown in Figure 1.[1,2] The free ends of the dipoles can be tied to different supports to keep the wires separated or insulators can be used between the wires. When the antenna is operated on a given band, one dipole is resonant having a low feed-point impedance while the other dipole is out of resonance, presenting a high feed-point impedance.

Our experience has shown that interaction between the two dipoles tends to pull the frequency away from the theoretical resonant length described by the usual dipole equation. Tuning the antenna is required by trial and error adjustment of the length of each dipole to get the best standing wave ratio (SWR). The antenna also requires making a number of insulating spacers to ensure the parallel dipoles do not touch one another on windy days.

- *Multiband trap antennas.* A second method to design a multiband antenna is to use *traps*. A trap is simply a parallel resonant circuit consisting of an inductor and capacitor.[3,4] In a two band parallel resonant trap dipole, one end of the traps is connected to the ends of the 40 meter dipole and the opposite ends of the traps are connected to extension wires forming the 80 meter dipole as shown in Figure 2. The trap is designed to resonate on 40 meters. The trap impedance at resonance is very high, electrically disconnecting the 80 meter section of wire while on 40 meters. When the antenna is operated on 80 meters the traps are not resonant. The trap then acts as an inductive reactance electrically extending the length of the extension wire forming the balance of the 80 meter dipole.

Traps are somewhat lossy, more involved to fabricate and can be affected by moisture. The traps also affect the ideal resonant length of the antenna making trial and error adjustment of the wire lengths necessary.

Multiband Antenna Using Switched Wire Segments

The ideal multiband antenna would use remotely controlled low loss switches to extend the length of the antenna for multiband use. On 40 meters the switches are open and on 80 meters the switches are closed.

Wired Relays

Our first thought was to simply put relays at the end of the 40 meter dipole legs to allow remote connection to the 80 meter wire sections. The problem is the control wires oper-

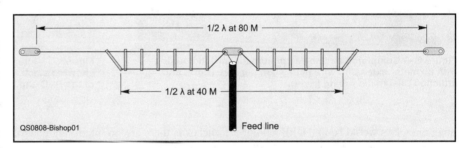

Figure 1 — Configuration of a multiband antenna made from two parallel dipoles.

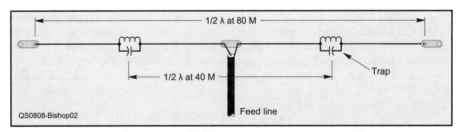

Figure 2 — Configuration of a multiband dipole using traps to separate the segments.

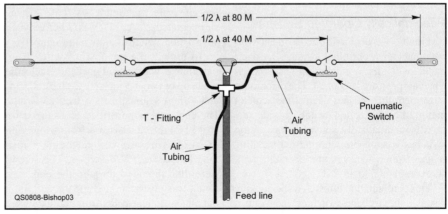

Figure 3 — Diagram of the design of a multiband antenna using pneumatically controlled switches.

[1]Notes appear on page 29.

Figure 4 — Surplus Micro Switch snap action switch used for band changing.

Figure 6 — Completed and sealed pneumatic switch housing with 80 meter extension wire (left), 40 meter wire (right) and attached pneumatic tubing (right).

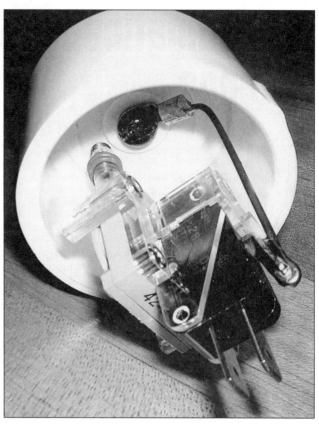

Figure 5 — Interior view of protective switch housing showing electrical and pneumatic connections through one of the PVC end caps.

ating the relays would be in the RF field of the antenna and interfere with the operation of the antenna.

RF Activated Switch

The next idea was to develop wireless RF activated switches. The idea was to design a circuit that could sense the RF frequency and automatically close the switches when operating on 80 meters and open the switches when on 40 meters. This would require battery powered RF sensing switches mounted at the ends of the 40 meter dipole. Although we did develop a rough prototype of this concept, it is not ready for prime time.

Pneumatically Operated Switches

Finally, we decided to experiment with pneumatically controlled switches. A pneumatic switch has a diaphragm that expands when air pressure is applied. The diaphragm movement then pushes against the actuator button of a snap action switch. A wide variety of pneumatically actuated snap action switches is available with current handling ranges from 3 to 25 A and operating pressures from 0.05 to 45 PSI.[5]

This configuration offers a cleaner looking installation, fast band switching and requires no coaxial switches to flip between antennas.

The advantage of pneumatically operated switches is there are no interfering control wires but only plastic tubing running up along the antenna. The idea was to place a pneumatic switch at the end of each leg of the 40 meter dipole and run pneumatic tubing from the switches into the ham shack as shown in Figure 3. To switch bands from 40 to 80 meters, simply apply air pressure to the tubing causing the remote switch to actuate, thereby extending the length of the dipole.

Construction of the 80 and 40 Meter Pneumatically Switched Dipole

For this application we selected surplus low pressure pneumatic switches having an integrated 20 A, 277 V ac Micro Switch snap action switch as shown in Figure 4.

To protect the pneumatic switch from moisture, it was housed inside an enclosure made up of two 1.5 inch PVC pipe end caps and a short segment of 1.5 inch PVC pipe. The end caps were drilled and tapped for size 12-24 machine screws. Round lugs with extension wires were slipped onto 1 inch long brass size 12-24 screws. The screws were then threaded through the end caps. Caulk was placed around the threads and a nut attached. The wires from the lugs were soldered to the normally open (NO) switch contacts on the pneumatic snap action switch as shown in Figure 5.

To route the air control line into the sealed pneumatic switch, a pneumatic bulkhead feed-through fitting was fabricated from a size 12-24 brass machine screw by cutting off the head, drilling a 1/16 inch diameter hole down its length and machining off the threads on the ends. One of the PVC end caps was drilled and tapped for a size 12-24 thread and the fitting was installed, sealed with caulk and locked with nuts. A short length of tubing was connected from the bulkhead fitting to the port on the pneumatic switch. The opposite side of the bulkhead fitting attaches to pneumatic tubing running back to the radio shack. If necessary, the design can be simplified by passing the tubing through a hole drilled in the end-cap eliminating the bulkhead fitting.

To complete the design, the PVC pieces were cemented together with PVC cement, forming a watertight seal as shown in Figure 6. The extending brass screws are attached between the 40 meter and 80 meter wires of the dipole using brass nuts. The dipole segment lengths were determined using the usual 468/f relationship.

The air tube feeding the pneumatic switches was 1/8 inch OD, 1/16 inch ID clear PVC tubing (McMaster Carr part number 5233 K514). This low cost tubing is trans-

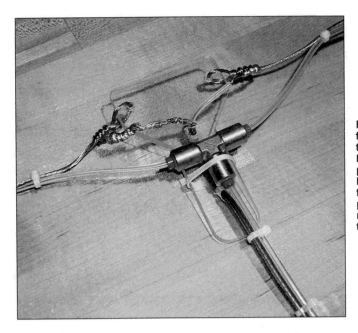

Figure 7 — Coaxial feed line attached to center of dipole. Left and right pneumatic tubing lines attached to T fitting and a single pneumatic line running down to the shack.

parent and has good ultraviolet resistance. A single length of tubing was taped along the coaxial feed line up to the dipole center insulator. A pneumatic T fitting was then used to split off the air line to the left and right segments of the dipole as shown in Figure 7. The tubing was attached along the dipole wires using electrical tape and then attached to the air bulkhead fitting on the pneumatic switch housing.

Low pressure air is required to activate the pneumatic switch from the shack. Low pressure pneumatic switches can even be activated by blowing into the air line. (This is not recommended, especially for SSB, since you will have to hold your breath while operating on 80 meters!) We simply used a small balloon hand pump to activate the switch for 80 meter operation and vented the air line for 40 meter operation. A balloon, bicycle pump, small fish pump and other air pressure providers could also be used as the air source.

Performance

Our dipole was erected between two large oak trees. One hundred feet of coax and pneumatic tubing ran down to the shack. We pulled out our old trusty MFJ Antenna Analyzer and to our surprise found the 40 meter antenna resonated with 1:1 SWR exactly at our design frequency.

We switched over to 80 meters by applying air to our pneumatic line. Checking the SWR again showed a 1:1 SWR on our 80 meter design frequency. There was no interaction between the 80 and 40 meter wires and no further adjustment was required.

On-air testing of the antenna was our next concern. Was the high voltage at the ends of the 40 meter dipole going to flash across our little snap-action switch? We fired up our 100 W transceiver and called CQ on 40 meters. Jack, K9GZK, responded to our call and we talked with no problems and no switch arcing.

Our final concerns were how long the pneumatic connections will last and whether moisture will condense in the tubing? After six months of operation, the only problem was that water entered one of the PVC enclosures via the capillary action along the brass screw threads, due to a poor caulking job. The switch was dried out and silicon caulk was reapplied over the threads. Since then, the antenna has worked fine through a variety of hot and cold weather conditions.

Other Ideas

The successful operation of the pneumatic switches generated other possible uses to explore in the future:

■ *Phone/CW broadband dipole* — Use pneumatic switches to slightly extend the length of a dipole allowing broadband operation in both the phone and CW portions of the band. This is particularly suitable for 80 and 75 meter operation.

■ *Multiband vertical* — Use pneumatic switches and the PVC housing to make a multiband vertical. Run the control air up the center of the antenna tubing to create a sleeker design.

■ *Switching directions of a wire beam* — Use pneumatic switches to change the length of the reflector and driven elements on a three element Yagi or quad to rapidly change antenna direction by 180°.

We will leave it up to our fellow amateurs to explore other uses for low cost pneumatic switches. Meanwhile, work continues on our second generation multiband antenna design using RF activated switches.

Notes
[1] R. D. Straw, Editor, *The ARRL Antenna Book*, 21st Edition, p 7-9. Available from your ARRL dealer or the ARRL Bookstore, ARRL order no. 9876. Telephone 860-594-0355, or toll-free in the US 888-277-5289; **www.arrl.org/shop/**; **pubsales@arrl.org**.
[2] Dipole length in feet = $468/(f_{MHz})$.
[3] J. Carr, *Practical Antenna Handbook*, 2nd Edition, TAB Books, 1994, p 141.
[4] See Note 1, p 7-11.
[5] If surplus switches are not available, another source is Air-Logic (**www.air-logic.com**). Their switch number F-4100-50-B80-15A should be suitable. Others may be available from Micro Technologies, SA, Pompano Beach, FL; **www.pressureswitch.com**.

Photos by the authors.

Gary S. Kath, N2OT, was first licensed in 1968 as WN2EPP and currently holds an Amateur Extra class license. He earned a BSEE from Widener University and an MSEE from Carnegie Mellon University. Gary has 28 years of experience as an instrumentation and automation engineering manager. He enjoys DXing, contesting, low power (QRP) operation, circuit design, software development and experimenting with HF wire antennas. Gary can be reached at 2671 Sky Top Dr, Scotch Plains, NJ 07076 or at **njklepper@att.net**.

Craig Bishop, WB2EPQ took his first license exam with Gary in 1968 and was assigned consecutive call WN2EPQ. After earning his Advanced class license, Craig focused primarily on antenna experimentation, DX and contesting. He was also very involved in his high school and college radio clubs. Craig holds a BSEE from Lafayette College and is an information technology executive at a large corporation. You can reach Craig at 28 Black Birch Rd, Scotch Plains, NJ 07076 or at **cbishop@att.net**.

An All Band HF Dipole Antenna

Use relays without extra wires to select your dipole length.

Jim Weit, KI8BV

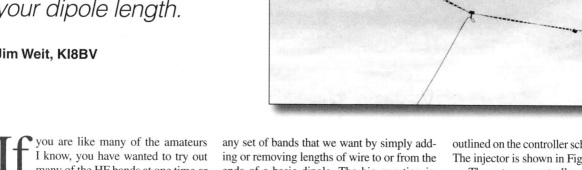

If you are like many of the amateurs I know, you have wanted to try out many of the HF bands at one time or another. Here is an antenna that can cover any or all of the HF bands that you might want to operate on. This antenna does not have strange radiation patterns or narrow bandwidth as do some multi-band antennas.

[This antenna should provide similar performance to the pneumatically switched multiband dipole presented in August *QST*.[1] The control systems provide a strikingly different approach to the switching mechanism. — *Ed.*]

Over the years I have put up many dipole antennas in my yard. I am lucky in that my lot is large enough for a full size 160 meter dipole. There are lots of large trees to hang dipoles between. Even on a large lot it is hard to arrange eight or nine dipoles in such a way that minimizes the interaction between them. The cost of all the coax needed to feed such a large number of antennas can get expensive. Then there is also the problem of the visual clutter, at least in the eyes of the neighbors.

An Idea Emerges

One day while trying to figure out where to hang one more antenna, it occurred to me that the only difference between a 10 meter and a 12 meter dipole was 14 inches of wire added to each end. The addition of 19 inches of wire at each end of the 12 meter dipole makes it a dipole for 15 meters. If there were a way to increase or decrease the length of the dipole whenever I wanted, I would have three dipoles in the same place, using the same supports, and using a single coax feed line. There would be no interaction between them, and they would have all the same characteristics as a dipole, because each one is a dipole. Well, I am sure that you can see that we could cover any set of bands that we want by simply adding or removing lengths of wire to or from the ends of a basic dipole. The big question is, how can we do this from the comfort of the ham shack anytime that we want?

One way to do this is to place relay contacts along each leg of the antenna at the points at which each dipole would end. Energizing pairs of relays connects lengths of wire to each end of the antenna, and de-energizing pairs of relays disconnects the lengths of wire and shortens the antenna. By making each leg of the dipole from two parallel wires, it is possible to get power and control signals from the shack, through the coax feed line to the relays. Since a number of relays must be controlled, some electronic components are needed at each relay to decode the control signals that are carried along the parallel antenna conductors. The relays and their control circuits must be housed in weatherproof enclosures. I call these assemblies *relay modules*.

We also need an enclosure with circuitry to generate the control signals that are sent to the relay modules using the same coax feed line that carries RF between the station and the antenna. I call this unit the *antenna controller*.

Figure 1 is a block diagram of the complete multi-band antenna system. Only two pairs of relay modules are shown, but additional pairs can be added to cover as many bands as you would like. With just the two pairs of relay modules shown, this would be a three band antenna.

A module called a *splitter* is located at the center of the antenna. This module also acts as the center insulator. The splitter uses RF chokes and capacitors to separate (or split) the RF power from the dc power and control signals on the feed line.

Another part of the system is called the *injector*. The injector allows dc power and control signals to be injected onto the feed line at the operating position. The injector circuit is outlined on the controller schematic (Figure 2). The injector is shown in Figure 3.

The antenna controller provides dc power to the relay modules, and generates the control signals that turn pairs of relay modules on or off. The controller and injector are located in the shack. The only wires that run between the antenna and the ham shack is a single coax feed line, just like a regular dipole antenna.

Basic Operation

Refer to Figure 1. At power-on, +12 V is applied to the + terminal of relay module 1A through Q1, L1, L2 and up the center conductor of the feed line. It also passes through the inductor in the splitter module to relay module 1B. The negative side of the power supply is connected to relay module 1B through the outer braid of the feed line. It is also connected to relay module 1A through the splitter. The relay module operation is described below.

At this point dc power is applied to the control circuits in the first pair of relay modules (1A and 1B). Initially the relays in these modules are not energized so the relay contacts are open and no power gets to the next pair of relay modules. The antenna is now set for the highest frequency band, band 1. The dc power to the relay modules passes through the inductors, but RF does not. Injector capacitor C1 allows RF from the transceiver to flow to the antenna and prevents dc from the antenna controller from flowing to the transceiver. The capacitors in the splitter keep both of the parallel antenna conductors at the same RF potential.

Making it Work

The control circuits in modules 1A and 1B look for a momentary zero voltage condition between the parallel antenna conductors (Q1 turns off and Q2 turns on for 100 µs). This action causes the control circuit to

[1]Notes appear on page 34.

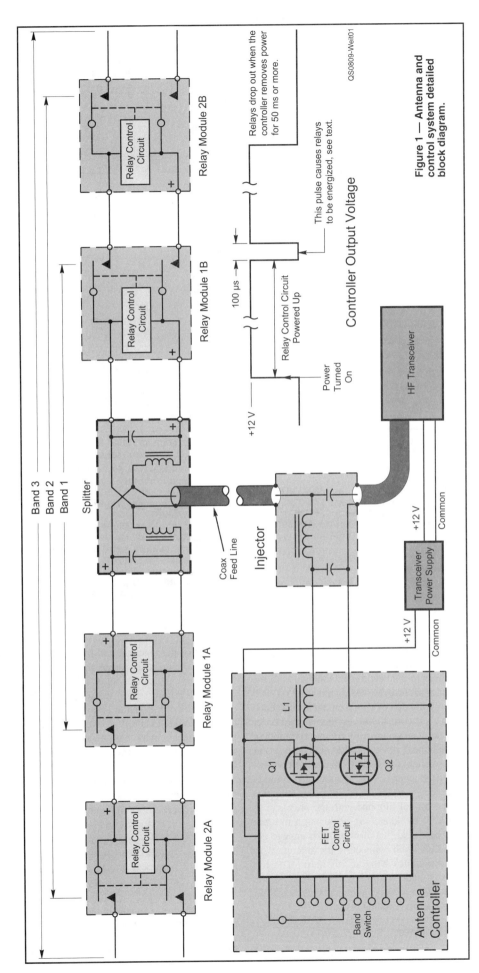

Figure 1 — Antenna and control system detailed block diagram.

energize the relays in the first pair of modules (refer to timing diagram on Figure 1). A 10 µF capacitor in each relay modules maintains power to the relay control circuit during the 100 µs that dc power is removed. Now the antenna is set for band 2, and power is applied to modules 2A and 2B through the relay contacts of modules 1A and 1B. On the next negative going pulse, the relays in the second pair of modules are energized, and the antenna is set to band 3. Any number of relay modules can be sequentially energized in this way. For practical reasons the 100 µs pulses must be about 40 ms apart. This means that eight pairs of relay modules (for a nine band antenna) can be turned on in about 320 ms, or less than a third of a second. By removing power to the relay modules (Q1 OFF and Q2 ON) for 50 ms, all relays will drop out, and the desired band can be selected with another string of 100 µs negative going pulses. With this control scheme, the circuits in all the relay modules can be identical regardless of their position along the antenna wires.

The Relay Module

Figure 3 is the schematic diagram of a relay module. The heart of the circuit is the PIC12F508 microcontroller. This chip is available in an 8-pin dual inline package (DIP). The industrial version is good for temperatures from –40 to 185°F. The basic function of the software is very simple. When power is first applied, the processor does nothing for 18 ms. This is enough time to make sure that any relay contact bounce from the module ahead of it is over. The processor then goes into the sleep mode. This shuts down the chip's internal 4 MHz oscillator and minimizes the current drawn by the processor. The next time the input (pin 7) goes low, the processor wakes up, energizes the relays, and goes back to sleep. It never does anything again unless it is reset by removing and re-applying power.

Two single contact relays are used. The contact rating of the relays is 10 A at 250 V ac. Since the relays don't interrupt RF power, it is the contact withstanding voltage rating of 750 V ac that is important. Simulations of the antenna using *EZNEC* predict that at 100 W of power to the antenna, the maximum RF voltage across any relay contact is 733 V.[2] This maximum occurs on the last relay module of an antenna that covers 160 meters while transmitting on 80 meters. I have measured the breakdown voltage across the contact of many of these relays and found that they can withstand a voltage of well over 1000 V ac. As long as your antenna is not built to cover 160 meters, the simulations indicate that you can use up to 200 W of RF power with these relays. My transceiver is rated for 100 W so I have not stressed the system beyond this power level.

The LED is not necessary, but it is very

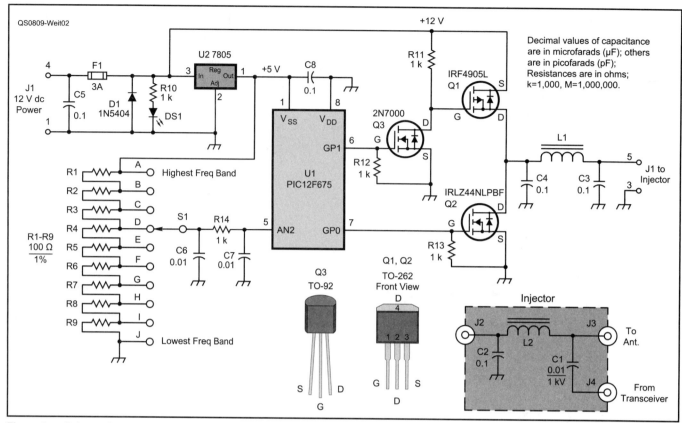

Figure 2 — Schematic and parts list for the controller and injector. Parts are available from distributors such as Allied Electronics at www.alliedelec.com, Digi-Key at www.digikey.com, McMaster Carr at www.mcmaster.com and Mouser at www.mouser.com.

C1 — 0.01 µF, 1 kV ceramic disk capacitor.
C2-C5, C8 — 0.1 µF, 50 V ceramic capacitor, type Z5U.
C6, C7 — 0.01 µF, ceramic capacitor, type Z5U.
D1 — 1N5404 silicon rectifier (Mouser 821-1N5404).
F1 — 3 A, 5 × 20 mm fuse.
Fuse clips for F1 (Digi-Key 283-2335).
J1 — DIN jack, 5 pin, (Mouser 161-0505).
J2 — Phono jack (Mouser 16PJ052).
J3, J4 — UHF jack (Mouser 523-83-878).

L1, L2 — 100 µH RF choke (Digi-Key M8271).
LED1 — Red LED (Mouser 638-333ID).
P1 — Plug to fit J1 (Mouser 171-0275).
P2 — Phono plug (Mouser 17PP052).
Q1 — P channel FET (Digi-Key IRF4905L).
Q2 — N channel FET (Digi-Key IRLZ44NLPBF).
Q3 — N channel FET (Mouser 2N7000D75Z).
R1-R9 — 100 Ω, ¼ W, 1% resistor.

R10-R14 — 1 kΩ, ½ W, 5% resistor.
S1 — 12 position rotary switch (Digi-Key CT2123).
U1 — Microprocessor (Digi-Key PIC12F675-I/P).
U2 — +5 V regulator (Digi-Key LM78L05ACZFS).
Controller enclosure, extruded aluminum (Mouser 546-1455N1201).
Injector enclosure, diecast aluminum (Mouser 546-1590A).
Knob, 1 inch (Allied 543-1105).

handy while testing modules. Even with the antenna in the air you can see if it is working properly by observing the LEDs, most effective at night.

Figure 4 shows a completed relay module circuit board as well as two completed modules. The enclosure is composed of three pieces. The base is made from ¼ inch thick PVC that is 2 inches wide by 3 inches long. The base has holes at the ends for antenna wire attachment. The sides of the module are made from 2 inch square PVC tubing that is cut into pieces 1 inch long and glued to the base plate using PVC cement. After the square tubing piece is cemented in place, the circuit board mounting holes can be located by dropping a blank PC board into the enclosure, and then using the PC board as a template to drill the holes. Note that the PC board is not a perfect square and must be oriented properly before drilling the holes.

The completed PC board is mounted in the enclosure using four #6-32 × 1 inch stainless steel screws. The screws are also used as terminals to connect the antenna wires to the modules. Before the outside nut is put on each screw, put a dab of PVC cement around each screw as it comes through the base, in order to make sure water can't get into the module through the screws. Another nut and two star lock washers are used to make the connection to the antenna wire as shown in Figure 5. After the PC board is installed, mark the plus input terminal (the one with the plus sign in Figure 3) by scratching a plus sign into the PVC base near that terminal. It is easy to get mixed up when connecting the antenna wire to the modules without this mark. The top cover is made from clear PVC sheet, so the LED can be viewed, and can be cemented in place after the module is tested.

The Splitter

The splitter assembly acts as the center insulator of the antenna, and the connection point for the coax. It houses the RF chokes (L3 and L4) and capacitors (C4 and C5) that split the RF power from the dc power. The construction of the splitter is similar to that of the relay modules. Drill an extra hole in the base to attach a nylon cord that will be taped to the coax to act as a strain relief for the coax connector. Be sure to waterproof the connector after the coax is connected to the splitter. Board and interior views along with a completed splitter is shown in Figure 6.

The Controller

Refer to Figure 2. The controller is powered from the 12 V transceiver power supply (typically 13.8 V). The FETs, Q1 and Q2, are controlled by an eight pin 12F675 microprocessor. This processor has an analog input to a 10 bit analog to digital converter. The band selector switch connects to a voltage divider (R1 to R9) that produces a particular voltage level

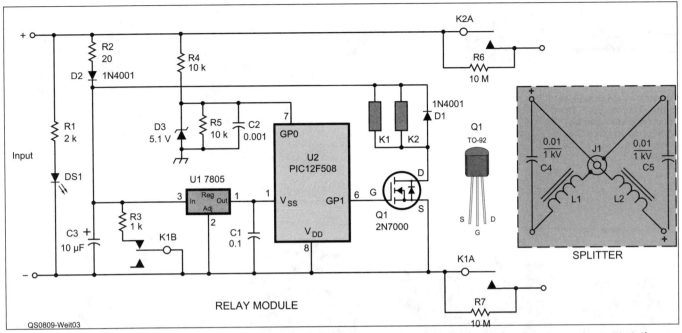

Figure 3 — Schematic and parts list for the relay module and splitter. The 10 MΩ resistors across the relay contacts prevent static buildup on unused antenna sections.

C1 — 0.1 µF, 50 V ceramic capacitor, type Z5U.
C2 — 0.001 µF, ceramic capacitor, type Z5U.
C3 — 10 µF, 50 V electrolytic capacitor (Digi-Key P10316).
C4, C5 — 0.01 µF, 1 kV ceramic disk capacitor (Digi-Key 399-4309).
D1-D2 — 1N4001 or equivalent silicon rectifier (Mouser 863-1N4001G).

D3 — 5.1 V Zener diode (Digi-Key 1N4733ACT).
DS1 — Red LED (Mouser 638-333 ID).
J1 — UHF jack, SO-239.
K1, K2 — Relay (Digi-Key Z1012).
L1, L2 — 100 µH RF choke (Digi-Key M8271).
Q1 — N channel FET (Digi-Key 2N7000D75Z).
R1 — 2 kΩ, ½ W, 5% resistor.
R2 — 20 Ω, ½ W, 5% resistor.

R3 — 1 kΩ, ½ W, 5% resistor.
R4, R5 — 10 kΩ, ½ W, 5% resistor.
R6, R7 — 10 MΩ, ½ W, 5% resistor.
U1 — +5 V regulator (Digi-Key LM78L05ACZFS).
U2 — Microprocessor (Digi-Key PIC12F508-I/P) with author's firmware.
Enclosures fabricated from type 1 PVC materials (McMaster Carr).
Stainless steel hardware (McMaster Carr).

for each band. The processor reads the voltage three times over a one second period to make sure you have finished turning the switch. If a band change is detected, the processor will kill power to all relay modules long enough for them to drop out. It then turns power to the relay modules back on and then generates the correct number of pulses to turn on the right number of relay modules for that band.

The controller does not know if you built your antenna without including a pair of relay modules for a particular band. For instance you might decide not to include relay modules for 30 or 60 meters. In this case, be sure to label the selector switch sequentially for the bands that you are using. Do not provide switch positions for bands that you are not using. When the switch is fully counterclockwise, the controller does not send any pulses to relay modules. Mark this position for the highest frequency band that your antenna is to cover. In the next switch position the controller will energize the first pair of relay modules. Be sure to mark this switch position for the band that is selected by the first pair of relay modules, and so on.

There is a 5-pin DIN connector on the back of the controller. Two of the pins are used to connect to the 12 V dc power supply. Two other pins are used to run the dc power and control signals to the injector. The control signal is connected to the injector using a standard phono connector. Controller and injector circuit boards are shown in Figure 7. The assembled controller is seen in Figure 8.

Assembling the antenna

After all the assemblies are built, everything can be tested by temporarily connecting the relay modules together using hookup wire. After all of the modules are built and tested, it is time to connect them together with antenna wire. I used 450 Ω ladder line with copper coated steel conductors for strength. You can use individual strands of wire as long as one conductor is insulated or spaced in such a way that the wires cannot short together. In one of the earliest versions of the antenna, I used 14 gauge hard drawn copper covered steel antenna wire, for one conductor, and 20 gauge insulated stranded hookup wire for the other conductor. I taped the two wires together every few feet. Having the conductors spread apart, as in the window line, actually increases the bandwidth of the antenna slightly.[3] A single conductor can be used for the run from the last relay module to the end insulator.

Because of the capacitive coupling across the relay contacts, each section of the antenna ends up a little shorter than the standard calculations indicate. It is best to make each

Figure 4 — Relay module. Shown is a completed PC board and front and side views of completed relay modules. The antenna wires will be connected to the studs on the back of the relay modules.

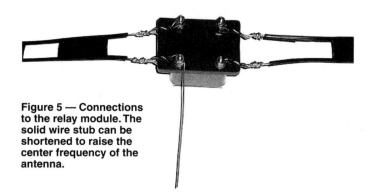

Figure 5 — Connections to the relay module. The solid wire stub can be shortened to raise the center frequency of the antenna.

Figure 7 — Controller PC board and the injector with the covers removed.

Figure 6 — Splitter module. The splitter acts as the center insulator of the antenna. The coax feed line and antenna wires connect to the back of the module.

Figure 8 — Completed antenna controller. This one is set up to cover all HF bands except 30 and 60 meters.

section shorter than the standard calculation. Each section can then be tuned by adding a length of stiff wire to one of the relay module screws on the input side of the module (refer to Figure 5). Keep in mind that shortening the length of a section also shortens the length of any lower frequency bands. The lowest band that your antenna is built for will be the normal length of a standard dipole. Table 1 shows the lengths that I ended up with for an antenna covering the bands listed.

After the antenna is raised, check the SWR on the lowest frequency band first and adjust the overall length to get the desired center frequency. Then go to the highest frequency band and adjust the length of the first pair of stubs for the desired center frequency. Then go to each higher frequency band in order, and adjust the stub lengths to get the center frequencies that you want.

Conclusion

Various versions of this antenna system have worked well for me for more than 5 years. I hope that this antenna system will make it possible for you to enjoy as many of the HF bands as you would like. Source code for the controller and relay module microprocessors are available from the ARRL Web or at the author's Web site, **www.mactenna.net**.[4] It also includes additional construction details, programmed processor chips and complete parts kits.

As with any antenna, make sure that it is disconnected from your transceiver and grounded when not in use.

Thanks to WA1FXT for his help with this article.

Notes
[1] G. Kath, N2OT, and C. Bishop, WB2EPQ, "A Pneumatically Switched Multiband Antenna," *QST*, Aug 2008, pp 30-32.
[2] Several versions of *EZNEC* antenna modeling software are available from developer Roy Lewallen, W7EL, at **www.eznec.com**.
[3] J. Hallas, W1ZR, "The Fan Dipole as a Wideband and Multiband Antenna Element" *QST*, May 2005, pp 33-35.
[4] **www.arrl.org/files/qst-binaries/**.

Photos by the author.

Jim Weit, KI8BV, was first licensed as K3CMN in 1957 and currently holds an Amateur Extra class license. A member of the ARRL, Jim graduated from Cleveland State University with a BSEE degree in 1967 and has worked in development engineering for most of his career. He is presently CEO of a small corporation.

His ham radio interests include fox hunting and experimenting with antennas. He is a VE and an active member of the Sandusky Radio Experimental League. Jim can be reached at 3410 Tiffin Ave, Sandusky, OH 44870 or at **ki8bv@mactenna.net**.

Table 1
Length Measurements for Seven Band Antenna at a Height of 50 Feet Over Average Earth

The antenna length is measured from center to center of the relay modules. The lengths for your antenna may be different depending on which bands are covered, antenna height, wire size and type of ground.

Band (Meters)	Center Frequency (MHz)	Antenna Length (Feet)	Stub Length (Inches)
10	28.85	14	4½
12	24.96	17.7	3¼
15	21.30	20	5¼
17	18.15	23.5	4¼
20	14.25	30	4½
40	7.225	62	7
80	3.85	121.8	

A No Compromise Off-Center Fed Dipole for Four Bands

An easy to build single wire antenna for 40, 20, 10 and 6 meters.

Rick Littlefield, K1BQT

Figure 1 — The 2.8:1 transformer.

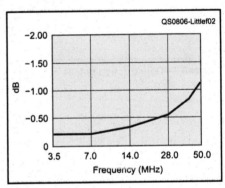

Figure 2 — Total loss of transformer and balun versus frequency.

Many believe the off-center fed dipole (OFCD) is a compromise antenna, but that appraisal may not be deserved. When done right, these antennas can really perform!

Understanding the OCFD

Half wave (λ/2) dipoles are generally fed in the center, a point at which the driving resistance is low enough to provide a convenient match for coaxial feed line. Dipoles will, however, efficiently accept RF power at any point along their length as long as the source is matched to the load. The key to a successful OCFD design is finding that magic point where similar driving resistances appear for multiple bands. Opinions may vary about where that best point is, but most designers locate it roughly ⅓ of the way down the wire and transform it down to 50 Ω using a broadband transformer.

The trouble begins when builders try to cover multiple bands with the antenna too close to ground, or use matching transformers with incorrect ratios. After modeling various designs on *EZNEC* and evaluating a prototype, I found driving resistances tend to converge in the 120 to 140 Ω range at the 33% feedpoint location.[1] These values suggest a transformation ratio of under 3:1, which is significantly lower than the 4:1 or 6:1 transformers often encountered.

Building a 2.8:1 RF Transformer

The simplest way to achieve a suitable match to the OCFD may be with a conventional 2.8:1 transformer as shown in Figure 1. This device has a 3:5 turns ratio and provides a match at the secondary to 138 Ω. Mutually coupled transformers require more careful design than their transmission line counterparts and generally exhibit slightly higher insertion loss. Once the right combination of inductance and core permeability is found, however, construction becomes easy because you don't need to link multiple windings together through a labyrinth of phasing connections.

I made the transformer using a binocular core consisting of two 1⅛ × ¼ inch ID 43-mix EMI sleeves (Fair Rite 2643540002 or equivalent).[2]

The relatively high core permeability of 850 yields good performance over a wide frequency range with a minimal number of turns. The cores are relatively inexpensive and widely available since they are often used as feed line chokes for RG-8X and LMR-240 coax cable.

I used 16 gauge stranded wire covered with a Teflon jacket for the 3-turn primary because it provides a high dc breakdown voltage across the device. The secondary is wound with 5 turns of 18 gauge double coated enameled wire. I found it easier to install the solid wire secondary first, saving the slippery jacketed Teflon wire for when space becomes tight inside the cores. Note that EMI sleeves may have sharp mold seams that can scrape off enamel coating, so use caution when winding.

To test the transformer for SWR response, I attached two 68 Ω resistors in series across the secondary to make up a 136 Ω load. I then connected an analyzer to the primary winding and swept it from 1.8 to 50 MHz. The transformer delivered virtually flat SWR from 2.2 to 24 MHz. The SWR began to slowly creep up beyond that point.

In order to test for insertion loss and power handling, I wound a second identical transformer and connected it back-to-back to the first. Using a signal generator and spectrum analyzer, I measured approximately 0.2 dB of insertion loss per device through 14 MHz, with losses slowly increasing beyond that point. The plot shown in Figure 2 tracks the combined loss for the binocular transformer plus a tandem 1:1 current balun (described below). This small amount of attenuation should have negligible impact on real world signal strength or antenna performance.

Finally, to test power handling, I connected a dummy load to the transformers and applied a 14 MHz, 1000 W test carrier for a 10 second interval. The cores became quite warm to touch but never too hot to handle. More importantly, there were no telltale changes in SWR to signal core saturation. At 0.2 dB insertion loss, a 1000 W carrier will result in about 47 W of heat, or roughly three times what the transformer can safely handle over time allowing 7 W dissipation per core. Based on this finding, I use my AL-80A linear amplifier when I need to, but limit high power operation to casual SSB or CW contacts. I also avoid prolonged amplifier tune-ups.

The 1:1 Current Balun

Because OCFDs are fed asymmetrically, they are especially prone to radiate RF energy from the feed line. To prevent this undesired condition, I installed a 1:1 current balun in tandem with the balanced matching transformer. While the ferrite matching transformer may provide some limited blocking of the undesired common-mode path, it lacks sufficient cross sectional area to provide really good isolation. To enhance isolation, I added a

[1]Notes appear on page 37.

MULTIBAND 35

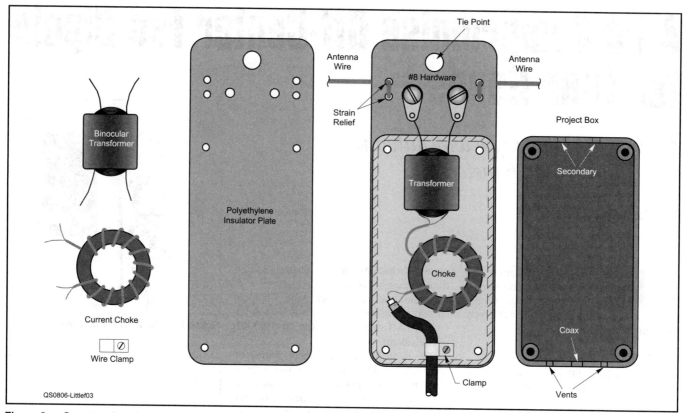

Figure 3 — Construction details of center insulator assembly.

lightweight 1:1 transmission line style current balun in tandem.

The balun core is made from two 1¼ inch outside diameter 43-mix toroids (Fair Rite 5943001601 or FT120-43) stacked together and secured with high-temperature Kapton tape. A light coating of 5 minute epoxy could be used to secure the cores if you don't have tape. The transmission line consists of 18 gauge high-temperature armature wire wound together at 4 to 6 turns per inch with an electric drill. I wound 12 turns of this twisted pair onto the form to complete the balun. Later checks with an RF current probe confirmed good common mode rejection along the feed line on all four bands. Construction details are shown in Figure 3.

Center Block and Weather Enclosure

The center insulator was made from a ⅛ inch thick piece of black marine polyethylene. Other materials may be used, but this particular plastic is very strong and provides good UV protection. I mounted the transformer, balun, and feed line attachment directly onto the polyethylene base and covered it for weather protection with an inexpensive styrene project box. The box is attached via mounting holes normally used to secure its cover. The cover isn't used, but does provide a useful drilling template. I added two ¼ inch vent holes on the bottom side of the project box to permit air circulation and used a round file to create a mouse hole to admit the coax. I also added two small notches at the top to pass the secondary transformer lugs. A couple of dabs of sealant around the secondary leads at the top will prevent water from running in around the lugs.

Making the Antenna Flat Top

I used jacketed wire and, from mid-center block, cut the legs to 22 feet 1½ inches and 44 feet 3½ inches for a total span of 66 feet 5 inches (see Figure 4). If you use bare copper with a higher velocity of propagation, increase these measurements by roughly 2.5% for a total span length of 68 feet.

Note that the antenna wire is wrapped through strain relief holes and attached on the back side of the insulator block with solder lugs. The support tether at the feed point may be used to reduce stress across the span of the flat top. By shopping around, you may be able to locate some inexpensive Teflon jacketed wire that does a very nice job of shedding water and ice. For end insulators, I used two 6 inch strips cut from black polyethylene and ⅛ inch parachute cord for support.

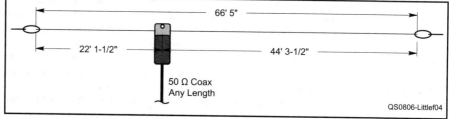

Figure 4 — Cutting dimensions for OCFD.

OCFDs and Mounting Height — the Elephant in the Room

If the OCFD has been touted as a compromise antenna, it may be because builders fail to consider the profound impact of ground proximity on the lower frequency bands. With that caveat in mind, please resist the temptation to double the wire lengths for this project to add 80 meters! It's true that the OCFD is an even-harmonic radiator and that 160, 80, 40, 20 and 10 meter bands are all harmonically related. At normal backyard mounting heights, however, Mother Earth perturbs the fundamental response more than the harmonic responses (see OCFD mounting height data in Table 1). As a result, unless you have very tall trees, you can count on 80 meters resonating

Table 1
Antenna Height versus Resonant Frequency (MHz) and Load Impedance (Ω)

Height (feet)	40 Meters		20 Meters		10 Meters		6 Meters	
70	7.11	87	14.24	150	28.68	128	50.33	139
60	7.12	108	14.18	147	28.64	127	50.34	139
50	7.06	122	14.20	127	28.70	132	50.3	137
40	6.95	114	14.29	135	28.64	125	50.33	137
30	6.87	84	14.26	175	28.67	129	50.33	140
20	6.88	47	14.06	156	28.71	137	50.38	138
10	6.99	15	14.05	63	28.42	124	50.26	151

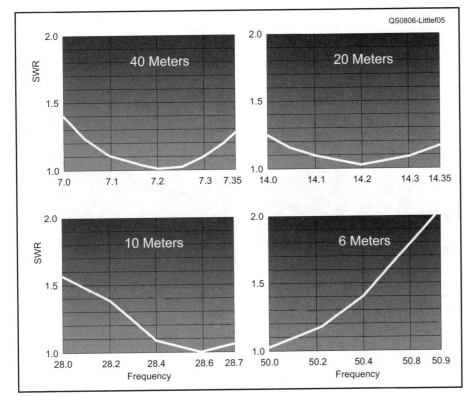

Figure 5 — OCFD SWR versus frequency plots.

below the edge of the band at well under the anticipated 130 Ω driving resistance.

What about Other Bands?

This antenna is not particularly usable on the 30, 17, 15 or 12 meter bands. The lowest modeled SWR I found was 23:1 on 17 meters. If the antenna is fed through 100 feet of RG-8X coax, the cable loss of almost 6 dB would result in an SWR at the radio of about 6:1 — likely usable with a wide range antenna tuner. There would likely be additional loss in the balun and transformer. Thus something less than 25% of the transmitter power would reach the antenna. On the other bands the mismatch is considerably worse.

Going on the Air

Figure 5 shows the measured SWR readings for my 45 foot high installation as seen through 100 feet of RG-8X. These favorable plots confirm *EZNEC*'s prediction that the 2.8:1 transformation ratio and 50 foot mounting height are a winning combination.

When it comes to on-air performance, the OCFD has the advantage of being electrically large, efficient and broadbanded. These qualities translate into having the ability to work almost any station you can hear — plus the freedom to hop from mode to mode or band to band without suffering power reduction from radio's final amplifier reducing power due to high SWR.

On 40 meters, the OCFD functions like any dipole with peak current occurring at mid element. As such, it models with 5.7 dBi gain at 42° elevation and works well for both domestic and DX contacts. On the harmonic bands, the radiation patterns develop progressively more peaks and nulls at higher octaves — much like a G5RV or a center fed dipole. As a result, the antenna will favor some directions with upward of 7.8 dBi gain on 20 meters and 9.2 dBi gain on 10 meters. Note that it is not omnidirectional and will exhibit weaker performance in directions at which nulls occur. The radiation angle on 6 meters is very low and SWR favors the bottom end of the band where horizontally polarized SSB, CW and AM signals prevail.

Finally, because this antenna has low visibility when tucked away among the trees, it might work well for hams living with covenants or apartment dweller restrictions. If you don't mind slitting turf and burying low loss cable in the dark of night, you could install the OCFD up to several hundred feet from your building. You'll lose a couple of dB to feed line loss on the higher bands, but you should suffer no additional transmission losses from high SWR. Best of all, the electrical racket from your complex as well as any consumer gadgets your signal might disable, will be several wavelengths away. Food for thought for the brave of heart!

Conclusion

This article presents a practical approach for achieving excellent multi-band performance and low SWR on its bands between 40 and 6 meters using a simple OCFD design. It doing so, it describes an alternative OCFD matching solution and raises awareness of the potentially negative impact of ground proximity on lower-frequency OCFD performance.

There have been many OCFD configurations described in the amateur literature. Serge Stroobandt, ON4AA, provides an excellent compendium of them on his Web site at **www.stroobandt.com** I also recommend reading the recent paper by L.B. Cebik, W4RNL, *The Isolated Off-Center-Fed Antenna: Some Less-Explored Facets*, available on his Web site at **www.cebik.com**. This comprehensive discussion of OCF behavior offers a wealth of new and useful information to OCF modelers and designers.

Notes
[1] Several versions of *EZNEC* antenna modeling software are available from developer Roy Lewallen, W7EL, at **www.eznec.com**.
[2] **www.fair-rite.com**.

Rick Littlefield, K1BQT, has an Amateur Extra class license. He was first licensed at age 13 in 1957. An avid builder and writer with over 100 technical articles in print, Rick especially enjoys designing antenna and low power projects and was an early inductee into the ARCI QRP Hall of Fame. His professional resume includes extensive work for familiar Amateur Radio manufacturers such as MFJ Enterprises, Ten-Tec and Cushcraft Corporation. He holds a master's degree from the University of New Hampshire and is currently employed as a product design engineer at Laird Technologies in Manchester, New Hampshire. You can contact Rick via e-mail at **k1bqt@arrl.net**.

Six Band Loaded Dipole Antenna

W8NX's unique design technique makes trap look-alikes do double duty. Here's a wire antenna that covers 160/80/40/30/17/12 meters!

Al Buxton, W8NX

Introduction

This article presents a new loaded wire dipole antenna. It covers the classic 160, 80 and 40 meter bands, plus 30, 17 and 12 meters. I call it the *W8NX Special*. Any amateur who installs this antenna and who has a triband beam for 20, 15 and 10 meters has a very good antenna system for working all the amateur high frequency bands from 160 through 10 meters. I installed my W8NX Special as an inverted V, using the tower holding up my triband Yagi as the center support. See Figure 1.

This antenna is based on the highly efficient *dominant element principle*, requiring only two pairs of load elements to give six bands of operation.[1] The radiation patterns have a single pair of broadside lobes on the classic 160, 80 and 40 meters bands but are similar to those of long wire antennas on the 30, 17 and 12 meter bands.

Radiation takes place along the entire length of the antenna on all bands, providing small but useful antenna gains. Good bandwidth is provided on all bands when used in conjunction with an antenna tuner. With the exception of the 160 meter band, full band coverage is provided on all bands. On 160 meters the effective working bandwidth is typically limited by the size of the capacitors in the antenna tuner. The built-in antenna tuner in my FT-1000MP Mark V transceiver can cover 55 kHz on 160 meters using this antenna.

The antenna length is 134 feet, suitable for installation on most city lots. Mine is installed as a "droopy" inverted V dipole, with the apex at 47 feet on the beam tower and drooping to a height of 20 feet at each end. There is little mutual coupling between the triband beam and the six band dipole, since the working frequencies of the two antennas are sufficiently separated to prevent interaction. Some bending and folding at the ends of the dipole antenna is permissible to accommodate installation on a short city lot.

Figure 1 — W8NX Special antenna mounted at 47 feet on tower used to hold triband Yagi. This is an efficient antenna system that covers 160/80/40/30/17/12 meters with the dipole and 20/15/10 meters with the triband Yagi.

Antenna Performance

Figure 2 shows the schematic diagram of the antenna. The schematic looks the same as that of a standard three band trap dipole. However, the loads do not use the truncating capability of tuned parallel resonant traps. This new type of load acts as either a pair of inductors or capacitors to supply the necessary reactance to bring the antenna into resonance with a low feed-point impedance, on both fundamental and odd-order harmonic modes. This makes the antenna suitable for feeding via a 1:1 current balun with either 50 or 75 Ω coaxial cable.

I advise that you use 75 Ω cable because it makes a typical antenna tuner more effective, especially on 160 meters where the size and cost of the large high voltage tuner capacitors is the limiting factor in the effectiveness of a tuner. The innermost pairs of loads create fundamental resonance on both 160 meters and 80 meters. The outermost pairs create fundamental resonance on 40 meters and third harmonic resonance on 30 meters. The overall antenna gives fifth harmonic resonance on 17 meters and seventh harmonic resonance on 12 meters.

The loads are large physically, with significant stray capacitance. They exhibit a parasitic series resonance at approximately 45 MHz (not shown in the Figure 2 schematic). These parasitic stray effects make small increases in the electrical length of the antenna, slightly lowering the antenna operating frequencies. The loads are necessarily large to achieve high Q, low loss performance. Wide air gaps between turns of the load windings and the use of thin walled

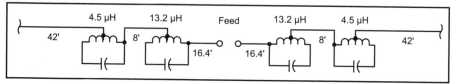

Figure 2 — Schematic for six band W8NX Special using dominant element principle dipole.

---

[1] A. Buxton, "Dominant-Element-Principle Loaded Dipoles," *QEX*, Mar/Apr 2004, pp 20-30.

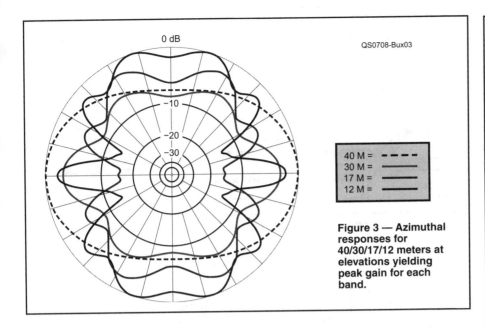

Figure 3 — Azimuthal responses for 40/30/17/12 meters at elevations yielding peak gain for each band.

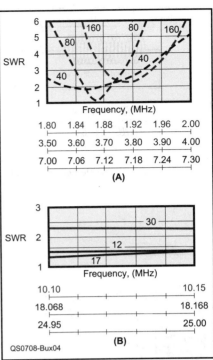

Figure 4 — At A, SWR curves for 160/80/40 meters. At B, SWR curves for 10/17/12 meters.

PVC coil forms minimize dielectric losses in the load elements. The use of RG-8U coax cable with large diameter stranded wire center conductors minimizes skin effect I^2R losses.

The Q of each 160/80 meter load is 260, and the Q of the 40/30 meter loads is 325. Load losses on 80 through 12 meters are less than 0.5 dB, but on 160 meters the loss approaches 3 dB. On 160 meters the radiation resistance of the antenna is low because of the relatively short length of the antenna, reducing the overall radiation efficiency to about 50%.

The radiation patterns have a single pair of broadside lobes on 160, 80 and 40 meters. Figure 3 compares the azimuthal patterns for 40 through 12 meters, at the peak elevation angles for each band. The patterns on the higher frequencies display numerous lobes, characteristic of long wire types of antennas. The peak gain on 40 meters is 1.5 dB above an ordinary dipole. As is the case with an ordinary dipole this has only two lobes. The gain on 12 meters is about the same as on 40 meters but the pattern has 10 lobes.

The measured SWR curves for the 160, 80 and 40 meter bands are shown in Figure 4A; those for the 30, 17 and 12 meter bands are shown in Figure 4B. The SWR curves are those measured at the rig end of an 80 foot long, 75 Ω RG-59 feed line. The curves pretty much speak for themselves.

Those of you interested in getting as much effective working bandwidth as possible on 160 meters can employ the trick of extending the feed line length when operating on 160 to that of a quarter-wave impedance inverter. The length of the extension must bring the total length of the RG-59 feed line to about 100 feet. This maximizes the effectiveness of the antenna tuner, reducing the required size of the tuner capacitors. The tuner now has an easier matching job of keeping your rig or linear amplifier happy. However, you have increased your feed line losses and even though your rig is happy over a broader bandwidth you have somewhat degraded the radiation efficiency of your antenna system. If you carry this trick to extreme measures under high power linear amplifier operation, you could conceivably incur current or voltage breakdown in your antenna feed line. The safe upper limit on 160 meters for SWR for RG-59 feed line is about 6:1 at maximum legal power operation corresponding to a maximum usable bandwidth of 130 kHz.

Remember your rig or linear amplifier never sees this SWR — the antenna tuner shields it from this level of mismatch. Your

Figure 5 — At left, construction techniques for 160/80 meter load element. At right, construction techniques for 40/30 meter load element.

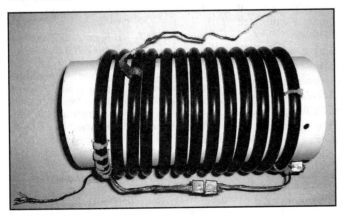
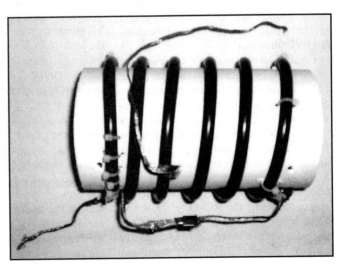

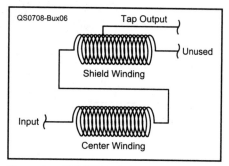

Figure 6 — RG-8U load element schematic.

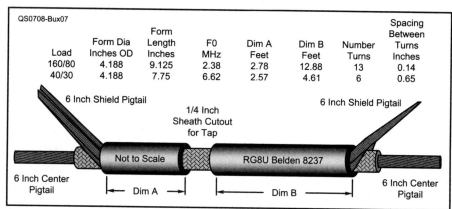

Load	Form Dia Inches OD	Form Length Inches	F0 MHz	Dim A Feet	Dim B Feet	Number Turns	Spacing Between Turns Inches
160/80	4.188	9.125	2.38	2.78	12.88	13	0.14
40/30	4.188	7.75	6.62	2.57	4.61	6	0.65

Figure 7 — Details of the load element coax.

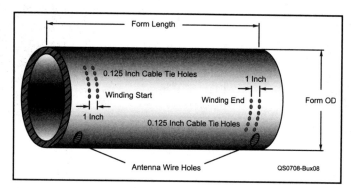

Figure 8 — Details of coil form.

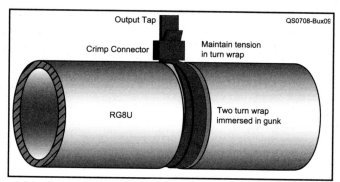

Figure 9 — Output tap detail.

antenna tuner does not reduce the SWR on the feed line. While some amateurs frown upon using this trick, it does give considerably more effective working bandwidth for 160 meter operation.

Construction

The toughest part of constructing this antenna is making the load elements. Figure 5A shows the 160/80 and 40/30 meter load elements. The load element schematic is in Figure 6. Note how the pigtail at the output end of the center winding is fed backward to the pigtail of the input end of the shield winding. The loads are made of RG-8U coaxial cable (Belden 8237) wound on a form made of 4.188 inch outside diameter PVC drain pipe.

Figure 7 shows details of the coax used for the loads. Figure 8 shows the load forms, the critical ones being the lengths and diameters of the forms and the 1 inch edge margins of the windings on the forms. Dimensions A and B fix the output tap location, with the RG-8U laid out flat and straight on a table. The tap is a 15 inch length of silvered braided shield wire cannibalized from RG-58 coax cable. The tap requires two turns tightly wrapped around the RG-8U wire at the ¼ inch break cut in the PVC sheath. Cover this break with anti corrosion gunk (Burndy Products, Penetrox A will do) to prevent resistance developing at the tap.

Care is required in making the output tap to hold the two turn wrap around the RG-8U permanently in tension using a crimp connector. Figure 9 shows the details of the 15 inch output tap of the loads. Unfortunately, soldering at the tap would weaken the electrical properties of the RG-8U coax cable so a mechanical-only connection is necessary.

The input terminal of any load is the near end (nearest the feed line) of the center conductor winding of the coax cable. The far end of the center conductor is fed back to the near end of the shield winding. The output of the load is taken at the tap on the outer shield winding. The output tap acts as an auto transformer, giving the needed L/C ratio for the load. You should fine tune the loads to within 1% of the specified frequency. I used a dip meter and an accurately calibrated receiver for fine tuning the loads.

Air gap spacing between the turns of each load reduces dielectric load losses and permits fine tuning of the load resonant frequency. Expanding the air gap increases the load resonant frequency; reducing the gap lowers the frequency. Do not hesitate to increase the gap between turns as much as necessary to achieve the resonant frequency of the load, even though you may distort the appearance of the load. After completion of the fine tuning, the location of the turns must be stabilized by cable ties, as shown in Figure 5. More cable ties are actually required than are shown, especially around the first and last turns of the load winding. Stabilizing the interior turns is not as critical, as they have less effect on the load's resonant frequency than the outermost first and last turns.

Although making the loads for this antenna may seem like a challenging task, your efforts will be well rewarded. There is nothing as satisfying in ham radio as the successful completion of a good, hands-on homebrew project.

I wish to thank my friend and colleague, Mel Vye, W8MV, whose help and constructive comments are greatly appreciated. I also wish to thank Jeremy (KB8QVF) and Angie Holland for their help with the photography of the antenna and the load elements.

Al Buxton, W8NX, has been a radio amateur since he was first licensed as W7GLC in 1937. A registered professional engineer, Al holds BSEE and MSEE degrees from Tulane University. His career spans industry and academia: 26 years in the defense industry with Goodyear Aerospace, six years with Tulane University and 11 years with the University of Akron. He's an Associate Professor Emeritus of Akron University. In industry, Al worked on the development of computers, automatic controls, radar, aircraft guidance, and navigation and space antennas. You can reach Al at 2225 Woodpark Rd, Akron, OH 44333 or **buxtonw8nx@aol.com**.

An All-Band Attic Antenna

Nothing beats an "aluminum cloud" on a tall tower, but when choices are limited, an indoor antenna can be amazingly effective.

Kai Siwiak, KE4PT

If zoning rules or aesthetic considerations make outside antennas prohibitive, an indoor antenna might just provide enough performance for casual operation on all bands ranging from 80 to 6 meters. With only 100 W, I've managed contacts with hams in over 130 DXCC countries and all 50 states, including 25 states and 13 countries confirmed on 6 meters. I've even made contacts on the 160 meter band, but the efficiency there is poor, and I don't recommend operating on 160 meters with this antenna.

This isn't a design article for a specific indoor antenna, but rather a description of the performance of one indoor antenna, and some guidelines that might help you understand the limitations, performance and RF safety aspects of antennas of this type.

The KE4PT Attic Antenna

I've been operating with an indoor inverted-L antenna in my attic for several years. I drive the antenna with an ICOM IC-706MKIIG running 100 W through a current balun and an ICOM AH-4 automatic antenna tuner located at the antenna feed point.[1] The tuner is what makes this antenna capable of operation on all of these bands. The basic idea was to place as much of the wire as possible into the clearest space of a cluttered attic in my one floor home in south Florida, as seen in Figure 1.

Design Approach

My basic design approach was to provide a fat radiating conductor using two parallel conductors of fairly thick wire spaced nearly 3 feet apart. This tends to smooth out impedance variations versus frequency and lets the automatic tuner do its work smoothly. I chose aluminum wire for its availability and cost. These

[1]Notes appear on page 45.

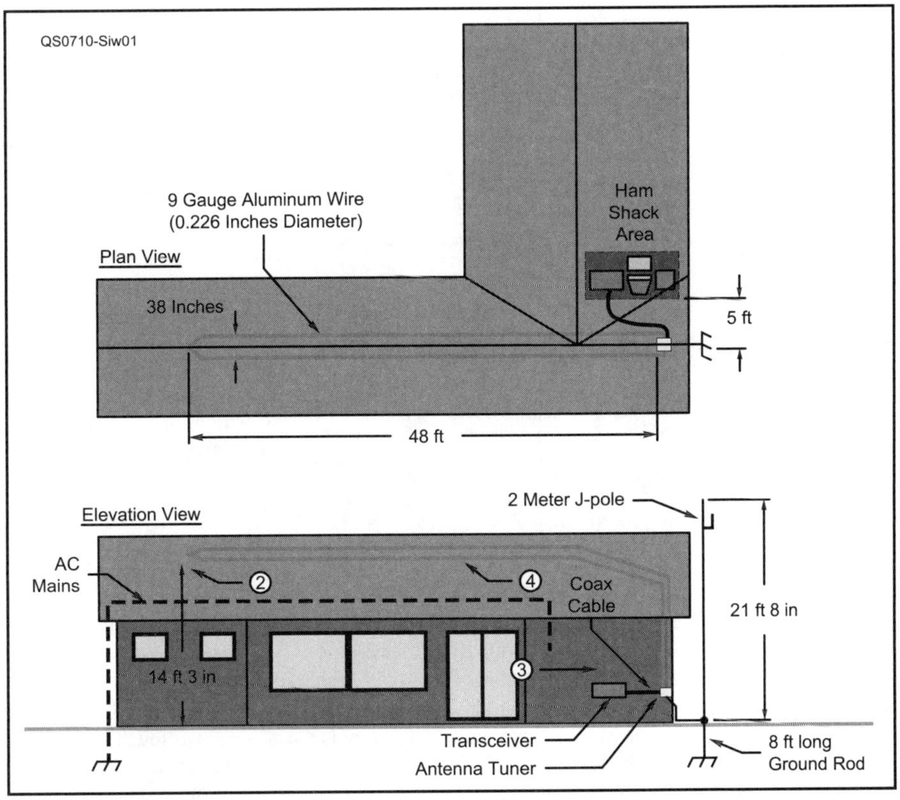

wires were placed as far as physically possible from other conducting objects in the attic.

I wanted an antenna that could be operated over the widest frequency range possible; so the L length was chosen as long as possible to obtain reasonable efficiency at the lowest frequencies, but with tolerable antenna pattern ripples at the highest frequencies. The actual length was constrained by the available attic space. Next, I used an antenna ground post to act as a counterpoise element. The whole system was match tuned at the feed point with an automatic tuner.

It All Came Together

The horizontal part of the L element comprises two parallel lengths of 9 gauge aluminum wire shorted at the far end, and spaced about 38 inches, as shown in Figure 2. The horizontal portion is about 48 feet long, and a bit more than 14 feet above the ground, under the roof of the house. The horizontal length is approximately a wavelength at 21 MHz so the antenna pattern is very nearly omnidirectional from the 20 down to 80 meters.

The parallel wires are brought together and emerge from the ceiling on a far wall of the house in a storage closet, as shown in Figure 3. Both of the parallel wires are joined together and connected to the antenna post of the AH-4 tuner. A copper ground wire runs from the tuner ground connection to an outside 8 foot deep ground rod. The antenna shares this ground rod with a conductive mast supporting a 2 meter J-pole that tops out at 21.7 feet. This mast also functions as part of the HF radiating system. A length of 50 Ω coaxial cable connects the tuner through an eight turn 5 inch diameter choke balun to the transceiver at the operating position in the ham shack on the other side of the wall of the storage closet.

We're Not Alone

The antenna isn't alone in the attic. There are air conditioning ducts as well as the ac mains power distribution for the house, which are marked by the heavy dashed line in Figure 1. This conduit can also be seen in Figure 4. I modeled the inverted L, the ground post with the attached J-pole mast, and the ac mains including its own ground post by using 4nec2 antenna modeling software.[2] The pro-

Figure 1 — Plan and elevation views of the attic inverted L antenna. The numbers are keys to the photographic views.

MULTIBAND 41

Figure 2 — The inverted L element is supported by egg insulators suspended from the rafters in the attic.

Figure 4 — The ac conduit parallels the antenna elements.

Figure 3 — The ham shack and transceiver are 6 feet to the left of the AH-4 tuner shown in the lower part of the photo.

Indoor Antenna Performance

What can be better that an extended on-the-air test? I kept track of many of my contacts (QSOs) by plotting them using *DxAtlas* by Alex Shovkoplyas, VE3NEA.[3] The results can be seen by the color-coded points on the maps in Figures 5, 6 and 7. The QSOs are between my south Florida location and the mapped points. Figure 5 shows QSOs in the 160 meter band (a few dark red marks), and in the 80, 60, 40 and 30 meter bands. The very close distances are covered well, although there were contacts as far away as Australia, South Africa and India and into Europe on 40 and 30 meters. The green points shown in Figure 6 show 20 meter coverage. A distinct skip zone occurs around my location. Coverage beyond that is worldwide. Figure 7 shows dark blue points for 17 and 15 meter band QSOs, light blue points for 12 and 10 meter QSOs and distinctive gold points marking the 6 meter "magic band" QSOs with 14 states, Puerto Rico and Spain. The 17 through 10 meter coverage has a prominent skip zone of about 1000 km around my location.

Propagation predictions using *HAM-CAP* freeware basically confirm the actual performance of the antenna over the long term, including the skip zones and the tendency for the 17 through 10 meter bands to dominate coverage into South America.[5]

I get my fair share of the rare and distant ones (VU7, 9Q1, VK9N, 1AØ, VQ9 and KH8/S on all five bands), not because of awesome RF power — I use just 100 W — or a high "aluminum cloud" antenna, but by listening and operating carefully, although those rare DX catches are as much a testament to the operating skills of the DXpedition operators! I also take advantage of the extra 2 to 3 S-units of signal-to-noise enhancement that operating on CW provides.

The Advantage of CW

With a maximum of 100 W from my transmitter, my CW average power is 40 W, but with SSB it is an average of only 20 W (3 dB advantage for CW). At the receiver end of the propagation link the CW receiver noise bandwidth is typically 300 Hz compared with 2700 Hz for SSB (9.5 dB more for CW). Finally, the CW operators appear to listen a bit more intently to my CW, especially many of the DXpedition operators, perhaps tolerating 6 dB SNR whereas comfortable SSB listening needs 10 dB SNR (another 4 dB advantage for CW). The net advantage of CW over SSB might be as much as 16.5 dB or the equivalent of about 3 S-units!

gram uses the *NEC2* (Numerical Electromagnetic Code) calculation engine, and is available for free. I started the *NEC* based analysis to make sure that I could adequately assess the RF exposure that results from this unusual antenna. As a by-product of that effort I was able to learn about the antenna patterns and radiation efficiency of this antenna.

The *NEC* modeling revealed that substantial RF currents exist on the J-pole mast, and they contribute significantly to the overall radiation from the antenna. The J-pole mast contributes a vertical polarization component to the overall radiation pattern that helps keep the far field patterns relatively omnidirectional, especially at the higher frequencies. This was an unplanned benefit, with the interesting lesson that all conductors radiate, even when connected across an earth ground connection!

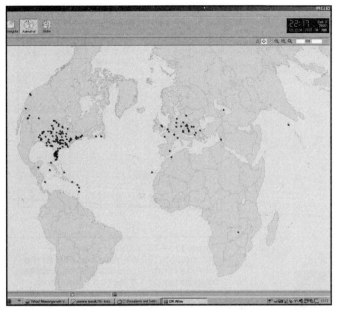

Figure 5 — Some contacts from KE4PT in South Florida. Dark red 1.8 and 3.6 MHz, red 5.4, 7 and 10.1 MHz.

Figure 6 — Contacts from KE4PT in the 14 MHz band.

What NEC says

The proof is in the antenna currents. I modeled the antenna and ground system, along with the ac mains and the J-pole mast using *4nec2,* which employs the *NEC2* calculation engine. The basic radiation pattern in the lower bands is a flattened cardioid pattern pointing upward as seen in the 10.1 MHz pattern shown in Figure 8. The antenna pattern in the figure is centered on the feed point of the antenna. To a receiver anywhere on the horizon, the pattern at 10° elevation varies less than an S-unit for 20 meters and longer wavelengths.

As frequency is increased the antenna pattern on the horizon develops more ripples, and the 2 meter J-pole mast contributes more vertically polarized energy to fill in horizontally polarized pattern dips. At 51 MHz, shown in Figure 9, multiple antenna pattern lobes are evident, but coverage again is still roughly omnidirectional in azimuth — effectively within 2 S-units. The total antenna system polarization is randomly elliptical, having both vertical and horizontal components. This can be seen in Figure 10 in which the polarization axial ratio is shown in color on the 51 MHz pattern. Blue indicates a linear polarization, and a trip through the color spectrum shows elliptical polarization culminating in circular polarization in the directions corresponding to the purple colored pattern areas. Informal S-meter tests by a local ham within 20 miles of my location verified that there was

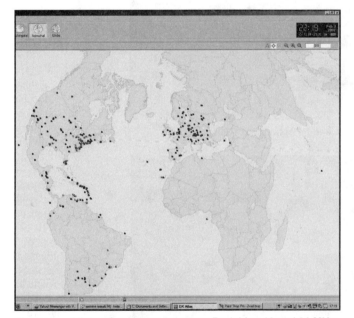

Figure 7 — Higher frequency contacts. Dark blue 18 and 21 MHz, light blue 24 and 28 MHz, gold 50.1 MHz.

substantial energy in both the horizontal and vertical polarization components during an impromptu 6 meter band test.

The antenna radiation efficiency can be defined as the total power radiated into space (that is, above the ground) divided by the transmitter power. Efficiency, predicted by *NEC2,* is between about –7 dB and –1 dB across 3.5 to 54 MHz. Efficiency dips to a dismal –20 dB in the 160 meter band, so the antenna is not too useful there, although I've made a few contacts in several states on that band. I tried modifications of the design by modeling various ground radials attached to the ground post. Efficiency was not significantly improved, however. At my location, the ground radials could be physically placed only perpendicular to the horizontal element, but that configuration produced undesirable deep nulls in the azimuth pattern.

No attempt was made to predict the antenna input impedances because (1) I always intended to use an automatic tuner, and (2) there were simply too many non-modeled coupling effects in the attic, including a substantial barrel-tile roof which sits inches above the antenna wires. As expected, the *NEC* analysis revealed that the currents on the antenna wires, the ac mains wires, and the J-pole structure are indeed standing waves starting with a null at the open end of each wire. This motivated a relatively simple RF exposure analysis described next.

Some Words about RF Safety and RFI

Indoor antennas should be very carefully considered from the RF safety point of view, especially for those within the dwelling. In addition, there is always potential for RF interference within the home. This applies as much to wire antennas as it does to small loops. Two possible hazards exist: the potentially high RF voltage that can exist on the antenna conductors and exposure to electric (E) and magnetic (H) fields. Both potential hazards are avoided by keeping one's distance!

But How Close is Safe?

I initially evaluated this antenna by real-

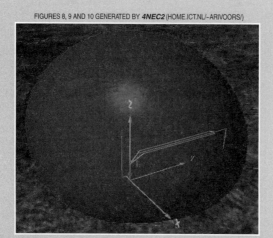

Figure 8 — The antenna and its 10.1 MHz pattern.

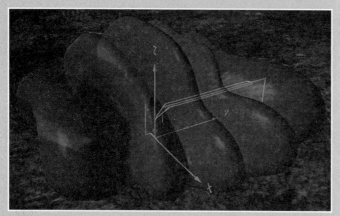

Figure 9 — The antenna and its pattern at 51 MHz.

Figure 10 — Polarization axial ratio at 51 MHz.

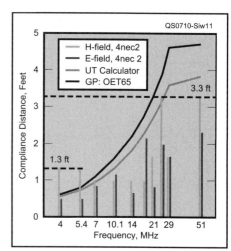

Figure 11 — RF safety compliance distance (at 100 W) from any part of the antenna ranges from 3.3 feet on 6 meters down to under 1.4 feet on 80 meters.

izing that at any particular frequency the currents and voltages along the conductors would be standing waves — just as on a dipole. As verified by *NEC* modeling, the electric charge accumulations are "out of phase" with the currents on the wire. Thus, where the standing wave current in the wire (and hence the H fields around the wire) goes through a null the voltages (and hence the E fields) peak, and vice versa.

To estimate the RF exposure, I then assumed that at any point on the antenna wire the currents would resemble those of a resonant dipole with the full power applied at that point. Then I tried the very simple-to-use University of Texas online calculator to determine a compliance distance.[6] I used the "occupational/controlled environment" since I have full control of access to the RF exposed areas.

Crunching the Numbers

The calculator needs very few inputs — 100 W RF power, an assumed 2.2 dBi gain of a dipole and a choice of whether there is a ground contribution (I selected no ground contribution). The largest compliance distance of 3.8 feet from any part of the antenna occurs in the 6 meter band, and that was initially the number I used for the compliance distance *at all frequencies*.

As an added check, I also used the "General Purpose Tables" in *RF Exposure and You*, with 100 W, 0 dBi and a controlled environment.[7] Finally, I calculated the near E and H fields using *4nec2* with a "real ground" and 100 W. The composite results are shown in Figure 11 in the form of compliance distance versus frequency. The University of Texas calculator and the general purpose tables give similar results. They appear to be adequate above 7 MHz, but they underestimate the exposure compliance distance at lower frequencies for this particular antenna.

A Second Opinion

The *4nec2* calculations predict compliance distances that are up to a factor of two larger than those obtained with the other approximations for frequencies below 7 MHz. The magnetic fields near the ground on the vertical portion of the antenna are the source of this discrepancy.

The *NEC2* engine in *4nec2* does allow connections of wires to ground, but does not model wires underground such as the ground post that's part of this antenna. It also does not correctly handle the charge distributions at the wire-ground interface, except for the case of a perfect ground. Bill Guy, W7PO, kindly helped me by using *NEC3*, which correctly accounts for buried wires, to check my antenna including the actual buried ground posts.[4] *NEC3* is still under export restrictions and is not generally available.

And the Answer Is —

A spot check of near fields of my antenna both near the vertical and near the horizontal parts of the wires shows that away from the ground connection *4nec2* (using the *NEC2* engine) and *NEC3* predict the same relative field strengths, typically within 10%, for a given radiated power level. Near the ground post connection, however, ground-level field values are similar only if a perfect ground is selected in *4nec2*. For practical RF exposure evaluations, especially for unusual antennas such as this one, modeling should be tried with both a real ground and with a perfect ground, then the most conservative compliance distance should be used.

For this antenna, the 6 meter band *4nec2* result of 3.3 feet gives sufficient compliance distance safety margin on all lower frequency bands. *Lesson: Evaluate unusual antennas very carefully, especially if a ground or ground post is part of the system!*

RFI Rears its Head

Because this indoor antenna is extremely close to wiring in the house, RF interference within the home is a strong possibility. I've noticed coupling RF energy to the ADSL, computer connection, side of my phone line, but only during 160 meter operation. That RFI potential and the generally poor antenna efficiency keep me off the 160 meter band. There is also noticeable coupling to my TV and audio systems, which is remedied by restricting operating during prime family TV viewing times.

Conclusions

An indoor antenna such as this one is not the contester's dream antenna, nor is it a DX hunter's "special," but it can be a useful and effective "stealth antenna" that will get you on the air on all ham frequencies between 3.5 and 54 MHz. Careful operating practices and the use of narrow-band modes, such as CW and digital modes, can yield delightful results. The use of an antenna automatic matching tuner at the feed point allows great flexibility in positioning attic wires, and in my case, allowed for an effective all-band design. Modeling with *NEC* provides great insight into the performance. Finally, great care must be taken in the RF safety analysis.

I'd like to acknowledge and thank Bill Guy, W7PO, for his help with the *NEC3* modeling, and Bob McGraw, K4TAX; Bob Walker, N4CU; Tom Kneisel, K4GFG, and Diana Siwiak, KE4QXL, for their helpful reviews and suggestions.

Notes

[1]R. D. Straw, Editor, *The ARRL Antenna Book*, 21st Edition, pp 26-21. Available from your ARRL dealer or the ARRL Bookstore, ARRL order no. 9876. Telephone 860-594-0355, or toll-free in the US 888-277-5289; **www.arrl.org/shop/**; **pubsales@arrl.org**.
[2]A. Voors, "NEC Based Antenna Modeler and Optimizer," **home.ict.nl/~arivoors/**.
[3]*DX Atlas*, **www.dxatlas.com/**.
[4]K. Siwiak and W. Guy are both members of the ARRL RF Safety Committee, **www.arrl.org/rfsafety/**.
[5]*HAM-CAP*, **www.dxatlas.com/HamCap/**.
[6]Online RF exposure evaluation, **n5xu.ece.utexas.edu/rfsafety/**.
[7]E. Hare, *RF Exposure and You*, ARRL, Newington, CT, 1998.

Kai Siwiak, PhD, KE4PT, was first licensed in 1964. He is a consulting engineer specializing in antennas, propagation, communications systems and ultra-wideband (UWB) wireless technology. Kai has authored several text books on those subjects and also wrote the electromagnetic theory chapter in ARRL's RF Exposure and You. *He holds more than 30 US patents, has been a frequent contributor to IEEE 802 standards, and was an advisor to the US delegation to the ITU-R on UWB technology. He is a member of ARRL, SAREX (Space Amateur Radio Experiment), a life member of AMSAT and a member of the ARRL RF Safety Committee. Kai prefers CW, usually on 40 through 6 meters, depending on those elusive sunspots. He can be reached at* **ke4pt@amsat.org** *for any questions or comments.*

A Wire Antenna Combination for DX

KT0NY takes two vintage flat-tops with tuned feeders, adds a wire Yagi and gets DX performance suitable for the 21st century. Will it work at your location?

Tony Estep, KT0NY

Many hams are faced with cold realities that force a compromise antenna installation. This article is dedicated to amateurs who are in that situation, but still want to be competitive in DX pileups. It describes one amateur's approach to a low-visibility antenna setup that covers a lot of directions, gives acceptable gain, and works on a wide range of frequencies. As you'll see, my scheme involves switching among three inconspicuous antennas. Two are combined into an "over-and-under" two-radiator long wire-dipole combination and the third is a Yagi that lies flat on the roof.

In my neighborhood, a tower is out of the question. Even an end-fed vertical won't do, since there's no way to have a radial system in my yard. Fortunately, however, antenna supports in the form of trees are conveniently provided. Looking at the two trees that are close enough to my shack, I tried to sketch out something that would give me a chance of a reasonable signal to DX locations. I wanted to get decent performance in as many directions as possible, with a low-visibility installation. Moreover, I want to work all bands from 80 to 10 meters.

I could readily see how I could put up at least one pretty good wire antenna between trees, but it appeared that my geographical coverage would be limited. The wire would run North-South, so I'd be shooting a good signal to Africa and Australia, but Europe would be 45° off of the perpendicular, and Asia would be right off the end of the wire. I didn't want an antenna that would give good gain in one or two directions while leaving the rest of the world unreachable. After scratching my head over this dilemma, I invested in Roy Lewallen's *EZNEC*[1] antenna analysis software. The $89 was some of the best money I've ever spent in ham radio.

The KT0NY Solution

I started with the most obvious choice,

[1]*EZNEC* software available from **www.eznec.com**.

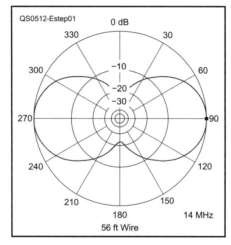

Figure 1—20 meter pattern of a 56 foot wire, oriented N/S and center-fed, at 40 feet; the low-angle radiation is E/W. (Important note: All patterns shown are for 8° take-off angle.) The length is chosen because this forms an extended double Zepp on 15 meters. This dipole will give limited directional coverage at low angles on 40, 30, 20, 17 and 15 meters.

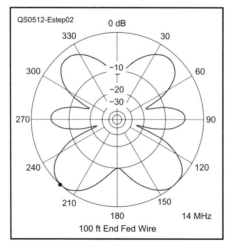

Figure 2—20 meter pattern of a 100 foot N/S oriented long wire, fed 13% from the north end, at 40 feet. This gives coverage that nicely complements that of the center-fed dipole.

a center fed dipole running from the north tree to the south tree. I chose a length of 56 feet, equal to an extended double Zepp on 15 meters. This antenna gives a figure-8 pattern pointing East and West. Its 20 meter pattern is shown in Figure 1.

Some tinkering with *EZNEC* gave me an idea for a way to supplement this pattern. Consider Figure 2. But the two antennas can't occupy the same space—or can they? I quickly concluded that they could. I sketched out the arrangement shown in Figure 3.

Both antennas are fed with tuned feeders. Figure 4 shows the support details. At first I brought the feeders into the shack and tuned them with a balanced tuner. At present, the lines lead to 4:1 current baluns right outside the shack window; a 6 foot length of coax brings them in to a standard unbalanced tuner. Both systems work, but I prefer having only coax inside the shack. My Ten-Tec 238A antenna tuner has a convenient antenna switch that lets me select my directional pattern—the poor man's rotator!

The idea is that I can switch back and forth between antennas, so that one of the major radiation lobes will be pointed (more or less) at the DX I'm trying to work. When you put the two patterns together, the coverage is as shown in Figure 5.

This looks good. The gain is a little higher to SE and SW than to NE and NW, which is the opposite of what I would like, but that's an unavoidable consequence of feeding the longwire 13½ feet from the north end. Of course, at your station the wires may have to run in a different direction. No matter. You should be able to cover many compass points, however your house and lot might be oriented.

The story is not quite as favorable as Figure 5 depicts, however. Using *EZNEC*, I modeled the actual shape of the system, including the droop in the center, the effects of transmission lines in the radiation field, and the interaction between the two antennas. These effects reduce the gain somewhat.

This is unfortunate, but can't be helped. Figures 6 and 7 give a realistic appraisal of

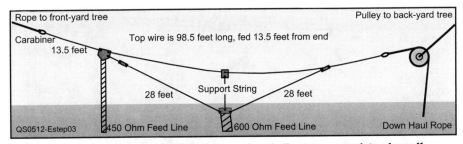

Figure 3—As constructed, the KTØNY "over-and-under" antenna consists of an off-center-fed 98.5 foot wire with a 56 foot center-fed dipole hanging below it. The ends are at about 42 feet, the low point (at the center of the dipole) is at about 32 feet.

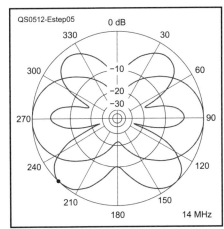

Figure 5—Total coverage of theoretical wire combination on 20 meters. Patterns on 15, 17 and 30 meters have generally similar shape.

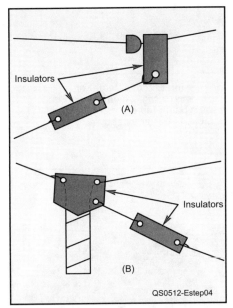

Figure 4—Details of the fittings for hanging the dipole below the long wire. Parts are made of ⅜ inch thick Delrin. At (A) right end support, at (B) left end support.

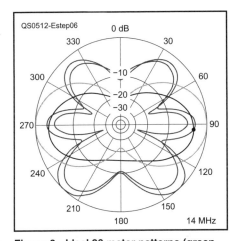

Figure 6—Ideal 20 meter patterns (green, red) and predicted pattern (black, blue) superimposed. The droop in the middle and the effect of interactions degrade the results, especially for the center-fed dipole.

the gain achieved. Very roughly speaking, on both 20 and 15 meters, the gain of the antenna system in the direction of its favored lobes is almost as good as that of a 2 element Yagi at 25 feet as shown in Figure 8.

Due North

The composite pattern figures reveal that the antenna so far puts little signal directly north. This bugged me, because some truly juicy DX (4S7, XW, XX9, and others) lie right in that northerly null. So I hit on a desperate idea for one last DX antenna. It is good for only one direction, on one band, but on the plus side it is almost completely invisible.

I built a single-band, single-direction wire Yagi, for 20 meters only, consisting of two wires lying right on the roof. They are about 20 feet above the ground, one on either side of the peak of the roof (in other words, the interaction between the elements takes place through the roof). Because the feed line has to exit to the south, I had to use a driven element/director combination, which is not as good as a driven element plus reflector. But it does work, and the resulting 20 meter pattern is shown in Figure 9.

A little experimentation with *EZNEC* will reveal that the pattern and gain deteriorate rapidly as you go above the optimal frequency. Therefore, the best setup is to tune the antenna for the high end of the 20 meter band. The SWR and gain will be acceptable across the whole band. I discovered that there are some tricks involved in actually constructing this antenna. After some trial and error, I found a simple procedure that worked well. (It will be much easier if you have an antenna analyzer.)

Make the two elements as shown in Figure 10, and cut them a bit oversize (note that dimensions are for insulated 14 gauge wire). Take them up to the roof, along with a short length of coax and your analyzer. Lay out the driven element, hook it to the analyzer, and find the frequency at which it displays lowest SWR. Trim it until the lowest SWR is at 14.300, even if you plan to operate mostly CW.

Now lay out the director right next to the driven element, and cut it to be 15 inches shorter. Then install it 13½ feet in front of the driven element. You now have a full-size, wide-spaced 20 meter Yagi.

The SWR curve will probably be pretty flat across the band. The *EZNEC* modeled curve has a fairly pronounced dip, so the "improvement" is due to losses caused by proximity to stuff in the near field. If you're going to put the antenna right on the roof, this can't be avoided. Coupling to the household wiring is a bad thing, of course, and the more you can elevate the wire Yagi, the better it is likely to perform. But low and lossy as it is, mine gives a boost of up to 10 dB over my long wire on signals coming from due north.

DX Results

The total setup is unobtrusive. Few notice it. From the viewpoint of the neighbors, all that is really visible is some window line running up into the front yard tree. The rooftop Yagi is almost impossible to see.

And, yes, it does work DX. After a long period of inactivity, I put up my first version of this antenna and became active in February 2004. In the ensuing 12 months, operating after work in the evenings, usually with limited power, I've worked 251 countries. I have snagged DXCC on phone, cw and digital, and I just completed DXCC on QRP. My wires have propelled my signal through the pileups on just about every DXpedition that has been on since I've been active. And best of all, I have managed that most elusive of my personal goals, WAZ.

The complete configuration is shown in Figure 11. There are limitations and frustrations, of course, but they are a lot less than I expected when I first contemplated a wire antenna. I hope that this article contains some ideas that may be helpful to others in similar situations.

Tony Estep, KTØNY, was first licensed in

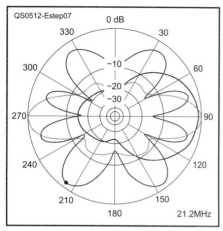

Figure 7—On 15 meters, the radiation in favored directions is roughly comparable to a 2 element Yagi (black) at 25 feet.

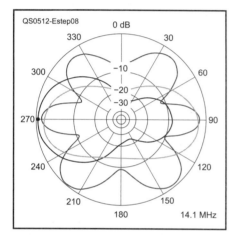

Figure 8—On 20 meters, the best gain is again similar to a low 2 element Yagi. It doesn't have much gain over a dipole, but covers more territory. On 40 and 80 meters, coverage is essentially omnidirectional. On 12 and 10 meters, it's mainly NE/SW and NW/SE.

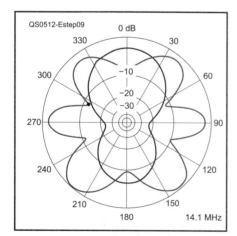

Figure 9—The wire Yagi on the roof works only on 20 meters, and only in one direction (black), but it fills in the null left by the other antennas, in the direction of the DX I need most! For construction, see Figure 10.

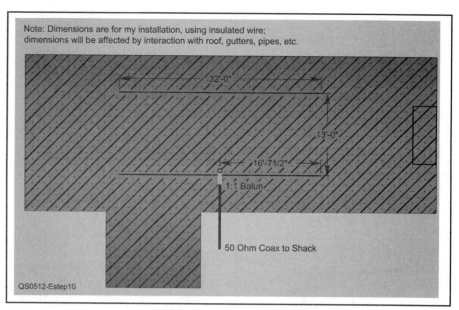

Figure 10—Two wires lying right on the roof, and running E/W at a height of 22 feet, form a fixed, single-band Yagi. The southern wire is the driven element, and the northern one is a director. To build it, make a balun-fed dipole resonant at the high end of the band, then add a director 15 inches shorter as shown. Dimensions shown are for PVC insulated wire.

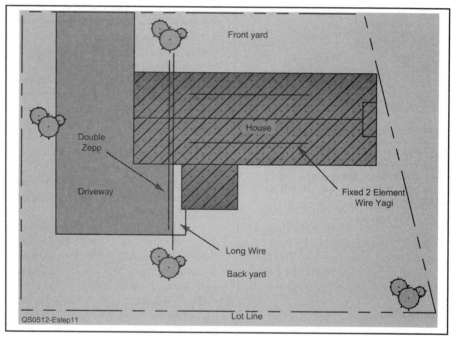

Figure 11—My house and yard are in a typical suburban configuration with neighbors on both sides. Still, I wound up with an antenna installation that performs well, without creating any neighborhood strife.

St Louis, Missouri in 1957 as KN0LTB at age 17. The sunspots were going crazy at the time, very different from today's conditions. Tony managed to complete his DXCC as a Novice with a Hallicrafters SX-96 receiver and a homebrew transmitter.

He later moved to London, where he held the call G5ANZ. When he returned to St Louis, he got his Amateur Extra class license, set up a shack, and after various tries with wire antennas eventually evolved the antenna scheme described in this article. It has accounted for WAZ, DXCC with QRP, and a lot of fun.

Tony holds a BA degree from Washington University and recently retired from a 43 year career on Wall Street, most recently as Managing Director of Bank of America Capital Management. While Tony is the author of many publications in the field of finance, this is his first in Amateur Radio. Tony can be reached at 541 Hickory Ln, St Louis, MO 63131 or kt0ny@arrl.net.

The Horizontal Loop — An Effective Multipurpose Antenna

The horizontal loop need not be resonant and can work well in a number of ways

Scott M. Harwood Sr, K4VWK

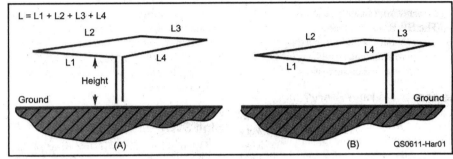

Figure 1 — At A, corner of angle-fed (AF) configuration showing key parameters. At B, center-fed (CF) configuration.

It's been well documented that a large horizontal loop will perform well as an amateur radio antenna. It may also be one of the most misunderstood of antennas. Many hams believe a loop must be resonant on the lowest operating frequency to work well at the design and higher frequencies. The fact is, as I will show later, a loop need not be resonant at all to perform well.

One purpose of this article is to demonstrate how to use computer modeling to perfect a loop for one's needs and location. This paper is not an antenna modeling tutorial. Programs such as *EZNEC* and *NEC Win-Plus* are relatively inexpensive and readily available.[1,2] Thus, I assume readers have a sufficient working knowledge of their respective modeling program to allow modeling the antenna and ground conditions and will be able to interpret the program outputs. Those wishing to learn more should look at the excellent ARRL Antenna Modeling Course, authored by L.B. Cebik, W4RNL, (L.B.) or at least visit his Web site.[3,4]

The Misunderstood Loop

L.B. has written several excellent papers on loops that can also be found on his Web site.[5] These should be required reading for anyone contemplating building one. He points out two general misconceptions; the

[1]Notes appear on page 51.

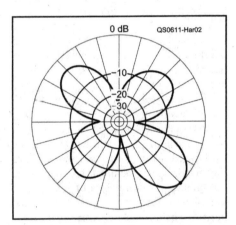

Figure 2 — Azimuth pattern of 300 foot loop on 14.2 MHz at elevation of 25°. Peak gain is 12.5 dBi.

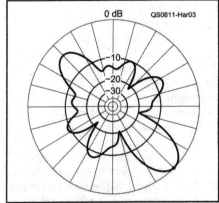

Figure 3 — Azimuth pattern of 320 foot loop on 14.2 MHz at elevation of 20°. Peak gain is 13.3 dBi.

longer the loop the more the gain, and that the loop gives an omnidirectional pattern on all HF bands. The truth is that low angle gain is proportional to height — the higher the antenna, the higher the gain at low angles.

Also, at higher than design frequencies, a loop is not omnidirectional. The loop radiation patterns and performance are affected by its shape and feed point location. The key parameters are shown in Figure 1.

Table 1
Loop Performance by Shape and Feed Point

	Circular Loop		Square Loop AF		Triangle Loop AF		Square Loop CF		Triangle Loop CF	
	Gain (dBi)	Elev	Gain (dBi)	Elev	Gain (dBi)	Elev	Gain (dBi)	Elev	Gain (dBi)	Elev
1.9 MHz	3.93	90°	3.46	90°	2.88	90°	3.70	90°	2.67	90°
3.9 MHz	8.47	90°	8.13	90°	7.76	90°	8.23	90°	8.04	90°
7.2 MHz	7.76	50°	7.35	50°	7.98	45°	7.64	45°	7.30	45°
10.1 MHz	8.34	35°	10.68	35°	7.35	30°	8.17	35°	7.24	30°
14.2 MHz	10.44	25°	12.50	25°	11.27	25°	10.25	25°	8.50	25°
18.1 MHz	11.18	20°	14.03	20°	12.32	20°	11.40	20°	8.84	20°
21.2 MHz	10.16	15°	14.55	15°	12.42	15°	11.28	15°	8.29	15°
24.9 MHz	10.77	15°	13.69	15°	14.09	15°	10.58	15°	10.10	15°
28.5 MHz	11.39	15°	12.85	10°	13.84	10°	11.19	10°	12.66	10°

Is This Antenna For You?

The first step in our planning is to determine if a loop is the right antenna for your needs. If you are interested in 160 and 80 meter DX and can only erect a horizontal loop 30 to 50 feet off the ground, you may be better off with other choices. At those frequencies, and heights below λ/4 to λ/2, most radiation will go skyward, making the loop ideal for near vertical incidence skywave (NVIS) propagation out to distances of a few hundred miles. This provides reliable coverage for emergency and other medium range communications, but not for DX. They do perform well as DX antennas on the higher frequencies. The loop makes a fine antenna for the ham who has space for only one antenna. In my case, I already had very good antennas for 160 and 80 meters, but I wanted something that would perform as a backup for these bands and give me good DX performance on the higher bands. I was particularly interested in 20 and 17 meters.

A good rule of thumb is to start with a loop about 5 λ at the highest desired DX operating frequency. Therefore, using the usual formula for a 1 λ loop, 1005/freq (MHz), a 1 λ loop for 18.1 MHz would have a circumference of approximately 56 feet, so our model loop should be about 280 feet in circumference. I then modeled a square loop 40 feet above real/high accuracy ground with dimensions of 70 feet per side.[6] After some experimentation, I found a leg length of 75 feet with the feed source in a corner of the loop would produce the clean cloverleaf pattern shown in Figure 2 on 20 meters, which was what I desired. Any longer leg length would give more gain, but would make the antenna more bi-directional as shown in Figure 3. Such a pattern may meet your needs. What about other shapes and feed points? Table 1 gives a comparison of these, showing circular, square and triangle loops, with the square and triangle loops being fed in the corners (AF) and midway along a leg (CF).

The circular and triangle loops developed a more omnidirectional pattern on the lower bands, and if that is what one desires, then

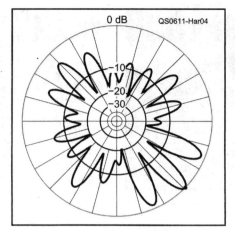

Figure 4 — Azimuth pattern of loop on 29 MHz at elevation of 10°. Peak gain is 12.6 dBi.

more experimentation with these types would be beneficial. For my purposes, the apex or corner fed square loop was the best. It gives nice performance on 80 through 30 meters and really shines on 20 and 17 meters. Looking at the figures for 10 meters, one might think it to be an excellent omnidirectional DX antenna. A close look at the actual azimuth pattern (Figure 4) shows that it has just about as many sharp nulls as gain lobes. Also, these lobes are relatively narrow. A windy day or varying atmospheric conditions can cause signals to fade in and out of the nulls. We want these nodes to be as broad as possible with the fewest nulls, so a frequency range of around 5:1 is the best range for a loop. For the DX enthusiast, a loop with a resonant frequency just below 7 MHz should perform well for 40 through 10 meters.

Optimizing the Antenna for Your Location

Now that we have a model of the kind of loop we want, the second step is to determine what size and shape loop we can erect. This means conducting a survey of one's antenna space. Take a long tape measure to the site and record distances to trees, towers, fences, other buildings, etc. Take this data and draw out a diagram of the maximum loop antenna possible. Once this is done, you can then attempt to fit your model into your actual location. If you have the supports in the right places, you are indeed fortunate. If not, don't be discouraged. The idea here is to utilize the modeling program, changing source point, shape, leg lengths, height (within limits of the overall yard dimensions), etc, until we have the best antenna for your location that will perform as well as possible on the bands you desire to operate.

Also play with adding loads (inductance and capacitance) at various points. For instance, adding an inductance may enhance performance on 160 meters, while adding a small capacitance may make it perform better on 80 meters. These components can also be utilized to "tame" the antenna on certain bands where matching is difficult. Nothing is sacred here, and playing with models certainly is easier than raising and lowering the loop many times!

One might ask why not erect a vertical loop, since this type of antenna only requires two supports and would seem to also generate good patterns on all bands? Well, as pointed out by W4RNL, loops have a strange behavior. At frequencies of twice design frequency and above, radiation is increasingly off the side of the antenna. Thus, on higher frequencies a vertical loop antenna would tend to radiate straight up and down! This is also why horizontal loops have lower radiation angle at higher frequencies.

Resonant vs Non-Resonant Loops

Now, let's deal with the issue of resonance. Table 2 compares performance of my loop against resonant 160 and 80 meter loops, as well as an inverted V. The non-resonant loop seems to be the better overall performer. One may ask, "What about SWR! Have you considered that? How are you going to feed this thing?" Well, first some basics. In his book, *Reflections*,[7] Maxwell states that all power fed into the transmission line (minus line loss) is absorbed by the load, regardless of the mismatch. Secondly, with open-wire tuned feed lines, we can ignore this mismatch at the junction of the feed line and the antenna, and all matching can be done at the transmitter itself.

One might think, "Isn't this bringing a high SWR (and problems) into the shack?" Well, Maxwell also tells us reflected power by itself is unimportant in determining how efficiently power is being delivered to an antenna. Put another way, if our antenna tuner can properly match the impedance of the input of the feed line, using open wire line, we can transfer just about all power to the antenna. Therefore, with a little planning, our loop can work on all amateur bands utilizing open line feeders and the proper tuner.

Table 2
Loop Performance vs Resonant Antennas

	160 Meter Loop		My Loop		80 Meter Loop		Inverted V	
	Gain (dBi)	Elev	Gain (dBi)	Elev	Gain (dBi)	Elev	Gain (dBi)	Elev
1.9 MHz	6.72	90°	3.46	90°	1.64	90°	2.09	90°
3.9 MHz	5.69	55°	8.13	90°	7.88	90°	5.03	90°
7.2 MHz	9.65	40°	7.35	50°	6.54	50°	4.23	45°
10.1 MHz	12.09	25°	10.68	35°	9.51	40°	5.18	25°
14.2 MHz	12.05	20°	12.50	25°	10.96	25°	6.30	20°
18.1 MHz	12.98	20°	14.03	20°	13.89	20°	7.07	15°
21.2 MHz	14.43	15°	14.55	15°	14.11	15°	6.97	35°
24.9 MHz	13.48	10°	13.69	15°	14.61	15°	7.18	10°
28.5 MHz	14.55	10°	12.85	10°	14.25	10°	7.07	10°

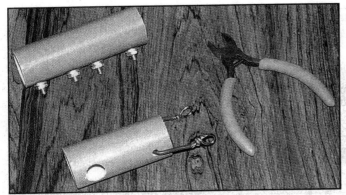

Figure 5 — PVC feed line and corner insulators.

Table 3
Antenna Z_0

	At Antenna	At End 65 Ft. 450 Ω Line
1.9 MHz	127.9 $-j$4282 Ω	2.029 $-j$310.1 Ω
3.9 MHz	230 $+j$691.1 Ω	71.72 $-j$160.5 Ω
7.2 MHz	188.3 $+j$475.3 Ω	286.2 $+j$619 Ω
10.1 MHz	313.3 $+j$0.03295 Ω	638.3 $-j$7.773 Ω
14.2 MHz	700.1 $+j$804.4 Ω	1620 $+j$424.2 Ω
18.1 MHz	2452 $-j$578.7 Ω	99.57 $+j$168.9 Ω
21.2 MHz	2280 $+j$609.2 Ω	737.4 $-j$1124 Ω
24.9 MHz	1579 $-j$1257 Ω	107.3 $+j$187.6 Ω
28.5 MHz	815.9 $-j$954.3 Ω	158.9 $-j$460.3 Ω

Tuner Considerations

We must consider the resistive and reactive components presented at the input of the feed line. Our tuner must be able to match these components of the line impedance (Z_0) to an unbalanced 50 Ω resistive load. Table 3 shows the impedances calculated by our modeling program for our loop at the antenna and at the end of 65 feet of 450 Ω transmission line. Here again, one can vary the line type, length, etc. to yield the best combinations for their location and needs. Using a 4:1 balun to a typical unbalanced tuner may work in some cases, but leaves a lot to be desired and will create a lot of problems. One needs a true balanced line tuner to match the antenna to the load properly.

It is not within the scope of this article to go into detail on the design and construction of such a tuner. *The ARRL Antenna Book*, *The ARRL Handbook*, and many other antenna journals have information on such a tuner. I personally prefer the tuner designed by AG6K using two variable inductors and a variable capacitor with a balun on the input side.[8] For those not willing to take the time and effort to design and build a tuner, there are several commercial tuners available.[9] The Palstar BT1500A is a commercial version of the A6GK tuner.[10] It is pricey but very well built, has an excellent metering system and is rated at 1500 W. MFJ has a balanced line tuner for a more attractive price that is rated at 300 W.[11] A surplus Johnson Matchbox should also work well, but likely won't provide a match on 30 meters.

Loop Construction and Erection

Once we have decided on the final design, the next step is construction and erection of our loop. Use your favorite method of putting up rope at the support points, but there should be some method of strain relief at each support such as pulley-counterweights or springs. Loops take a lot of stress from wind and swaying supports. Many years' experience have taught me that in most areas, large loops need to be put up one leg at a time. Therefore, I recommend carefully measuring and cutting each leg of the loop.

Feed line and corner insulators can be fabricated from short lengths of PVC pipe, as shown in Figure 5. These should be spray painted to protect them from the sun. My feed line insulator has short internal jumpers running from the center terminals to the outside terminals. The corner insulators should be connected to the antenna legs by brass or stainless steel hardware.

Lay out the legs and insulators on the ground in the manner they will be part of the antenna. Connect the open wire line and the two extending legs to the feed line insulator and raise this up part of the way. Connect the next leg to one corner insulator. Keep working around the loop until all legs are up and connected and up in the air.

Measure out the proper length of open wire line, and route it along its path to the tuner. Open wire feed line is affected by nearby objects, especially metal objects such as gutters and other wires, so make every attempt to keep it free and clear. It should also be secured as much as possible to eliminate flopping and swaying around. I found 2 inch screw-in porcelain electric fence insulators very handy for making runs along the wall of the house.

There are many ways to run open wire line into the shack. Replacing a window pane with Plexiglas and drilling holes in it is one method. Another way is to run two short pieces of RG-8 coax with the center conductor of each coax connected to one of the open wire feeders. By connecting the shields together a shielded balanced line of twice the coax Z_0 is formed. Note that this transmission line will have the loss associated with the mismatched coax, so make the length of such a section as short as possible.

Final Thoughts

So there you have it. All the information needed to create that new station antenna that will suit your needs and location. Please remember modeling software is a great aid in discovering new high performance antennas, but it is not the absolute gospel. It can point us in the right direction and save a great deal of time in our quest for the "perfect" antenna, but its results need to be tested and verified.

One last thing: L.B. Cebik has stated, "The advantage of the [horizontal loop] will not show itself in any one contact or in a short period. Satisfaction with the antenna grows with time and changes in the propagation paths, a successful communication with almost everywhere shows up in the log." I couldn't agree more. I have enjoyed my loop for some time, and have worked many countries and received excellent signal reports.

Notes
[1] *EZNEC* is available from **www.eznec.com**.
[2] *NEC-Win Plus* is available from **www.nittany-scientific.com/plus/index.htm**.
[3] Information on ARRL modeling course available at **www.arrl.org/cce/courses.html**.
[4] **www.cebik.com**.
[5] For starters read "Horizontally Oriented, Horizontally Polarized Large Wire Loop Antennas" and "Horizontal Loops: How Big? How High? What Shape?"
[6] ASCII files of antenna models used in this article are available from the author.
[7] M. Walter Maxwell, W2DU, *Reflections: Transmission Lines and Antennas*, (Out of print). The entire text of *Reflections II* is available at **www.w2du.com**.
[8] R. Measures, AG6K, "A Balanced Balanced Line Tuner," *QST*, Feb 1990 (updated at **www.somis.org/bbat.html**).
[9] J. Hallas, W1ZR, "Product Review: A New Generation of Balanced Antenna Tuners," *QST*, Sep 2004, pp 60-66.
[10] Available from **www.palstar.com**.
[11] MFJ Enterprises **www.mfjenterprises.com**.

Scott M. Harwood, K4VWK, has been interested in radio since childhood. In the seventh grade he built a two tube regenerative receiver using #30 tubes as a science project. He obtained his Novice license in 1958 and has retained the same call for over 40 years. He now holds an Amateur Extra class license. After college and a tour in the USAF, Scott returned to Virginia where he now resides. An avid antenna experimenter, his main area of interest has been small portable antennas for 160 and 80 meters. He has given talks at local radio clubs on antennas, and has written articles for CQ and AntenneX magazines. You can reach Scott at PO Box 523, Farmville, VA 23901 or at scotth@hsc.edu.

The Horizontal EWE Antenna

The original EWE shepherd goes in a new direction for low noise reception.

Floyd Koontz, WA2WVL

This antenna was designed to solve a major reception problem at this location by maximizing the received signal to noise ratio (SNR) of 75 meter phone signals coming from Europe.

Background

In 1999 I had up a six element switchable vertical array hung from some of the many 100 foot pine trees in my yard. The array appeared to have good directivity but never received the good signal reports I expected. Eventually I put a dipole between trees at 80 feet elevation as a reference antenna. On nearly every contact the dipole was 10 dB better than the 6 element array. Even though the vertical array wires were 20 feet or more from the trees, the trees seemed to be absorbing the signal. In northern locations, the trees drop their sap to the roots in the winter (DX season on the low HF bands) and many stations have good luck with verticals hung from trees. Here in Florida the sap stays up all year round and the trees are quite conductive (and longer than λ/4 at 75 meters). Vertical polarization simply doesn't seem to work in my yard.

Recently I decided to look at the EWE antenna[1] in a horizontal plane and discovered that it worked very well. With vertical EWEs, a single element has a deep null off the back. A single horizontal EWE, on the other hand, would have that null at 0° elevation instead. Over real ground, the single horizontal EWE has a front to back ratio (F/B) on 75 meters as shown in Figure 1 for 30° elevation. The low angle gain increases with height above ground, as with most horizontal antennas, but the pattern remains nearly the same at 10 to 30 foot heights. The size can be chosen to fit the available space but four supports (trees, towers, house, etc) are needed to hold up the corners.

Of the different sizes and shapes that can be used, one is optimum. It is a square, λ/8 on a side (a total of λ/2 around). For this size (30 × 30 feet for 75 meters), the feed is non-reactive and can be matched with a simple broadband transformer. The calculated feed impedance was 1337 Ω and was matched with a 26:5 two-winding transformer. The F/B was more than 11 dB on 75 meters and 15 dB on 160 meters.

Two Element Design

As noted, a single EWE antenna gives a modified cardioid pattern with a usable, but not dramatic, front to back ratio. The front to side ratio is only about 4 dB so a two element design was established to improve the back and side rejection. Available trees allowed a spacing of 100 feet. Figure 2 shows the layout of this array including the location of the feed points and terminations. Figure 3 is the modeled pattern of the two element array, again at 3.8 MHz and 30° elevation. As is evident, the two element array resulted in a sharpened beamwidth and a significantly improved F/B. While the pattern for 30° elevation is shown, it is similar with lower output at lower elevations.

The antenna was to be 25 feet off the ground. This was determined to be the maximum height that I could safely reach from my 24 foot extension ladder. Vinyl insulated

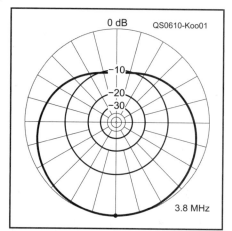

Figure 1 — *EZNEC* modeled pattern of a single element horizontal EWE at 3.8 MHz and 30° elevation.

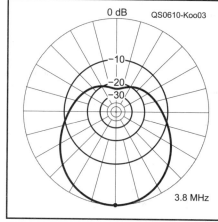

Figure 3 — *EZNEC* modeled pattern of a two element horizontal EWE configured as in Figure 2 at 3.8 MHz and 30° elevation.

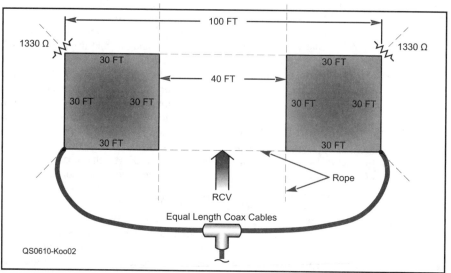

Figure 2 — Orientation of the two element horizontal EWE antenna array.

[1]Notes appear on page 53.

14 gauge "speaker wire" was used, but any wire strong enough to be pulled tight without stretching could be used.[2] The loops were tied at the corners (every 30 feet) by 1/8 inch Dacron ropes. The knots were taped with black electrical tape to prevent the knots from coming untied. The input matching transformer was mounted on a 2 × 4 × 1/4 inch piece of UHMW material.[3] The feed coax (RG-58A/U) was woven through three tight holes vertically in line about 5/8 inch apart to support its weight.

The termination was also mounted on a 2 × 4 × 1/4 inch piece of UHMW. Both types of boards had lifting holes at the top for attaching the ropes. After all the soldering was completed, the boards were coated with silicone window sealing except for one of the 50 Ω transformer connections. The two loops must be fed in phase to develop the pattern. I had a 50% chance of getting it right. If I guessed wrong, the pattern would have a 30 dB null off the front and receiving performance would be poor. I was successful the first time and did not have to reverse the connections, so I proceeded to coat these connections as well.

During the assembly process the wire is lying on the ground in the space where it will be pulled up. In my case the SE loop enclosed only one tree while the NW loop has three trees inside the loop. A ladder was placed against the trees to be used for supports and a small hole was drilled in each tree. A screw eye was installed as high as I could reach at each support point. A piece of the 1/8 inch Dacron line was fed through each screw eye and pulled back to ground and tied to another screw eye at 4 feet. After doing this on eight trees, I was now ready to lift the antenna in place without further climbing.

Both feed points had equal length coax cables attached. The length was determined by the location of the ninth tree to which both coax cables would go (I used 100 feet for each run length). I ran the cables overhead at about 12 feet from tree to tree. A BNC T was used to parallel the 100 foot coax cables and the third port connected to the coax that went to the shack.

Antenna Output Level Considerations

The calculated gain of the two element horizontal EWE (at 20°) at 3.8 MHz was about −18 dBi (a λ/4 vertical has a gain of about 0 dBi). For a height of only 10 feet the gain drops to −24 dBi. Most modern receivers and transceivers have sufficient sensitivity so that even at this level there is sufficient gain that the signal to noise ratio is limited by external noise.

If the noise level doesn't increase by at least 10 dB when replacing a dummy load with the receive antenna, you will need to have additional gain to get full benefit from this antenna. In order to directly compare the performance of this antenna to your transmitting antenna, you may want to add gain so that the signal levels are similar and the S-meter moves in the same way. A preamplifier with a gain of 18 to 25 dB should be just what you want for 80 meters, more if you use the antenna on 160.

A suitable amplifier for 160 meters was included with a recent antenna article.[4] A dual band amplifier was also published in an earlier issue of *QST*.[5] Gary Nichols, KD9SV, has assembled preamps for either 160 meters or 160 and 80 meters available through Radio-Ware.[6,7]

It also might be that switching your receiver's preamp on provides just the amount of gain required to bring the signal level up to that from your transmitting antenna, and that is a suitable way to equalize the gain. Whatever preamp option you take, make sure that the preamp is protected from pick up of RF from your transmitting antenna. In many cases, the receive antenna will bring it directly into the preamp, if provisions aren't made to the contrary.

Operation with this system has been gratifying with the SNR often being improved by 10 to 20 dB on 75 meters compared to my reference antenna. On 160 meters, many SSB stations can now be copied that were below the noise before.

Notes
[1] F. Koontz, WA2WVL, "Is This EWE For You?" *QST*, Feb 1995, pp 31-33, and "More EWEs For You," *QST*, Jan 1996, pp 32-34. Available on **www.arrl.org**. The antenna gets its name from its resemblance to an inverted U.
[2] "Speaker wire" is available from Home Depot in 250 foot lengths.
[3] Ultra High Molecular Weight (UHMW) Polyethylene is available from plastics suppliers for less than $15 per square foot.
[4] D. Stroud, W9SR, "An Effective Receiving Loop," *QST*, Jun 2006, pp 35-38.
[5] D. DeMaw, W1FB (SK), "A Preamplifier for 80- and 160-Meter Loop and Beverage Antennas," *QST*, Aug 1988, pp 22-24.
[6] G. Nichols, KD9SV, "A Variable Gain 160-Meter Preamp," *Ham Radio*, Oct 1989, pp 46-48.
[7] Click **KD9SV Preamps** at **www.radio-ware.com**.

Floyd Koontz, WA2WVL, is a retired electrical engineer with 40 years' experience designing communications systems, radio transmitters and antennas. He was first licensed in 1955 as WN9JQA and has been WA2WVL since 1961. He has written numerous QST articles about antennas over the years. An ARRL life member, he can be reached at 8430 W Park Springs Pl, Homosassa, FL 34448, or **wa2wvl@tampabay.rr.com**.

The Fan Dipole as a Wideband and Multiband Antenna Element

It's broadbanded and operates effectively on several HF bands—a nice combination for a ham antenna.

Joel R. Hallas, W1ZR

Multiband HF antennas are certainly an attractive concept, especially as new bands are added to our authorized set of frequencies. Now with 9 bands between 3 and 30 MHz, it is difficult to have separate antennas for each band on a reasonably sized piece of property without significant interaction. Over the years there have been a number of common approaches to multiband antennas:

• *Antennas that take advantage of multiple resonances in a single element structure.* This category includes 40 meter dipoles operated on 15 meters and G5RV dipoles. Although these can be effective, the feed impedances are generally different on different bands, often resulting in potentially significant transmission line losses if coax is used.

• *Antennas using resonant circuits as traps to isolate sections.* These can often be effective as well. The traps may restrict the frequency range on each band and will contribute to system losses, however.

• *Antennas using parallel dipoles resonant on each band.* These have been used successfully by some, although I have not been very successful with this approach. Unless elements are orthogonal (two antennas at right angles), the coupling can restrict the frequency range and make adjustment difficult. Mutually orthogonal dipoles for more than three bands are hard for me to visualize.

• *Antennas using tuned feeders and low-loss line.* The "double zepp" approach has gained in popularity with the common use of "no tune" restricted matching range transmitters and the availability of wide range antenna tuners. The typical antenna is a half wave at the lowest band, center-fed with open wire or ladder line. The impedance on any band is considered irrelevant since the tuner can deal with the resultant impedance at the bottom of the low loss line and transform it to the 50 Ω unbalanced impedance needed by the transmitter. This can be a very effective system. The fact that the pattern changes from broadside to a complex multi-lobe pattern above a full wavelength can provide additional geographic coverage from the single antenna. In addition, the whole antenna is always used, providing gain in some directions at the higher frequencies. The typical configuration is shown in Figure 1.

The loss can be low if connections are made carefully. As shown below, however,

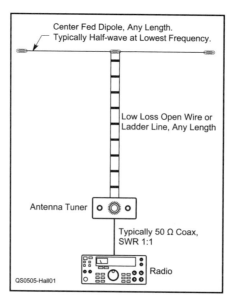

Figure 1—"Double Zepp"—typical configuration.

the SWR can be above 10:1 on the transmission line on some bands. *The ARRL Antenna Book*[1] indicates that a matched 100 foot length of clean, dry (people used to wax their twin lead!) ladder line has a loss of 0.15 dB or less at HF *if matched*. An SWR of 10:1 adds about 1 dB of loss,[2] still probably less than typical trap antennas.

Another potential area of concern is the impact of the SWR on the voltage and current within the tuner. A high SWR can result in maximum currents and voltages on the line equal to the matched value times the square root of the SWR. These will occur at different spots along the line depending on load, line length and operating frequency. With all the different frequencies involved, it is likely that the maximum of each will be near the tuner on one band or another, however. For a 100 W output and a 10:1 SWR, this results in a maximum of 630 V or 1.6 A. For 1.5 kW it increases to 2.5 kV_{rms}, 3.5 kV_{peak} or 6.1 A, however, which can explain the arcing or smoking observed in some tuners!

Enter the Fat Cylindrical or Biconical Dipole

John Kraus, W8JK, shows the way to solve this problem and simultaneously reduce the frequency sensitivity of such antennas in his classic text *Antennas*.[3] Figure 9-9 indicates that while a cylindrical dipole with a length to diameter ratio of 2000 (about #4 AWG wire at 20 meters) will have an impedance variation between its half wave and full wave resonances of

[1]Notes appear on page 56.

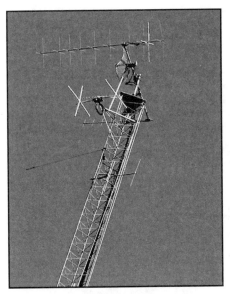

Figure 2—Looking up the tower at the center spreaders of the Cage antenna at W1AW.

Figure 5—W1ZR 20 meter biconical array, hidden in the trees.

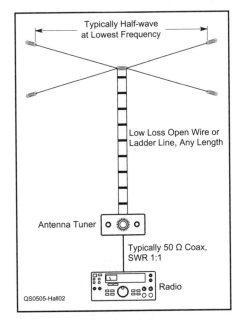

Figure 3—Biconical (fan) dipole configuration.

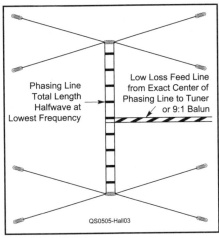

Figure 4—Biconical lazy-H antenna configuration.

70 Ω to about 3300 Ω, with corresponding variation in reactance, the 2 λ resonance is at about 2300 Ω and the average is 873 Ω. In contrast, the figure shows that for a length to diameter ratio of 60 (a 6.6 inch cylinder at 20 meters) the half wave impedance is about the same while the full wave is reduced to around 900 Ω, with the average a convenient 454 Ω.

This approach has been used frequently to broaden the bandwidth of a half wave antenna, for example, to allow better coverage of both 80 and 75 meters with a single dipole, but has even more impact on harmonic operation where the concept has not often been employed in amateur service.

The straightforward approach to this is to use larger diameter wire or tubing for the elements. This can work for VHF, but supporting an 80 meter dipole made with 2 foot diameter tubing is hard to imagine! Fortunately, the same effect can be accomplished with a skeleton structure, and a "cage" antenna has been popular in various applications (it was used for the first transatlantic ham QSO and one is now in use at W1AW; see Figure 2). The cage typically uses a crossed spreader and four wires for the elements (six were used for the T/A tests). W1AW Station Manager Joe Carcia, NJ1Q, designed the one at the ARRL HQ station to operate well on all W1AW 80 and 75 meter frequencies. Joe used 3 foot PVC spreaders (reinforced with dowels and sealed using PVC caps and tees) at right angles with #14 stranded wire to construct this highly effective antenna.

An alternate is to use a skeleton biconical dipole as shown in Figure 3. This has the advantages that only two wires are used per side, and that the spreader structure is much simpler. I use a single 6 foot spacer on each end of the elements of a 20 meter array as described below. An 80 meter antenna might require some intermediate spacers to avoid tangles during raising. Note that while the upper wire must support the antenna weight, the lower wire needs only to provide conductivity. Although the amount of wire required is comparable to a parallel dipole antenna, the performance is better.

Fortunately, Kraus provides the capability to transform between the cylinder structure, the thin rectangle (equivalent radius is $1/4$ of the width) and the biconical. The impedance of a biconical, or fan, with an end radius of 2.8 times the cylinder radius (in this range) has the same impedance characteristics, yielding a half angle of 2.7°. Extrapolating to the flat biconical (triangle), we would expect to need a triangle base of $4 \times 2.8 = 10.2$ times the cylinder diameter. For a 20 meter fundamental antenna this is a manageable 5 foot 7 inches. I also considered a "mini-cage" made of 400 Ω ladder line (typically sold as "450 Ω" ladder line, but really measuring closer to 400 Ω) with the wires connected together at the feed point.

Why Bother?

What does it buy us? I have run EZNEC[4] simulations of 80 meter fundamental and 20 meter fundamental skeleton biconical dipoles and compared the results with that of a single wire dipole. To make comparison easy, for each case, I "trimmed" the length to provide best SWR from band edge to band edge. At 80 meters, using Kraus' factors, the predicted end spacing is about 22 feet, so I also ran it at a more reasonable 6 feet to find the difference.

I was glad I did, since EZNEC predicts that beyond a few feet the additional spacing

Table 1
Comparison of SWR of 80/75 Meter Dipoles of Various Cross Section

SWR at 50 Ω, *EZNEC* prediction. Single band coax fed.

Antenna Type	3.5	3.6	3.7	3.8	3.9	4.0 MHz
Thin, #14 wire dipole	5.9	2.8	1.6	2.1	3.6	5.8
Ladder line "cage"	3.8	1.9	1.2	1.7	2.7	3.9
3 foot fan	3.2	1.9	1.1	1.5	2.3	3.2
6 foot fan	3.0	1.8	1.1	1.5	2.3	3.1
22 foot fan	3.3	1.9	1.3	1.7	2.4	3.4
NJ1Q cage	2.5	1.6	1.1	1.4	1.9	2.5

SWR at 400 Ω, *EZNEC* prediction. Multiband ladder line fed.

Antenna Type	80	60	40	30	20	17	15	12	10 Meters
Thin, #14 wire	7.2	6.5	12.9	14.7	8.3	9.0	5.8	9.2	5.0
Ladder line "cage"	8.5	4.1	7.0	10.7	4.7	7.0	3.6	5.2	3.5
6 foot fan	8.2	3.6	4.8	8.0	3.8	4.5	2.8	4.0	2.7
NJ1Q cage	9.1	2.4	2.1	6.6	2.3	2.6	3.6	1.3	4.1
Max gain over 1/2 λ dipole	0.85	1.2	2.2	4.9	2.5	3.5	1.7	2.2	4.7
Azimuth of main lobe (number of significant lobes)	90 (2)	90 (2)	90 (2)	90 (2)	129 (4)	118 (4)	152 (10)	138 (6)	149 (10)

doesn't matter. The results are interesting at the fundamental as well as on the harmonics (see Table 1). At 80/75 meters, while a thin wire dipole's SWR across the band may be outside of the range of many in-rig auto tuners, even the easiest to make multiwire configurations are within the usual 4:1 range of such devices on this tough band.

Note that with ladder line feed as a multiband antenna, on the higher bands where losses are highest, the SWR variation is reduced significantly. We still have the SWR at the first resonance to deal with and it is very similar to that with the single wire, typically around 8:1 at resonance. Note that the reduction in impedance variation will generally also mean less retuning as frequency is changed across any band. Tables 1 and 2 tell the story.

The Biconical Lazy-H

At my station, I have solved the problem of high SWR at the fundamental (half-wave) on the 20 meter fundamental antenna by making a "stacked biconical" (a popular TV antenna in the '50s) or "biconical lazy-H," if you prefer. This consists of two 20 meter biconical dipole elements, the second a half wavelength below the first and fed in phase with 400 Ω ladder line. By transforming each element's low impedance at 20 meters through the resulting quarter-wave matching section to the center of the phasing line, and feeding them in parallel, I end up with about a 4:1 SWR across 20 meters.

This configuration, shown in a diagram as Figure 4 and a hard-to-see photo in Figure 5, provides broadside gain on 20 meters. It also acts like a well matched 4 element combination broadside and collinear array on 10 meters. The downside of this is that I now have higher SWR on some of the intermediate bands. On the plus side, broadside gain is provided on all bands 14 through 30 MHz. It will tune and operate on 30 meters as well, but watch the SWR!

At W1ZR, this antenna is fed with about 150 feet of ladder line and then a 9:1 balun. The SWR readings were taken with a Bird 43 wattmeter at the balun. I expect that the difference between predicted and measured results is due to some combination of loss in transmission line and balun and measurement error. The antenna does seem to perform well.

Table 2
Comparison of SWR of 20 Meter Dipoles of Various Cross Section

SWR at 50 Ω, *EZNEC* prediction. Single band coax fed.

Antenna Type	14.0	14.1	14.2	14.3	14.35 MHz
Thin, #14 wire	1.7	1.6	1.6	1.65	1.7
Ladder line "cage"	1.3	1.25	1.3	1.3	1.36
6 foot "fan"	1.2	1.1	1.03	1.16	1.22

SWR at 400 Ω, *EZNEC* prediction. Multiband ladder line fed.

Antenna Type	30	20	17	15	12	10 Meters
Thin, #14 wire	40	5.1	6.0	6.7	10.5	10.6
Ladder line "cage"	32	6.5	5.3	4.5	5.9	5.4
6 foot "fan"	26	7.8	4.6	4.4	4.2	4.2
Max gain over #14 dipole (dB)	0.8	1.1	1.4	1.8	2.3	

All at 90/180°

Table 3
Performance of Biconical Lazy-H at 73 Ft Elevation

Gain and SWR	30	20	17	15	12	10 Meters
Gain dBi	8.5	10.3	12.0	12.7	11.4	12.4
Gain over dipole	1.1	2.5	4.7	5.1	3.9	4.4
Gain over 20 m fan	0.6	2.2	3.8	4.0	2.5	2.8
EZNEC SWR	31	4.2	10.6	13	4.9	2.6
Measured SWR	4.6	1.3	1.4	2.7	2.5	1.7

Notes

[1] R. D. Straw, N6BV, Ed., *The ARRL Antenna Book*, 20th edition, p 24-20.
[2] *The ARRL Antenna Book*, 20th edition, p 24-10.
[3] J. Kraus, W8JK, *Antennas,* New York: McGraw-Hill Book Co Inc, 1959.
[4] *EZNEC* is a registered trademark of Roy W. Lewallen (**www.eznec.com**).

*Joel Hallas, W1ZR, is QST Assistant Technical Editor and Product Review editor. You can reach him at **jhallas@arrl.org**.*

Modernizing the V Antenna

Want multiband performance with some gain? Try this update of a classic wire antenna.

John S. Raydo, K0IZ

I have found that one of the old-time wire antennas—the horizontal V antenna—has much to offer. It has gain in two major directions, needs no ground radials and exhibits a low angle of radiation for good DX. A practical advantage is that the apex (center point) of a V antenna can be a roof peak or tree adjacent to the house, making for a short feed line. The end points can be positioned more or less wherever suitable supports (trees) are located.

Traditional designs require open-wire feed line and a tuner.[1] My V antenna uses coax feed and covers 80, 40, 20, 15 and 10 meters with low SWR and significant gain in various lobes. Operation on 17 meters is also possible with excellent gain, but SWR may be about 3:1.

The keys to the multiband resonance are three homemade coaxial traps[2] in each leg, one each tuned to 15, 20 and 40 meters, and an impedance transformer at the feed point. Each leg is identical and represents 5.25 wavelengths (λ) on 10 meters, 3.75 λ on 15, 2.25 λ on 20, 1.25 λ on 40, and 0.75 λ on 80. Please note that these legs are horizontal (parallel to the ground), unlike the more common inverted V antenna. My installation uses four legs, with pairs of legs selected by remote relays to "rotate" the antenna for optimum directivity.[3] A two-leg antenna also works well in most directions.

Construction

Dimensions are shown in Figure 1, cut to favor the phone bands. Each inside (20 meter) segment is made of two #14 hard-drawn stranded copper wires separated by one-foot spacers. This makes the segments appear to be "fat" and noticeably broadens the antenna. It also lowers the resonant frequency, allowing these sections to be slightly shorter than a single wire. The 40, 15 and 80/10 meter sections use single lengths of #12 stranded copper.

Coax for the traps is marine-grade RG-8X with a solid dielectric to handle maximum legal power.[4] Do not use regular RG-8X with foam insulation because the voltage rating is inadequate for power above about 400 W (I speak from experience). Gray PVC conduit

[1]Notes appear on page 60.

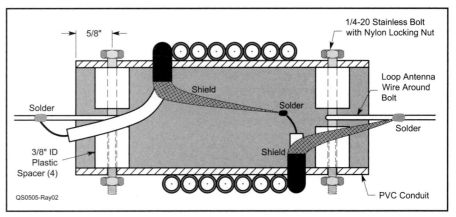

Figure 2—All traps use marine-grade RG-8X coax with solid (not foam) insulation, close-wound on gray PVC conduit (see text). PVC sizes are nominal inside diameters.
40 meter trap: $9^{1}/_{4}$ turns on 4.5 inch length of 1.5 inch PVC conduit.
20 meter trap: 6 turns on 4 inch length of 1.25 inch PVC conduit.
15 meter trap: $4^{1}/_{8}$ turns on 3.25 inch length of 1.25 inch PVC conduit.

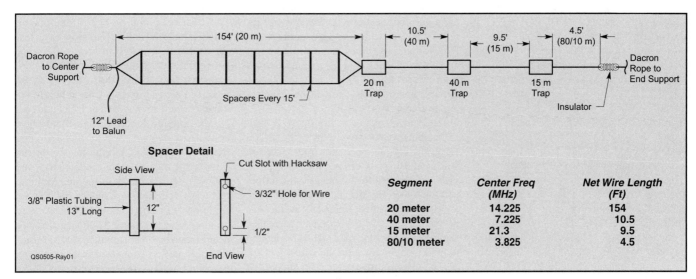

Figure 1—Each leg of the horizontal V antenna is about 180 feet long. The longest (20 meter) section is made of two conductors separated by spacers (see text). Only one leg is shown, but all legs are identical.

MULTIBAND 57

Figure 3—Here are the finished 40, 20 and 15 meter traps. The 15 meter trap is shown before installing the bolts and covering the coax winding with RTV silicone sealant.

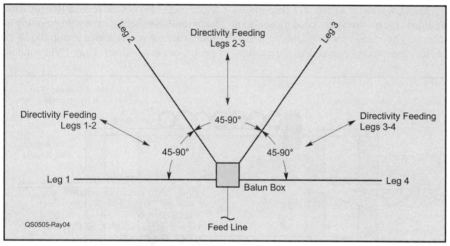

Figure 4—The basic V antenna is bidirectional. A four-leg V antenna can cover six directions by switching among the legs (1-2, 2-3, 3-4). Feeding legs 1-4 creates an extended doublet.

is UV resistant and is a better choice for trap forms than white PVC water pipe. See Figures 2 and 3. Tuning of the traps is not critical. If a dip meter is available, adjust resonance of each trap to the desired center frequency by adjusting the spacing of the coax turns.

The end bolts have two small plastic spacers cut from $3/8$ inch PEX tubing or similar material.[5] The antenna wire loops will fit in the gap between the spacers, keeping the wire centered on the trap bolts. I also filed the bolt threads a little in the center to smooth the sharp thread edges. When connecting the traps to the antenna wire, orient each trap so that the center-conductor lead is connected toward the antenna apex (feed point).

After fabrication and adjustment, the coax windings are covered with a neutral-curing black silicone rubber to hold windings in place. (Use GE RTV5223 or equivalent non-acetic sealant.[6] If it smells vinegary, don't use it.) Also put some sealant where the center conductors separate from the braid to avoid water infiltration into the coax.

Installation circumstances may affect resonance, so cut each antenna wire segment at least 2 feet longer than the shown finished lengths to allow for adjustment. To aid in adjustments during initial setup and tuning, I recommend using split-bolt connectors (Thomas & Betts 9H or equiv) to make easy temporary connections. Later, you can remove these connectors and solder the wires. Finished lengths shown make allowance for a 1 foot connecting lead (#12 stranded wire) from leg ends to balun box. If your installation requires longer leads, shorten the 20 meter legs accordingly.

The spreaders are cut from gray $3/8$ inch PEX tubing. If you buy 30 inch lengths you can get two 13 inch spreaders from each. You will need 10 spreaders per leg. Drill a $3/32$ inch hole through the tubing at $1/2$ inch from each end, then slot the end to the hole using a hacksaw. Install the spreaders at intervals of about 15 feet in the 20 meter segments. Squirt some hot glue into each spreader end to hold them in place on the wires. A $1/8$ or $3/16$ inch Dacron rope is ideal for supporting the antenna legs. Polyethylene rope is not recommended since it is not UV-resistant. To counteract tree sway and keep antenna tension I used three 48 inch bungee cords in parallel at the end of each leg. Don't worry if your terrain has a slope as this will tend to lower the radiation angle in the downhill direction and make long-haul DX even more favorable in that direction.

Figure 4 shows one possible configuration for a four-leg V antenna. Optimum apex angle between legs for 20 meters is about 67° and is a compromise for the other bands. Almost any angle between 45° and 90° will work (90° works well to optimize 40 and 80, and 45° would be better for 10 and 15 meters). My antenna uses four legs so I can switch among three different V directions (using legs 1-2, 2-3 or 3-4) plus a fourth direction using two opposite legs (legs 1-4) as an extended doublet.

Balun and Relays

Figure 5 shows the circuit of the balun box that I use to match the antenna to a 50 Ω feed line and to switch among the four legs of my antenna. To match the antenna impedance of about 100 to 130 ohms, a 1:2.25 impedance transformer is connected at the antenna feed point. My transformer consists of two toroids: a Guanella 1:1 balun followed by a Ruthroff 1:2.25 unun transformer (see Figure 6). Construction was based on information in Jerry Sevick's excellent book on transmission line transformers.[7] This transformer has virtually no loss and has a flat SWR from below 1.8 MHz to above 40 MHz. For safety reasons, use low-voltage relays. I selected relays with 24 V dc coils since dc relay coils require less current than ac and thus less voltage drop on a long control cable (mine has #22 conductors and works well). Small chokes connected between each antenna terminal and ground help to eliminate static buildup on legs not in use. You will also need a control box. Mine is a simple 24 V dc supply and switch mounted in a small RadioShack box (Figure 5B).

A Carlon brand 4×4×2 thermoplastic junction box (available from most electrical supply houses) makes an ideal waterproof housing for the balun. If you install more than two legs, heavy-duty relays can be placed in a larger 6×6×4 Carlon box to remotely switch among the legs (see Figure 7).

My antenna location is in the Sangre de Cristo mountain range of Colorado and frequent storms make lightning protection a must for any antenna, particularly one with so much wire up in the air. Multiple pathways to ground will reduce risk to your equipment. The balun box has a heavy wire running down to ground. The coax connector on the balun box has a gas tube surge arrestor (U2 in Figure 5) connected from center pin to ground (use two in series for power above 500 W). Near the base of my center tree, I cut the coax feed line and installed a coax

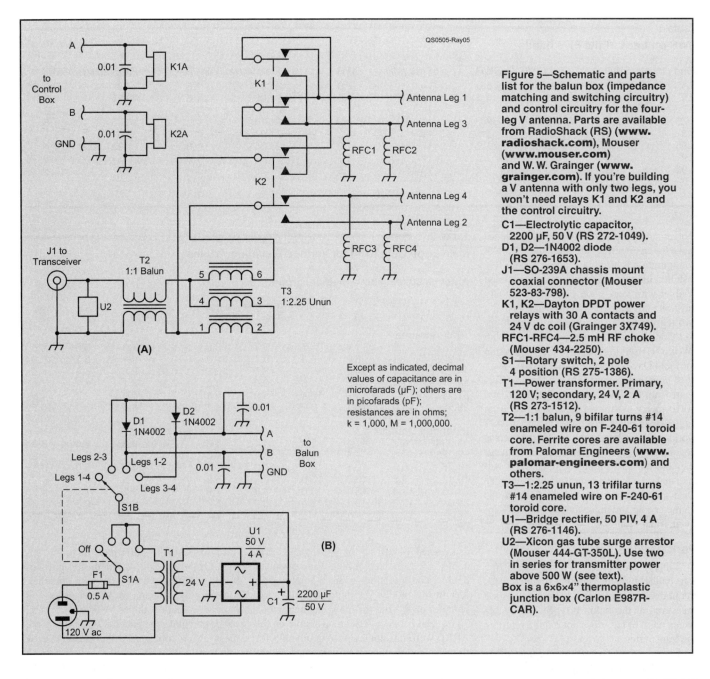

Figure 5—Schematic and parts list for the balun box (impedance matching and switching circuitry) and control circuitry for the four-leg V antenna. Parts are available from RadioShack (RS) (**www.radioshack.com**), Mouser (**www.mouser.com**) and W. W. Grainger (**www.grainger.com**). If you're building a V antenna with only two legs, you won't need relays K1 and K2 and the control circuitry.

C1—Electrolytic capacitor, 2200 µF, 50 V (RS 272-1049).
D1, D2—1N4002 diode (RS 276-1653).
J1—SO-239A chassis mount coaxial connector (Mouser 523-83-798).
K1, K2—Dayton DPDT power relays with 30 A contacts and 24 V dc coil (Grainger 3X749).
RFC1-RFC4—2.5 mH RF choke (Mouser 434-2250).
S1—Rotary switch, 2 pole 4 position (RS 275-1386).
T1—Power transformer. Primary, 120 V; secondary, 24 V, 2 A (RS 273-1512).
T2—1:1 balun, 9 bifilar turns #14 enameled wire on F-240-61 toroid core. Ferrite cores are available from Palomar Engineers (**www.palomar-engineers.com**) and others.
T3—1:2.25 unun, 13 trifilar turns #14 enameled wire on F-240-61 toroid core.
U1—Bridge rectifier, 50 PIV, 4 A (RS 276-1146).
U2—Xicon gas tube surge arrestor (Mouser 444-GT-350L). Use two in series for transmitter power above 500 W (see text).
Box is a 6×6×4" thermoplastic junction box (Carlon E987R-CAR).

junction connector. A short, heavy ground wire is connected between this junction and the same ground rod that grounds the balun. The coax is routed through 50 feet of buried flex aluminum conduit, the end of which is grounded where the coax enters the station. A coax lightning protector connected to the same ground completes my antenna protection system.

Tuning

An antenna analyzer or noise bridge is highly recommended to do a good job of adjusting resonances. If possible, connect the unit directly to the coax connector on the balun box. Since the impedance of wire antennas varies with installed height, the best balun match will be achieved if the antenna is at least 30 feet above ground. Adjust the length of the 20 meter section on each leg first, then 40, then 15, and finally the short 80/10 meter end section. As a guide for adjustment, one foot of wire (per leg) affects resonance by about 80 kHz on 20 meters, 40 kHz on 40, and 120 kHz on 15. Since both 80 and 10 meters utilize the entire antenna, adjusting the last segment affects resonance on both of these bands (20 kHz per foot on 80 and 160 kHz on 10 meters).

After adjusting my first two legs, I found that I could duplicate the dimensions for my third and fourth legs without further adjustment.

Variations

Not everyone has the space to install a multiple-leg V antenna of this size. However, this antenna works fine with only two legs. One or

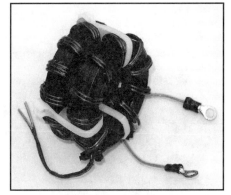

Figure 6—Impedance transformation is accomplished with a 1:1 balun and a 1:2.25 unun, each wound on a separate ferrite core and held together with cable ties. In this photo, the 1:1 balun (with bifilar winding) is toward the front. See text and Figure 5 for details.

MULTIBAND

Table 1
SWR on Each of the Five Bands

Freq (MHz)	SWR	Freq (MHz)	SWR	Freq (MHz)	SWR	Freq (MHz)	SWR	Freq (MHz)	SWR
3.5	5.0	7.0	5.0	14.0	2.0	21.0	1.8	28.0	3.0
3.6	4.0	7.05	4.0	14.05	1.6	21.05	1.6	28.25	2.6
3.7	3.0	7.1	2.9	14.1	1.4	21.1	1.5	28.5	2.2
3.75	2.3	7.15	2.2	14.15	1.3	21.15	1.4	28.75	1.8
3.8	1.4	7.2	1.5	14.2	1.2	21.2	1.4	29.0	1.4
3.85	1.0	7.25	1.2	14.25	1.2	21.25	1.3	29.25	1.4
3.9	1.3	7.3	1.5	14.3	1.3	21.3	1.3	29.5	1.6
3.95	1.6			14.35	1.5	21.35	1.4	29.7	1.8
4.0	2.0					21.4	1.4		
						21.45	1.5		

more main lobes and a number of minor lobes make for an effective antenna. A horizontal V configuration is also not necessary. WØVRW installed his two-leg version as an extended doublet with very good performance. Only have one tall support? No problem. Install a two leg version as an inverted V. The Johnson County (Kansas) Radio Amateur Club (WØERH) used the inverted V configuration for Field Day with exceptional results.

If your end supports are less than 180 feet apart from the apex, you can let the 15 and 80/10 meter sections dangle down or at an angle. If so, black #14 house electrical wire works well for these sections. If 80 meters is not of interest, you can eliminate the 15 meter trap and the 80/10 meter segment (this will also make 10 meters nonresonant, however). Or if 15 meters is not needed, eliminate the 15 meter trap and make the 80/10 meter segment 16 feet long.

Table 2
Main Lobe Gain (dBi) for Various Elevation Angles

Antenna 60 feet above medium ground

	Elevation Angle (degrees)								
	5	10	15	20	25	35	45	55	65
70° V Antenna									
3.9 MHz	−7.1	−1.4	1.7	3.7	5.0	6.7	7.3	6.9	5.6
7.225	1.1	6.6	9.3	10.7	11.3	10.7	8.1	3.7	−0.3
14.25	9.8	14.2	15.2	13.9	10.2	0.9	3.8	5.5	4.6
18.1	11.4	14.8	13.8	10.0	4.0	7.1	7.1	1.7	−7.4
21.25	11.7	15.0	13.4	5.9	5.1	7.1	1.9	−2.2	1.8
29.0	15.0	15.1	6.2	9.9	11.7	−2.6	6.8	−3.3	−0.7
Extended Doublet									
3.9 MHz	−6.7	−1.1	2.1	4.1	5.6	7.4	8.3	8.6	8.8
7.225	−1.4	4.1	6.9	8.4	9.3	9.5	8.4	6.5	4.2
14.25	6.5	10.6	11.2	10.0	7.3	−2.9	4.5	6.0	5.8
18.1	9.6	13.3	13.0	9.9	5.9	7.2	8.5	4.0	−5.0
21.25	12.4	15.1	13.0	9.3	7.9	8.7	3.2	−1.5	4.2
29.0	13.3	13.1	9.4	8.0	8.7	−0.6	6.8	−0.8	1.3

Performance

Table 1 shows the SWR on each of the five bands with the antenna optimized for the phone segments. These SWR values are measured at the balun box. Switching between pairs of legs does not require retuning the transmitter.

I used *EZNEC* 4.0 antenna modeling software[8] to calculate main lobe gain, which can exceed 14 dBi on the upper bands. See Table 2 for gain data for both V and extended doublet configurations using a height of 60 feet in the model. Azimuth and elevation plots for each band for the V antenna with a 70° spread between legs are available on the ARRL Web site, along with azimuth plots for the extended doublet configuration.[9] As expected, the V antenna patterns are bidirectional with some significant minor lobes. The extended doublet configuration azimuth plots look similar to that of traditional harmonic dipoles.

In both configurations the radiation angles are quite low. For chasing 20 meter DX it's hard to beat a 14 dBi gain at a 10° angle. Or how about a 40 meter gain of 9 dBi at 15°? As with most wire antennas, lowering the antenna to 35 feet or so will increase radiation angles by 5° to 10° on all bands and make the patterns somewhat more messy. Main lobe gain will also decrease by 2 to 3 dB.

Actual on-the-air operation confirms the model data. The antenna "gets out" very well and I've received many extremely favorable DX reports and "strongest on the band" comments. If you have the space for at least two legs, this antenna or one of its variations will likely work for you too.

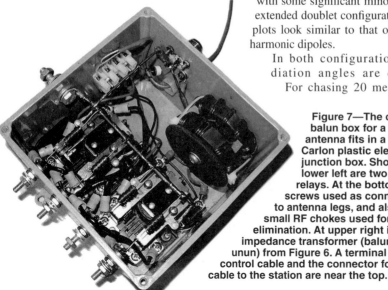

Figure 7—The completed balun box for a four-leg V antenna fits in a waterproof Carlon plastic electrical junction box. Shown in the lower left are two DPDT relays. At the bottom are four screws used as connections to antenna legs, and also four small RF chokes used for dc static elimination. At upper right is the impedance transformer (balun plus unun) from Figure 6. A terminal strip for the control cable and the connector for coaxial cable to the station are near the top.

Notes

[1] Information on classic V antennas from older editions of the *ARRL Antenna Book* is reproduced in *ARRL's Wire Antenna Classics*, pp 5-1-5-3. Available from your local dealer, or from the ARRL Bookstore, ARRL order no. 7075. Telephone toll-free in the US 888-277-5289, or 860-594-0355, fax 860-594-0303; **www.arrl.org/shop/; pubsales@arrl.org**.

[2] R. Sommer, "Optimizing Coaxial-Cable Traps," *QST*, Dec 1984, pp 37-42.

[3] L. Colvin, "Multiple V Beams," *QST*, Aug 1956, pp 28-29. This article is reproduced in *ARRL's Wire Antenna Classics*, pp 5-4-5-5 (see Note 1).

[4] I got my RG-8X Marine Coax from The RF Connection (**www.therfc.com** or tel 800-783-

2666). Their part number is WIR-117. Solid dielectric RG-8X is available from other suppliers as well—check with your favorite cable supplier.

[5]PEX is a type of polyethlyene (plastic) tubing commonly sold as inexpensive water supply line at many hardware stores and home centers.

[6]I got mine from MSC Industrial Supply, 75 Maxess Rd, Melville, NY 11747, **www.mscdirect.com**. Manufacturer's part no. RTV5223 12C, MSC order no. 06904841.

[7]J. Sevick, *Transmission Line Transformers*, 4th edition (Noble Publishing: 2001), Figures 7-14 and 9-3. Available from your local dealer, or from the ARRL Bookstore, ARRL order no. TLT4. Telephone toll-free in the US 888-277-5289, or 860-594-0355, fax 860-594-0303; **www.arrl.org/shop/; pubsales@arrl.org**.

[8]*EZNEC* 4.0 software available from W7EL at **www.eznec.com**.

[9]Visit **www.arrl.org/files/qst-binaries/Raydo.zip** for *EZNEC* azimuth and elevation plots of a V antenna with 70° leg spacing and an extended doublet, both at 60 feet.

Photos by the author.

John Raydo, K0IZ, received his Novice license in 1957 at the age of 13. He worked his way up through the licensing steps as K0LMZ and changed to a vanity call a couple of years ago. From early on he has enjoyed designing and building ham radio equipment and in the mid sixties he authored two construction articles for QST and the Mobile Manual. *After an extended period of amateur radio inactivity he recently purchased some classic Collins equipment (KWM-2A, 75S-3B, 30L-1) and set up his four-leg V antenna at his Colorado station. He is a graduate electrical engineer and also has a liberal arts degree in math and science, plus an MBA. He started his career working for TWA in the engineering department and later headed their information services and purchasing departments. He is currently president and CFO for a securities broker/dealer that he helped start several years ago. You can contact the author at* **kcflyers@yahoo.com**.

By Steve Ford, WB8IMY

The Classic Multiband Dipole Antenna

It's easy to understand why hams have had an almost 100-year love affair with wire antennas. They are inexpensive and remarkably easy to install. And for such little effort and expense, they are capable of surprising performance.

One of the simplest wire antenna designs is also one of the oldest: the random-length dipole fed with an open-wire feed line. You can put this antenna up almost anywhere, in almost any configuration and get on the air right away. The only trick is matching the input impedance of the antenna system to the output impedance of your transceiver (± 50 Ω). More about that in a moment.

Building the Antenna

Begin by cutting two equal lengths of stranded copper wire. These are going to be the two halves of your dipole (*di* pole = "two poles"). Don't worry too much about the total length of the antenna. Generally speaking, make it a half-wavelength long at the lowest frequency you hope to operate. Using the formula...

468 ÷ Frequency in MHz

...you'd make the antenna about 66 feet in total length if you chose 40 meters (7 MHz) as your lowest frequency band.

Connect one end of a length of 450-Ω *ladder line* (available from most ham dealers) to the center insulator of the antenna (see Figure 1). Feed the ladder line into your house, taking care to keep it from coming in contact with metal.

The next step is to connect the feed line to the transceiver. One way to do that is through an adjustable matching device known as an *antenna tuner*. Not just any tuner will do, though. Look for a "balanced" tuner, or a tuner with a *balun* (a balanced-to-unbalanced transformer) built in. The ladder line connects to two terminals on the back of the tuner and a short length of coaxial cable connects the tuner to your radio.

Tuning Up

Ladder line offers low RF loss on HF frequencies, even when the SWR is relatively high on the feed line going to the antenna. Just apply a signal at a low power level to the tuner and adjust the tuner controls until you achieve the lowest SWR reading. (Anything below 2:1 is fine.) You'll probably find that you need to readjust the tuner when you change frequencies. (You'll *definitely* need to readjust it when you change bands.)

You may discover that you cannot achieve an acceptable SWR on some bands, no matter how much you adjust the tuner. Changing the length of the feed line may resolve this problem.

But what if you own a radio with a built-in antenna tuner? These tuners aren't designed to work with open-wire feed lines, but a compromise is possible. Many *QST* advertisers sell external baluns. You can attach the ladder line to one side of the balun, then run a short (less than 10 foot) section of coax from the balun to the radio. As with the manual tuner, the built-in tuner may not achieve a match on all bands.

The Ladder Line Mystique

It's fair to ask why more hams don't use open-wire feed lines. The reason has much to do with convenience. Ladder line isn't as easy to install as coax. As I've already noted, you must keep it clear of large pieces of metal (a few inches at least). Unlike coax, you can't bend and shape ladder line to accommodate your installation. And ladder line doesn't tolerate repeated flexing as well as coaxial cable. After a few months of playing tug o' war with the wind, ladder line may break.

Besides, many hams don't relish the idea of fiddling with an antenna tuner every time they change bands or frequencies. They enjoy the luxury of turning on the radio and jumping right on the air—without squinting at an antenna tuner's SWR meter and twisting several knobs.

Even with the hassles, you can't beat a ladder-line fed dipole when it comes to sheer lack of complexity. Wire antennas fed with coaxial cable must be carefully trimmed to render the lowest SWR on each operating band. With a ladder line dipole, no pruning is necessary. Simply throw it up in the air and let the tuner worry about providing a low SWR for the transceiver.

Steve Ford, WB8IMY, is the editor of QST. *You can contact him at* **sford@arrl.org**.

By Charles W. Pearce, K3YWY

A 3-Band No Trap Dipole for 40, 15 and 6 Meters

A quick mod for that 40 meter dipole can turn you into a "magic band" aficionado.

Many modern rigs now come with 6 meter capability, but that may be just another unused feature of your radio because of the lack of an antenna. Even if you had a desire to work the "magic band," you may not have had a way to erect a beam antenna, thinking that was what was needed to work 6 meters. You can now transform your existing 40 meter dipole into an antenna for 6 meters with the simple addition of two capacitance hats.

The Theory

Using a 40 meter dipole on its 3rd harmonic is a time-tested technique to work 15 meters. In looking for a way to get on 6 meters, it occurred to me that 6 is more or less the 7th harmonic of 40 meters. My 40 meter dipole is resonant around 7.25 MHz and has capacitance hats, as described in *The ARRL Handbook*, to improve its characteristics on 15 meters.[1] The seventh harmonic should have been a resonant point of 50.75 MHz. In fact, I measured a resonant point of about 51.8 MHz at an SWR of 1.55:1. The resonant point was about 1 MHz or 2% higher than simple harmonic theory would have predicted. Consultation with the *Handbook* indicated that this effect is to be expected and is due to the end effect. The effect is implicit in an empirical equation for long wire antennas in the *Handbook* and is also modulated by the effect of finite wire size on antenna reactance.[2] To investigate this phenomenon further, the antenna was modeled with *MININEC*, the antenna-modeling program.[3]

I first modeled a free-space dipole similar in length to my own. Table 1 contains the results of those calculations. As expected, the feed point impedance at resonance is close to the theoretical value of 72 Ω and, using a 50 Ω feed line, should yield an SWR of 1.43:1. Notice, however, that the resonant point of the 3rd harmonic is higher by 1.8% than that predicted by a simple tripling of the 40 meter resonant point. The same is true at 50 MHz, where the resonant point is 2.5% higher than would be predicted by multiplying the 40 meter resonant point by 7 and is consistent with the experimental observations.

The modeling was repeated with the dipole 5 meters above a perfect ground to approximate my actual installation. The 40 meter resonance point did shift downward, but the upward shift of the nominal 3rd and 7th harmonic resonant frequencies above the simple expectation of tripling and septupling did repeat and was even somewhat accentuated. The shifts were now 3.6% and 4.9%. Table 1 contains these results along with those calculated from the *Handbook* formula. This formula does provide a good estimate of the resonant frequency, as well. Also, notice the rise in feed-point impedance with increasing frequency, in all cases. This places some practical limitations on using the 7th harmonic, depending on your tuner and feed line.

The increase in resonant frequency is an interesting aspect of the antenna system, but it poses an obstacle to using it in the more favored section of the band, especially if you don't have an antenna tuner. To remedy this, I decided to try capacitive loading, like that used to alter the 15 meter point.

Capacitance Loading Modification

Using alligator clips, as shown in Figure 1, I positioned 18 inch wires approximately a quarter wavelength or 4.5 feet on either side of the feed point, following what had been done for the 15 meter optimization. This lowered the resonance below 50 MHz. Further pruning of the wires and subsequent measurements indicated that the resonant point would shift at the rate of about 122 kHz/inch of wire length. I finally settled on a length of 12 inches for a resonant frequency of about 50.5 MHz. The measured SWR was 1.65:1.

Figure 1—Temporary attachment of capacitance wires to the antenna using an alligator clip.

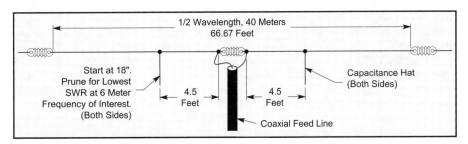

Figure 2—The modified 40 meter antenna with 6 meter capability.

[1]Notes appear on page 64.

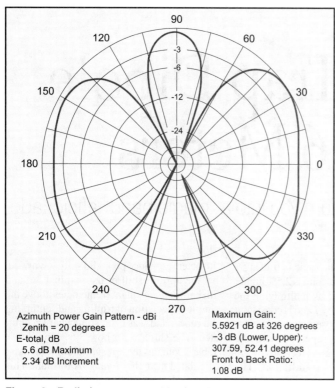

Figure 3—Radiation pattern at 20° elevation.

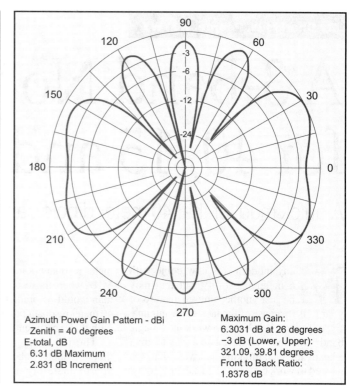

Figure 4—Radiation pattern at 40° elevation.

Table 1
40 Meter Half-Wave Dipole with a Wire Radius of 0.0005 M Using MININEC

Model (Harmonic)	Free Space Resonance (MHz)	Free Space Impedance (Ω)	5 Meters Above-Ground Resonance (MHz)	Above-Ground Impedance (Ω)	Modeling Segments Used (Number)	Handbook Formula Resonance (MHz)
1st	7.24	71.6	7.08	27.5	6	7.05
3rd	22.12	105.0	22.01	125.5	18	21.90
7th	51.93	127.0	51.99	143.0	48	51.60

Figure 2 shows a drawing of the modified 40 meter antenna.

Performance

The addition of the wires had no discernable effect on the 40 meter or 15 meter characteristics. *MININEC* predicted a 3:1 SWR bandwidth of 0.41 MHz at the feed point. I measured something in excess of 1.6 MHz in the shack at the end of the feed line. So, if you use a tuner, it should not be too difficult to achieve operation over a wide fraction of the band.

MININEC also predicted a number of side lobes, as would be expected for operation at such a high harmonic. Figures 3 and 4 show the azimuthal patterns at zenith elevations of 20° and 40°, respectively.

Fortuitously, the band was open when I first went to use the antenna, and I was able to work California. Since then, I have worked more DX, including North Dakota and some locals, as well. This may not be the best antenna for 6 meters, but it will get you on the band with a minimum of fuss.

What Needs Doing

The end effects, ground plane effects and finite wire size will all impact your actual installation, but it is likely that even with a dipole having a resonant point at the low end of 40 meters, the 6 meter resonant point will be above 51 MHz.

Assuming you already have a 40 meter dipole, measure the SWR on 6 meters to determine where your antenna is resonant or use an antenna analyzer. If the resonant frequency is above the point at which you would like to operate, proceed as follows: Solder 18 inch lengths of wire, to points 4.5 feet on either side of the feed point and remeasure the SWR. Prune as necessary to move the resonant point to your desired location using the rule of thumb of 122 kHz/inch. If you have a feed line with high loss at 50 MHz such as RG-58/U, you may want to consider replacing it with something at this frequency. Welcome to 6 meters!

Notes

[1] See, for example, *The ARRL Handbook,* 1996 edition, Chapter 20, pp 20.17 and 20.18 and *The ARRL Handbook,* 2004 edition, p 20.17. Also see *The ARRL Antenna Book,* 20th edition, Chapter 6, p 6-23. Both current editions are available from your local dealer or the ARRL Bookstore. Order nos. 1964 and 9043, respectively. Telephone toll-free in the US 888-277-5289 or 860-594-0355; fax 860-594-0303; **www.arrl.org/shop; pubsales@arrl.org**.

[2] R. G. Brown, R. A. Sharpe and W. L. Hughes, *Lines, Waves and Antennas*, New York: The Ronald Press Co, 1961.

[3] *MININEC* is available at **www.emsci.com**.

Chuck Pearce, K3YWY, was first licensed in 1963 and received a PhD in Electrical Engineering from Lehigh University in 1988. He retired from Agere Systems after 33 years as a semiconductor process engineer and now divides his time between consulting and teaching. Chuck's current Amateur Radio interests include VHF-UHF contesting and homebrewing. He can be reached at 410 S 12th St, Emmaus, PA 18049; **cpearce@fast.net**.

By Brian V. Cake, KF2YN

The "C Pole"—A Ground Independent Vertical Antenna

KF2YN takes the vertical to new heights with this folded design that doesn't require a counterpoise.

When I moved to my new home on the coast of northeast Florida, it was into a deed-restricted community, where "unsightly antennas" were forbidden. I enjoy occasional operation on the HF bands (principally 14 MHz and above) and the location was just begging for the use of vertical antennas, where the proximity to the water would help with good low radiation angles. The verticals could be hidden in the upper deck support structure and everybody would be happy, including my wife.

Unfortunately, the old saw about vertical antennas radiating equally poorly in all directions has a lot of truth to it and losses in the ground system can eat up much of your power. I made the mistake of attempting to measure the ground conductivity in my backyard. That was after I compared the on-air performance of a vertical half-wave dipole for 10 meters with a simple quarter-wave vertical with no radials. I was shocked at the quarter-wave vertical performance. I was even more shocked when I measured 30 kΩ between deep rods spaced 2 feet apart in my back yard.

Conventional solutions to this problem involve the use of radials or counterpoises, but I didn't want to sprinkle the lawn with wires. A full-size vertical dipole, at 30 plus feet for 20 meters, is too high for this location.

With all of these considerations in mind I went looking for another solution, and found an interesting configuration. It is ground independent, has a ground-level 50 Ω feed point, is less than half the height of a full-size half wave dipole, is very efficient, and has a 2:1 SWR bandwidth of about 3 percent. It can be suspended from any convenient support, rolls up into a tiny space and makes a good Field Day antenna.

Basics

The antenna consists of a vertical half-wave dipole that has been folded virtually in half, as shown in Figure 1. By erecting this just above ground level the ground currents are reduced dramatically over those of a quarter-wave ground-mounted monopole. The H-plane radiation pattern for this antenna is virtually omnidirectional.

As shown in Figure 1, the antenna is symmetrical about the feed point and is known as an open folded dipole. The feed-point impedance can be altered by changing the ratio of the diameters of the vertical wires. My intention, however, was to use suspended wire as the elements. The antenna can be analyzed in much the same way as a conventional folded dipole, and it turns out that it can be treated as a short dipole loaded by means of a short-circuited length of transmission line. I decided to take the easy way out and model it using EZNEC, however.

There are two practical problems with the antenna in Figure 1: The feed-point impedance is too low and the feed point is in the wrong place. The feed-point impedance depends on the geometry, but for spacing between the vertical wires of about 20 inches on 15 meters the feed-point impedance is about 25 Ω. This has to be transformed up to 50 Ω. Also, it is highly desirable to have the feed point at ground level, since

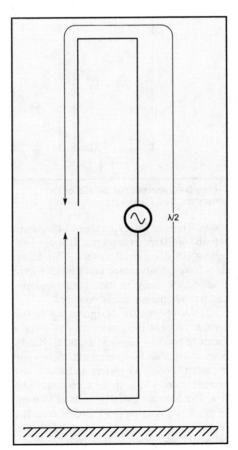

Figure 1—A vertical half wave dipole bent virtually in half.

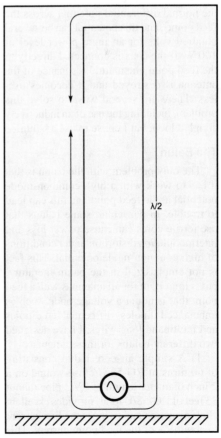

Figure 2—The bent dipole with a shifted feed point.

Table 1
Dimensions (in Inches) of the Modeled Antennas
Wire diameter is $1/16$-inch.
Height of lower horizontal wire is 12 to 24 inches (non-critical).
See Figure 3 for dimensional details.

Band (Meters)	2:1 SWR Bandwidth (kHz)	Dimension A	Dimension B	Dimension C	Dimension D	Dimension E
20	400	177	85	84	8	40
17	540	137	66	67	4	31
15	600	124	60	60	4	20
12	800	100	53	43	4	23
10	800	87	46	37	4	20

otherwise the feed cable has to be dressed away from the antenna such that currents are not induced into the feeder. These currents can lead to undesirable effects of RF in the shack and a modification of the radiation pattern. A ground-level feed point is nicer too, because the cable can be buried a short distance under the lawn.

Both of these problems can be fixed by rearranging the antenna as shown in Figure 2. Moving the feedpoint away from the voltage node at the antenna center increases the feed point impedance and an exact match to 50 Ω can be obtained by shifting the position of the gap at the dipole ends. Unfortunately, doing this places the feed point at a position where there is a substantial common-mode potential. That is to say, the two antenna feed-point terminals have the same potential on them relative to ground (in addition to the normal differential potential across the feed point), and this potential can be several hundred volts for an input power level of 100 W. If the coax is connected directly to the feed point, the natural resonance of the antenna is destroyed and it becomes useless. There are several ways to solve this problem, including the use of an inductively coupled loop, but I chose to use a balun.

The Balun

The only problem with the balun is that it has to work with a high common-mode potential at the feed point and this can lead to trouble. In particular, some baluns that use ferrite cores can cause power loss and intermodulation distortion under conditions of high common-mode potential. This fact is not emphasized in the balun literature, but is important for all antennas with a feed point that is not at a voltage node, such as unbalanced dipoles, off center fed dipoles and multiband long wires. I have designed two different baluns for these antennas:

1) A simple air-core balun consisting of 60 turns of RG-58/U close-wound on a 2 inch diameter length of PVC pipe (about 33 feet of RG-58/U total) provides excellent choking action and reduces the line current to about $1/10$ of the feed point current. This will work fine from 14 MHz to 30 MHz, but soaks up a fair bit of power, mostly in cable

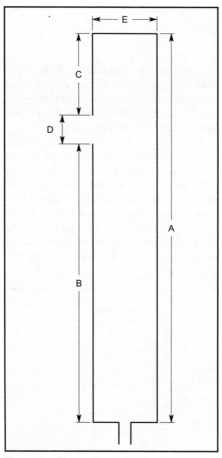

Figure 3—Dimensional details of the antennas. See Table 1.

losses. The total losses are about 14% (about 0.6 dB) on 20 meters and rise to about 18% (about 0.8 dB) on 10 meters. This balun does have the advantage that a quick trip to RadioShack and your local hardware store can provide the materials you need.

2) An alternative design using ferrite toroids reduces the power loss by over a factor of two to <7% (0.3 dB) on all bands. Two different designs, one for 20 meters and the other serving 17 meters and above, are needed in order to keep the core power loss low. The 20 meter balun consists of 19 turns of RG-174/U coax on an FT-240-61 core. For higher frequencies use 15 turns of RG-174/U on an FT-240-67 core. It is possible that a close-spaced winding of the same number of turns of 14 gauge or similar wire will give

lower loss than the RG-174/U and will also handle higher power, but I have not tried it.

Antenna Construction

The dimensions for the 20, 17, 15, 12 and 10 meter bands are shown in Table 1. Refer to Figure 3 for the dimensional key. You will note that the spacing between the vertical wires is 20 inches for 15 and 10 meters, but 40 inches for 20 meters. This is because I wanted to squeeze the antenna into available space. Twenty inches would also work fine for 20 meters as long as you adjust the vertical length of the wires.

The dimensions given are those used in the models. Note that the actual dimensions will vary from these. This is because of the effects of support structure, the proximity to objects nearby and the effects of ground on the feed point impedance. My antennas for both 15 and 20 meters resonated too low in frequency and had to be shortened quite a bit. This was partly because I used PVC covered wire and partly because they were hung close to the upper deck. The dielectric constant of the wood reduced the antenna's resonant frequency.

The antenna element can be made of anything from thin, PVC covered copper wire up through aluminum tubing, with suitable small changes in the element lengths. Thin wire will have higher losses than fat wire and will also have a higher common mode potential at the feed point. On 15 meters the loss attributable to the element resistance is 0.57 dB (14% power loss) when 32 mil (20 gauge) copper wire is used. This drops to 0.3 dB (7% loss) when using $1/16$ inch copper, and to 0.15 dB (3.5% loss) for $1/8$ inch copper. I used PVC covered wire because bare copper wire looks ugly after exposure to a beach atmosphere for even a short while. Also note that the balun choke reactance will change the resonant frequency of the antenna somewhat. An inductance of 25 μH on 20 meters will shift the resonant frequency upward by about 1.7%, or 250 kHz.

Assembly

The assembly method I used is shown in Figure 4. Here, suitable lengths of $3/4$ inch schedule-40 PVC pipe are used as the top and bottom spreaders, with the element wire simply pushed through the tubes. The spacer in the gap is a 6 inch piece of the same tubing, with holes drilled right through at 4 inch spacing (10 inches and 8 inches respectively for the 20 meter version). Start construction by cutting each piece of the element wire to the dimensions shown, plus 2 feet or so. This additional length allows for securing the wires to the spacer and for adjustment of the resonant frequency and of the SWR. Make the spreaders and the spacer as shown. Drill suitable holes in the top spreader for a suspension cord, if that is the way you are supporting it. Drill two holes near the center of the lower spacer to allow the wires to exit the spreader at the feed point. It is also advisable to drill a few holes in the spreaders to allow water to exit.

Lay the spreaders out in their approximate positions on the ground and thread the wires through them. Temporarily secure the wires at the feed point with tape. Make the balun and solder the feed point wires to the balun cable. Once you have made any adjustments necessary you should seal these joints against the ingress of water. Hoist the antenna into position, and pull on either vertical wire in order to get the lower spreader horizontal. The base of the antenna can be anything from 1 foot or so off the ground to as high as desired. The ground rod shown is not essential—it is useful for anchoring the balun so the base of the antenna doesn't flap in the breeze.

You can now test for resonant frequency and SWR. It is unlikely that you will get it exactly right the first time but, if you are using bare copper wire and the antenna is in the clear, then with the dimensions given it should be pretty close. If the resonant frequency is too low, lower the antenna (or use a stepladder), untwist the wires above and below the spacer, and shorten the element by an equal amount on either side of the spacer, then retwist the wires.

Once the resonant frequency is right, check the SWR. If your SWR meter indicates that the feed-point resistance is too high, then it is necessary to raise the position of the spacer. This is easily done by untwisting the wires, and moving the spacer farther up the top wire. Be sure to keep the total wire length unchanged, or the resonant frequency will shift. Then retwist. A low feed-point resistance will require the spacer to be lowered. If your SWR meter does not indicate whether the resistance is high or low, you will have to guess which way to move the spacer.

This sounds like an arduous setup procedure but it is actually very quick and easy to do, especially where the spacer is easily accessible from the ground. With the antenna vertical it should be possible to get an SWR of very close to 1:1 on your favorite frequency. If you can't get the SWR down below 1.5:1 then suspect that something is wrong. Also, once you have the antenna in position, check the 2:1 SWR bandwidth. It should be roughly that shown in the dimension table. If it is substantially wider than this, you should suspect that losses are higher than they should be. Finally, when all appears well, find an unused frequency and apply power for a minute or so, then check that the balun is not getting hot. This is a big advantage of a ground-mounted feed point!

Additional Notes

It is likely that a "sloper" version will work well and it is obviously easy to support, but I have not tried it.

If you are running more than 100 W out I suggest you use air-core baluns. As pointed out earlier, ferrite-core baluns can be problematic in situations where there is considerable common-mode potential. The hysteresis losses are strongly dependent on frequency and on the flux density. For a given frequency, the hysteresis losses are proportional to somewhere between the square and the cube of the flux density. This can cause distortion and heating problems. The ferrite-cored baluns described here will loaf along at 100 W but I wouldn't recommend that you go too much above that.

The name I came up with for this antenna is the "C pole," because of its shape and because the popular "J pole" is so-named for its resemblance to the shape of that letter.

Does it Work?

The evidence I have that this is an effective antenna is part scientific and part observational. The scientific part refers to the observation that the antenna Q, as measured by the 2:1 SWR bandwidth, is as expected, and the expected Q includes the effects of identifiable loss mechanisms. The observational part is simple—it is very easy to work DX stations, even though I never run more than 100 W out. Part of that is no doubt because of my excellent location, but the antenna does play a significant role. I'm sure you can tell when you are using a good antenna system—with an effective antenna, operating is a pleasure, not a struggle. That is the way it has been with this antenna design, and if you put it together carefully I'm sure you will get the same enjoyment out of it that I have.

Brian Cake, KF2YN, was born in England and first licensed as G8AFH. He received an EE degree from City University, London. Brian is now retired after 15 years as Chief Technical Officer at LeCroy Corporation, where he was manager of the Advanced Development Group. He now lives on the Matanzas Inlet, near St Augustine, Florida where he designs and tests new antenna ideas and builds miniature live-steam locomotives. Brian can be reached at 248 Barrataria Dr, St Augustine, FL 32080; **bcake@bellsouth.net***.*

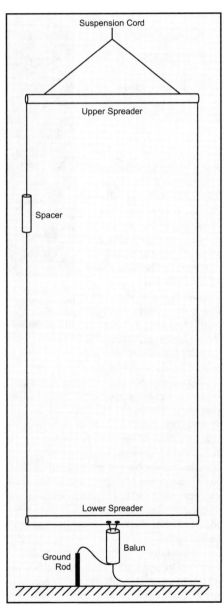

Figure 4—The antenna constructional details.

By Sam Kennedy, KT4QW

A 10/17 Meter Hanging Loop Antenna

Loops work! Build a hanging loop for 10 and 17 meters that will give almost 3 dBd of gain. It's compact, horizontally polarized, has a broad azimuth pattern, requires no matching network and can be easily rotated.

Figure 1—At a radio club meeting, the author explains the hanging rectangular loop using a scale model of the antenna. The antenna shown is a workable 2 meter loop. Although the antenna has relatively low gain at VHF, the smaller model serves well to illustrate the design.

I have experimented with several "hanging" antenna designs because the numerous tall trees in my yard furnish good support for hanging antennas. As most of my hanging antennas up to this point have been vertically polarized, I decided to try my luck with a horizontally polarized loop. A square loop proved to be too unwieldy for a hanging design and could not be easily matched on a multi-band basis using a single coax. As a result, I researched the available material and noticed the single rectangular 10 meter loop design in *The ARRL Handbook*.[1] Basic loop antenna design dates from the 1930s, but loops work just as well today as they did then!

Design

One big advantage of this antenna is that it has a feed-point impedance of 50 Ω. This same design can, of course, be scaled to any frequency, and more than one loop can be hung within the same frame. In this case I combined the 10 and 17 meter bands. I also tried to include a 15 meter element. It resonated okay, but it interacted with the 17 meter element, so I could not achieve a flat SWR on either band. Using *The ARRL Handbook* design as a launch point, I used *NEC4WIN95* modeling software and rescaled it to 17 meters.[2]

After careful examination, and a series of optimizing sequences, my new design, which theorized results that were very pleasing, emerged. I used 18.140 MHz as the 17 meter center frequency to ensure a low SWR across the entire phone band. Covering all of 17 meters was no problem, as it is a narrow band. Later, I included the 10 meter element and embedded it in the hang-up harness. I centered the 10 meter loop at 28.500 MHz and, of course, it could not cover the entire band without supplemental tuning. It does, however, cover the popular low-phone portion with a favorable SWR.

Figure 1 shows a scaled 2 meter model of the antenna, sized for demonstration purposes only, as the relative gain at VHF is low. The radiation pattern is essentially that of a dipole. The gain of this antenna is realized by compression of its vertical lobes into the main lobe and the take-off angle is low. The antenna has very good performance characteristics and it suits the needs of 10 and 17 meter communications for both distant and local coverage. Figure 2 shows the antenna's basic layout.

A "rotator" string has been included, attached to one bottom corner of the loop. This allows you to stabilize the direction of the loop or to rotate it, if desired. You'll need only to rotate it about 45° to get stations out of its deep side nulls or to null an undesired signal. A rotation angle of 90° is the maximum that would ever be necessary. I did try the loop both with and without a balun and found no measurable difference in SWR or in radiation characteristics. I chose to use the simplest approach and eliminated the balun. While not a critical consideration, if the antenna wires make contact with foliage, the loop may become detuned.

The ARRL Handbook has a good description of the slingshot method of launching lines into trees.[3] I've found that I can usually launch a line over the desired limb with a few tries. That tree in the backyard isn't a tower, but it's the next best thing to it.

Figures 3 and 4 show the elevation and azimuth radiation patterns. Note that the blue outside trace is the loop and the red trace represents a half wave horizontal reference dipole at the same frequency and height. Referring to the current distribution plot, Figure 5, you'll note that the bottom half of the loop forms a virtual half-wave dipole joined to and feeding the top half, which is also a virtual half-wave dipole. The two dipoles thus form a one-over-one horizontal array. This compresses the higher vertical lobes into the main lobe. As a result, small (but worthwhile) gain is

[1]Notes appear on page 71.

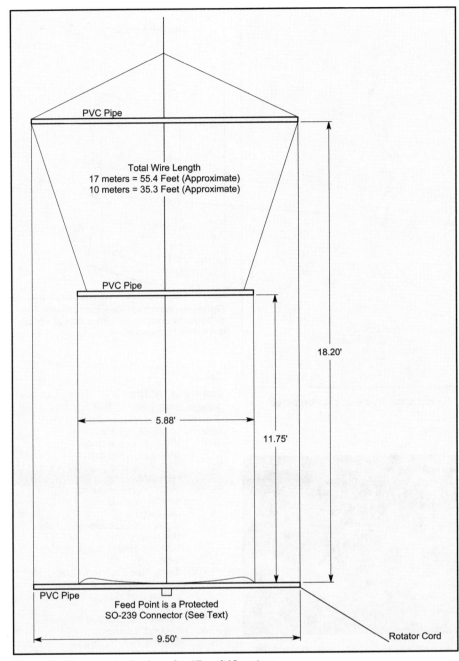

Figure 2—The rectangular loop for 17 and 10 meters.

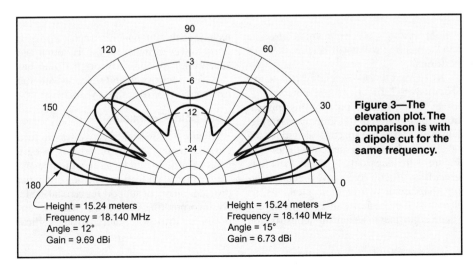

Figure 3—The elevation plot. The comparison is with a dipole cut for the same frequency.

realized compared to a single dipole, close to 3 dB. As with any antenna, the higher you hang it, the lower the radiation angle. This usually improves the performance of the antenna, depending on distances and propagation conditions. This antenna gives a better impedance match to 50 Ω cable at the feed point than a simple dipole at the same height (72 Ω).[4] You can actually "tune" the feed point impedance by slightly changing the aspect ratio of the rectangle. The wider the horizontal dimension is, the higher the impedance.

Construction

Table 1 gives the materials needed for building the antenna and a step-by-step guide for constructing the antenna follows below.

1) Prepare the two 10 foot schedule 40 PVC spreaders and place them at the proper points in the ground. Drive four small stakes in the ground corresponding to the dimensions of the loop. See Figure 6.

2) Unspool the 14 gauge stranded copper wire and apply it around the ground stakes. This forms the rectangular loop and allows the PVC spreader pipes to be correctly positioned at the top and bottom. Start and end the wire at the center of the bottom of the loop, leaving enough extra to connection to the feed point. *Be sure to allow enough extra length for pruning, as necessary.* The total length of the wire used is calculated by the following formula: Length in feet = 1005/MHz. Always cut a little longer than calculated, then adjust.

3) Connect the antenna wires to the feedpoint connector temporarily. Do not solder until you have completed the tune-up procedure.

4) Carefully measure the wire and temporarily tape it in place on the spreader PVC pipes. Tape it in enough places to ensure that it holds its shape. Note that the antenna wire is fastened to the surface of the PVC pipe. The wire does not go through the PVC; only the feedpoint assembly is positioned through the PVC pipe.

5) Build the hanging harness by paying attention to Figure 7. It is advisable to melt the rope instead of cutting it, to avoid end fraying. *Caution*—be very careful when melting synthetic rope!

6) Hoist the antenna up to your prepared test location so that the bottom of the antenna is at least a half wave above the ground, if possible. Using an antenna analyzer, minimize the SWR at the center operating frequency. To avoid being misled by the analyzer's indications, use 50 Ω coaxial cable, cut to a multiple of a half-wave length at the center design frequency. Make sure to use the correct value of velocity factor (VF) in your calculations. The formula for a half-wave length of coax in feet is: Length=

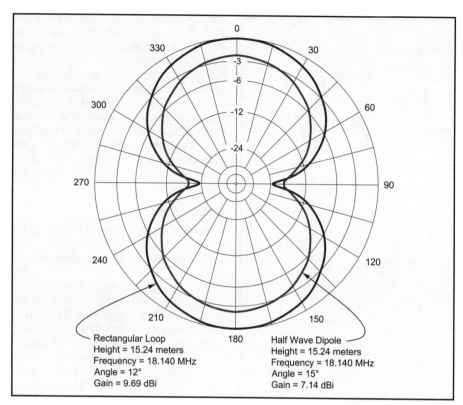

Figure 4—The azimuth plot. Again, a dipole cut for the same frequency is compared.

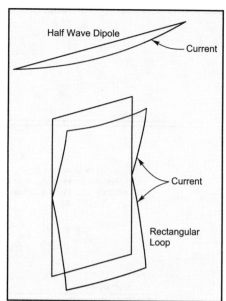

Figure 5—A current distribution plot. The antenna is compared with a dipole cut for the same frequency.

Table 1
Materials for the 10/17 Meter Loop

2 each	PVC pipe, 10 feet, 1/2" schedule 40 (use uncut—full length).
4 each	End cap, 1/2" PVC.
100'	Wire, #14 stranded copper, green vinyl insulated.
25	Tie wraps or equal, black UV resistant.
50'	Rope, nylon or dacron, 1/4" or smaller (for harness fabrication).
50'	Cord, construction-type, nylon (for rotator cord).
1	Silicone sealer, medium size tube.
1	Tape, electrical, vinyl black roll.
1	Container, durable plastic pillbox type design for quick disconnect.
1	Connector, SO-239 for coaxial cable disconnect.
1	Brazing rod, 1/8" brass.
1	Solder, 60/40, rosin core.
1	Paint, camouflage green, Plasti-Kote #17035.

Figure 6—The layout technique used for quick wire measurement and assembly of the loop and its associated hang-up harness. Note the use of PVC pipe stakes, carefully positioned and squared, for forming the structure. Both the 17 and 10 meter elements can be put into place during this operation.

(491.8/MHz)×VF, where VF is the velocity factor of the coaxial cable used. The VF for RG-8X is 0.75 and for RG-8/U it is 0.66. For other types of cable see *The ARRL Handbook*. If you use, for example, RG-8X, one half wave would be 20.3 feet in length. Since you would need it a bit longer than that for testing, you would probably want to use two half wavelengths or 40.6 feet.

7) If you choose to minimize visual attention of the completed antenna, spray paint the entire unit, including the rope, with flat olive green paint. Protect the SO-239 connector from overspray by masking. A light "hazing" of spray paint is adequate and the painting will not affect the antenna's performance.

Note that PVC spreader pipes are specified in Table 1. To prevent bowing, use Schedule 40 PVC pipe for this application. Construction of this antenna is simple; however, a large flat space is needed for the layout. The harness arrangement shown in Figure 7 includes details about the knots used. It is difficult to achieve a good hanging shape with two or more elements, so it is important to have an easy means for shape adjustment. Using this construction technique the antenna may appear flimsy. It does, however, make for a very tough and survivable structure. My original unit has survived a hurricane and severe weather at my location for over three years.

Feed-point Connector

Figure 8 shows an effective way to feed the rectangular loop. I found this to be a practical way to build a strong, durable and weather resistant feed-point connection that provides plenty of support for coaxial cable. By incorporating a standard SO-239 connector, a "drip skirt" and a strong vertical

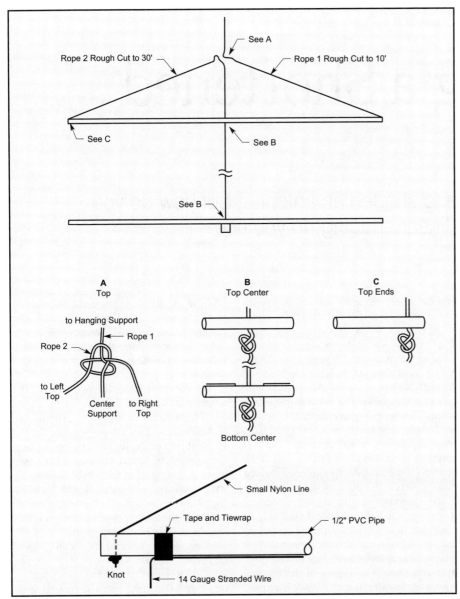

Figure 7—The rope harness is necessary for a stable hanging loop. For clarity, the knots are shown before tightening. The overhand knot is used because it holds firmly and is easy to adjust when necessary. Note that the antenna wires are fastened to the exterior of the PVC pipe.

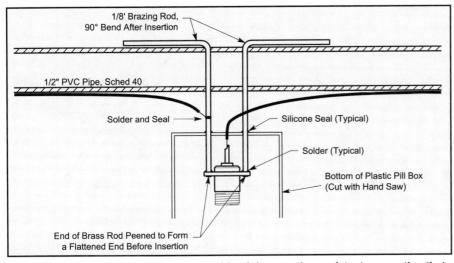

Figure 8—The feed-point connector assembly—it is a weather resistant connection that does not require taping and sealing.

support member, this method for making a quick disconnect feed-point connector for the hanging rectangular loop has worked well. While other techniques can be used, this one has proven to be satisfactory. No sealing compounds or tape are necessary to protect the connector from the weather, although protection can be applied, if you so chose. Note that it is helpful to heat the general area of the 90° bend on each section of brazing rod with a propane torch until it becomes somewhat discolored. This will anneal the brass and make it much easier to make the bend. To avoid "melt-down," the annealing process is accomplished before installing the rods into the connector, the cover and the PVC pipe.

Conclusion

Although I have no facilities for scientific measurement of the actual antenna gain, this antenna consistently gives more than 1 S unit higher received signal level than my inverted V or my 17 meter vertical. If you do decide to build one, you will be pleased with its performance. When I started using this antenna I was pleasantly surprised with results that truly lived up to, and frequently exceeded, its theorized prediction. It's the best simple wire antenna in my inventory.

Notes

[1] The rectangular loop design used here is based on a design in the 2004 as well as earlier editions of *The ARRL Handbook*, Newington: ARRL, 2004, "A Simple Gain Antenna for 28 MHz," p 20.43.

[2] My computer modeling used the *NEC4WIN95* modeling program by Orion Microsystems (**www.orionmicro.com**).

[3] A good description of this method of launching lines into trees is covered in the 2004 as well as earlier editions of *The ARRL Handbook*, "The Trusty Slingshot," p 20.7.

[4] [*Editor's note*: The feed impedance will depend upon the antenna's height above ground and its frequency of operation. Many hams use full wave low frequency loops as multiband antennas on the loop's harmonic frequencies. The feed impedance will vary with frequency when a loop is used this way. In that situation, it is best to feed the loop with open wire or ladder line into an antenna tuner, one preferably designed for link coupling.]

Photos by the author.

Sam Kennedy, KT4QW, was first licensed in the 1950s as K4DEP, but has been interested in radio since the age of 7. Relicensed in 1996, Sam was assigned his current call, and earned the Amateur Extra ticket shortly thereafter. He attended both commercial and US Navy electronics schools and has worked with military radio, radar and navigation equipment. Sam enjoys the technical aspects of ham radio. You can contact him at 57 Huxley Pl, Newport News, VA 23606 or at **kt4qw@arrl.net**.

By Luiz Duarte Lopes, CT1EOJ

Designing a Shortened Antenna

Loading coils can be used to shorten an antenna, but how do you design the coils and what linear spacing do you use?

Many amateurs cannot install the antennas they'd like because the physical space they have available is simply not large enough. Erecting a classic half-wave dipole for 40 meters, which requires approximately 20 meters of wire length, may prove to be difficult for many hams. One solution could be the installation of a so-called "shortened antenna."

There are several ways to shorten an antenna (the half-wave dipole will be considered here) and the techniques to use in each case have been covered before. No new antenna is presented here; this article focuses only on the way in which a shortened dipole can be tailored to fit available space.

The antenna we are going to design is a horizontal half-wave dipole, which is shortened with loading coils. Although the subject has been covered before in some detail[1,2] the purpose here is to clarify the basics behind the use of loading coils to do that job.

Current Distribution

In the classic half-wave dipole, at resonance, the current distribution along the antenna wire is sinusoidal—the maximum value is at its center (the feed point) and the minimum (almost zero) is at its ends. This fact assumes that the wire diameter is very small in relation to its length. At this point we won't consider the end-effect; we will assume the current at the extremities of the antenna wire is zero. The maximum current is determined by the amount of power delivered to the antenna and its *radiation resistance*—the antenna's ability to transfer power to free space—and its efficiency.

Let's assume the antenna wire is divided into very small segments. Consider that the signal strength at any particular point in space is the sum of the radiation coming from each

[1]Notes appear on page 76.

of these small segments, and the final result comes mainly from the elements at the center of the antenna, where the current is greatest. The contribution from the segments with currents very near zero is negligible. As the reduction of the antenna length is based on the replacement of part of the antenna wire by a coil, the question is: What part(s) of the antenna are we going to remove?

The physical length of a horizontal half-wave dipole is equivalent to an electrical length of π radians (2π radians equal 360°) or 180°. If we consider this antenna divided into six parts of 30° each, as shown in Figure 1, and remembering what we said previously, it is evident that the parts making the least contribution to the total radiated power are the two labeled C. Although we could be tempted to remove them, their replacement by a coil at each extremity of the antenna wire is not feasible, because it would require a very large, practically infinite inductance.

[As the electrical distance (in degrees, ß) to the antenna's end approaches 0°, the cotangent of that distance becomes very large, thus increasing the reactance (hence inductance) needed. This will become more evident later.—*Ed*.]

On the other hand, the two parts of the antenna at A, where the RF current is both maximum and near maximum, should not be touched, as they are responsible for the greatest part of the radiated power. In fact, the amount of power radiated by the two parts at A is equal to the power radiated by the remaining four parts, B and C, taken together.

As a good compromise, the part that should be removed from each side of the antenna (to be replaced by a coil) should be part B. We then will arrive at an antenna length that is $2/3$ of the full half wavelength. If this length reduction won't be enough, we'd also have to consider removal of a part of C

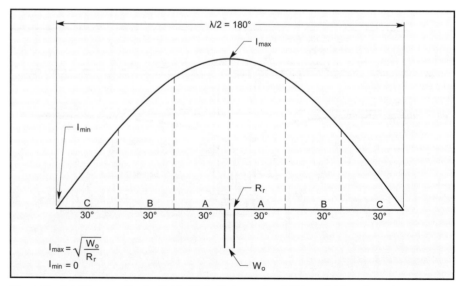

Figure 1—A half-wave dipole divided into 6 elements of 30° each. The sinusoidal current distribution is shown above the antenna.

(not all) and, eventually, of part of A. The final decision depends on the particular space occupied by each segment and the practicality of the coil inductance used. In any case, it would be best to keep part A untouched.

Reactance Along the Antenna Wire

Suppose we intend to have an antenna shortened to $2/3$ the length of a half-wave dipole and the coils are to be located just in the middle of each antenna half. As an example, for a frequency of 7.070 MHz, such an antenna is represented in Figure 2.

First of all, by analogy with transmission line theory,[3] we will use Equation 1 to determine the reactance in both extremities of the piece of wire that will be replaced by the coil:

$$X = -j Z_0 \cot \beta \qquad [\text{Eq 1}]$$

where

X is the reactance we are looking for,
β is the distance in electrical degrees from the extremity of the antenna wire to the point under consideration, and
Z_0 is the characteristic impedance of a one-wire transmission line using the same wire diameter and height above ground as the antenna.

We obtain two values: X_1 (at the junction of C with B) and X_2 (at the junction of B with A). In each arm of a half-wave dipole, β is always less than 90° (λ/4) and we obtain two negative values: $-jX_1$ and $-jX_2$ (see Figure 2). The coil reactance, X_L, to be introduced in each arm of the antenna, comes from Equation 2:

$$X_L = X_2 - X_1 \qquad [\text{Eq 2}]$$

or

$$X_L = -jX_2 - (-jX_1)$$

and

$$X_L = jX_1 - jX_2$$

As the quantity X_1 is always greater than the quantity X_2 [X_1 is closer to the end of the antenna than X_2, β is smaller and thus cotan β is larger.—*Ed.*], the value of X_L is positive (+*j*), which corresponds to a coil, as we expected. (Remember that positive reactance is inductive.)

For the expression in Equation 1 we still need the value of Z_0. We will use Equation 3.[4]

$$Z_0 = 138 \log (4h / d) \qquad [\text{Eq 3}]$$

where h and d are the antenna height above ground and the wire diameter, respectively, in the same units.

In practice, the value of h is not easy to know accurately. In the majority of situations, the value we can measure with a measuring tape is not equal to the real electrical height. It is affected by the nature of the soil and, mainly, by the close proximity of other objects and antennas. Typically the electrical height is smaller than the physical height, but the physical height will be used for the approximate value of h.

A First Example

Using the antenna of Figure 2, we can now determine the coil inductance and the wire lengths, with 7.070 MHz as the antenna's resonant frequency. The antenna wire diameter will be 2.0 mm (12 gauge) and 6 meters (20 feet) will be the estimated height to the ground. This height value looks small but, as previously discussed, we have to be aware of not only the distance to ground but also the distance to nearby objects and other conductors.

Using Equation 4, with the frequency f in MHz, we obtain the length l in meters of the horizontal half-wave dipole before being shortened:

$$l = 150 / f \qquad [\text{Eq 4}]$$

$$l = 150 / 7.07 = 21.22 \text{ meters}$$

As stated previously, we are ignoring the usual reduction of this length due to the end effect. Antenna trimming (with an RF analyzer) at 7.070 MHz will take care of that later.

Using Equation 3, we can calculate the characteristic impedance (Z_0):

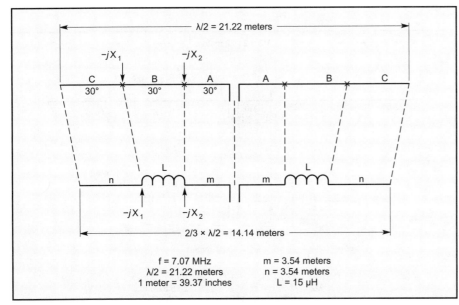

Figure 2—The first shortened example. A half-wave dipole reduced to $2/3$ of its normal length.

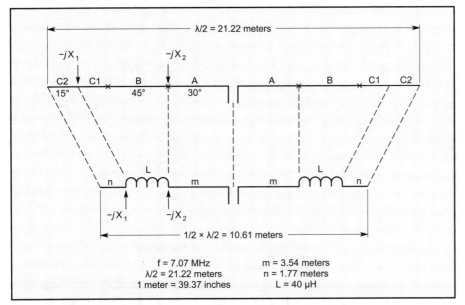

Figure 3—Example two. A half-wave dipole reduced to half its normal length.

$Z_0 = 138 \log [4 (6000/2.0)]$

[6000 mm is about 20 feet and 2.0 mm is about the diameter of 12 gauge wire. —Ed.]

$Z_0 = 138 (4.08)$
$Z_0 \approx 563 \, \Omega$

Now, with Equation 1, we can determine the values of X_1 and X_2 (see Figure 2). The distance, β, from the extremity of the antenna to the junction of the segment C with B and to the junction of B with A is 30° and 60°, respectively.

Then,
$X_1 = -j563(\cot 30°) = -j563(1.732)$
$X_1 = -j975$

And
$X_2 = -j563(\cot 60°) = -j563(0.577)$
$X_2 = -j325$

Finally, using Equation 2, we have:
$X_L = -j325 - (-j975)$
$X_L = +j650$

With the frequency f in MHz, the value of the coil L, in μH, is obtained with Equation 5:

$X_L = 2\pi f L$ [Eq 5]

$L = 650 / [2\pi (7.07)]$

$L = 14.63 \, \mu H \approx 15 \, \mu H$

Then, with the insertion of one coil with an inductance of 15 μH in the middle of each arm of the dipole, the antenna length will be reduced from 21.22 meters to 14.14 meters, or $2/3$ of its classic length. The end effect will reduce this even more.

A Second Example

We consider the previous antenna, but this time shortened to half of its classic length. We start by dividing each element C of the dipole into two elements C_1 and C_2 of 15 electrical degrees each, as shown in Figure 3. As the central elements, A should be preserved as much as possible; the elements to remove are now B and C_1, that is 30° + 15° = 45° on each side of the dipole.

We already know, from the previous example, that:
$Z_0 \approx 563 \, \Omega$ and
$X_2 = -j325$

We need a new value for X_1. Using Equation 1 for β =15°, we have:
$X_1 = -j563 (\cot 15°) = -j563 (3.732)$
$X_1 = -j2101$

From Equation 2:
$X_L = -j325 - (-j2101)$
$X_L = +j1776$

And, from Eq 5:
$L = 40 \, \mu H$

The total length of the horizontal dipole has thus been reduced from 21.22 meters to 10.61 meters. That is half its normal length, but this reduction does require greater inductance and hence larger coils (40 μH).

One may consider that 40 μH coils are physically too large. Because of that, we present a third example, for an antenna reduced to half the classic size, but using smaller coils.

The Third Example

Keeping the antenna half size, but looking for smaller coils implies that we have to move each coil to a position closer to the center of the antenna. This is shown in Figure 4, where the full length of the dipole is divided into 8 segments of 22.5° each. The values of X_1 and X_2 are now calculated for 22.5° and 67.5°, respectively.

Doing the calculations as in the previous examples, we get the following results:
$X_1 = -j1359$
$X_2 = -j233$
$X_L = +j1126$ and finally,
$L = 25 \, \mu H$

The size of the coil is now smaller than it was in the second example. But this was only possible because we jeopardized part A of the dipole, reducing it from its original 30° length to 22.5°. The question is: Can we use this 25 μH coil without touching part A of the antenna? The answer is presented in the next, and final, example.

The Fourth Example

Figure 5 illustrates the final example, with A equal to 30° and L = 25 μH. How long should C_2 be? We already know that:

$X_2 = -j325$ (from example 1)
$X_L = +j1126$ (from example 3)
Then:
$X_1 = X_2 - X_L$
$X_1 = -j325 - j1126$
$X_1 = -j1451$

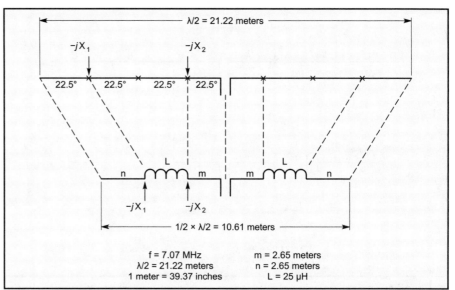

Figure 4—The third example. A half-wave dipole half its normal length, but with smaller coils. The lower inductance coils must be moved closer to the center of the antenna. The dipole is divided into 8 segments of 22.5° each.

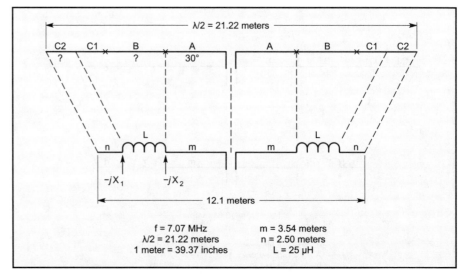

Figure 5—Example four. The dipole is slightly longer than half its classic length, but the coils are now moved so that the critical length A is not affected. Segment A is the area of maximum radiated current that we want to avoid by the loading coils.

As
$X_1 = -jZ_o \cot \beta$
$\cot \beta = 1451/563 = 2.577$
And
$\beta = 21.20°$
Then:
$C_2 = 21.20 (21.22 /180) = 2.50$ meters

The antenna now has a total length of about 12.1 meters, which is a little bit longer than half the classic half-wave, but part A of the dipole is untouched and is left with its original electrical length of 30°. The end effect and the trimming of the antenna will allow us to have a final length very near 10.6 meters (half of the half-wave length).

The examples we have shown so far are only four possible cases that may be encountered. In the real world there are many different situations and the use of loading coils could be a satisfactory solution to shorten an antenna. The procedure we've shown can be used for any one of those possible cases. [A program for calculating the loading coil inductances, **K1TD.EXE**, can be found at the ARRL Web site **www.arrl.org/files/qst-binaries/lopes1003.zip**. This will simplify the calculations considerably.—*Ed.*]

Building the Antenna

To confirm the calculations, an antenna was constructed using the parameters of the fourth example. The antenna was built with ordinary plastic insulated 12 gauge copper wire, commonly used for electrical house wiring. The final lengths, after trimming, are shown in Figure 6. The values were very close to those calculated, although they do have some uncertainty in a couple of parameters (antenna height and end effect).

Building the loading coils was the most difficult part of the job. [An inductance bridge or a Q meter would be a big help here.—*Ed.*] For the forms, white PVC tubing of 10 cm length and 46.5 mm outside diameter were used, on which was wound 33 turns of 12 gauge enamel wire. The length of the coil was 70 mm. The number of turns was determined with the aid of Equation 6.[5]

$L = [(a^2) (n^2)] / (18a + 40b)$ [Eq 6]

where
L is in µH
a and b are the diameter and the length (in inches) of the coil, respectively,
and n is the number of turns

Using the values found earlier, a 25 µH coil was made. A piece of Plexiglas was introduced inside the coil to support the tension of the antenna wire. Figure 7 details the coil construction and Figure 8 shows the completed coil before the Plexiglas wire support was installed.

The Results

The receiving and transmitting performance of the antenna was very good. During several contacts the reports received were very similar, or slightly lower than the reports with my main antenna (a W3DZZ type). The difference did not exceed –3 dB (half an S unit), principally because the short antenna was tested at a lower height. In theory, if the losses in the coil are small, the amount of radiated energy is very close to the energy radiated by a full-length half-wave dipole. However, a short antenna has a lower radiation resistance; this is the main reason for the reduction in efficiency.

Efficiency

In free space, the radiation resistance of a classic (full-length) half-wave dipole is about 73 Ω. In actuality, near ground, the radiation resistance depends on the height above ground and, in most cases, it is closer to 50 Ω, as the antenna is usually relatively low.[6]

When we reduce the length of a dipole in relation to its half-wave length, the radiation resistance decreases, which, in a loss-free world would be of no significance. In fact, with the same amount of power delivered to the antenna, the antenna current would increase in such a way that the radiated power would be the same as with a full-length half-wave dipole.

In the real world, losses in the antenna system do exist. They are in the conductors, the insulators and the ground and they are also in associated items, such as baluns, transmission lines and antenna tuners.

The antenna system efficiency is the ratio between the radiated power and the power delivered to the antenna system and is determined by the following equation:

$\eta = [R_r / (R_r + R_t)] \times 100\%$ [Eq 7]

or

$\eta = [1 / (1 + R_t / R_r)] \times 100\%$ [Eq 8]

where
η is the antenna system efficiency,
R_r is the radiation resistance and
R_t the equivalent resistance of all the losses in the antenna system.

Assuming that the total losses R_t remain the same, this last equation shows that the decrease in the radiation resistance R_r implies the increase of the ratio R_t / R_r and, consequently, the decrease of the antenna efficiency η.

For example, we can assume that a half-wave dipole antenna with a radiation resistance of 50 Ω and a total loss resistance of 5 Ω has an efficiency of 50 divided by 55, that is, 91%. A short version of this dipole may have 25 Ω of radiation resistance and, assuming no change in the loss resistance, the efficiency would be 25 divided by 30, or 83%.

Actually, the introduction of the loading coils implies some increase in the antenna losses due to the resistance of the coil wire. Additionally, an antenna tuner (adding further loss) would probably be used with the shortened dipole. If we thus consider a higher value of 10 Ω rather than 5 Ω for the loss resistance (including the tuner loss), the efficiency would be 25 divided by 35, which is 71%. How important is this efficiency reduction? In fact, it corresponds to a decrease of only 1 dB.

Several calculations and tests were run to determine the radiation resistance of this antenna. Using specific formulas from different sources[7, 8] a value of about 25 Ω was calculated. Finally, with a noise bridge and a computer to solve the *transmission line equation*,[9] a similar result was achieved. The SWR goes up to 2.0 at this low value of radiation resistance. With the use of RG-58 (50 Ω) coaxial cable as a feed line, the use of an antenna tuner is strongly advised. [Two lengths of paralleled RG-58 (total $Z_0 = 25$ Ω) could be used to feed the antenna, however. This would bring the SWR close to 1.0 and would eliminate the need for a tuner, if your transmitter can handle the lower load impedance. In place of this, a quarter-wave transformer could be

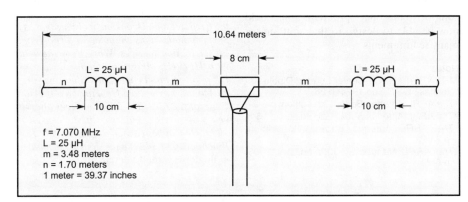

Figure 6—The completed shortened half-wave dipole after frequency trimming at 7070 kHz.

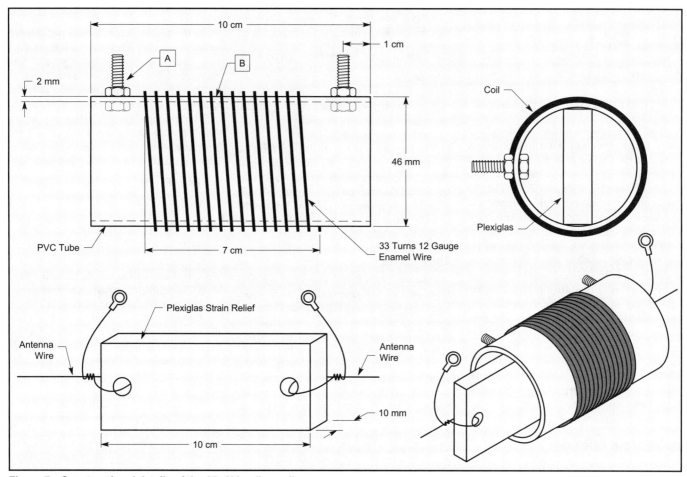

Figure 7—Constructional details of the 25 μH loading coils.

Figure 8—The completed loading coil before the addition of the tension support.

used, consisting of 27 feet of 2 lengths of RG-59 cable (70-75 Ω) in parallel (with a resulting effective impedance of about 35-37 Ω), the whole in series with the 50 Ω feed line, at the antenna. A further option would be a series matching section of 75 Ω coaxial line inserted into the 50 Ω feed line to match impedances and, again, get around the tuner requirement. [See The *ARRL Antenna Book* (19th edition, p 26-4) for design details on these useful matching techniques.[10]—*Ed.*]

Conclusion

The claim is not made that a shortened antenna with coils is as good as a classic half-wave dipole. Although the reduction in efficiency is low, the classic half-wave dipole is still a better solution, if you have enough space for its installation. That's a big "if," however, and we've shown that the loaded coil dipole offers an effective solution to that space problem. You should now be able to design to that solution for many requirements.

Notes
[1] J. Hall, K1PLP, "Off-Center Loaded Dipole Antennas," *QST*, Sep 1974, p 28.
[2] *The ARRL Antenna Book*, 19th edition, p 6-27.
[3] *The ARRL Antenna Book*, 19th edition, p 16-8.
[4] *The ARRL Antenna Book*, 19th edition, p 24-22.
[5] *The ARRL Handbook*, 80th edition, 2003, p 6-22.
[6] *The ARRL Antenna Book*, 19th edition, p 3-2.
[7] Laport, *Radio Antenna Engineering*, McGraw-Hill, 1952.
[8] *The ARRL Antenna Book*, 19th edition, p 16-6.
[9] *The ARRL Antenna Book*, 19th edition, p 24-11.
[10] *The ARRL Antenna Book*, 19th edition, is available from your local dealer or the ARRL Bookstore. Order no. 8047. Telephone toll-free in the US 888-277-5289, or 860-594-0355, fax 860-594-0303; **www.arrl.org/shop/**; **pub-sales@arrl.org**.

Luiz Lopes, CT1EOJ, is an Electrotechnical Engineer who graduated from the Oporto University in Portugal in 1953. Luiz joined the Civil Aviation Department of Portugal as a telecommunications engineer for airports and air navigation services. While there, he dealt with HF/VHF air-ground communications, HF point-to-point communications and radio aids for air navigation. He retired as Director-General for Air Navigation Services after 40 years of service. Luiz was first licensed in 1993. He can be reached at Rua do Vale 13A, Rinchoa, 2635-342 Rio de Mouro, Portugal or at **luizlopes@mail.telepac.pt**.

By Mike Loukides, W1JQ

A Dipole Curtain for 15 and 10 Meters

W1JQ tackles the construction of a version of one of the largest types of HF antennas. It's the main radiator at some of the most powerful international shortwave broadcast stations—the curtain array.

Looking at a shortwave broadcaster's Web site, I noticed that their antenna was a "dipole curtain." I wondered what a dipole curtain was as I'd always wanted an antenna that I could call a "curtain"… Sterba, Bobtail—whatever. I've had a lot of fun with my G5RV multiband dipole, but it's clearly not the antenna to use as the sunspot cycle declines.

At around 2 AM of a sleepless night, I decided that a dipole curtain must be an array of dipoles, fed in phase. Jim Peterson, K6EI, pointed me to a Web site (**www.tcibr.com/NewFiles/hfbroadants.html**) that showed I was correct. Dipole curtains have long been the "gold standard" of shortwave broadcast antennas. They are among the largest antennas I've ever seen. An array can have up to two dozen dipoles, stacked up to six high, with a design frequency as low as 5 MHz. A commercial dipole curtain looks like the backstop for a baseball field, designed for 100 foot-tall players. They can yield a gain of 20 dBi or more—as much gain as an EME antenna, on frequencies as low as 60 meters! These arrays typically use a nonresonant reflecting screen to give a unidirectional pattern. It's common to put a set of driven elements on either side of the reflector, so the pattern is switchable. Curtains with two or more stacks of dipoles are also slewable; that is, the pattern can be steered by changing the phasing between the stacks.

Could some of the world's largest antennas, with price tags in the millions of dollars, be adapted to amateur service? I didn't know, but there were many reasons to try. Dipole curtains are very broad; their properties don't change very much as you move across a band or even

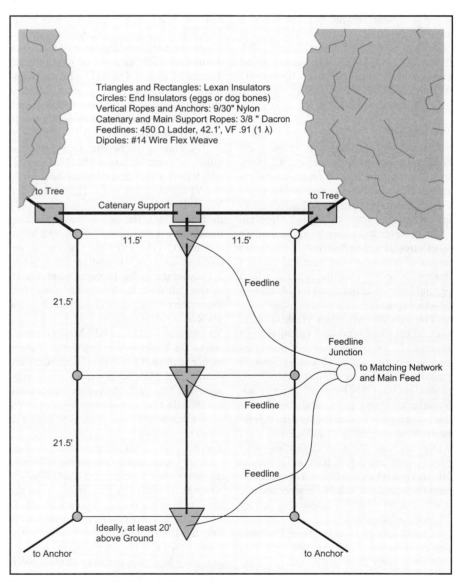

Figure 1—15-meter dipole curtain geometry.

band to band. They have excellent low-angle radiation characteristics and they are ideal antennas for DX work. The optimum radiation angle for DX propagation is 10 to 20°,[1] and that's where curtains show their maximum gain. Additionally, they have a very broad beamwidth, particularly compared to antennas with equivalent gain. Although they deliver high gain, their radiation pattern allows them to cover a lot of territory without any rotation.

I decided to see whether I could trim the dipole curtain down to size and build an antenna that would fit into a suburban backyard. A few things go away immediately—the reflecting screen looks difficult to build and, at least for a first antenna, a single stack of dipoles is sufficient. With a design frequency in the 15 meter band, closer than ideal spacing and ground proximity lower than ideal, a stack of 3 or 4 dipoles can be made to fit easily in a backyard. Figure 1 shows the general idea of my dipole curtain. Its gain is competitive with a beam and its radiation characteristics are in some ways superior. It didn't cost much, it didn't require a tower (just some good trees) and it's even "stealthy." Dollar for dollar, I don't think it's possible to buy or build a more effective antenna for the upper HF bands. It's the only wire antenna I know about that has both high gain and broad beamwidth.

The Design

I started by stacking four 15 meter dipoles at 15 foot intervals, starting at 20 feet, with the top dipole at 65 feet. That height sounds arbitrary, but it represented the highest elevation I thought I could achieve. My trees are mature maples, close to 100 feet tall and I've never been able to use more than $2/3$ of a tree's height effectively. A minimum height of 20 feet was an educated guess; I thought it represented the point at which ground loss would outweigh the advantages of wider spacing.

The four-dipole design yielded decent gain, an excellent maximum radiation angle of about 12°, a nice broad beamwidth and very similar performance on 12 and 10 meters. I traded e-mail with Dean Straw, N6BV, who pointed out that I'd be better off if I cut the antenna back to two dipoles. With four dipoles that close together, coupling between the elements would significantly reduce the gain. I really did want those extra dipoles—so I tried putting one dipole back in (dipoles at 20, 41.5 and 63 feet). The third dipole didn't help 15 meters but it didn't hurt, either, and it was exactly what the antenna needed for 10 meter performance.

I spent lots of time tweaking the basic design shown in Figure 1, but my initial guess was fairly close to optimal, given my assumption that I could get the top dipole to 65 feet. If I made the spacing between dipoles larger, the bottom dipole was too low and performance suffered; if I made the spacing smaller, the elements were too close together and, again, performance suffered.

So, I stuck with dipoles at 20, 41.5 and 63 feet, cut for 21.25 MHz (23 feet total length). This array yields 11.38 dBi gain over real ground on 15 meters, and 13.34 dBi on 10 meters, according to *EZNEC*. The half-power beamwidth is 80° on both bands and the takeoff angle is around 13°.

Now, how to feed it? For the two-dipole array, N6BV suggested equal lengths of 50 Ω coax to the dipoles and then a quarter wave matching section of parallel 75 Ω coax (with an effective impedance of 37.5 Ω). That would work reasonably well for the three-dipole array—except it wouldn't work on 10 meters. My strategy was to feed the dipoles with some number of half waves of transmission line on 15 meters. Regardless of the transmission line's impedance, its input impedance will equal the load impedance every half wave. That way, I had a workable feed system for 15 meters: the impedance at the junction of the transmission lines was about 25 Ω, and it could be matched to 50 Ω with a quarter-wave transformer. I played with different combinations of transmission line length and impedance to find something that would yield a reasonable match on 10 meters.

The winning combination turned out to be full-wavelength feeders of 450 Ω ladder line, which is 42.1 feet (according to the formula $\lambda = VF \times [984/f]$, where f is 21.25 MHz, and VF is the velocity factor; I assumed 0.91 for ladder line). The quarter-wave matching transformer is 9 feet long (assuming a VF of 0.78 for RG-11). *EZNEC* predicts a minimum SWR of about 1.3:1, and an SWR below 2:1 across the entire 15 meter band. On 10 meters, full-wave feeders conveniently yield a secondary resonance with a reasonably low SWR at 28.5 MHz—about 1.75:1, and below 3:1 between 28.125 and 29 MHz (Figure 2 shows the feed line construction). That's a higher minimum SWR than many hams are comfortable with, but it's really not a problem. Walt Maxwell's *Reflections*[2] argues that we shouldn't be scared away by high SWR or, for that matter, waste our time trying to tune our antenna systems for a perfect 1:1 match… that's what antenna tuners are for.

Still, I spent some time seeing if I could do better—and found some interesting red herrings. It turns out that, if you feed the top dipole or the bottom dipole with 300 Ω line, and the other two dipoles with 450 Ω line, the 10 meter SWR drops significantly. I discovered that this configuration had significantly less gain, however. A good SWR wasn't worth a few dB of signal strength. While I never analyzed why the 300 Ω line improved the SWR but reduced the gain, the answer is almost certainly that it upset the current distribution between the elements.[3] I tried other transmission line impedances, from 200 Ω up to 800 Ω, and none worked as well as 450 Ω.

So I stuck with full-wave feeders of 450 Ω line, and a quarter wave section of two lengths of RG-11U in parallel, all fed with 50 Ω coaxial cable. Since the SWR on the transmission line is on the high side, particularly on 10 meters, I chose to use high-quality low-loss cable. I settled on one of the many Belden 9913F7-equivalent (buriable, low-loss foam, RG-8-style) cables.[4] To ensure that the feed system could handle high power, I simulated all the feed lines using N6BV's *TLW* program, and satisfied myself that, when used on 15 and 10 meters, the antenna and feed system are capable of 1500 W—though it's getting close to the maximum voltage for RG-8 style foam coax. If you really want to run high power, you might be better off using "solid" RG-8, rather than foam.

If you're more adventurous, here are some other ideas for feeding the antenna. Perhaps the most obvious is using ladder line end-to-end. That's no doubt the best solution for those who have figured out how to route parallel line inside their house. A recent *QST* article[5] suggested another interesting possibility…a weatherproof, automatic antenna tuner mounted in the trees. Several vendors, most notably SGC and LDG, have tuners that will fill the bill. They are relatively expensive and I thought long and hard about whether to spend the money. I decided against it—but you might not.

Building It

This antenna proved to be the most complex piece of aerial engineering I've ever tried. Getting it up into the air without turning it into a tangled mass of wire and rope was a challenge.

I started by making center insulators from 6×6 inch squares of $1/4$ inch Lexan (from the McMaster-Carr Supply Company, another vendor I've come to love[6]) using a design suggested by Joe Wonoski, N1KHB. Figure 3 shows the basic design. I cut each square diagonally (to be precise, Joe cut the squares diagonally for me), making two insulators from each piece. To prevent abrasion, I used a small rat-tail file to round off the edges of the holes through which the wires pass; I also sanded down the edges of the insulators slightly. When you've made an insulator, punch some holes in the "webbing" of the ladderline, and lace it to the insulator using black cable ties. The insulator thus serves as a strain relief. You could also use the WA1FFL Ladder-Locs for the same purpose.[7]

Once I had a piece of ladderline tied

[1]Notes appear on page 81.

to an insulator (without the dipole), it was time to cut the feed line to 1 wavelength at 21.25 MHz. The antenna's behavior is fairly sensitive to getting the feed lines the right length, and the velocity factor of parallel transmission line can vary quite a bit, even within the same piece of cable. Rather than cut blindly, I borrowed N1KHB's MFJ Antenna Analyzer, which allowed me to measure a full wave precisely: cut the cable at about 45 feet, short it at the insulator end, tie the insulator up in the air (it doesn't have to be high), stretch the cable out so it was above ground, and trim the loose end for minimum impedance. Repeat until you have three insulators with roughly 42 foot long pieces of ladderline attached.

I became a complete convert to Flex-Weave antenna wire (available from Radio-Ware[8] and other suppliers). That wire just doesn't want to tangle! You can tie knots in it as easily as in nylon rope.

I used standard egg insulators at the ends, though these turned out to be a poor choice given the antenna's geometry. If I build another curtain, I'll make triangular Lexan insulators for the ends (one hole for the wire, one hole for the upper support rope and one hole for the lower support rope). For pruning, I left some extra wire at the ends, tied back so as not to lengthen the dipole. I didn't try pre-tuning the dipoles with the MFJ Analyzer. Hoisting the dipoles to their eventual height purely for tuning was too much work, and at more convenient heights of 4 or 5 feet off the ground, the resonant frequency and impedance of a dipole is significantly different from what it will be in the air, making the value of "low-altitude" measurements questionable. *EZNEC* showed that the antenna wasn't particularly sensitive to the length of the dipoles—and the FlexWeave was so easy to work with that it was easy to measure the dipoles fairly precisely.

After reading some articles in *More Wire Antenna Classics*,[9] I decided to use a catenary rope at the top of the antenna. The catenary gives the antenna additional strength in windstorms and ice storms, both frequent in New England. The catenary—which is basically a "dipole" made out of rope, about 3 feet longer than the real dipoles—gave me a point from which I could support the center insulators, and allowed me to use more tension than I would have dared otherwise.

The trickiest part of the antenna was the junction between the main feed line and the ladder lines to the elements, as shown in Figures 4A and 4B. I made a square of Lexan, on which I mounted two SO-239 coaxial sockets (for the matching section). I drilled holes that allowed me to lace the ladder line to the insulator, placing the three feed lines on top of each other. A few extra holes allowed me to attach ropes for suspending the junction in the air, and for hanging the matching section underneath; one hole allowed me to feed the right side of the three feed lines through to the bottom junction, where I attached them to the SO-239 bodies using spade lugs. I soldered the left side of the transmission lines to a stiff wire that ran between the center conductors of the two sockets.

There are three things to keep in mind when building the junction:

• The SO-239 connectors must be facing down, as you want the matching section and the main (coaxial) feed line to hang from the junction. Use epoxy to prevent water from getting into the sockets. I don't know whether water can get through an SO-239, a PL-259 and into your coax, but if you live in a cold climate, I guarantee you that water collecting in the "well" made by the SO-239 will break the junction apart. I used coax sealant liberally at all junctions. [Trust the fact that water *will* get into an unprotected PL-259 and SO-239 connector and eventually into the coax; these are not waterproof. Seal these connectors and their mating surfaces well.—*Ed.*]

• You must make sure the dipoles are all in phase. This is easy enough. Roll the ladder line for each dipole into a flat coil, stack the coils on top of each other and lace the lines to the junction, making sure that nothing has flipped over. Mark the same side (let's say the left side) of each center insulator. Then, at the junction, solder the ladder line to the SO-239 connectors. When you haul the antenna up, make sure the marked sides of the center insulator are all facing the same direction.

• Once you attach the feed lines to the junction, you have determined the array's stacking order. The top feed line goes to the top dipole, and so on. Label the dipoles so you don't spend lots of time tracing a tangle

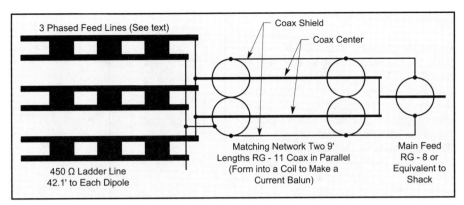

Figure 2—Transmission line schematic.

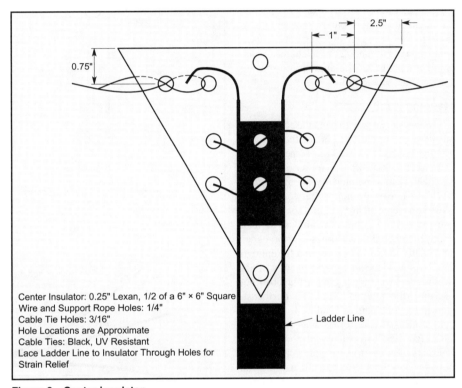

Figure 3—Center insulator.

of cable and wire.

The matching section itself was simple. I used the Antenna Analyzer to cut two quarter-wave pieces of RG-11 cable. Cut pieces of cable that are roughly 10 feet long. Leave one end open, attach the analyzer to the other end and trim the other end for minimum impedance. To make things modular, I used PL-259s on both ends of each piece. At the antenna end, they mate with the SO-239s on the junction; on the other end, I used a "T" connector to attach them to the main feed line. Once you have the matching section built, wind the cables into as tight a coil as possible to form a current balun.

The final step, prior to hoisting the antenna in the air, was to pre-cut 23 foot lengths of rope to use between the elements. I used masking tape to mark 21 foot lengths, which made it easy to set the appropriate spacing between the elements.

Hanging It All

Now you're ready to hang the contraption in the air. The hardest part of the job was finding the right trees. After some hunting, I found a pair of large maples on the edge of the forest, separated by about 25 feet, with no major branches between them. With some careful archery and some friends who are better with a bow and arrow than I am, I managed to get ropes over branches at roughly the 65 foot level and far enough apart to spread the antenna adequately. And I was lucky; I was able to choose branches that "swung" the antenna a bit to the northeast, giving me a 60 degree heading I wanted.

Raising the antenna was routine—although there was plenty of potential for snarls. When the upper dipole got to the 40 foot level, it was time to start hauling the junction into the air. I was fortunate to find a convenient branch to support the junction just when I needed it; this was one detail I had tried hard not to think about. To allow the ladder lines to reach the individual dipoles and to keep the ladder lines from tangling, the junction should be 30 to 40 feet above ground and at least 20 feet away from the antenna. To avoid disturbing the antenna's radiation pattern, the junction should also be centered on the antenna.

Disaster struck when the south side of the antenna got stuck at the 45 foot level. The rope was high enough, but was going under a branch that prevented me from raising it further. You probably know the routine. Drop the antenna, shoot another arrow, pull another rope through the tree and start again. This time, I got stuck with the top of the antenna somewhere between 55 and 60 feet above ground...and there was nothing to be done. The obstruction was a long branch that was passing over the antenna, right in the middle. The antenna isn't as high as I had hoped it would be and I'm sure that ground loss is

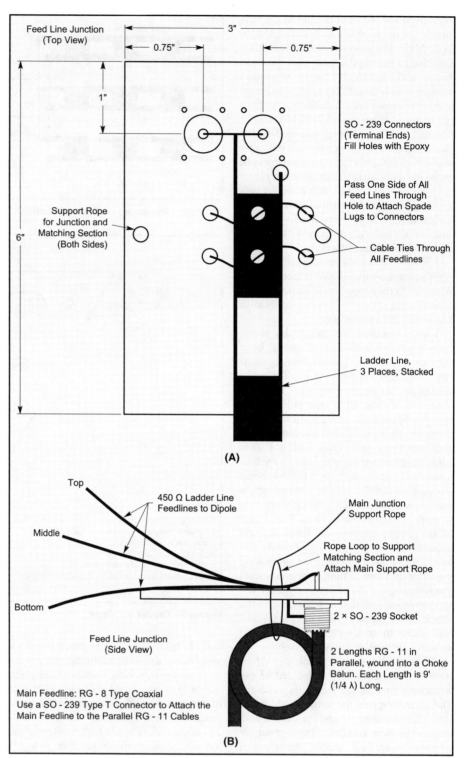

Figure 4A and 4B—Feed line junction, top view and side view.

higher than I'd like, but the bottom element is still 12 or 14 feet off the ground, and that seems to be enough.

A number of problems I had expected just never materialized. I was worried that the weight of the transmission lines would pull the centers down and forward, giving me a stack of Vs skewed at an odd angle. In retrospect, elevating the feed line junction was critical to the antenna's geometrical integrity...the rope suspending the junction bore the weight of the transmission lines, not the dipoles themselves. It proved easier than I expected getting the feed line junction into the air without tangling the individual transmission lines.

Does It Work?

This is the part of the article where I'm supposed to write about how I worked YA and P5 on the first call, etc. I'm not going to do that. (Well...just a little.) As exciting as those stories sound, we all know that you can work DX running QRP into a dummy load if the conditions are right. And 100 W running into an antenna with 11-13 dBi of gain is not 1500 W feeding stacked, wide-spaced, monobanders. Antennas radiate; they don't work miracles.

What's the best way to evaluate an antenna? Ultimately, I go by what I hear. If I can hear stations, there's a good chance they can hear me. On 15 meters, signal strengths are literally 6 S-units better than with my G5RV—although I've already implied that the G5RV wasn't the best performer on 15. I worked ZK2TO under very poor conditions, when I couldn't even hear her on my other antenna. And I've gotten a couple of compliments for being one of the loudest signals on the band...something I'd never heard before. Comparing the curtain to an admittedly bad antenna doesn't prove a whole lot, but I'm satisfied that I accomplished what I wanted, which is rough parity with other stations running low power and a Yagi.

I've been reasonably satisfied with the G5RV on 10 meters, so the improvement isn't as striking, but the curtain is usually better by 2 S-units or more. Sometimes the improvement is as much as 4 S-units, sometimes less. On 10 meters, the G5RV has a gain of about 9 dBi, in the right direction. That more or less agrees with my observations. I see the smallest improvements (an S-unit or so) into the South Pacific, where the G5RV has one of its lobes.

On 15 and 10 meters, the SWR is satisfyingly close to what *EZNEC* predicted. The antenna, as I've built it, is a little long—but, given what I've said previously, you shouldn't be surprised that I haven't bothered to tune it. I'd rather spend time operating than minimizing my SWR. The SWR "in the shack" is still below 2:1 across the entire 15 meter band, and below 3:1 between 28 and 29 MHz.

I can't resist pushing my luck and trying my antennas on other bands. The curtain performs decently on 20 meters. The elements and element spacings are really too small to provide a lot of gain, but they're still good for 9 dBi, according to *EZNEC*. *EZNEC* also predicts a resonance in the 20 meter band, where the SWR is high (5:1 to 10:1 and in agreement with what I observe) but not unusable if you have a tuner. I wouldn't make this my only 20 meter antenna but it's something else to try when you're in the middle of a pileup or a contest. Its low radiation angle is a definite asset and it's been very effective. (I can't resist saying that I worked JY on my second call.) On 17 meters the antenna accepts power about as willingly as a rock. On 12 meters, the SWR is also very high, but the antenna delivers about 12 dBi of gain, so it's well worth trying; the only real question is how much additional loss you incur in the feed system due to the high SWR. Since I hadn't planned on either 12 or 20 meters, I feel like I got two extra bands "for free."

Without a real antenna range, about the only way to evaluate an antenna is subjective. So maybe that's the real bottom line. Do I still feel at a disadvantage compared to stations running equivalent power and a triband beam? The answer is an unequivocal "No!" Whether I'm in a pileup or a contest, I'm now competitive—and with far less expense than a beam, a tower and a rotator.

The Antennas I Didn't Build (But Might Have)

This article wouldn't be complete without mentioning some of the antennas that "got away"—my hope is that these will give you some ideas. So here goes:

• If you can figure out how to get 1500 square feet of chicken wire into the air, about 0.3 wavelengths behind the driven elements, please let me know! A non-resonant reflecting screen roughly 20% larger than the antenna in each direction should give you an additional 2.5 dB gain, or so.

• If you scale the design frequency from 15 meters to 17 meters, the "secondary resonance" obligingly moves from 10 to 12 meters, making a very nice antenna for the 12, 17 and 30 meter bands. (Don't forget to scale the transmission lines and elements heights, too.)

• Scaling the 3-element dipole curtain to 20 meters yields an antenna that's probably too big, unless you have really large trees in the right place. However, a 2×2 curtain looks like it might be practical—and, with an appropriate phasing network, it is slewable about 25 degrees off the center axis.

• Finally, if you have an aluminum farm with multiple towers, the curtain looks like an ideal fixed antenna to me. With optimal spacing and at a greater height, the antenna looks like a real winner, producing gains up to 14 dBi—even without a reflector.

But those antennas are for the future. For now, I'm satisfied with an excellent wire antenna for 10 and 15 meter DXing and contesting—the curtain array.

Notes
[1] *The ARRL Antenna Book*, 19th edition, chapter 23. Available from your local dealer or from the ARRL Bookstore, order no. 8047; tel 888-277-5289; **www.arrl.org/shop**.
[2] M. W. Maxwell, *Reflections II*, Worldradio Books, 2001. Available from the ARRL Bookstore, order no. REF2; tel 888-277-5289; **www.arrl.org/shop**.
[3] One would think that the best performance would come when the currents are equal on all elements. I set up an *EZNEC* model with this property, however, and this wasn't the case; equal currents yielded slightly less gain than my final design.
[4] Davis Bury-Flex (available from many vendors; I bought mine from RadioWare), Wireman CQ-102 or CQ-106; **www.radio-ware.com**; **www.thewireman.com**.
[5] S. Ford, WB8IMY, "One Stealthy Delta," *QST*, May 2002, pp 47-48.
[6] McMaster-Carr Supply Company, **www.mcmaster.com**. The 6×6 inch sample squares I used are PN8574K11. Half inch Lexan is also available in 12×12 inch squares (PN 8742K117) and only slightly more expensive.
[7] **www.thewireman.com**; **www.radio-ware.com**.
[8] **www.radio-ware.com**.
[9] R.Olsen, N6NR, "The NRY: A Simple, Effective Wire Antenna for 80 through 10 Meters," pp 3-26 to 3-28. This article appeared, as well, in *QST*, Mar 1993, pp 22-24. In addition to the catenary support, the "NRY" is also interesting because it's another stacked wire antenna–two 20 meter extended double Zepps, which is (if you think about it) essentially a 2×2 curtain. *More Wire Antenna Classics* is available from your local dealer or from the ARRL Bookstore, order no. 7709; tel 888-277-5289; **www.arrl.org/shop**.

Mike Loukides, W1JQ, was first licensed in 1969, at age 13. After a lapse of 15 years with renewal not possible, he retook the amateur exams and became a new Extra class ham in 2001. His recent attention to Amateur Radio revolves around the HF bands with a particular interest in wire antennas. Mike says they are among the few things in Amateur Radio he can build with his near nonexistent metalworking skills. He's written a software contest-logging program in Java and says he'd like to experiment with the satellite digital modes. Mike has a BSEE from Cornell and a PhD in English Literature from Stanford, and is a senior editor for a major computer book publisher. He can be contacted at 30 Hungry Hill Circle, Guilford, CT 06437 or at **mikel@oreilly.com**.

By Marc C. Tarplee, N4UFP

Two Bands from One Dipole

A dual-band dipole design using no traps or coils.

My quest for a simple two-band dipole began when I decided to become active on the 17 and 12 meter bands. I wanted to operate on both bands, but did not have room for two separate dipoles. A single antenna design that would operate on both bands was required; it also had to be lightweight, simple to construct and reliable.

Adding a Second Band to a Dipole—The Techniques

There are several ways to modify a dipole for multi-band operation. The first is to tie two dipoles to a common feed. Plastic or wooden spreaders can be used to keep the two dipoles apart or separate sets of supports can be used for each antenna. Spreaders add weight, and unless the wires are fairly widely spaced ($\lambda/100$ or more), the antenna can be difficult to adjust.

It is possible to add a parasitic dipole for coverage of a second band. While only one dipole is directly fed, the closely coupled parasitic radiator makes tuning difficult. There are no simple design rules for this type of antenna, so a successful design is normally the result of considerable experimentation. [R. Dean Straw, N6BV, points us to "The Coupled-Resonator Principle: A Flexible Method for Multiband Antennas" by K9AY in *The ARRL Antenna Compendium, Vol 5*[1] for detailed design information on parasitic coupled-dipoles.—*Ed.*]

Many amateurs have used trapped dipoles for multi-band operation. Low-loss traps that can withstand the elements are not easy to construct and the traps greatly increase the weight of the antenna. Additionally, the traps, no matter how well designed, introduce some additional loss.

[1]Notes appear on page 83.

The Transmission Line as a Transformer

When a transmission line is terminated in any impedance other than its characteristic impedance, the impedance measured at the input of the line depends on its electrical length. The input impedance for a specific load impedance, line length, and frequency may be computed from the following equation:

$$Z_{in} = Z_0 \ [(Z_A \cos\Psi + j\ Z_0 \sin\Psi) / (Z_0 \cos\Psi + j\ Z_A \sin\Psi)] \quad [Eq\ 1]$$

where:

$$\Psi = 2\pi\ f\ x\ /\ 983.6\ f_v$$

and,

Z_0 = characteristic impedance of the transmission line (Ω)
Z_A = antenna load impedance (Ω)
Z_{in} = input impedance (Ω)

Table 1
Two Band Dipoles Using 450 Ω Ladder Line and 14 Gauge Copper Wire

Bands (Meters)	Dipole Length (Feet/Inches) (L)	Ladder Line Length (Feet/Inches) (T)	Lower Resonant Frequency (MHz)	Lower Frequency Input Z	Higher Resonant Frequency (MHz)	Higher Frequency Input Z
75/40	144/10	89/6	3.87	89 Ω	7.25	32 Ω
30/17	54/9	36/2	10.12	88 Ω	18.12	39 Ω
20/17	77/8	76/2	14.13	33 Ω	18.11	83 Ω
20/15	51/0	50/8	14.17	53 Ω	21.27	41 Ω
20/12	68/0	46/8	14.15	33 Ω	24.92	82 Ω
17/12	28/7	46/8	18.11	77 Ω	24.95	75 Ω
17/10	33/4	62/6	18.08	88 Ω	28.42	87 Ω
15/10	102/0	70/6	21.25	48 Ω	28.32	64 Ω
10/6	16/6	33/5	28.40	69 Ω	50.10	64 Ω

Table 2
Two Band Dipoles Using 300 Ω Ladder Line and 14 Gauge Copper Wire

Bands (Meters)	Dipole Length (Feet/Inches) (L)	Ladder Line Length (Feet/Inches) (T)	Lower Resonant Frequency (MHz)	Lower Frequency Input Z	Higher Resonant Frequency (MHz)	Higher Frequency Input Z
40/20	96/9	101/0	7.02	30 Ω	14.23	48 Ω
20/10	48/3	50/6	14.08	34 Ω	28.40	50 Ω
15/10	23/0	41/0	21.20	68 Ω	28.40	46 Ω

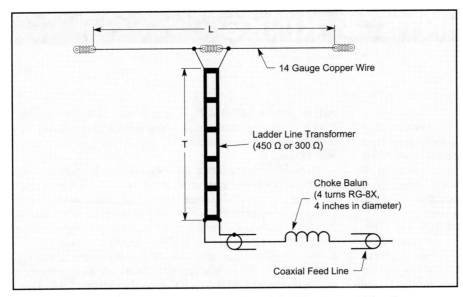

Figure 1—The antenna consists of a dipole of length L with a transmission line transformer of length T. The antenna is fed with coaxial cable through a choke balun.

x = line length (feet)
f = frequency (MHz)
f_v = velocity factor of the line

A transmission line can be used as a matching network that transforms an antenna's impedance to a more desirable value. In principle, it should be possible to find a length for the antenna and matching section that results in an input impedance near 50 Ω on two frequencies by using Equation 1. In practice, this can be difficult; Z_A, the antenna impedance, cannot be computed from a simple formula and is usually found by simulation. An optimization program using impedance data from simulation software must be used to determine the proper lengths for the dipole legs and the matching section.

Actual Designs

Table 1 shows dimensions for several two-band dipoles. *EZNEC 3.0*,[2] in combination with *MathCAD 2000*[3] was used to develop the designs. All designs using 450 Ω ladder line were tested, except for the one for 75/40 meters. The designs are based on a velocity factor of 0.90 for the transmission line used as an impedance transformer.

The antennas were fed with 50 feet of RG-8X-type coax. A choke balun was formed at the connection to the ladder line by winding a coil of 4 turns of RG-8X that was approximately 4 inches in diameter. When the antennas were pruned to resonance, the measured input impedance was within 10% of the theoretical value. [Where the input Z for both bands is closer to 75 Ω, rather than 50 Ω, the use of 75 Ω coax (RG-6) as a transmission line would be advised, such as in the 17/12, the 17/10 and the 10/6 meter antennas. The choke balun should be made from the same cable.—*Ed.*]

It is not possible to design two band antennas for all band combinations using 450 Ω ladder line as the matching network. Additionally, some 450 Ω designs result in inconveniently long matching sections.

Table 2 shows some designs based on 300 Ω parallel line:

These antennas are very simple to construct and erect, but there are some points that should be kept in mind:

1. These antennas are usually somewhat longer than other two-band designs using multiple wires or traps.
2. The bandwidth of these antennas is lower than a half wave dipole cut for the same frequency.
3. The radiation patterns on the two bands may be very different.

Summary

Figure 1 shows the basic antenna layout, which consists of the dipole, the transmission line transformer, the choke balun and the coaxial feed line. This two-band dipole is lightweight, easy to build and tune, and requires no special components such as traps or spreaders. They are ideal Field Day antennas for 12, 17 and 30 meter operation. Other band combinations besides those presented in the tables are possible. The combinations chosen result in dimensions of the antenna and matching section that are feasible for many amateurs.

Notes

[1]Available from your local dealer or the ARRL Bookstore. Order no. 5625. Telephone toll-free in the US 888-277-5289 or 860-594-0355, fax 860-594-0303; **www.arrl.org/shop/**; **pub-sales@arrl.org**.
[2]**www.eznec.com**.
[3]**www.mathcad.com**.

Marc Tarplee, N4UFP, has a PhD degree in electrical engineering from the University of South Carolina. His research interests include semiconductor device modeling and computational electromagnetics. Marc is presently the Dean of the Engineering Technologies Division of York Technical College, Rock Hill, South Carolina. He has been a licensed ham for 15 years and is ARRL Technical Coordinator for the SC Section. He can be contacted at 4406 Deer Run, Rock Hill, SC or at **mtarplee@yorktech.com**.

HINTS & KINKS

BUILD A PARALLEL-WIRE DIPOLE

◇ Figure 1 shows a multiband dipole antenna I've been building for some folks around here. Table 1 shows measured values from one I built for Brian, K4BKG, who lives in Sampson County, North Carolina. I put the dipole up between a few pine trees at about 40 feet above ground level. It is mounted in a flat-top configuration with the center supported via an eye-ring on the center insulator. It could be built in an inverted-V configuration also.

The center insulator (no balun) that I use is from The Wireman (#800 at **www.thewireman.com**), but there are many others available elsewhere. [If you're concerned about antenna-pattern uniformity, use a balun at the feed point.—*Ed.*] You can also get the bare #14 AWG hard-drawn copper wire, end insulators and pulleys from there. My contributions to the original concept are the weed-trimmer line, spreaders and wire sizes. The trimmer line is stiffer and neater than string or twine. The spreaders are made from small-diameter PEX or PVC tubing secured by filling them with hot glue. The wire passes through them via holes positioned to stabilize the antenna. The bare stranded 80 meter wire serves as a messenger cable to support shorter wires via the spreaders. The other wires are #16 AWG insulated wire I purchased at the local hardware store.

When you purchase the wire, check the diameters of both sizes before you buy the drill bits. Keep the hole size as close as possible to the outer diameter of the wire; you'll see why later. The bottom wire holes are spaced a bit from the top wire (see Figure 2) to lower the center of gravity. This helps keep the antenna from twisting on itself! After drilling and cleaning the holes, I used a .22-caliber gun-cleaning rod and bore-brush to remove the plastic burrs from the center of the tubing. Next, cut two wires for each band, but be sure to allow a little extra length. You'll need it for terminations at the center and pruning at the end insulators.

I've found it best to cut the wires and thread them through the spreaders first. Lay your wires out as shown in Figure 1, 80 meters on top and the higher frequency wires downward in succession. Thread the first spreader on, making sure you are using the *top* hole and the bare wire for 80 meters. Once you have all the wires started through all the spreaders on that side, grab each wire and pull about 2 feet through the spreaders from that end. You may want to do this work a few spreaders at a time, depending on how well the holes are aligned. Now, strip about 4 inches of insulation from each of the bottom wires. If you are not already using wire thimbles on your wire antennas, I suggest their use. They reduce wire fatigue.

Place the thimble through one of the eyes on the center insulator. Tin about 6 inches of the bare 80 meter wire using a high-wattage soldering gun or a small gas torch and some rosin-core solder, then let it cool. Wrap the tinned wire around the thimble and leave about 3 inches extra from the thimble junction before you begin the wrap (see Figure 3). Compress the thimble ends as much as possible, but *do not* use pliers! Pliers may nick the thimble edges. Start a tight wrap, one turn right next to the other! When finished, apply more heat and solder to the junction if needed to fill any voids. Don't use too much heat, as you don't want to soften the wire! Make sure to check for voids and fill where the wires come together at the thimble ends; this will improve the strength.

Next, place all the wires flat as they would hang from the top: 80-40-20-10. *Make sure the thimble and center insulator are oriented properly before you start!* The PL-259 should be at the bottom, just as it would hang when in use. Hold the bottom wires by the insulation, keeping them flat, perpendicular and underneath the end of the 80 meter wrap. The 40 meter wire should be the first and outermost wire, next to the beginning of the 80 meter wrap. Do a flat spiral wrap from each wire around the double wire leading back to the thimble. Keep the wires as flat as possible, and wrap towards the thimble. Snip any extra and solder. Do the same for the other side. Now, attach and solder the pigtails from the center insulator to each side.

It's just about time for testing, but before you do, ensure that the lengths of both antenna sides are equal. I did this by folding the antenna over onto itself, but measuring would be simpler and should be sufficiently accurate. Check each set of wires according their band, and be careful not to cut the wrong wire.

Now, grab a couple of end insulators and install them on the 80 meter wires. Pull $1\frac{1}{2}$ feet of wire through the end insulator and loosely wind it back onto itself; then do the same on the other side. Connect the feed line, and your antenna is ready for tests. If you use coax, make a shield choke near the transmitter by wrapping six loops of the coax at about 8 inches in diameter and taping them together. [Eight inches is good for small-diameter coax, but always conform to the minimum bending radius specification for the cable

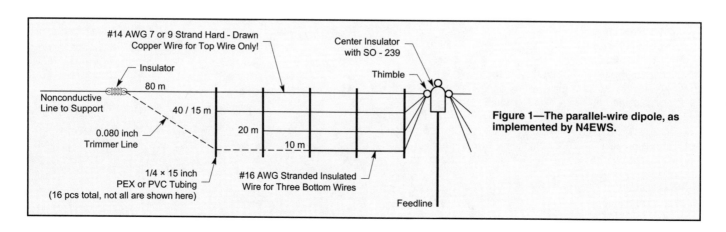

Figure 1—The parallel-wire dipole, as implemented by N4EWS.

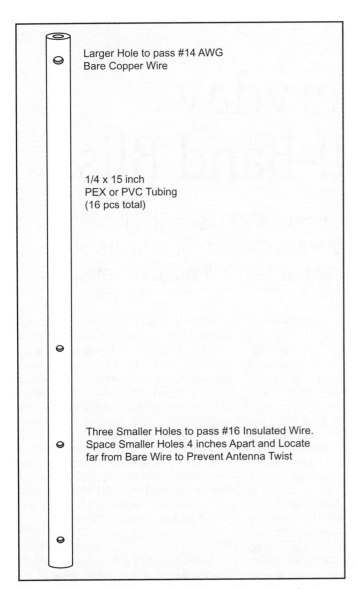

Figure 2—Spreader holes are drilled to space shorter wires well below the 80 meter wire. This places the center of gravity well below the point of support and prevents the antenna from twisting.

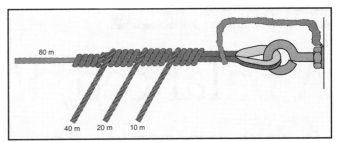

Figure 3—Details of the wire connections and thimble at the center insulator. The 80 meter wire is wrapped about 3 inches from the center insulator, and the shorter wires are wrapped around the double wire in that 3 inch space.

Table 1
Parallel Dipole Data

Band (m)	Leg Length	f_0 (MHz)	SWR@MHz (Phone Subband)	
80	60' 8"	3.880	1.1@3.850	1.3@3.980
40	33' 6"	7.225	1.4@7.230	1.9@7.300
20	17' 0"	14.260	1.2@14.200	1.1@14.345
15	(See 40 m)		1.7@21.300	1.8@21.450
10	8' 7"	29.000	1.1@28.200	1.5@29.000

you're using.—*Ed*.] This ensures that your SWR measurements won't be disturbed by stray shield current.

Hoist the dipole into operating position and give it a test. Remember, the antenna height and configuration affects the impedance. When testing, measure the SWR on all the bands and record the results after every test. You need to see how much the wires interact before final pruning for resonance. When you start cutting, keep a close eye on 10 meters. I have found that it can really interact with the other bands. [I have not experienced this with the wires spaced apart by 4 inches or more and when pruning in order from shortest wire to longest.—*Ed*.] Leave an extra $1^1/_2$ inch on the outer ends of the insulated wires. This is for securing the wire end at the spreader. To do this, strip the insulation from that $1^1/_2$ inch of wire previously mentioned, twist the stripped wire into a small ball and then apply some solder. You don't need to cut the 80 meter wire yet; just unwrap, move the insulator in or out and rewrap until the adjustments are complete.

When adjustments are complete, it's time to run the string trimmer line and glue everything down. Lower the antenna and position the spreaders evenly. Fire-up the 80 W hot-glue gun while you're feeding the string-trimmer line through the holes in the spreaders.

Allow some extra line for tying to the end insulators. When you get to the end of the 10 meter insulator, you can either make a loop around it and/or drill another hole to terminate it there. You can drill it about an inch above the 10 meter hole, pass the line through it, make a knot and glue it. It's kind of like bobbing the ends of the wires, but you use hot glue instead of solder.

Now grab your heavy-duty glue gun and get to work on the spreaders. Make sure the glue gun has a full reservoir, a fresh stick in the feed handle and there's a good supply on hand! You'll need a lot of glue to fill the centers of the spreaders. Wear work gloves to do this next part, and be very careful; it can get hot. Start with the first spreader near the center on either side. Hold the spreader from the top, horizontally with your covered hand between the 80 and 40 meter wire or lay the spreader on a table. Tilt it upward slightly, so that the 10 meter wire end is slightly elevated. Be careful not to let the wires slip from side to side, as this will cause one or more wires to be slack. Insert the glue-gun nozzle firmly into the top of the spreader. Squeeze the trigger, filling the entire length of the tubing. Don't stop until you see glue coming out the other end and don't move it until the glue cools and starts to solidify!

Some of the glue will be squeezed out the holes, where the wires and string trimmer line are passing through the insulator. This is okay. In fact, it's the reason why I used bare stranded wire for the 80 meter span! The glue forced into the wire strands will help it stay in place.—*Joe Deaton, N4EWS, 107 Nature Trail, Louisburg, NC 27549;* **n4ews@mindspring.com**

Hints and Kinks items have not been tested by *QST* or the ARRL unless otherwise stated. Although we can't guarantee that a given hint will work for your situation, we make every effort to screen out harmful information. Send technical questions directly to the hint's author.

QST invites you to share your hints with fellow hams. Send them to "Attn: Hints and Kinks" at ARRL Headquarters, 225 Main St, Newington, CT 06111, or via e-mail to **h&k@arrl.org**. Please include your name, call sign, complete mailing address, daytime telephone number and e-mail address on all correspondence. Whether praising or criticizing an item, please send the author(s) a copy of your comments.

By Kirk A. Kleinschmidt, NTØZ

A Balanced, Everyday Approach to All-Band Bliss

Feed lines, antenna tuners, baluns, RFI, computer noise and all-band antennas—now there's a snake pit of potential conflict. After years of experimentation, the author has found the path to multiband nirvana.

For most of us, the Holy Grail of ham radio is antenna performance. It's often the key element in determining ham radio success and operating enjoyment. You can get by with a second-rate transceiver, a deep gravelly voice and even a severe lack of good looks and charm, but if you have an underperforming antenna, ham radio isn't nearly the fun it could be.

You've undoubtedly looked with longing, as I have, at magazine pictures that show fabulous contest "superstation" antenna farms, the few fortunate hams who have 350-foot towers festooned with big Yagis (or a smattering of 200-footers), the Northern California ham who has a dozen full-size rhombics strung between the tops of giant Sequoias, and so on.

After imagining an antenna system that qualifies as a navigation hazard, most of us will scale things down to the real matter at hand—how to put up an affordable, easy-to-build multiband antenna that works great and fits on an average-size lot. We're back to the search for the Holy Grail.

Horizontal Loop Antennas

What, you were expecting dipoles?

Although dipole antennas in all of their various shapes and configurations perform well, in my experience the *best* all-around multiband antenna is the horizontal loop. It's efficient, omnidirectional over most "real ground," it's quiet, it operates well on *all* HF frequencies above its design frequency (and even those below, as we'll see later), it fits on most lots and, contrary to tradition and many official-looking radiation pattern plots that can be found in various antenna manuals—can be an *outstanding* antenna for domestic *and* DX contacts alike.

As a kid I made my share of vertical loops/quads from bamboo poles and copper wire, but I didn't think about horizontal loops until I read Dave Fischer, W7FB's life-changing article, "The Loop Skywire," in the November 1985 issue of *QST* (back when Dave signed WØMHS). Shown in Figure 1, the loop is simply a full-wavelength of wire cut for the lowest band of interest. Feed it with coax or ladder line (feed lines are discussed in detail later).

I had previously used quad loops and dipoles (G5RV-type and conventional). Sure, they *worked*—and they still do—but I had always thought something was lacking, and I had a secret hunch about the Loop Skywire.

Now, Fischer's First Rule of horizontal loop construction is to enclose as much area as possible within the confines of the loop. A circular loop is ideal, but a square loop is much more practical and doesn't suffer performance-wise. My lot could only accommodate a triangular "loop," which is pretty much the geometric limit of what you can get away with. If you make the loop any more elongated or constricted, it loses its "loop-like" qualities.

Although my most recent loop could have been cut for 40 meters, my property and available skyhooks could contain a larger antenna (which should work better, especially on the low bands). It wasn't the 272 feet required for an 80-meter loop, but something in between. That's how I discovered another rule of thumb for building modern-day horizontal loops: Put up the largest possible horizontal loop your situation allows and forget about pruning it to resonance. The antenna tuner, which you'll need anyway for multiband operation, will take care of things.

Strung about 45 feet above the ground, I knew from past experience that my loop would be an excellent performer. Fed with 50 feet of RG-8 and my trusty old antenna tuner, the loop worked very well on 40 meters and up. As before, however, 80 and 160 were adequate, but just barely.

RFI was a big headache on the higher bands. In fact, 15 meters was almost impossible. Even at 5 W power levels, every key-down zapped the TV screen and all of the stereo and computer audio circuits in my office/shack. I had converted the garage to an office, and my shack is on the west wall. Just outside the wall is the base of my tower, which supports the feed point of the horizontal loop. Although the antenna itself is at least 50 feet from all of the PCs and consumer electronics, the feed line was in close proximity. The crud generated by three or four computers was also a headache and wiped out large chunks of the bands.

RFI

Despite the RFI and computer noise, I was pleased with the performance of the big loop.

I tried all of the standard RFI-fighting techniques. I made sure I had a good, short, low-impedance connection to an earth ground at my operating position. I installed ferrite cores and clamp-on chokes on seemingly endless numbers of audio and video cables. I installed ac line filters and connected some sensitive gear to the ac mains via an uninterruptible power supply, complete with RFI filtering, surge suppression and line conditioning.

I picked up a copy of *The ARRL RFI Book*, which is handy to have even if you're not besieged. I read up on common-mode interference, front-end overload, nonlinear rectification and even interference that's re-radiated by other affected components.

I disconnected dozens of speaker wires, audio and video leads, and coaxial TV cables. Is the RFI getting in through *this* wire or is it through *that* one? It was test, test, test—back and forth.

In the end, all of that poking and prodding made the RFI situation quite a bit better on all of the bands except 15 meters, which was still unusable.

Still, life was pretty good on 40, 30, 20 and 10 meters, and I was working lots of juicy DX and enjoying solid stateside ragchews.

Climbing the Ladder Line of Success

At this point I was feeding my loop through a standard antenna tuner and a 50-foot length of coax. I knew about open-wire line, TV twinlead and ladder line, but I'd never used the stuff to feed an antenna. Then I got wind of Steve Ford, WB8IMY's, excellent and eye-opening introduction to multiband antennas fed with 450-Ω ladder line. The article is "The Lure of the Ladder Line," from the December 1993 issue of *QST*. It's also available to ARRL members in PDF format from *ARRLWeb* (**www.arrl.org/**).

Steve tells us how he dramatically improved the performance of his multiband dipole, formerly fed with coax and a tuner, by replacing the feed line with 450-Ω ladder line (see Figure 2). There it was in black and white: A key piece of antenna system wisdom that I'd been lacking for years.

In that article I discovered that the loss figures commonly attributed to coaxial cables of various sizes and compositions *are only accurate under low-SWR conditions*. As shown in Table 1, when the SWR on the coaxial feed line between your antenna tuner and your antenna's feed point is high—as it usually is when feeding antennas on frequencies at which they're not resonant—the signal losses in the coax can be staggering.

No wonder my antenna worked great at the design frequency and on all higher HF bands, but fell off on 80 and 160 meters. On those bands, even a 40-meter full-wave loop is physically small *and* the high SWR on the line between the tuner and the antenna wasted most of the power.

But look at the loss figures for the ladder line. They are a lot better, especially on the lower bands.

Baluns and Conventional Antenna Tuners

Unfortunately, using open-wire feed lines isn't always as easy as simply swapping one cable type for another. Coaxial cables are unbalanced (which can make them vulnerable to common-mode RFI), and conventional antenna tuners are designed to handle them, so when they're matching coaxial cable loads, everything works out fine as long as the impedance at the tuner end of the feed line isn't too extreme.

Ladder-line and open-wire line are intended for balanced operation where equivalent currents flow through each of the two wires that make up the feed line. To accommodate balanced feed lines, conventional tuners almost always use a balun transformer at the tuner output to make the transition from balanced line to an unbalanced tuner network.

In a perfect world, this works pretty well and users can conveniently feed unbalanced and balanced loads without needing separate tuners. The problems arise when we consider how difficult it is to make a single balun that works well over a wide range of frequencies and power levels. In short, it's easy to build a tuner-output balun that works well on a single band or on a few adjacent bands, but when it comes to a single dc-to-daylight tuner-output balun, things often don't work so well.

Also, because of where the balun resides in the tuner/antenna circuit, output-style baluns are often subject to extreme RF voltages, which can cause arcing, sparking, burning and other undesirable behavior. Output-style baluns also tend to have a tough time staying electrically balanced over a wide frequency range.

All of these factors combine to decrease the tuner's efficiency and increase power losses in the tuner and balun that are *in addition* to the losses of the feed line. Of course, all antenna tuners have some loss, and that loss tends to vary by frequency and load impedance. Matching extreme impedances usually means more loss.

Steve experienced this when feeding his 40-meter dipole with ladder line on 80 and 160 meters (extreme impedances for a 40-meter dipole). At anything more than just a few watts, his tuner would arc, snap, sizzle and pop. To operate on those bands

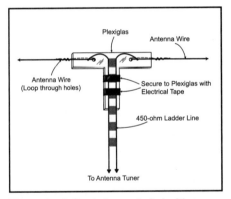

Figure 2—A dipole formerly fed with coax now has a ladder line feed.

Table 1

Loss Comparisons for Belden 8214 Coaxial Cable and 450-Ohm Ladder Line

Cable length: 50 feet.
Antenna: 66-foot dipole at 30 feet.
Calculated by Dean Straw, N6BV, Senior Assistant Technical Editor.

Freq (MHz)	Loss (dB) 8214	Ladder Line
1.9	26.9	8.82
3.8	13.7	1.37
7.15	0.19	0.07
10.14	2.85	0.07
14.27	5.30	0.15
18.14	6.96	0.31
21.40	0.78	0.12
24.90	3.94	0.13
28.50	5.69	0.18

Figure 1—Put up the largest horizontal loop your lot can support while keeping the "loop" as square as possible. Don't worry about perfect symmetry. For size reference, values are shown for 80 and 40 meters. See the text for additional information.

he could run QRP or switch to an expensive megapower tuner.

After a quick trip to the Twin Cities to fetch some ladder line, I dropped the feed point, made the switch to ladder line and hooked everything up to my time-tested—conventional—antenna tuner, making sure I connected the jumper wire that brought the output balun into the circuit.

With high hopes, I keyed the rig and, as usual, the impressive audio thumps and TV screen blackouts began. I still felt the lure of the ladder line, and I was now making easy contacts on 80 and 160 meters—electrically goofy feed line and all. I was gaining ground, but because of the RFI, etc, operating wasn't convenient.

Autocoupler to the Rescue

The next remedy I tried didn't cure all ills, but it became a piece of "can't do without" gear. In preparation for portable operation at the lake, I acquired an SGC SG-231 autocoupler, a computerized, automatic supertuner that can match practically any load from 160 through 6 meters in the blink of an eye.

The SG-231 has no controls and is designed to be mounted outdoors, even in harsh environments. You supply the dc power to operate the innards and some RF from your rig and the '231 does the rest. Simply key the mike on whatever frequency and the autocoupler matches the load in a jiffy, remembering the tuning solution so when you return to a nearby frequency, the tuner matches the load in about a quarter of a second—fast.

This amazing piece of hardware, called an autocoupler by the manufacturer, is designed to be *mounted at the feed point of the antenna*. When mounted in that fashion, the SG-231 matches the antenna to the 50-Ω impedance of the coax that runs from your rig to the tuner/feed point. Because the SWR on the cable between the tuner and the radio is low (matched), SWR losses are minimal and essentially of no concern.

The big problem for me was, I couldn't use the autocoupler at the lake if it was hanging 50 feet up in the air, precariously attached to my loop. And, even though it's designed for such service, I couldn't get myself to mount the coupler outside, exposed to the elements and those nasty Minnesota winters.

So, I snooped around on the Internet and saw that some ops were using their SGC tuners to feed balanced lines in a conventional sense (tuner in the shack, feeding a multiband antenna via 450-Ω ladder line).

I quickly connected the SG-231 to my rig and to my ladder line, fired it up and watched the magic happen with my own eyes. The autocoupler easily matched everything from 160 through 6 meters with the exception of a small chunk of 80 meters where the impedance at the shack end of the ladder line was

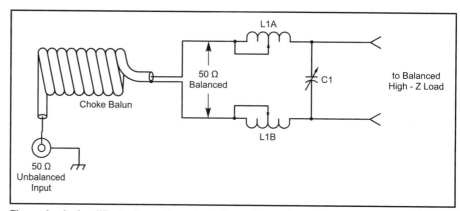

Figure 3—A simplified schematic of the balanced tuner as originally presented by Rich Measures, AG6K. The home-brew coaxial balun is on the input side of the network, which consists of two roller inductors that are adjusted in sync and a single variable capacitor. The capacitor, usually on the output side of the coils, can be moved to the input side to match some lower-impedance loads. Some builders use fixed, tapped inductors to save money. See the text and the References sidebar for more information.

probably weird.

I enjoyed using this arrangement for several years. It matched my loop, which is probably resonant at 5 MHz or so, in a snap, and RFI on 80 and 160 meters was pretty much eliminated. The 231 added tremendous convenience to the loop's superb performance.

The Final Balancing Act

Clearly, the horizontal loop, the ladder line and the autocoupler were working famously. I probably would have put up with the RFI/noise problems for a good long while if I hadn't run across a discussion during one of my late-night jaunts on 75 meters.

The guys in this roundtable were talking about how they'd built *balanced antenna tuners to feed their big horizontal loops with ladder line*. I knew I'd feel right at home chatting with these guys. They were spread out from the Carolinas to Arizona, and they were booming in on their own horizontal loop antennas. The guy from Carolina was running a kW and he sounded like a shortwave broadcast station.

The gist of our conversation centered around building a simplified version of the balanced antenna tuner detailed in, "A *Bal*anced Balanced Antenna Tuner," by Rich Measures, AG6K, in the February 1990 issue of *QST* (available to ARRL members in PDF format from *ARRLWeb*.

The tuner uses a balanced L network instead of the conventional pi network employed by almost every commercial antenna tuner in service today (see Figure 3). The balanced L network can directly feed 450-Ω balanced lines while maintaining a high degree of electrical balance on each leg of the ladder line. It's this balance, I learned, that's critical in keeping the ladder line from radiating RF.

And instead of being at the tuner output, the balun is placed at the tuner's input, where baluns really do work over wide frequency ranges and where RF voltages and RF losses are minimal.

So what's the catch? Well, although the balanced L network could hardly be simpler, Rich's version requires two matched roller inductors, which are difficult to find and somewhat expensive, and a turns-counting dial.

Still, it was clear from reading Rich's article that using a balanced tuner with the balun on the input was the *proper* way of doing things for antennas fed with ladder line. So, I decided to build one and see for myself.

Thankfully, I had two brand-new roller inductors on hand. I'd purchased them from MFJ several years ago when I was planning to build a pair of conventional antenna tuners. I also had a turns-counting dial I'd purchased almost 20 years earlier. The capacitor was a junkbox transmitting unit. The only parts I had to purchase were the sprockets (¼-inch shaft size) and the toothed belt required to turn each roller inductor in sync. These cost only a few dollars from McMaster-Carr (www.mcmaster.com).

Building this tuner seemed like carpentry, with a little radio thrown in for good Measures (pun intended). The tuner is built on a piece of plywood with a wooden (or other non-conducting) front panel because the capacitor and inductor shafts are hot with RF. Building on metal would have required stand-off insulators and a lot of tedious wrangling. With wood it's a no brainer.

The only accommodation I made in my prototype is the use of banana posts and jacks to let me occasionally switch the capacitor from the output side of the coils to the input side to match balanced loads that are less than 50 Ω (most are greater than 50 Ω).

The thing went together in a couple of hours, and once I synchronized the roller inductors I replaced the autocoupler with the balanced tuner. Figure 4 shows the completed tuner in all its glory.

Ahhh. The tuning was smoooooth, with no sharp, hard-to-find dips. It was also convenient because it had only two controls instead of the usual three. I methodically tuned up and down the bands with a 5-W signal and was pleased to notice that every spot on every band tuned up without a hassle, except for part of 75 meters—the same part that the SGC autocoupler didn't like.

The other thing I almost forgot to notice was that—as if by divine decree—there was no more RFI. Anywhere. On any band. At any power output from 5 to 100 W. Not even the faintest of audio thumps could be heard in any of the many electronic goodies just three feet away from the tuner and the stub of ladder line that pokes through the wall.

But there's more. The computer noise was reduced by a good 80%. Now I could operate anywhere. The noise pickup problem that I'd made incremental progress on over the past few years was now virtually eliminated, and what remained was barely noticeable. I rushed to get on the air.

Because I was familiar with how well the horizontal loop works as a DX antenna, I wanted to really push the new setup to the edge. I tuned up on 30 meters with about 1.5 W showing on the QRP wattmeter. As I tuned to the low edge of the band I heard a nasty pileup. Underneath it all (and a few kHz down the band) was 5U1A—a DXpedition to Niger, as I learned later. After re-remembering how to operate split, I jumped into the fray. It took me about 15 minutes to work through the pileup, but at that relatively low power level I was more than pleased (as I was the next night when I worked V51AS in Namibia on the same band).

After using the prototype tuner for a while I discovered a couple of minor things I need to iron out. The first is the funky part of 80 meters, which I hope to fix by lengthening the feed line. The second involves the wide tuning range I'm asking the L-network to accommodate.

Using the first capacitor I tried (a 15 to 300 pF unit) I can easily tune the bands from 160 through 20 meters, but there's apparently too much stray capacitance to match things on the higher bands. When I substitute a smaller capacitor I can tune 40 through 10, but not 80 and 160.

I think my eventual solution is to use the smaller capacitor and switch a fixed-value capacitor in parallel as needed, or to use the larger unit and switch a fixed C in series. My short-term solution, however, is to mount two tuning caps on the front panel and use their respective banana plugs to switch them in and out as necessary. Oh, the joys of breadboard construction.

Figure 4—The parts layout of the author's balanced tuner. At the right is an easy-to-build, 160-10 meter coax balun. At the center is a pair of roller inductors and the front-panel tuning capacitor. The larger banana jacks allow the tuning capacitor to be switched from the input to the output side of the coils. The smaller banana jacks are for connecting the feed line. The smaller variable capacitor was added to facilitate testing. See the text and References sidebar for more information).

The Path to Your Bliss

So, what have I/we learned so far?

(1) Horizontal loops are fabulous—if not the best—all-band non-resonant antennas. They noticeably outperform dipoles when used at frequencies above resonance and they're easier to match there as well (impedance wise). They're efficient, quiet and forgiving.

(2) As long as in-shack RFI and computer noise aren't part of your equation you can happily feed the loop with coax via a standard antenna tuner for use on the band of resonance and all HF bands above the fundamental frequency.

(3) If you want to operate your loop on bands below its fundamental frequency, you'll probably want to replace the coax with ladder line to minimize SWR losses in the feed line.

(4) In doing so you may discover firsthand that most conventional tuners don't work very well when feeding balanced lines, and that most tuner-output baluns don't keep things balanced over a wide range of frequencies.

If it isn't obvious by now, I'd like to offer my heartfelt thanks to Dave Fischer, W7FB; Steve Ford, WB8IMY; Rich Measures, AG6K; and the loopy guys on 75 meters.

You can reach the author at 16928 Grove St, Little Falls, MN 56345; **kirk@cloudnet.com**.

By Hal Kennedy, N4GG

The N4GG Array

Need a simple, nearly invisible wire antenna with reasonable gain, low-angle radiation (for DXing) and multiband capabilities? Check out this long-overlooked design that requires no antenna tuner.

Having been relegated to a "no antennas," deed-restricted neighborhood five years ago, I started a search that's unfortunately becoming more and more familiar to hams everywhere. It's the search for a stealthy multiband antenna that has decent DXing performance. Wire antennas seem right for invisibility, but on-air testing of dipoles mounted close to the ground confirmed what seasoned hams and antenna modeling packages will tell you: A dipole mounted less than $1/4$-wavelength above ground is essentially radiating straight up! The earth makes an effective, if lossy, reflector, and the emitted RF does a great job of warming the clouds. Low dipoles and inverted Vs are fine for local contacts, but are relatively poor performers for long-haul DX.

Searching through various antenna handbooks led me to consider verticals and a variety of vertical arrays, but the radial field usually required for efficient operation can't be practically implemented in my suburban setting. And even under the best of circumstances it's a major project. Ever try putting 60 radials for 80 meters on top of, or under, a grass lawn without your neighbors asking you what you're doing? Even the placement of ground-mounted verticals at my location was problematic. The vertical(s) would have to be inside a dense stand of trees or very near the house. Traditional verticals were out.

Self-contained verticals looked promising. These include delta loops and quad loops, among others. They yield low-angle radiation and do not require radials. They're also large and hard to operate on multiple bands without an antenna tuner. Closed loops cut for different bands often can't be fed in parallel. Most multiband approaches include some combination of relay switching, multiple feed lines, matching networks and antenna tuners. Did I forget to mention that in addition to gain, low-angle radiation and stealth, I wanted this antenna to be simple? Also, because I don't own a high-power antenna tuner, I wanted a reasonable SWR at the operating frequencies of interest.

Among the self-contained verticals is the *half square*, which looked like a nearly ideal approach except, again, for the difficulty in erecting a version that works on multiple bands without a tuner. The bobtail curtain also had possibilities, but it's usually shown fed at ground level against radials and is not inherently multiband in nature. It was time to fire up *EZNEC* and see if some new variation of a self-contained vertical could be devised. A few hours later the N4GG Array debuted—at least on paper!

Design Details

Technically, an N4GG Array consists of two top-fed, $1/4$-wavelength verticals spaced 1 wavelength apart, fed 180 degrees out of phase. Think of the array as a bobtail curtain with its center wire replaced by the feed line. Bobtails aren't particularly well-known, so if the bobtail analogy is hard to grasp, think of the N4GG Array as a $3/2$-wavelength horizontal dipole with the last $1/4$ wavelength of wire on each dipole leg bent at 90 degrees (hanging vertically). Figure 1 shows a bobtail antenna (A) and the single-band version of the N4GG Array (B).

Not too familiar with a $3/2$-wavelength dipole? If you've ever used a 40-meter dipole on 15 meters, you were using a $3/2$-wavelength dipole. Figure 1B shows the current distribution along the wires. Note that maximum current (and therefore maximum RF radiation) is at the *top* of the antenna. The antenna is center-fed with coax and should include a 1:1 current-type balun.

The elevation radiation patterns for an N4GG Array and a dipole at the same height are shown in Figure 2. The outer circle in the figure is +5.96 dBi. The gains of the antennas are equal at a 23.5-degree take-off angle, but

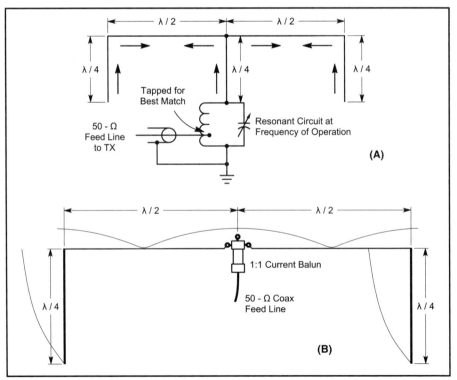

Figure 1—A bobtail curtain (A) compared to the N4GG Array (B). The diagram of the N4GG Array shows current distribution. The antenna is essentially a $3/2$-wavelength dipole with the outer $1/4$-wavelength part of each dipole leg hanging vertically.

the gain of the N4GG Array is approximately 3.4 dBi higher than that of the dipole at elevation angles of between 10 and 15 degrees, and a whopping 11 dBi higher at 5 degrees.

For DXers, the Array's dismal performance at high take-off angles is just as important as its excellent low-angle performance. For DXers, high-angle reception is simply a source of interference and additional atmospheric noise. Straight up, the gain of the N4GG Array is more than 20 dB below that of the dipole. All of the data presented in this article was obtained using *EZNEC* 3.0, with the ground model set to "average, pastoral heavy clay." The elevation plots shown in Figure 2 are for the azimuth angle yielding maximum gain, which is 90 degrees (broadside) for the dipole, and 40 degrees from the plane of the horizontal wires for the N4GG Array.

A tremendous amount of information has been published lately about the effects of the number of radials used in a particular antenna, elevated radials and ground characteristics on the performance of vertical antennas. Restating it all here is beyond the scope of this article but, in summary, ground radials and the earth itself provide two things for verticals mounted near the ground: (1) a return path for antenna current and (2) a surface that reflects the lower half of the free-space radiation pattern upward, adding to the upper half.

Return-current losses are usually minimized by the use of radials, while radiation reflection losses are determined by the ground conductivity out to 10 wavelengths or more from the antenna (in most cases reflection losses are out of our control). Verticals work well over good-conducting earth and particularly well over or near saltwater. The N4GG Array follows these same principles, and radials aren't required, as the "return current" is within the antenna and nearly lossless.

The actual gain of an N4GG Array over a dipole, however, particularly at low elevation angles, will depend on the height of the antenna above ground and the conductivity of the ground underneath it. Figure 2 shows an installation with average ground conductivity and near-worst-case proximity to the ground. If your location has average ground conductivity you should be able to achieve at least the gain performance shown in Figure 2. Increased height and/or increased ground conductivity will yield even better performance.

Depending on your point of view, the azimuth radiation pattern of an N4GG Array could be considered one of its two drawbacks—the other being that the horizontal size is twice that of a standard dipole. The azimuth radiation pattern for an N4GG Array at an elevation angle of 25 degrees is shown in Figure 3. As you can see, the phased verticals produce nulls both broadside

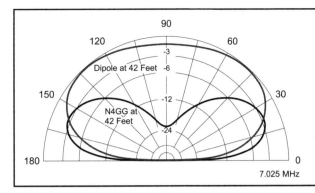

Figure 2—Comparison of the elevation radiation patterns of an N4GG Array and a dipole, both mounted at the same height, close to the ground. The outer ring is +5.96 dBi.

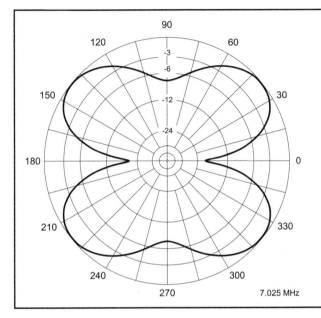

Figure 3—Azimuth radiation pattern for a "close to the ground" N4GG Array at an elevation angle of 25 degrees. Note the dipole-like nulls along the horizontal wires and the pattern dips broadside to the horizontal wires. As modeled, the antenna is not omnidirectional.

and along the plane of the horizontal wires, together with four peaks that occur at 40 degrees from the horizontal wires. If a truly omnidirectional antenna is what you want, this antenna doesn't quite fill the bill. But how bad is it?

As modeled, the −3 dBi azimuth beamwidth of the antenna is 187 degrees out of 360 degrees, and the deep nulls along the horizontal wires are very narrow and not much different than those of a dipole. The "as modeled" pattern could actually be used to your advantage. At my mid-Atlantic location, an N4GG Array could be positioned to provide peak gain toward Europe, Africa, VK/ZL and JA—not bad! But maybe not so good, either, as the broadside pattern dips would be toward South America and parts of Asia.

The real answer to how objectionable the departure from an omnidirectional pattern is lies in a fuller investigation of the modeled performance, the difference in real antenna performance compared to idealized models and some on-air observations.

The model indicates that the broadside pattern dips lessen as elevation angle increases. Some DX signals arrive at higher elevation angles, particularly during band openings and band closings on the lower frequencies. More importantly, the models are idealized in all respects except for the characterization of the earth, which is set to a point-estimate that may or may not accurately reflect a specific location. The actual radiation pattern for a real N4GG Array will depend on proximity to local objects, local topology, actual ground characteristics, and so on.

I decided simply to put one up to get some real-world results with respect to the modeled antenna and its theoretical radiation pattern. My on-air observations are at the end of the article, but I can assure you that the strength of long-haul DX signals—from any direction—is nearly always better on my N4GG Array than on a reference dipole at the same height, and is *never* worse than equal. On a receive signal-to-noise basis, the N4GG Array is always better, which is understandable given its lower gain at high elevation angles.

The dimensions for an N4GG Array are L_1 (feet) = 489/f (MHz), and L_2 (feet) = 257/f (MHz), where L_1 is the length of each of the two horizontal wires, and L_2 is the length of each vertical wire. These formulas are correct for a height of approximately 0.3-wavelength above ground and will vary slightly as a function of height.

As with most wire antennas, it's reasonable to make the antenna a bit larger than the formula suggests (in this case the vertical sections) so the antenna can be trimmed for minimum SWR at the desired operating frequency. Beyond trimming for SWR, the dimensions are not critical to performance. At resonance and at 0.3-wavelength above average ground, the feed-point impedance is 73 Ω, providing a near-perfect match for 75-Ω coax and less than 1.5:1 SWR when fed with 50-Ω coax. Using 50-Ω coax, the 2:1 SWR bandwidth on 20 meters is greater than 200 kHz.

Table 1 provides dimensions and some operating characteristics for single-band HF N4GG Arrays. The table values are for arrays where the bottom of the vertical wires are 7 feet above the ground (out of harm's way) and for resonant frequencies where the 2:1 SWR envelope starts at the lower band edge (for bands other than 30, 17 and 12 meters), or at the center of the band (for 30, 17 and 12 meters, which are entirely contained in the 2:1 SWR envelope). The 2:1 SWR bandwidths shown are for 50-Ω feed line.

An important consideration in achieving reasonable performance is to keep the feed line from radiating and becoming an additional antenna element. This can happen by not using a balun at the feed point to make the transition from an unbalanced transmission line to a balanced antenna. A high-quality 1:1 current-type balun should be used at the feed point to prevent this problem.

A nice feature of an N4GG Array is that the fields from the two vertical radiators cancel at the center of the antenna, resulting in no parasitically induced current on the shield of the coax feed line (at least in theory). In practice, the near-field radiation pattern from the verticals may not perfectly cancel, and the feed line placement may deviate somewhat from the ideal. Induced current on the coax shield should be sufficiently small to not affect the antenna's performance significantly, however.

Let's Build an Array

Construction of an N4GG is straightforward. Physically this is just a center-fed dipole of twice the traditional length, with vertical wires at the dipole ends. "Invisibility" *and safety* dictate the exact construction techniques.

A few words about "invisible" antennas might be useful at this point. My various wire antennas have been built using 18 or 19-gauge galvanized steel wire, which is available at home supply stores and is very inexpensive. Copper would be somewhat better electrically, but the galvanized wire has good strength at nearly invisible diameters. Galvanized wire has only moderate life, however, and will eventually rust and fail mechanically. Copperweld is probably the best choice for strength and life, and it is good electrically.

Strength is particularly important if you're going to build a multiband N4GG, and a critical necessity if you do not have a center support for the feed line and balun. The vertical wires in an N4GG Array only support themselves and can be of a smaller gauge if necessary. Remember, however: the smaller the wire gauge, the narrower the bandwidth.

The galvanized wire takes on a dull gray finish after a few days outdoors, which helps with invisibility. I paint the insulators and the balun with flat gray spray paint. Feeding with RG-8X also helps, and I have found that RG-8X will handle 1.5 kW without problems as long as the feed line SWR is low enough (as it is with this antenna).

My multiband N4GG Array uses trees for skyhooks and a line tossed over another tree limb to support the balun and feed line at a height of 66 feet. The balun is very close to the center support tree limb and the coax runs down the side of the tree that can't be seen from the street. The antenna has been up for three years and has been detected only once, by a neighbor who strayed onto the property.

The vertical wires can be terminated with insulators and held taut by tying them to ground stakes with nylon or heavy-duty monofilament line. This approach is prone to breaking, however, if you are using trees for end supports, as the wind will cause the antenna to move up and down, stressing the lines and wires. I prefer to simply let the vertical wires hang, using two-ounce fishing weights at the bottom to keep them somewhat taut. This way, the vertical elements tend to swing in a breeze, but this isn't noticeable on the air.

N4GG Arrays can be installed as low as a 1/4-wavelength above the ground, but two hazards arise when the vertical ends are lower than about seven feet above the ground. First, the bottom end of the vertical wires are obstacles for people and animals to run into (the use of "invisible" components makes this problem worse). Second, the lower end of the vertical elements are the high-voltage points in the antenna and can cause RF burns to people or animals that may be in contact with them while you're transmitting.

Use common sense during your installation and, if at all possible, install the antenna high enough to keep the bottom ends of the vertical elements above harm's way. If the ends *must* be near the ground, running the wires inside a few feet of 1-inch (or greater) PVC pipe can add significantly to safety, at some expense to stealth. N4GG Arrays can actually be installed even closer to the ground if linear loading, loading coils or capacitance hats are used to shorten the length of the vertical elements.

Simple Multiband Operation

What about multibanding? Simple fan-dipole construction allows connecting multiple N4GG Array wire sets to a common center insulator/balun. Figure 4 shows the schematic of a triband 10, 15 and 20-meter N4GG Array. Figure 5 shows the actual antenna, suspended about 3 feet off the ground during assembly. Half-inch PVC pipe was used to hold the wire sets 4 inches apart. Figure 6 provides details of how the PVC spreaders were installed.

This is actually a four-band antenna, as the wires that make up the 15-meter N4GG Array are the length of a standard 1/2-wavelength dipole on 40 meters. The antenna displays a low SWR on that band, but does not function as an N4GG Array there. On 40, the setup is simply a dipole with bent ends, and offers commensurate

Table 1
HF N4GG Arrays—Dimensions and Characteristics

Resonant Freq (kHz)	Height (feet)	L₁ (feet)	L₂ (feet)	Bandwidth (kHz) (2:1 SWR at 50 Ω)	Max Gain (dBi)	Takeoff Angle (degrees)
1810	147.5	268	140.5	40	4.03	22.5
3525	80	137.5	73	45	3.54	23
7050	43.5	69	36.5	100	3.58	23
10,125	32.6	48	25.6	140	3.89	23
14,100	25	34.9	18	210	4.19	22.5
18,118	21.25	27	14.25	290	4.48	21.5
21,200	19.1	23.2	12.1	340	4.65	21.5
24,940	17.35	19.6	10.35	420	4.79	20.5
28,250	16.3	17.2	9.3	480	4.91	20

Note: The figures here assume that the bottom of the vertical elements will be 7 feet above the ground.

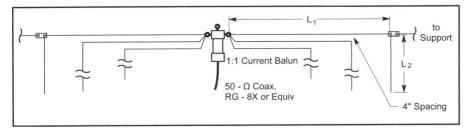

Figure 4—Fan-dipole construction of a 10, 15 and 20-meter N4GG Array.

Figure 5—A tri-band N4GG Array stretched out 3 feet above the ground for easy assembly. Half-inch PVC spreaders are used to separate the wires by 4 inches.

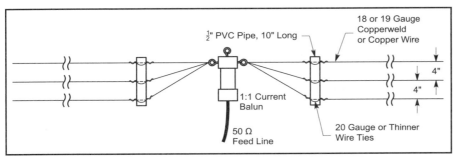

Figure 6—The Array wires travel through the spreaders and are secured with 20-gauge wire ties.

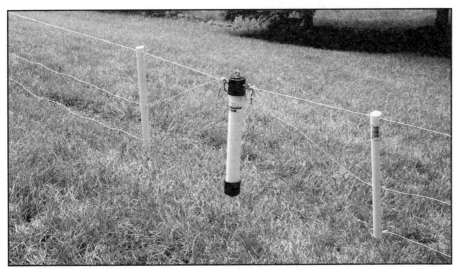

Figure 7—Close-up of the center insulator/balun of a tri-band N4GG Array. Note that all support of the lower wires is provided by the uppermost wires.

performance. The antenna's SWR is below 2:1 on all four bands and does not require the use of an antenna tuner.

Figure 7 shows a close-up of the center insulator/balun. After these pictures were taken, the balun and PVC spreaders were spray painted flat gray.

There is a second approach to multibanding that can yield an N4GG Array from an existing low-band dipole. Figure 8 shows the addition of the vertical wires for a higher-frequency N4GG Array directly onto the horizontal wires of a lower-frequency dipole. In this case no spreaders are used and there is only one connection to each side of the balun. This arrangement works because the vertical wires act as low-impedance stubs, inserted onto relatively high-impedance points on the horizontal dipole.

I added a set of 15-meter $1/4$-wavelength vertical wires onto an existing 160-meter dipole using this method, getting a second band essentially "for free." The addition of the 15-meter wires had no measurable effect on the 160-meter dipole. This approach can be used for adding one—or perhaps more than one N4GG Array—onto existing large dipoles. Before you start stitching vertical elements onto your monster dipole, be sure to see how things might play out by modeling the antenna first. For example, a 15-meter N4GG Array can't be added to a 40-meter dipole because they're both resonant on that band!

Actual Performance

Okay, so how well does one of these things actually work? Based on my observations, signals from stations that are more than 3000 miles away are typically a few dB stronger on my N4GG Array than on my dipole at the same height. For long-haul DX, this is the difference between working them and not. I added XU and XW as new countries lately—and I couldn't hear either station on the dipole. When 15 meters is hot, as it is now near the top of cycle 23, I can sometimes call CQ on the N4GG Array and start a pileup of European and Asian stations, something I've never accomplished with the dipole!

Your first impression operating with an N4GG Array may not be good—mine wasn't. Tuning quickly, the whole band sounded down, both stations and noise. "Something's broken," or "These things don't work as modeled," were my first thoughts. If you put up an N4GG Array and it sounds dead at first, it's working—it's supposed to sound somewhat dead! Most of the signals we tend to hear when quickly tuning a band are close in. These signals—and much of the band noise—arrive at high elevation angles, where an N4GG Array can be 20 dB down from a dipole. After you get over how quiet the band sounds, find a DX station and switch between an N4GG Array and a dipole. That will put a smile on your face! Then try one in a major DX contest and get ready for even more smiles.

Make no mistake, this antenna isn't nearly as good as a decent Yagi. It is, however, the best DX antenna design I've found to date that offers stealth, low-angle radiation (even when installed close to the ground), tuner-free multiband operation when fed with 50-Ω coax, radial-free installation, simplicity and affordability. That's a lot of benefits in one package!

Photos by the author.

Hal Kennedy, N4GG, is the Vice President for Technology Commercialization at Lockheed Martin Corporation. He was first licensed in 1961 and holds an Amateur Extra license as well as a General Radiotelephone license. He received a BSEE degree from Lafayette College and an MS in Management from The Sloan School at MIT. An ARRL and PVRC member, Hal spends his time DXing, contesting and trying to improve his signal from a suburban lot. The author may be reached at 110 Fox Trail Terr, Gaithersburg, MD 20878; **n4gg@hotmail.com**.

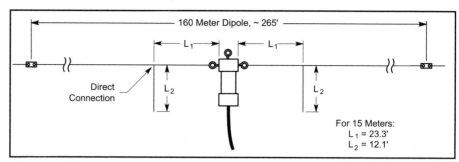

Figure 8—A higher-frequency N4GG Array can be formed by adding 1/4 wavelength vertical wires to a lower-frequency dipole.

By Dave Benson, K1SWL

Taming the Trap Dipole

A self-supported dipole for 10/15/17 meters can be a fine thing—if it's designed right.

After our recent move from a city location to several acres of wooded bliss, it was only natural that a young man's fancy would turn to thoughts of . . . antennas! I've experimented with any number of antenna configurations over the years, but multiband operation always seemed to involve tuners used to press non-resonant wires into service. With the "clean slate" afforded me with the new location, I decided I wanted to pursue the "hook up the coax and forget it" approach. I'm also reluctant to spend my limited discretionary funds on commercial antennas when the homebrew approach works well.

One approach to a multiband dipole design is the so-called "fan dipole" wherein a separate electrical half-wavelength of wire is added in parallel at the feedpoint for each band of interest. This can become mechanically cumbersome after the first several bands and interaction between bands becomes noticeable, at least with close wire spacings. I elected instead to pursue the trap approach. This article describes the development of a self-supported 10/15/17 meter trap dipole.

This project moved from the back burner to the "gotta try it" category when I found that the local home-improvement emporium carried 8-foot lengths of ³/₈-inch aluminum C-channel stock. This material has one important advantage: all surfaces are flat, which eases a number of construction details. The joints between the element sections need to be an insulating material and of sufficient strength to carry the weight of the outboard sections. The ideal material for this application turned out to be ³/₈-inch square black Delrin (plastic) stock, which has good tensile strength properties.[1] This material is also available in sizes up to 4 inches square (at daunting prices) for applications where higher strength is required.

Figure 1 shows the dimensions of the trap antenna. The innermost dipole section (10 meters) is decoupled from the rest of the antenna by a pair of traps tuned to 28.1 MHz. The next pair of sections is decoupled from the outer wires by a pair of traps ad-

[1]Notes appear on page 97.

justed to 21.1 MHz. Although the dimensions shown are for the 10/15/17-meter bands, there's nothing to prevent you from developing other combinations.

The traps themselves are quite simple—a parallel-resonant tuned circuit adjusted to the center of each amateur band of interest. I constructed each of these from iron-powder toroidal cores and a pair of silver mica capacitors. Each trap uses two 1 kV-rated capacitors in series and T94 cores, the largest that would fit in the "low-profile" trap enclosures I chose. I used Serpac C-series enclosures available from mail-order distributors, and a number of choices are also available through RadioShack. Figure 2 shows the construction details—a pair of machine screws exits through the rear wall of the trap enclosure and passes through holes drilled through the insulator stock and the aluminum C-channel.

The traditional tool for adjusting traps has been a grid-dip meter, and this has been supplanted more recently by antenna analyzers. If you don't have access to either of these tools, though, despair not!

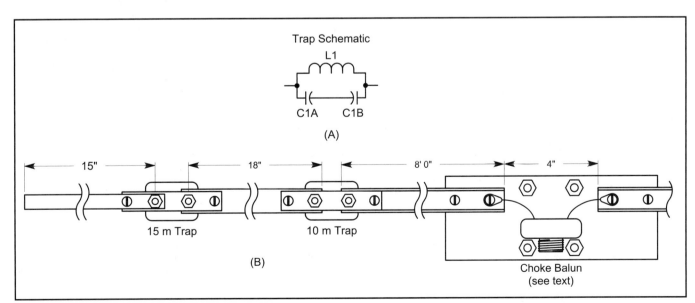

Figure 1—The dimensions of the trap antenna. Other dimensions can be devised for bands other than 10, 15 and 17 meters. At A, the schematic of the trap. At B, dimensions for one side of the dipole antenna.

C1A, C1B—100 pF, 1 kV silver mica capacitor.

L1—*10 meters*: 9 turns on a T94-10 toroidal core; *15 meters*: 11 turns on a T94-6 toroidal core. The coils must be tuned to resonance.

The Noise Bridge

Diode D1 is a source of broadband noise. This noise is amplified to useful levels by the two-stage circuit comprising Q1, Q2 and associated components. Although there's no attempt made to frequency-compensate this noise source, there's plenty of signal for our purposes—its output level ranges from S9+20 dB at 1.8 MHz to S7 at 30 MHz. In practice, when the impedances connected to points B and U are equal, this "bridge" circuit is in a balanced condition and output to the receiver is at a null. The only "tricky bit" in this circuit consists of the trifilar winding T1. [The circuit board project offering uses color-coded wire for this toroid, so hookup is pretty much foolproof.]

So Now What?

Let's put this to practical use: Connect a 100-Ω ¼ W resistor across the "unknown" terminals and connect to your receiver with a length of coax. Apply dc power (8-15 V) to the noise bridge circuit and you should hear a loud rushing noise in the receiver. Adjust control R1 for minimum S-meter indication and then C1. Once these are both adjusted carefully, the noise level in the receiver should drop to its internal noise level alone. The noise bridge is now adjusted for a null—the impedance presented by the 100-ohm resistance and stray capacitance is now balanced by the bridge's R1 and C1 settings.

Putting it all Together

If you add the trap—a parallel L-C circuit—at its resonance frequency across that 100-ohm resistor, there'd be no disturbance to the null since its impedance at the intended operating frequency is theoretically infinite. Away from the resonance frequency, the noise level will rise as the receiver is tuned off to either side. Finding the trap's resonant frequency amounts to tuning your receiver until you've located the noise

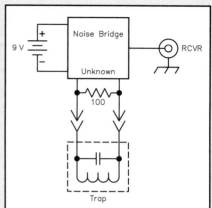

Figure B—How to hook up the noise bridge.

null. This null will be fairly broad; however, it should be easy to locate using 1-MHz and then 100 kHz tuning steps.

Once you've found the null, bunch the toroid turns together to lower the trap resonance frequency or spread the turns apart to raise the resonance frequency. There's a fair amount of adjustment possible without resorting to changing the toroid turns count—the 21 MHz traps, for instance, could be tuned in this manner to cover a range of 19-22 MHz.

Caution

My initial attempts at repeatable resonance measurements were inconsistent—the "casual" approach using clip leads yielded well over a MHz of variation in resonance frequency at 25 MHz! It's critical to make the leads from the "unknown" terminals on the bridge to the traps as rigid as is practical. I used 2-inch lengths of no. 20 magnet wire to the 100-Ω parallel load and installed solder lugs outboard of that resistor. This allowed the traps to be added and removed with a minimum of change in stray capacitance, which affects the resonance measurement significantly. Once these precautions were taken, the measurements became reassuringly repeatable. *Note:* Once these trap hookup connections are ready to go and prior to adding the traps, be sure to readjust C1 for a noise null—this effectively tunes out the test setup stray capacitance.

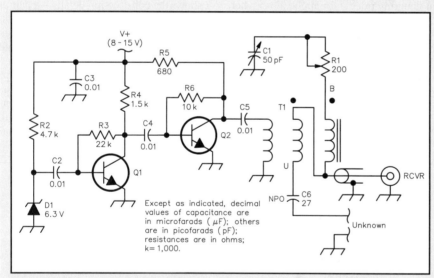

Figure A—The schematic diagram of the noise bridge, based on a design that appears in *The ARRL Antenna Book*. All resistors are 5%, ¼-W carbon composition.
D1—6.3-V, 0.5-W Zener diode, 1N753A or equiv.
Q1, Q2—High-speed NPN switch, PN2222A, 2N4401 or equiv.
T1—4 turns trifilar-wound on FT37-43 toroid; observe phasing.

If you have an HF transceiver with general coverage capability, you've already got most of what you need.

The remaining piece of equipment required is a noise bridge. Despite the arcane-sounding name, this is a simple circuit that is easily duplicated. The sidebar shows the schematic diagram for this circuit, and this is taken largely intact from *The ARRL Antenna Book*.[2] A printed circuit-board kit was developed as a club project and is available to interested builders.[3]

Antenna Adjustment

This antenna was developed by starting with the innermost (10-meter) section and working outward one band at a time. With a 4-inch spacing between the ends of the 8-foot channel sections, the 10-meter antenna simply worked on the first try. Resonance for this dipole was at 28.1 MHz and SWR characteristics were fairly broad due to the element thickness.

Upon adjustment of a pair of 10-meter traps, these were added to the element ends and outboard sections for 15 meters were added. Rather than use the C-channel ma-

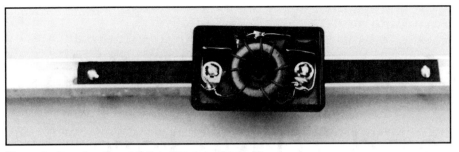

Figure 2—Construction details of the trap. See text.

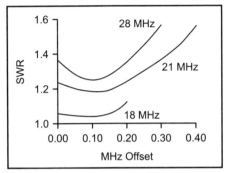

Figure 3—The SWR characteristics for the trap dipole. Since the author operates primarily CW and data modes, the lengths are optimized for the lower end of each band.

terial on the initial adjustments, I found it much more convenient to install outboard sections of ¼ inch aluminum rod stock. This material proved to be quite easy to trim to length with a pair of bolt-cutters! Tune-up was done at an initial height of 20 feet. Element lengths are adjusted using an SWR bridge and transmitter to determine the frequency at which SWR is minimum and adjusting accordingly. *A gentle suggestion: It's much easier to start "long" and subtract material rather the reverse!*

You'll find that the outboard lengths for each additional lower-frequency band do not meet the familiar formula for computing dipole lengths. The traps themselves present a very high impedance at their design frequency but below this frequency are inductive. This has the effect of shortening the resonant length of the antenna. [It has a modest effect in lowering feedpoint resistance as well, but is not significant within the context of this application.] With the trap components I chose, each outboard section length was shortened by 30-35% over the expected values for a dipole. For the adventurous, this length may be estimated by calculating the effective impedance of the trap at the lower band and applying it to any of several tools. This information is found in graphical form in *The ARRL Antenna Book*[4] or by use of *EZNEC*.[5]

With the length of the 15-meter section under control, I replaced the temporary rod sections with C-channel and added a pair of 15-meter traps. With the addition and adjustment of the outer 17-meter sections, this completed the design for my applications, so I elected to leave the outer antenna ends in the form of ¼-inch rod stock to reduce weight and lower the antenna's visible "profile."

The center insulator/mounting block is constructed from a ⅜ × 3 × 12-inch block of Delrin plastic. This provides sufficient rigidity for this antenna, although if the concept is extended to lower bands you'd probably want thicker plastic material. A small plastic box at the feedpoint contains a choke balun. I constructed this using a short length of RG-174 coax looped three times through a group of six FT37-43 ferrite toroids. There's nothing magical about this approach—any of a number of other methods can be used to achieve the same goal.

Construction

All fastening hardware for the trap dipole should be of stainless steel, and toothed lock washers are needed to maintain integrity of the tightened joints. Once the traps are adjusted to the desired resonance frequencies, the trap enclosures are sealed shut with an edge-bead of model airplane cement and resonance was re-checked. This final check ensures that adding the enclosure covers has not disturbed the trap frequencies—a possibility given the tight quarters afforded by the enclosures I chose.

Results

The SWR characteristics for this antenna are shown in Figure 3. I operate primarily CW and data modes, so my interest is in the lower end of each band; the lengths in this article reflect that preference. Whatever frequency you choose, you know you've done a careful job tuning the traps if the addition of these traps and outboard sections has no effect on resonance frequency of the inner antenna portion. Their presence, though, will narrow the effective SWR bandwidth as you move away from resonance—the trap-antenna bandwidths are lower than for that of a "plain-vanilla" dipole.

Trap Losses

Although I normally operate at 5 W output or less, that's not everyone's "cup of tea." I've tested this antenna at 100 W without incident. *EZNEC* analysis using the published "Q" values for the toroid trap material shows antenna gain at 28 MHz to be 0.8 dB down from the expected free-space values, and 0.9 dB down at 21 MHz. At 18.1 MHz, the loss is approximately 0.25 dB. These values would be somewhat improved with the use of higher-Q inductors. This design has traded "compact" and "low-profile" for modest gain penalties—proof indeed of the old adage about "no free lunch."

A point of interest—I calculate the peak voltage across the traps at that power level to be over 1 kV. This is no place for junkbox capacitors of questionable pedigree! A high-quality NP0 capacitor type is a "must"—the types typically available from your local electronics emporium may be quite lossy at high frequencies, and this will translate into considerable component heating and disappointing performance. The 500-V silver mica capacitors available from the large distributors are sufficient for lower-power (QRP) operation.[6]

I installed this antenna at the 35-foot level above my roof and have been very pleased with its performance. After years of "low-profile" QRP operation, my success rate snagging contacts on the first call has improved markedly. To a large extent, the old maxim of "Put it up high and in the clear" applies here! As a final "food-for-thought" consideration, the trap-construction scheme I've described would lend itself nicely to multiband vertical and ground-plane antennas.

Acknowledgments

Special thanks to Seabury Lyon, AA-1MY, for his assistance with the noise bridge project.

Notes

[1]Delrin plastic may be purchased in small quantities from McMaster-Carr, **www. mcmaster. com**; see "raw materials."
[2]*The ARRL Antenna Book*, 19th Ed., p 27-24.
[3]A noise bridge kit consisting of double-sided/silkscreened printed-circuit board, on-board parts and RG-174/U cable with BNC connector and instructions is available from the New England QRP Club for $17 ($20 overseas) postpaid. Checks or money orders payable to S. Lyon, AA1MY, 99 Sparrowhawk Mtn Rd, Bethel, ME 04217.
[4]Dean Straw, N6BV, Ed., *The ARRL Antenna Book*, 19th Ed., p 6-28.
[5]*EZNEC* is available from Roy Lewallen, W7EL, **www.eznec.com**.
[6]Toroids are available from Amidon Associates (tel 714-850-4660) or Palomar Engineers, **www.palomar-engineeers.com**. 1-kV silver mica capacitors are available from RF Parts Co (**www.rfparts.com**; tel 800-737-2787).

Dave Benson, K1SWL, is a frequent contributor to QST. He can be reached at **dave@ smallwonderlabs.com**.

By Rick Rogers, KI8GX

A "One-Masted Sloop" for 40, 20, 15 and 10 Meters

What started off as a compromise replacement for a "monster loop" turned out much better than expected. This antenna may prove to be an exception to the rule that "you get what you pay for."

Over 33 years of hamming, one of my favorite activities is building and testing antennas. Of all the types of antennas tried, I get the best bang for the buck from simple, horizontal loops.

Designing the Loop

An interesting property of loop antennas is that they are harmonically resonant. As shown by Doug DeMaw, W1FB, a loop designed for 7.1 MHz will also resonate at 14.2 MHz, 21.3 MHz, 28.4 MHz, etc.[1] See Figure 1. The ability to operate on multiple bands without retuning and the multidirectional nature of their radiation patterns make horizontal loops especially useful for DX, contest, and net control applications where having to wait to rotate a beam can be a disadvantage. Another advantage of the loop antenna is that it tends to be quieter on receive than some other designs, such as Yagis or verticals.[2]

The best antenna I ever built was a 160-meter full-wave horizontal loop. Even though the antenna was only up about 35 feet, it did a pretty good job on 160, is spite of radiating most of its energy skyward. Where this antenna was really effective, though, was on its harmonics. An *EZNEC*[3] model of this antenna shows, for example, that at 10 meters, it radiates multiple low-angle lobes, some with gain figures of more than 13 dBi.

Of course, a monster like this had (note past tense!) its problems. It required 4 masts, 540 feet of wire and a big chunk of land. As the reader might guess, antennas that big suffer a lot from the wind, even if made out of relatively strong wire. Mine was made of 17 gauge aluminum fence wire but it seemed like I was always repairing damaged masts and broken wires. [Solid wire is more likely than stranded wire to break as a result of repeated flexing.—Ed.] After about six months of constant struggle against the elements, the antenna and three of its four supports succumbed to wind-driven hail.

After the storm, and several unsatisfying weeks trying to get by with a home-brew vertical, I thought to try something a little less ambitious. What I had in mind was a loop that would use only the single remaining support. A quick session with *EZNEC* showed that a sloping loop, 140 feet in circumference (a full wavelength on 40 meters), with the feed point elevated on a single 30-foot support should resonate on 40, 20, 15 and 10 meters. The antenna should also produce reasonable gain in multiple directions, especially at the shorter wavelengths (see Figure 2). This "one-masted sloop," a *sloping loop* supported and fed at the top corner, turns out to be a good performer and costs almost nothing.

Building the Loop

Construction couldn't be easier. First, buy or build a dipole center insulator with coaxial connector as described in *The ARRL Handbook for Radio Amateurs* (see Figure 3).[4] Connect the opposite ends of the 140-foot wire to the center insulator. I prefer 14 gauge stranded and insulated wire because it is easy to work with. Tie 50-foot lengths

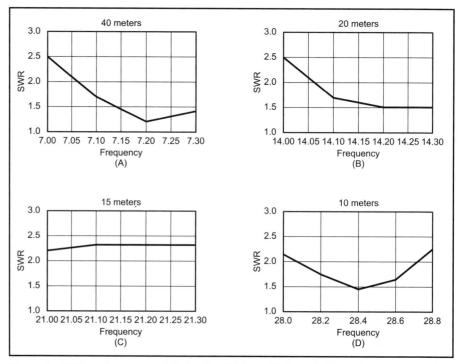

Figure 1—SWR vs. frequency plots for the 136-foot, 40 through 10-meter sloop. The SWR minimum for the four bands is easily adjusted by adding or deleting small lengths of wire from the loop.

[1]Notes appear on page 100.

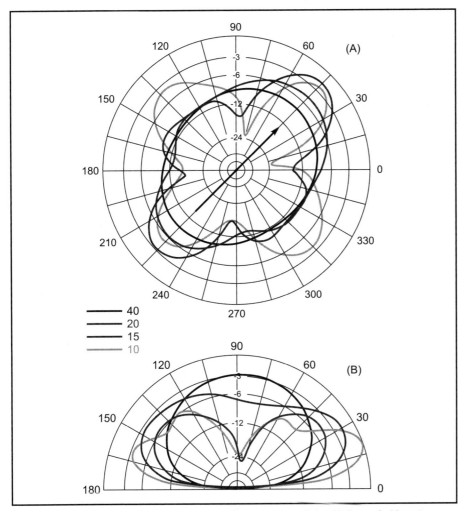

Figure 2—*EZNEC* study of the far field radiation patterns of the 40 through 10-meter "Sloop." The arrow indicates the direction of the slope. A is the azimuth plot at 30 degrees elevation. B shows the elevation plot along the axis of maximum gain, 45-225 degrees.

of 3/16-inch rope to the antenna at points 35 feet away from the center connector on each side. [You may wish to use a ceramic insulator at the side and bottom tie-line attachment points, particularly if high power will be used; see Figure 4.—Ed.] Connect 50-Ω coaxial cable such as RG-8 or RG-58 to the connector and raise the feed point to a height of 30 to 40 feet. Pull the side tie lines sideways and down until the upper half of the antenna forms a taut 90-degree angle and slopes at 30 to 45 degrees with respect to the ground (see Figure 3). Tie off these lines. Attach a short (2-3 foot) length of line to the bottom point of the loop and tie off the bottom of the loop to a stake or a fence post.

The loop will need to be pruned for the antenna to resonate at the desired frequencies. To do this without raising and lowering the antenna for each adjustment, remove lengths of wire at the bottom of the loop and then solder the ends back together. Shorten the loop a few inches at a time until the SWR approaches 1:1 at the desired 40-meter frequency. Adding wire will lower the resonant frequency on all bands.

In my case, a final length of 136 feet yielded SWR values lower than 3:1 over the entire 40, 20 and 15-meter bands. The loop also produced a 2:1 SWR over almost 1 MHz of the 10 meter band (see Figure 1). Since I typically hang out in the phone sections of these bands, my antenna was tuned for the best match there. My old Kenwood TS-830 and ancient Hallicrafters HT-41 kilowatt amplifier—both with adjustable pi matching output networks—easily tune

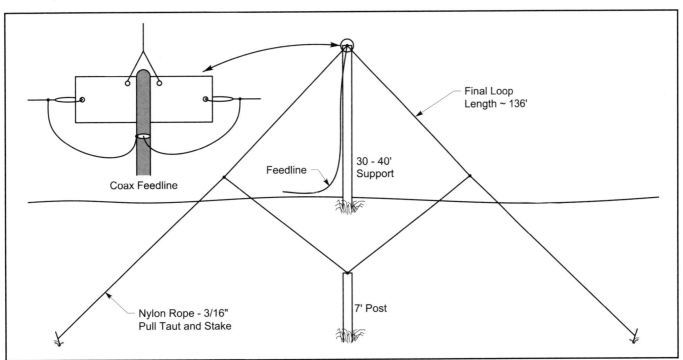

Figure 3—The vertical support of the Single-Masted Sloop can be a mast, tree, building, flagpole, and so on. The simplicity of the design and the multidirectional gain delivered at the harmonics make this antenna a good candidate for Field Day.

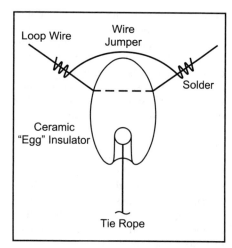

Figure 4—One simple method of attaching tie ropes to wire antennas.

to this antenna at any frequency on all four bands. Most recently manufactured rigs can handle the 2 or 3:1 SWR at the band edges. [To lessen the SWR, particularly at higher frequencies, the loop can also be fed with open-wire line.—Ed.]

Results

The results with this antenna are gratifying, especially given that it can be built in a couple of hours from scrap wire and hardware, tunes easily, doesn't need to be elevated to great height and occupies a reasonable "footprint." Stations in Europe, Japan, South America and the Azores were worked with 100 W on 20, 15 and 10 meters within an hour or so of completion and with good signal reports. I tried the antenna on 40 meters during the November 2001 Sweepstakes to get some idea of its performance on that band. I was pleased to find that contacts could be made with the antenna on both coasts from central Ohio at midday in spite of *EZNEC* showing much of the energy on 40 meters radiates straight up (see Figure 2). The performance, simplicity and cost of this antenna suggest to me that this would be the antenna I would roll up and take along on that low-budget DXpedition to the Caribbean.

Notes

[1] Doug DeMaw, W1FB, "A Closer Look at Horizontal Loop Antennas," *QST*, May 1990, p 28.
[2] See Note 1.
[3] *EZNEC* 3.0 Antenna Design Software by Roy Lewallen, W7EL (**www.eznec.com/; w7el@eznec.com**).
[4] Chapter 20 ("Antennas and Projects") of any recent *ARRL Handbook* contains drawings that illustrate ways of attaching a center connector.

Rick Rogers, KI8GX, was first licensed as WN-6HGY in 1968, followed by WA6EZT, N9COO and N7GEF. He is a professor of Neuroscience at Louisiana State University where he does research on, and teaches, neurophysiology and physiological instrumentation. A chance encounter with a neighborhood ham cleaning out his garage (Sam Westfall, K6PHH) in 1967 started Rick, then 13 years old, on his career in ham radio and science. Ham radio provided an ideal entry point into neurophysiology since the principal elements of the nervous system neurons "talk" to each other using frequency modulated electrical pulses. The ARRL Handbook for Radio Amateurs can be found on the bookshelves of quite a few neuroscientists, whether they are hams or not. You can reach the author at 9831 Bank St, Clinton, LA 70722; **rogersrc@pbrc.edu**.

By Sylvia Hutchinson, K8SYL

K8SYL's 75 and 10-Meter Dipole

On getting licensed, upgrading and entering the wide world of HF.

In June 2000, I retired after 36 years of teaching and moved from Connecticut to my native state of Michigan. At first, my days were completely consumed with getting settled into our house and working around the lawn and gardens. It wasn't easy, but it was fun.

As Labor Day approached, I had the feeling that it was time to get ready for school. The outdoor work, while not over, was under control. I had time for me, and because I wouldn't be teaching I decided to be the student.

Chuck, K8CH, had received his first ham license while we were still dating. Back then, I learned a phrase in Morse code because he would tap it out on my hand during church. Even today, I can recognize "I love you honey" at 25 wpm but I'm not sure if I'd recognize my own call sign at that speed. A few years later, I remember sitting in a school gymnasium with my husband of nearly a year as he handled messages for the Red Cross. It was interesting, but it wasn't for me—not then. I was a full-time student at Michigan State University, and my first son was on the way.

For 40 years I had watched Chuck enjoy operating his radio, and I knew he would like to share that with me. I too wanted to share it with him. It looked like fun, and now I finally had the time for Amateur Radio. Being a wife, mother and bilingual (Spanish) special-education teacher had been very demanding of my time. I decided to go for my Technician class license. We had a copy of *Now You're Talking!* on the bookshelf.[1] I spent about an hour a day studying, and in the process set the goal of achieving 100% on the exam.

In February 2001, I met my goal, passing the exam with a perfect score. (Thanks, HQ staff who wrote the book!) The first thing I did as a new ham was to send my money and application for life membership in ARRL. The second was to apply for a vanity call sign. I didn't want to be KC8QKB if I could be, say, K8SYL. Then I checked into the Ionia County ARES (ICARES) net on the N8ZMT repeater in Portland, Michigan. That's something I continue to do regularly. I had met these folks at their monthly Saturday morning breakfast meetings. They were all supportive and made me feel welcome.

One of the ICARES group is long-time family friend Donna Burch, W8QOY. As soon as I had that Technician class license, she and Myriam Gregg, K8ILN, began to encourage me to upgrade to General. I would have 75-meter privileges and could join The Auto State YL Net (TASYLs). That sounded like fun and besides I was ready to learn more code than "I love you honey."

Time to study for that General. Back to the books, this time *The ARRL General Class License Manual*.[2] I set the same 100% goal for the written exam as before, and thanks again to Larry, WR1B, and the ARRL HQ staff, I reached that goal.

I had learned the Morse characters a long time before, but now I needed to relearn the characters and build some proficiency. Chuck downloaded the program *Morse Academy* from the Internet and I got started. Soon after, we ordered *Morse Tutor Gold* software from ARRL and that became my favorite learning tool. Once my code speed began to approach 5 wpm, I started using W1AW code practice. I particularly liked the *Real Audio* files available online at: **www.arrl.org/w1aw/morse.html**. Those files allowed me to listen at my convenience. For other code learning ideas check out **www.arrl.org/FandES/ead/learncw/** on *ARRLWeb*.

My First HF Antenna

With my new General class license about to arrive, I wanted antennas for 75 and 10 meters. With help from Chuck, I put together a 120-foot center-fed dipole and we installed it about 35 feet high. This allowed me to join the other members of the TASYLs on their weekly 75 meter (3940 kHz) net. With leg lengths of 60 feet, my dipole was resonant at 3.900 MHz and the 2:1 SWR points were at 3.830 and 3.980; see Figure 1. It was good enough for my purposes, so we didn't bother pruning it further.

I was doing very well on 75 meters, but what was I to do for 10? Chuck had a partially built 10-meter ground-plane antenna in the basement that he was building for the book he was writing.[3] That was nice, but that ground plane wasn't going to do me much good until it was finished and he was

[1] Notes appear on page 103.

working on other chapters. I wasn't going to wait. One afternoon I was tuning across the 10-meter band when I heard KP4NU calling CQ from Caguas, Puerto Rico. I really wanted to have a QSO in Spanish, so I did what you would probably do—I called José using my 75-meter dipole (after first engaging the internal antenna tuner in my transceiver). I had a nice QSO. Was it luck, good conditions or what? After I bragged about my contact, I asked Chuck what he thought about it.

The Explanation

We both knew that a dipole is resonant on odd harmonics (3rd, 5th, 7th, etc), but 28 MHz is 8 times 3.5 MHz. That's true, but my dipole is cut for the high end of the band—closer to 4 MHz. Hmm, 4 times 7 is 28, and harmonic resonance is higher than one would expect. In other words, while you might expect that a 75-meter antenna that is resonant at 3940 kHz would have a 7th harmonic resonance at 27.58 MHz, it will actually be over a MHz higher.

We both understood the theory, but to better answer my questions Chuck next connected our MFJ-259B analyzer to the antenna feed line. The analyzer showed a resonance just below 29 MHz with an SWR of less than 3:1. He then modeled my antenna in *EZNEC*, which confirmed what the analyzer had just shown. At this point there were two options. The first was to leave well enough alone and use the transceiver's automatic antenna tuner.

The second option was to make my 75-meter antenna usable on 10 meters without the need of an antenna tuner. That's what we opted to do.

The Design

We had to deal with two issues in order to use my dipole on 10 meters. The first was to improve the 10-meter match without upsetting 75-meter operation. The second was to move the dipole's 10-meter resonance point a bit lower in the band.

At resonance on 10 meters, the feed-point impedance is about 120 Ω. We used a calculator to confirm that a quarter-wave transformer made with 75-Ω coax would take care of the 10-meter impedance match. At the same time, the length of this coaxial transformer is short enough to have no significant effect on the antenna's 75-meter operation.

I used RG-11 to build the series-matching transformer. For low-power operation, RG-59 can substitute. The physical length of the stub depends on the velocity factor. My RG-11 (Belden 8238) has a 66% velocity factor, which means the stub is 5 feet, 9 inches long. If you use 75-Ω coax with a 78% velocity factor such as Belden 8213 or 8212, you'll need to make your stub 6 feet, 9.5 inches long.

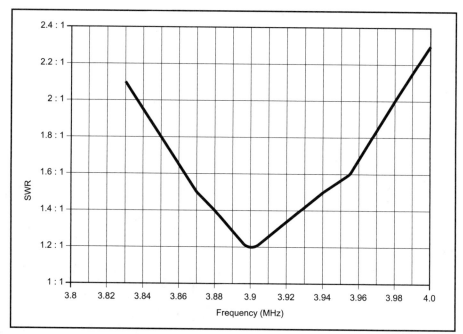

Figure 1—SWR of K8SYL's original 75-meter dipole with 60-foot legs.

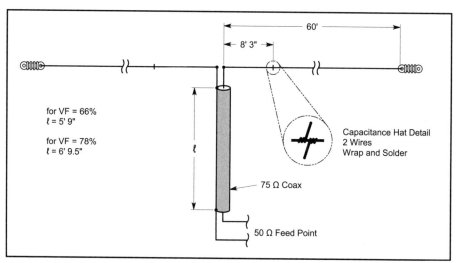

Figure 2—K8SYL's dipole as first modified for 75 and 10-meter operation. A quarter-wave section of 75-Ω coax transforms the 10-meter impedance. Capacitance hat wires wrap securely around the dipole and are soldered. They extend about 5 inches from the main dipole wire. See text for tuning instructions and final dimensions. This drawing is not to scale.

I had built my antenna to cover the upper (General class) end of the 75-meter band. Chuck and I thought about lengthening the dipole to move 10-meter resonance to the vicinity of 28.4 MHz. The *EZNEC* model said it would only require 4.5-inch extensions to each dipole leg. The downside to this is that it moves the 75-meter resonance to 3.89 MHz, and that's lower than what I wanted. I asked if we could find a method to lower the 10-meter resonance without substantially moving the 75-meter resonant frequency? Chuck had an affirmative answer.

He told me that Rus Healy had described adding capacitance hats on a 40-meter dipole to move the 3rd harmonic resonance lower in the 15-meter band.[4] We could use a similar technique to lower the 7th harmonic resonance of the 75-meter dipole. In the case of my antenna, *EZNEC* indicated that it took only the little bit of loading provided by a pair of short (3-inch) wires on each leg of the dipole. We modified my 75-meter dipole as shown in Figure 2. It was easy, and tune-up went smoothly.

Tuning the Antenna

First I'm going to explain the process to follow in tuning this two-band dipole. Then I'll tell you how it worked for me.

With the 75-Ω quarter-wave transformer section in place, tune the antenna for resonance in the upper part of the 75-meter band. As I found out through experience, you should do your tuning with the antenna in its final position. You'll need to trim for best

SWR above about 3.89 MHz or you're apt to lose some 10-meter coverage. If you tune for about 3.925 MHz, you should cover the entire General class band of 3.850 to 4.000 MHz with an SWR of 2:1 or better.

Next, check the 10-meter resonant frequency. (For the dipole dimensions given in Figure 2, it was just below 29 MHz.) If you need to lower that frequency, add the capacitance hats as shown in the drawing. You may want to make the wires a bit longer to start with. Check the resonant frequency again—it will be lower. To raise the frequency you can trim the fingers of the capacitance hat or you can just bend them a bit. It's that easy—at least in theory.

Chuck used the support mast for my dipole to hold a 2-element 17-meter Yagi (a project for his book). That meant we had to move my dipole, and it ended up being only 28 feet above the ground. Between that move and the addition of the 75-Ω quarter-wave transformer, my dipole's 75-meter resonant frequency shifted another 20 kHz lower. To compensate, I ended up shortening each leg by 8 inches, making the leg lengths 59 feet 4 inches. This gave me an SWR of 2:1 or better across the entire General class portion of the 75-meter band (see Figure 3).

As you might guess, that raised the 10-meter resonant frequency so that the simple loading wires were not sufficient to give me good SWR at the lower end of the band. I used a couple of 16-inch lengths of bare copper wire to make capacitance hats. I formed these into circles by wrapping them around a piece of 4-inch PVC drainpipe. I then fastened and soldered the circles to the loading wires as shown in the title photo. As you can see, I didn't bother to trim the extra loading wire. This gave me coverage of 28 to 29.1 MHz with an SWR of 2:1 or better, as you can see in Figure 4.

The Results

I have been using my dual-band dipole for nearly a year with very good results. I make 75-meter contacts with ease. Okay, I don't chase exotic DX, but I have no trouble talking with my friends. On 10 meters, I'm able to make contact with the US and most of the world. Amateur Radio is really fun!

In case you're wondering, Chuck completed that 10-meter ground-plane antenna shortly after we finished this project. In head-to-head comparisons, sometimes his ground plane works better, and sometimes my dipole comes out ahead. The reason for that is wrapped up in the antenna patterns and angle of arrival of the signals. I could show you the theoretical patterns of our antennas, but you will probably put yours up in a different configuration. The point for telling you this is to let you know that it's always good to have a choice between antennas—especially when you're talking about simple antennas like dipoles and verticals.

Around here, we're pretty much convinced that my dipole has become a permanent fixture in our ham station. I'd like to get up it a bit higher for better 75-meter performance, but it works very well on 10 meters. Perhaps this is what you should try for your next (or first) HF antenna.

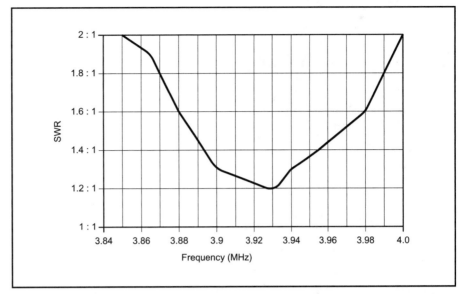

Figure 3—SWR of the modified K8SYL dipole after the two legs have been shortened to 59 feet 4 inches. The dipole now covers the entire General class portion of the 75-meter band with an SWR of 2:1 or better.

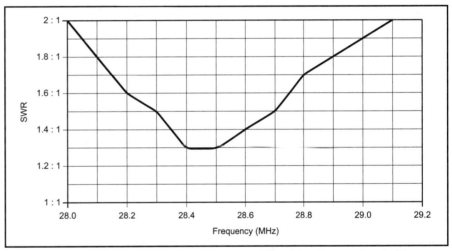

Figure 4—SWR of the K8SYL dipole covers over 1 MHz of the 10-meter band with an SWR of 2:1 or better. If you operate CW, you may want to lower the 10-meter resonant frequency by adding a bit more loading with larger capacitance hats.

Notes

[1] L. Wolfgang and J. Kleinman, *Now You're Talking!*, ARRL, Newington, CT, 2000.
[2] L. Wolfgang, *The ARRL General Class License Manual*, ARRL, Newington, CT, 2000.
[3] C. Hutchinson and R. D. Straw, *Simple and Fun Antennas for Hams*, ARRL, Newington, CT, 2002.
[4] J. W. (Rus) Healy, *Antenna Here is a Dipole*, QST, Jun 1991, pp 23-26.

In addition to Amateur Radio, the author enjoys reading, gardening and spending time with family—especially her granddaughter, Briana. You can contact Sylvia at 9145 Bliss Rd, Lake Odessa, MI 48849; k8syl@ starband.net.

Delta Loop Collinear Antennas

If one delta loop is good, more can be even better.

James K. Boomer, W9UJ

The full-wave delta loop antenna has been described in detail in the Amateur Radio literature.[1,2] We can get substantial directivity gain by building multielement delta loops in Yagi configurations. We can also get substantial directivity gain by stringing two or more full-wave delta loops end to end, forming a collinear array and feeding the loops in phase. These arrays are easy to build, and their bidirectional pattern provides usable gain over a single loop. While the peak response on harmonics is at higher than optimum angles, there is still usable gain at low angles.

Configuration of the W9UJ Two-Element Delta Loop Collinear Array

In 1994 I put up a two element delta loop collinear array that is still up there. I am blessed with 90 foot tall oak trees, and have room for a 40 meter, two-element collinear array tied between two of them (See Figure 1). The ends of the array are about 80 feet above the ground, with the center at about 70 feet. This antenna has been an excellent performer. It also performs well on harmonics of 7 MHz, which gives me 20, 15 and 10 meter coverage.

Construction

Selecting the proper wire is the key to wire antenna longevity. I have had the best luck with #12 AWG solid copperweld (copper plated steel) wire. It's a challenge to work with, and you have to be careful not to kink it, but I find it well worth the effort. [Some find stranded copperweld a good compromise that is more flexible and easier to work with. — *Ed.*] Of course, you can use larger gauge copperweld for longer antennas.

Wire Length

I calculated the delta loop wire length using the usual quad loop formula, L (feet) = $1005/f$(MHz). At a design frequency of 7.025 MHz, this results in 143 feet of wire per loop, or a 47 foot 8 inch length of wire on each of the three sides of an equilateral triangular delta loop. I had sufficient space to separate the loops by 23 feet 10 inches, however, you can separate them further if you desire.

To anchor the ends of the array, I ran a length of #12 AWG copperweld wire from each end insulator to the tree branch, threading it through a length of garden hose around the tree branch to keep the wire from embedding the tree. You can also use a large screw eye, instead of the garden hose approach. I did a standard wire wrap, being careful not to nick the wire. I also left enough sag in the system to avoid breakage in high winds. You can use any strain relief method you desire.

Antenna Feed Subsystem

For maximum weather and aging resistance, I used a coaxial cable feed system with a balun connected to each loop's apex feed point. I used 1:1 voltage baluns because I had them on hand, but I strongly recommend 1:1 current baluns, which provide superior current balancing performance and have less loss than voltage baluns.[3]

My feed apexes are some distance from the station feed line entry point, so I needed to use a length of transmission line from each loop to that entry point.

A half wavelength, or a multiple of a half wavelength of transmission line is a 1:1 impedance transformer, and the input impedance of each of my delta loops is about 150 Ω at the design frequency.[4] I used a half wavelength of coaxial cable from each loop balun to the station lead-in entry point outside the house. Since the impedance looking into each of the half wavelength lines is about 150 Ω, simply terminating the two lines in a coaxial T connector results in a 75 Ω impedance looking into the third port of the T connector. With the same length line to each loop, this provides the required in-phase feed for the two loops.

In addition, I used hooks under the rear eave of the house to support the half wavelength coaxial feed cables from the two loop baluns. Then I simply connected the coax T to them, and to the lead-in coax, which routes through the attic, down the inside of a wall and into the station.

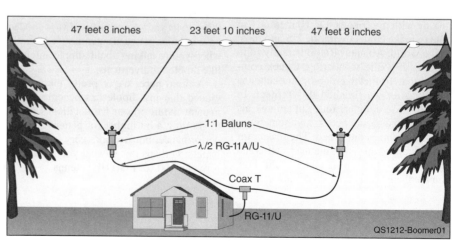

Figure 1 — The W9UJ two element delta loop collinear antenna array.

[1]Notes appear on page 106.

The physical length of a half wavelength of transmission line is calculated as $L (\lambda/2) = (491.8/f) \times V_F$. Where, L is the length in feet, f; the frequency in MHz and V_F is the relative velocity factor of the transmission line.[5]

You can use 50 or 75 Ω coaxial cable for the half wavelengths, or multiples thereof, and for the lead-in to the station. I used RG-11A/U 75 Ω coax since I had it on hand, but RG-11 (Belden 8238) will work just fine. Also, RG-213 (Belden 8267) is a good 50 Ω coax choice. The velocity factor of both of these cables is 0.66, so, a half wavelength of either of these cables is 46 feet 2 inches at 7.025 MHz. The matched loss in each half wavelength cable is about 0.2 dB at 7 MHz, and 0.6 dB at 30 MHz, which is reasonable.[6] The additional loss due to SWR is small, since the modeled SWR at the T connector is reasonable on all bands.

The stability and weatherproof characteristics of coaxial cable systems are hard to beat, but you can also use balanced transmission lines from the loop apexes to the station or its lead-in entry point. Remember, however, that snow, ice, rain, soiling and aging (in the case of window line) change the characteristic impedance and may increase the loss in these lines.

Ladder line has a velocity factor of 0.95, so, the physical length of a half wavelength at 7.025 MHz is 66 feet 6 inches. The loss in a half wavelength of this line is about 0.1 dB at 30 MHz. You can also use open-wire line (wire with spacer insulators), which has extremely low loss and a velocity factor of 0.97.

Insulators and Connections

Figure 2 shows how to string the wire through the end insulators. I used a wire tie to insure that the insulator stayed at a fixed point on the loop. Do this at each end of each loop's flattop and solder the wire wraps (four places total). Be careful not to nick the wire.

Use porcelain or similar insulators for each loop feed point. Thread each end of the loop through each end of the center insulator, loop it back and carefully twist the wire around the loop wire to secure it. Use a short length of wire to hang the balun from the center hole in the center insulator. Then, you can make the connections from the balun to each end of the loop wire, leaving a small "drip loop." Solder all loop wire terminations and wraps. To achieve in-phase feed, be sure that you connect the two baluns' terminals to like ends of the loops' center insulator terminations. Use coax connector sealant on all coaxial cable connections, to protect them from the weather.

If using balanced transmission line, connect the balanced transmission line directly to the loop center insulators, using appropriate strain relief (see below). Make sure you connect the lines so that like ends of the loops are connected in phase. That is, the left and right ends of one loop's center insulator terminations need to be electrically connected to the corresponding left and right ends of the other loop's center insulator terminations when the two transmission lines are paralleled at the station lead-in entry point, as described below.

Use a center insulator intended for the application that provides the required strain relief, such as the Ladder-Lock center insulator for window line (available from most dealers). Also, use appropriate anchors for the transmission line at the station lead-in entry point. In the case of window line, I use the plastic beverage/ladder line standoff insulators (available from Radioware in packages of 25). At the station lead-in entry point, connect the ends of the balanced transmission line together in parallel. Make sure you connect the wires to maintain the in-phase feed. If you elect to connect your equipment to the balanced line, simply splice the required length of transmission line lead-in to the point where the transmission lines from the loops are paralleled. Use a 75 Ω transmission line (75 Ω transmitting twin lead) to minimize VSWR in the station area, since the impedance looking into the paralleled half wavelengths or multiples thereof is about 75 Ω at the design frequency.

For the coaxial cable feed to the station equipment, install a 1:1 current balun at the station lead-in entry point by connecting the paralleled transmission lines to the balun terminals, and running coax to your equipment. You can also use 50 Ω coax if you desire with negligible performance difference.

Loop End-to-End Separation

The loop end-to-end separation is not critical, with increasing gain as the separation increases, until after about ½ wavelength the

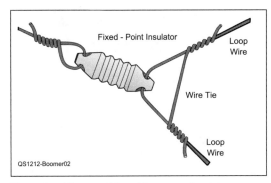

Figure 2 — The use of ties at the corner insulators, as shown, keeps the corners in place.

pattern starts to fragment as shown on 15 meters in Figure 4 (C). At 67 feet separation, for example, the 40 meter 15° elevation gain increases by almost 3 dB. This is obviously a trade off depending on how clean a pattern you want on each band. I used an egg strain insulator in the middle of the section of wire separating the two loops. You may need more strain insulators, depending on how far you separate the ends of the loops. Space the strain insulators at about 14 feet or less to avoid resonance at any operating frequency up to 30 MHz.

Three Element and Four Element Delta Loop Collinear Array Geometry and Feed

The geometry is similar to the two loop array, with the three or four elements positioned end to end and fed in phase. Note that the nominal resonant impedance looking into the combined (paralleled) half wavelength, or multiples of a half wavelength, transmission lines from the loop feed points will be 150/3 = 50 Ω for the three element array, and 150/4 = 37.5 Ω for the four element array. So combining the transmission line inputs will make a nominal 1:1 VSWR match for 50 Ω coax lead-in to the station for the three element array and 1.33:1 VSWR for the four element array.

Performance:

The standing wave ratio (SWR) of my array

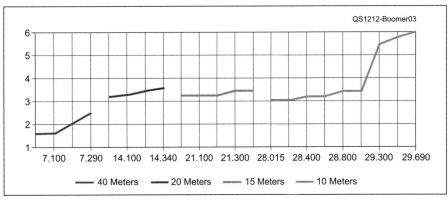

Figure 3 — Measured SWR of two element delta loop collinear array.

Table 1
Two, Three and Four Element Delta Loop Collinear Array Performance Data

Elements	Frequency (MHz)	Elevation Angle (°)	Intensity (dBi)	Beamwidth (°)
1	7	30	6.4	92
1	7	15	3.7	85
2	7	30	8.4	55
2	7	15	5.7	50
2	14	50	9.5	38.4
2	14	15	7.9	26
2	21	45	6.9	26
2	21	10	5.4	22
2	28	60	9.7	24
2	28	10	7.2	12
3	7	15	7.4	33
3	14	15	9.6	16
3	21	10	7.0	13.8
3	28	10	9.0	6.8
4	7	15	8.6	25
4	14	15	10.8	12
4	21	10	8.2	10
4	28	10	10.1	3.4

(see Figure 3) permits the use of a modest antenna coupler to achieve a very low SWR at the transmitter/receiver. The two element delta loop collinear antenna directivity patterns are shown in Figure 4.

The key two, three and four element delta loop collinear array performance data are shown in Table 1 in comparison with a single delta loop. The three and four element arrays provide more gain as expected. Their radiation patterns are similar to the two element array, but the lobes (beamwidths) are narrower, since the gain is greater. If you have some flexibility on positioning one of these arrays, you can set the system up to have particular lobes aimed at selected station locations.

Notes
[1] F. Koontz, WA2WVL, "A Quad Loop Revisited," *QST*, May 2006, pp 39-40.
[2] W. Orr, W6SAI, and S. Cowan, W2LX. *The Radio Amateur Antenna Handbook*, Radio Publications, Inc.
[3] W. Maxwell, W2DU, *Reflections II Transmission Lines and Antennas*, 2nd Edition, Chapter 21, "Some Aspects of the Balun Problem." Worldradio Books,
[4] *The ARRL Antenna Book,* 22nd Edition. Available from your ARRL dealer or the ARRL Bookstore, ARRL order no. 6948. Telephone 860-594-0355, or toll-free in the US 888-277-5289; **www.arrl.org/shop**; **pubsales@arrl.org**.
[5,6] See Note 4.

James K. (Jim) Boomer, W9UJ, has been licensed since 1947. He is active on 40 through 10 meters. Jim holds a BSEE degree from the University of Nebraska, and retired in April 2000 after 46 years in the electronics business.

He was a radio design engineer and project engineer at Collins Radio Company from 1954-1964. While at Collins, he was the project engineer on their 62S-1 VHF Converter for the Collins S-Line amateur radio equipment. He took a leave of absence from 1954 to 1957 to serve in the United States Air Force as a jet fighter pilot and instructor pilot.

From 1964 to 1966, Jim was employed at The National Cash Register Company (NCR) where he was project engineer on UHF rescue beacons and a state-of-the-art UHF Homing Receiver for NASA's early space shots.

From 1966 until 2000, Jim was employed at The Magnavox Company (now Raytheon) as senior staff engineer, project engineer, engineering section manager and marketing product manager. He was project engineer on the AN/URC-64 state-of-the-art survival radio used by airmen in Vietnam among other projects.

Jim can be reached at 4031 Dalewood Dr, Fort Wayne, IN 46815 or at **jkboomer1@frontier.com**.

For updates to this article, see the *QST* Feedback page at www.arrl.org/feedback.

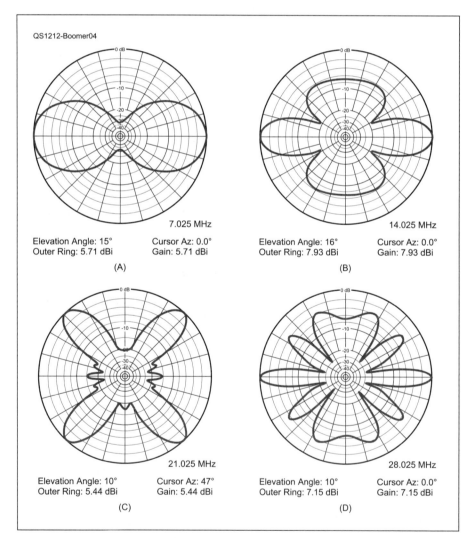

Figure 4 — Azimuth plots of the two element delta loop collinear on the 7- (at A), 14- (at B), 21- (at C) and 28-MHz (D) bands. For 40 and 20 meters, the azimuth pattern at 15° elevation is shown, while 10° was used on the two higher bands, corresponding to the Table 1 data.

Moving Yet Another Band Lower with that HF Loop

Through clever matching techniques, you can operate on 160 meters with your 40 meter loop.

Dave Robertson, KE5QWP

A couple of years ago *QST* published my article describing a method for using a selected transmission line length and a single capacitor to make a half wavelength HF loop resonate.[1] The original motivation was my desire to work 80 meters by way of the single 40 meter full wave loop I had managed to squeeze into the attic. That was after my initial attempts to make the loop bigger had resulted in putting my foot through the kitchen ceiling and a subsequent family ban on more attic wiring adventures.

Don't ask me why, but for some reason 160 meters, the band that I could not yet work, became my next *failure is not an option* tuning project. I started to stare at the *EZNEC* impedance characteristics of the full wave 40 meter loop at 1.8 MHz to figure out what the challenges might be to add that band.[2] Note that the perimeter of the loop is a quarter wavelength at this frequency. The model predicted impedance is in the vicinity of 6-7 Ω resistance and around 1000 Ω of inductive reactance (6 + j1000).

Part of the reason I went to the single capacitor method described in the earlier article is that I prefer capacitors versus inductors for the tuning of compromise antennas. That makes me like loops versus dipoles (short dipoles are capacitive and require series loading coils while short loops are inductive). Big, continuously tunable capacitors are still pretty easy to find and are not prone to the same resistive losses as the big coils needed at low frequencies to tune dipoles or verticals. I also like loops because a big array of ground radials is not required, as one would require for a 160 meter vertical monopole.

Sizing and Gathering the Pieces

Anyway, back to 6 Ω of resistance and 1000 Ω of inductance per the *EZNEC* model. I knew that a material part of this would be loss resistance (versus radiation resistance) but I resolved to make the best use of whatever radiation resistance was there.

[1]Notes appear on page 109.

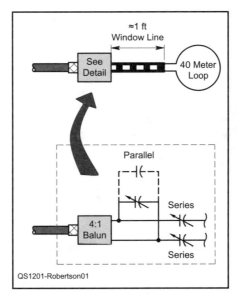

Figure 1 — Schematic layout of capacitor tuned 160 meter ¼ wave loop.

The challenge would be to cancel the inductance by adding series capacitance. What one needs to watch out for is high voltage and somewhat high current. If we want to get all the power into the 6 Ω, the current will be $\sqrt{(P/6)}$. For a power of 100 W, the current will be in the vicinity of 4 A. Due to the 1000 Ω of inductive reactance, there will be 4 kV between the antenna terminals.

With a voltage of 4 kV applied to the series capacitance, it helps to reduce the stress on the capacitors by splitting the voltage across two, one per feeding side. As I've visited swap meets and searched around on the Internet, I've found it relatively easy to gather an inventory of doorknob type and transmitting variable capacitors rated for several kilovolts and 5-10 A. I knew that I would need to fine tune the total series capacitance, but I decided not to be so concerned about exact balance and went for a reasonably close value fixed capacitor on one side of the antenna feed and a beefy air variable on the other. The required capacitance on each side would (in theory) be in the vicinity of 200 pF — a nice round value for fixed capacitors and nicely in the range of most of the air variables I've collected over time.

The Bulb Comes On

Then the "aha moment" based on my learning from the half wave loop exercise appeared. Having resonated the large inductance, matching to 50 Ω via a standard tuner would be practical but somewhat loss prone with the usual commercial T-network configuration. When I was tuning the half wave loop, I'd adjusted the length of the transmission line to achieve a relatively small inductive component, then used a single large parallel capacitor to achieve a final impedance match. What I came to realize was that I could add just a little less series capacitance than was needed to cancel all of the inductance (for the quarter wavelength loop), then use a single parallel capacitor to do the final matching. In effect, we create a balanced L network with series L and parallel C, a well known configuration for efficiently matching a very low impedance to a higher transmission line impedance. The L is leftover inductance of the antenna, once most it is offset by series capacitance.

So now I have two big air variables, one in series with one antenna leg and the other in parallel with the input. I also have a big fixed capacitor in the opposite antenna leg. Off I went to try for a match (see Figure 1). After lots of experimentation, juggling and more than a few sparks and minor RF burns (I eventually learned to wear gloves and safety glasses), I managed to get a nice match with capacitances somewhat higher than 200 pF per side and a parallel capacitance of a few thousand picofarads (see Figures 2 and 3). The size of the series capacitors implied that the actual inductance of my particular loop was somewhat lower than that predicted by the simulation. No doubt this has something to do with the fact that it is in an attic and wraps around all manner of other attic stuff.

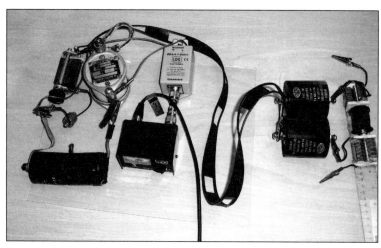

Figure 2 — Plexiglas breadboard contains series and parallel capacitors I normally use as well as balun and an SWR bridge for tuning feedback. The additional capacitors were added to reduce overall series capacitance and spread out the higher voltages (to the right of the window line) when I fed the temporary 200 ft loop.

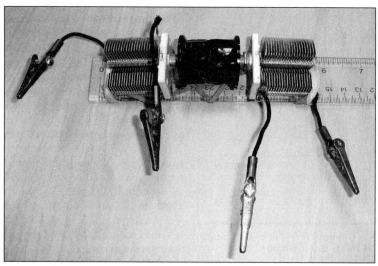

Figure 3 — I found a way to fudge a balanced, isolated pair of variable capacitors for series-C adjustment. The tuning knobs are taped together.

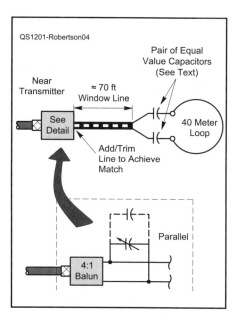

Figure 4 — Schematic of the remotely tuned loop antenna system.

Practical Simplifications and Generalization

One thing I learned was that trying to build the high value capacitor with a significant variable component can take quite a few parallel parts. The required capacitance can be significantly reduced by matching to a higher Z_0. I found insertion of a 4:1 balun prior to the capacitors (on the radio side) made life much easier. The size of the series capacitors hardly changes as this is done, since they are needed to cancel almost all of the antenna's inductance, in either case.

The above raises an entire range of medium size loop design options. There has always been something of a gray area in antenna literature between *large loops*, loops with perimeters greater than a half wavelength, and *small loops*, loops much smaller than a half wavelength. The latter, often referred to as magnetic loops, are often built with pipes and welds so as to minimize loss resistance — generally the major performance limitation of small loops with fractions of an ohm of radiation resistance.

Loops smaller than a half wavelength are always inductive so can be resonated with capacitors. Inductance and resistance decrease as the loop's size decreases. The smaller the loop, the more constant the radiating current around it. This leads to radiation pattern attributes that resemble the attributes of small magnetic loops. As the loop becomes smaller (relative to a half wavelength), where it is fed (side or bottom) becomes less and less important and some good low angle radiation characteristics can be achieved without a big ground radial array. Somewhere around a quarter of a wavelength, the radiation resistance drops to less than 1 Ω and wire and connection losses get to be an overwhelming factor with efficiency quickly dropping below 10% and the magnetic loop effects predominate.

More recently, I had opportunity to use some temporary space, sufficiently large to hang an oddly shaped, side fed 200 foot loop. This is nearly a half wavelength on 160 meters, and *EZNEC* predicted around 2500 Ω inductance plus around 10 Ω of resistance at the feed point. The analysis above helped me to tune this up in a snap. In this case, given even higher series capacitor voltages, I started using three layers of series capacitors (the additional two layers are to the right of the window line in Figure 2) in order to divide the high voltage.

All of the loop systems I tuned had a wide enough SWR bandwidth to allow operation over the most useful part of the 160 meter CW band without constant tuning. This is a plus for medium loops versus the small magnetic loops, which need to be tuned for even small frequency excursions but is also an indicator of lower efficiency, something the original choice of wire leaves me the victim of.

Getting the Tuner Closer to Home

The above three-capacitor discussion was all in the context of tuning elements placed at the loop feed point. That means elimination of all transmission line loss due to mismatch and simple calculations. Unfortunately, it is not always convenient or even possible to place a bunch of adjustable tuning components right at the feed point. My feed point is up in the attic and going in there every time I want to tune to a new frequency range gets old very fast. Here's the remote tuning strategy I chose,

Figure 5 — With the single tuning element used at the antenna feed point (see Figure 4), I can tune the system in the shack (letting ladder line do some of the tuning job). A little less power efficiency but fewer "moving parts."

which made use of all of my learning:

- Link the loop feed location to the shack (or wherever the variable tuning components are best located) via window line, so that power loss due to the high SWR can be minimized. The length of the 400 Ω line I started with was about 70 feet (around an eighth of a wavelength at 160 meters). I had quite a bit of slack and found myself trimming off several feet to achieve my final tuning objective, as described below.

- Put a fixed high voltage capacitor in series with each wire at the feed point. The capacitance is small enough to cancel all of the antenna inductance and add even more capacitive reactance to offset the phase and impedance shift imposed by the transmission line. My choice of a 150 pF capacitor added to each leg (for 75 pF total effective series capacitance) more than offsets approximately 1000 Ω of antenna inductive reactance (moving R + j1000 to R − j180). This impedance is then transformed to one with a positive reactance component after the transmission line is added. Note (again) that the antenna-capacitor-transmission line combination needs to present a net (and relatively small) inductance for the L tuning technique to work.

- Apply the L tuning strategy as described above. This is where I applied my earlier lesson that fine adjustment of transmission line length and parallel capacitance is a practical alternative implementation of the L matching network for impedances in the range of interest, the range of impedances on the top left quadrant of a Smith Chart (see Figure 4).

In my case, care in calculating the size of the feed capacitors considering the antenna impedance and transmission line length allowed me to just trim the length of the transmission line to a point at which an optimum inductive reactance plus resistance combination for matching was reached. Then I was able use a single variable capacitor, connected in parallel with the antenna side of my balun (an alternative could have been a large doorknob capacitor in parallel with a smaller air variable) to achieve the match. This was trial and error, though the math told me that my starting point was close.

In general, as long as R is well below the characteristic impedance one is trying to match to (200 Ω for my case, because of the 4:1 balun inserted prior to interface with the 50 Ω rig) and a relatively small residual inductive reactance, it will be possible to just trim or add transmission line (see Figure 5). This will mostly adjust the inductive component, though there is some small change in the real part as well. The parallel capacitance is adjusted at the end in order to achieve a perfect match.

Although window line minimizes loss pretty well, one wants to be mindful of the fact that some significant power loss will occur as a result of the high SWR on the run to the shack even with low loss line. This is a cost of this remote tuning design and sacrifices something on the order of 30% of the available power in order to provide tuning convenience.[3] Larger loops (with higher R values) or shorter transmission line runs would help reduce this. I thank Steve Hunt, G3TXQ, for bringing my attention to this type of transmission line tuning loss following my previous article and leading me to the referenced tool for estimation of transmission line impacts. I take 30% seriously, so I go to the trouble to remove this compromise and go back to the full tuner, right at the antenna, when conditions are not great or I'm going for maximum distance.

I've really enjoyed exploring top band (160 meters) with these compromise loops. My 100 W have allowed me to reach the farthest continental states and a couple neighboring countries — not so bad for an indoor 160 meter antenna. I am thankful for all of the big gun stations with Beverage receive antennas, kilowatt transmitters and huge outdoor antennas who offset my compromises. Locals are easy, as NVIS-type radiation is included at no additional cost.

Notes
[1] D. Robertson, KE5QWP, "Squeezing the Next Lower Band Out of Your Big HF Loop," *QST*, Oct 2009, pp 36-38.
[2] Several versions of *EZNEC* antenna modeling software are available from developer Roy Lewallen, W7EL, at **www.eznec.com**.
[3] Calculated using tool at **www.vk1od.net/calc/tl/tllc.php**.

Photos by the author.

ARRL member and General class licensee Dave Robertson, KE5QWP, received his first US call sign in October 2007, after multiple decades away from the hobby. His original experience with ham radio occurred when he was a teenager in the early 1970s using his original Canadian call, VE3HHR.

*Dave has a Bachelor's Degree in Electrical Engineering from the University of Waterloo and a Master's Degree in Electronics Engineering from Carleton University, Canada. Dave is Vice President of Engineering at ZixCorp (**www.zixcorp.com**), a provider of secure, hosted e-mail encryption services.*

Dave lives in Richardson (near Dallas), Texas with his wife and two daughters. He enjoys skiing and fishing when he's not moving wires and trying for DX. You can reach Dave at 3906 Sharp Ln, Richardson, TX 75082 or at **drobertson@zixcorp.com**.

The Shared Apex Loop Array

This compact directional wideband receiving antenna can reduce interference.

Mark Bauman, KB7GF

Effective receiving antennas are becoming an indispensible part of our amateur arsenal as we battle interference from both natural and man-made sources. Many of us do not have the acreage to erect directional antennas, especially on the lower bands, so we use shortened verticals and low hanging dipoles, which provide essentially omnidirectional response. As a result, our ears are bombarded with signals and interference from all directions when our transmitting antenna doubles as our receiving antenna.

Antenna Concept

To assist in this battle, I designed a compact directional receiving antenna that effectively reduces interference over a wide frequency range. The array described here is compact, having a loop spacing of only 2 inches, a 10 foot tall mast, an array length of 20 feet and a base height of 6 inches. In this configuration, the array delivers directivity over a frequency range of 500 kHz to 22 MHz and exceptional sensitivity above 6 MHz.

A ground mounted version of the shared apex loop array is shown in Figure 1 and schematically in Figure 2. The antenna utilizes two closely spaced loops that are interconnected via a delay line to deliver healthy front to side and front to back ratios over a wide frequency range. A non-conductive mast guides the vertical side of two identical right-triangular-shaped wire loops to form a common or shared apex. Each loop is draped in a symmetrical manner about the mast, oriented in a common vertical plane, and held in tension by an anchor forming a horizontal base that is spaced a few inches above the ground.

Each loop is constructed as an endless wire loop that is routed through a group of ferrite cores forming a current transformer acting as a coupling link. The coupling link is positioned at a distance from the mast and is connected so that the anchor side of the transformer is connected to the center coax conductor of a loop feed line. The loop feed line from loop 1 is connected to a reference line. The opposite end of the reference line connects to an input port of a combiner amplifier that will be described later in this article.

The loop 2 coupling link is positioned at a distance from the mast and is connected so that the anchor side of the transformer is connected to the center coax conductor of a loop feed line. The opposite end of the feed line is connected to a delay line. The opposite end of the delay line is connected to a second port of the combiner amplifier. The output signal from the array is delivered from the combiner amplifier to the receiver.

The array operates using the true-time-delay principle of operation by combining signals from loop 1 with delayed signals from loop 2. Using this principle, a time delay difference is selected so that signals arriving from a direction that is opposite the favored direction, when combined, are maximally attenuated. If the array is configured in this manner, signals arriving from the favored direction are attenuated less than signals coming from other directions. This directional effect is largely frequency independent up to a maximum frequency.

> **I designed a compact directional receiving antenna that effectively reduces interference over a wide frequency range.**

The array also benefits from its employment of electrically small loop elements that exhibit a profoundly bidirectional characteristic, with lobes off of their ends and sharp nulls to their broadside. The combination of the small loop element and true time delay operation join together to provide the horizontal response as modeled with *4NEC2* and shown in Figure 3. This pattern shape is largely preserved over the frequency range, but the forward gain decreases significantly as the operating frequency is lowered.

Combiner Amplifier

The combiner amplifier shown in Figure 2 is a three terminal device that must provide proper termination for the delay and reference lines, port-to-port timing and amplitude accuracy as well as amplification. It is essential to understand the port characteristics of the combiner amplifier before we consider its internal circuitry.

The input impedance of PORT A and PORT B of the combiner amplifier must closely match the characteristic impedance of the coax line (in this case 75 Ω) over the operating frequency range. This is essential to maintain a consistent time delay through the delay line, and help to ensure that signals are absorbed rather than reflected. The input impedance must also be maintained at PORT A and PORT B even though the source impedance from each loop may vary widely over the operating frequency range. So, it is beneficial that PORT A and PORT B be isolated from one another. Also, the input impedance of PORT A and PORT B must be maintained despite various OUT loading conditions.

In addition, the group delay and amplitude for signals entering from PORT A and PORT B to the OUT terminal should be closely matched over the frequency range to ensure proper operation. For this array, a group delay accuracy of 2 nanoseconds or better and an amplitude accuracy of 5% are desirable over the frequency range.

A block diagram of a matched amplifier version of the combiner amplifier is shown in Figure 4. The signal from PORT A is routed to the input of amplifier A1, and delivered to a winding of the transformer T1. The signal from PORT B is connected to the input of amplifier A2, and is delivered to a second winding of transformer T1. The OUT port is connected to a third winding of T1 and represents the sum of the signals from loop 1 and loop 2. For best results, both amplifiers should offer isolation between the input and output, be balanced to minimize second order harmonics and should have a high compression point.

Another version of the combiner amplifier utilizing a passive input combiner (C1) is shown in Figure 5. Here, the signals from PORT A and PORT B are combined in coupler C1. One suitable circuit for such a coupler can be found in an early edition of *The ARRL Handbook for Radio Amateurs*.[1] The output from the combiner is connected to the input of amplifier A1. Control of the group delay and amplitude accuracy between PORT A and PORT B and the output of the combiner C1 is essential for proper operation. For best results, amplifier A1 should offer isolation between the input and output, be balanced to minimize second order harmonics and have a high compression point.

Each implementation of the combiner amplifier has advantages and disadvantages. The matched amplifier version shown in Figure 4 offers more sensitivity at the expense of increased complexity, challenging inter-

[1] *The ARRL Handbook for Radio Communications*, 1994 edition, Chapter 25, p 37.

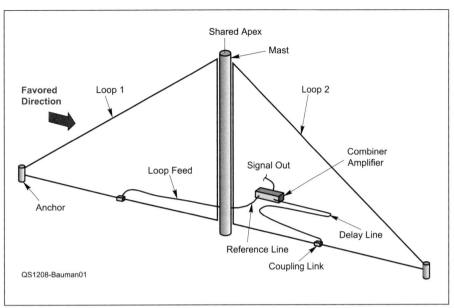

Figure 1 — Sketch of a basic two element shared apex loop array.

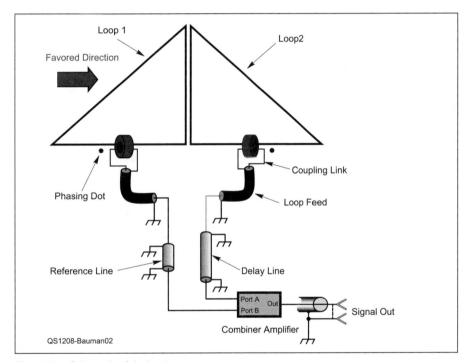

Figure 2 — Schematic of the basic array.

amplifier matching, and susceptibility to AM broadcast band intermodulation products. The passive combiner version shown in Figure 5 provides better immunity to AM broadcast band intermodulation products (since the signals are combined and attenuated before amplification). However, this version has reduced sensitivity (due to the 6 dB loss of the combiner, which adds to the overall noise figure of the system), and may exhibit compromised amplitude and group delay accuracy when applied over a wide frequency range.

Remember that any group delay difference between PORT A and PORT B must be combined with the delay difference provided by the combination of the reference line and the delay lines. For best results, it is helpful to measure the delay of the combination before deployment. Specifically, the delay can be measured by employing a function generator as a trigger input for an oscilloscope and routing the function generator signal between the delay line and the reference line to measure the time delay through the system. For this array, and using the combiner amplifier,

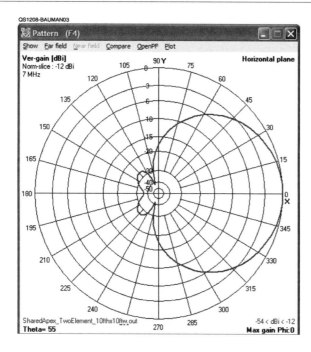

Figure 3 — Horizontal response of the array using a *4NEC2* Model at 7 MHz.

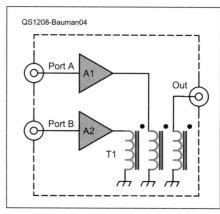

Figure 4 — Block diagram of an active version of a matched combiner amplifier.

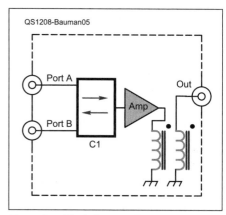

Figure 5 — Block diagram of a passive version of a combiner amplifier.

the combination time delay difference was measured to be 8 ns.

Loop Construction

The construction of a shared apex loop array is relatively straightforward and will be described in detail below. A close-up view of a coupling link is shown in Figure 6. The link is prepared by first selecting a group of six ferrite cores (Laird Technologies FB095051-000 available from Digi-Key, PN#240-2277ND) from a supply of cores, and stringing them together in a line to test their combined inductance using a single turn of wire. At room temperature, use a target inductance of 70 ±1 µH. To achieve this, it is often necessary to replace individual cores from the string with other cores, since individual core permeability can vary by as much as 30% from core to core. Once the proper inductance has been achieved, stack the cores on a dowel. Use a piece of heat shrink tubing or electrical tape to retain the cores. Then, route a piece of #18 AWG hookup wire through the cores and connect each end to a coax connector to form a secondary winding. Mark the end of the link that is connected to the center of the coax connector with a red piece of electrical tape to indicate the phase of the transformer. Prepare a second coupling link in a similar manner.

Next, prepare the mast by first obtaining a 10 foot length of 2 inch, schedule 40 PVC pipe. Drill a pair of ⅜ inch holes, spaced about 1 inch apart and near the top of the pipe, and 12 inches from the bottom of the pipe keeping the holes in vertical alignment along the pipe as shown in Figure 7. Also, perform this operation on the opposite side of the pipe so there are a total of eight holes drilled in the pipe. At this point, if you desire to make the antenna portable, you may cut the length in half and use a pipe coupler to reassemble the pipe so that it can be disassembled and easily transported in a car.

Now, prepare the loop wires for loop 1 and loop 2. It is important that each loop be constructed so that each has an identical length and shape. To accomplish this, first pre-cut two lengths of #18 AWG wire to a length of 32 feet 5 inches. Then, take one of the wires and route it through the guide holes formed in the mast so that the loop wire exits as shown in Figure 7. Take the same loop wire and route it through the pair of vertically aligned guide holes near the bottom of the mast so that the loop wire exits from the mast from the bottom-most hole. Repeat these steps for the second loop wire.

Next, select a location for your antenna. Ideally the ground should be reasonably flat and as far away as feasible from buildings and other structures. This is especially important for operation below 2 MHz, where a distance of at least 20 feet is recommended. Obtain four stakes to act as anchors for the guy ropes for the loop as shown in Figure 8, and secure the guy ropes at mid-level to the mast. Select a mast location and an orientation for the loop. Position each anchor at a quadrant and at a distance 11 feet from the

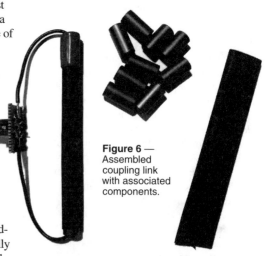

Figure 6 — Assembled coupling link with associated components.

Figure 7 — Top mast section showing guide holes and loop wire routing.

mast location. Next, secure the guy ropes and adjust the mast using a level so that it maintains a vertical stance.

Now, route the first loop wire through one of the coupling links so that the phasing dot is oriented to the anchor side of the loop. Next, splice the two ends of the loop wire to form an endless loop as shown in Figure 9. Then, take a short section of guy rope and prepare a loop tether and secure the tether to one of the anchors. Repeat these steps to prepare the second loop and position it so that it is in the same plane as the first loop. Adjust the loop tethers to ensure the mast continues to maintain its vertical stance.

Figure 8 — Partially constructed array during mast alignment.

Figure 9 — Base of completed array showing link distance and loop splice.

Figure 10 — Coupler stake and coupling link with phasing dot toward anchor.

Now locate a pair of coupler stakes that will support the loop feed and coupling links. Position each of these at a link distance of 60 inches from the mast. Secure the loop feed for each loop to the coupler stake as shown in Figure 10. You may use any suitable length of coax cable, although it is important that both loop feeds be identical. In this array, I used an 8 foot RG-6 cable (75 Ω) with F-Type connectors for each of the loop feeds. Connect a reference line, in this case a 3 foot RG-6 cable, to the loop feed for the favored direction and connect this to PORT B of the combiner amplifier. Also connect the delay line, which is a 12 foot RG-6 cable, to the other loop feed and connect it to PORT A of the combiner amplifier. Finally, route the output signal to the receiver.

We can enhance the operation of this array by adding a switch module to the system as shown in Figure 11. Here, the switch module is located between the loop feed lines and the

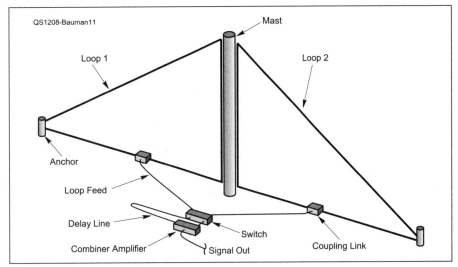

Figure 11 — Sketch of an enhanced two element shared apex loop array with a switching module.

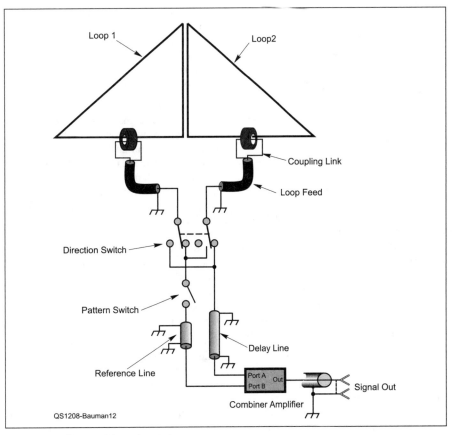

Figure 12 — Sketch of the enhanced array.

Figure 13 — Switching module, combiner amplifier and cabling for the enhanced array.

Figure 16 — Completed four element shared apex loop array utilizing two orthogonally positioned arrays identical to those described in this article.

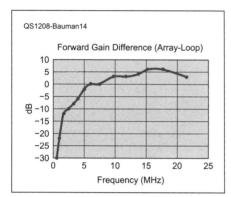

Figure 14 — Graph of the forward gain difference between the described array and single loop element over the operating frequency range.

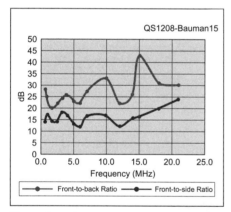

Figure 15 — Graph of the front to back and front to side measurements over the operating frequency range.

patch and delay lines as shown in Figure 12. In this configuration, the delay line is connected to PORT A and the reference line is connected to PORT B of the combiner amplifier. A double pole double throw (DPDT) DIRECTION switch is connected to each of the loop feed lines and acts to select the direction of the array. Signals coming from the direction of the loop that is connected to the reference line will be favored.

A second switch, in this case a single pole single throw (SPST) switch, can be used to select between a unidirectional pattern or bidirectional pattern as shown. This is especially helpful at frequencies below 3 MHz where the sensitivity of the array is much less than that of a single loop. The switch can be implemented as a manual or a relay switch directed by a remote control.

Cabling for the enhanced array is shown in Figure 13. All cables are 75 Ω, RG-6 using Type F connectors. In this picture, the loop feed lines are shown as connected to the switch module (in this case, a remote controlled relay switch). The delay and reference lines are connected between the switch module and the combiner amplifier. The signal out line from the combiner amplifier runs from the array to a receiver in the shack.

As mentioned earlier, the forward gain of the array decreases with decreasing operating frequency. To quantify this effect, I measured the difference between signals received by the array and a single loop element in the array over the frequency range as shown in Figure 14. By inspection, the zero gain point where the gain of the array is equal to a single loop element occurs at about 6 MHz. Above this frequency, the array exhibits some gain over the single loop element. Below this frequency, the forward gain drops dramatically, reaching a low of −30 dB at 500 kHz.

In practice, the noise figure of the combiner amplifier can become the limiting factor during quiet band conditions for frequencies below 5 MHz. During these conditions, and at lower frequencies, it is helpful to be able to remotely switch from the array to the single loop element to hear weak DX. When interference is prevalent, however, the array is useable even down through the entire AM broadcast band where it can parse competing stations sharing the same frequency. The antenna can even be scaled in size to improve the quiet band performance by increasing the size of the loops, increasing the distance from the coupling loops to the mast and increasing the delay line length.

In Figure 15 the front to back and front to side ratios are each plotted over the frequency range. The data used here has been gleaned from over the air testing of the array and an ICOM IC-R71A receiver using manual peak observation readings from the S-meter (assuming 6 dB per S-unit). The data conforms approximately to the chart generated by the 4NEC2 model shown in Figure 3 and confirms the wideband performance of the array.

Other Possibilities

A variation combines two of the two element arrays in an orthogonal manner to cover each of four primary directions. Such an array is shown in Figure 16. Another variation includes using balanced feed lines rather than coax feed lines. Here, the balanced feed lines connect to the coupling link on one end, and the opposite end is connected to a balun. The output of the balun connects to the switch as in Figures 11 and 12.

There is nothing magical about the aspect ratio and size of the loops, and they can be adjusted to meet individual needs. A smaller version would provide even less forward gain, but a higher frequency range. Some aspects of the array are novel. Although I have filed a patent on these features, I encourage amateurs to build and experiment with the shared apex loop array. My hope is that your ears will be pleased with the results.

An article in the September/October 2012 issue of *QEX* will provide additional design information including information on a suitable preamp. This article is available to all ARRL members by clicking on the sample issue at **www.arrl.org/this-month-in-qex**.

ARRL member and Amateur Extra class licensee Mark Bauman, KB7GF, has been licensed as an Amateur Radio operator since 1978. He is also licensed as a professional electrical engineer in the state of Washington and is a registered patent agent. He works as an electrical engineer and patent agent for Nelson Irrigation Corporation and is a small business owner. He lives with his wife and their four children in an antenna challenged neighborhood in College Place, Washington. You may contact Mark at 1910 SE Sunflower Ct, College Place, WA 99324-1781 or at **kb7gf@arrl.net**.

For updates to this article, see the *QST* Feedback page at www.arrl.org/feedback.

Nested Full Wave Delta Loops for 20 and 10 Meters

A full wave delta loop has less width and provides more gain than a dipole.

Don McMinds, K7DM

I moved from Oregon to my present location in Ocean Shores, Washington 3 years ago. In Oregon, I had over 2 acres to work with and was blessed with a five element tribander at 55 feet as well as a full wave delta loop for 40 meters. Unfortunately, my present location is situated on a very narrow lot that does not have adequate room for the tower. After considering several antennas, I decided that a delta loop would be the best solution. I built my previous 40 meter delta loop based on an excellent 1984 *QST* article by Doug DeMaw, W1FB (SK), and Lee Aurick, W1SE (SK).[1] The authors pointed out several advantages of a delta loop:
- It doesn't require a ground screen.
- It doesn't need to be perfectly vertical.
- It provides some gain over a dipole.
- It's much less noisy than a vertical.
- It can be fed at any of several points.
- Its segment lengths don't have to be equal.

Design

My original plan was to orient a 20 meter loop in an apex up configuration on a 30 foot mast mounted in a 5 foot A-frame tower on the roof. I chose the apex up configuration because a second supporting mast is not possible at my house. I then decided that adding a 10 meter loop would be fairly easy from a mechanical standpoint and would provide another band. The 10 meter loop fits inside the 20 meter loop and is supported by a short length of rope, one end of which tied to its apex insulator and the other end tied to the 20 meter loop apex insulator. The loops are raised and lowered by a halyard rope looped through a pulley at the top of the mast.

The feed point for both loops is at the lower left hand corner which, according to DeMaw and Aurick, provides vertical polarization and a low angle of radiation. The *ARRL Handbook*, 1984 edition, states that "…the main consideration for a good DX antenna is a low angle of radiation. It should be said, however, that most DX antennas for HF work are horizontally polarized." This suggested to me that an apex up corner fed delta loop would be good for DX. [The corner feed provides a mix of both horizontal and vertical polarization. Feeding in the center of the horizontal section will provide

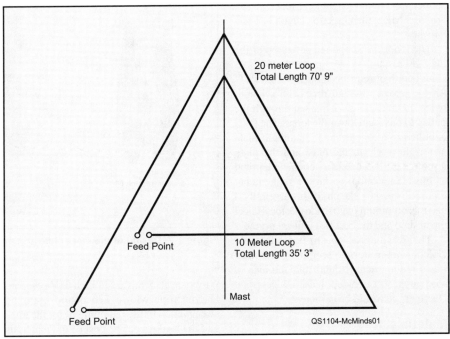

Figure 1 — Design layout of the 10 and 20 meter delta loops.

Hamspeak

Delta loop — Name used to describe a full wave loop antenna configured in triangular shape. The antenna can have its apex either pointing up or down. If fed in the center of its horizontal section it will have horizontal polarization. Often used by itself, it can also be part of a multielement directive array.

Q section — Popular name for a one quarter wave section of transmission line used to transform impedances.

Tribander — Antenna that works on three bands, usually 20, 15 and 10 meters through the use of separate elements per band, traps or a combination. Term is typically applied to commercial Yagi arrays for the three bands.

Yagi — Multielement directive antenna in which many of the elements are not directly connected to the driven element(s). The other elements are parasitic and receive and reradiate energy due to electromagnetic coupling. Often used as a rotatable antenna system in the upper HF through UHF regions.

---

[1]D. DeMaw, W1FB (SK), and L. Aurick, W1SE (SK), "The Full-Wave Delta Loop At Low Height," *QST*, Oct 1984, pp 24-26.

primarily horizontal polarization resulting in higher gain at low angles if the bottom is a reasonable height above ground, at least ½ wavelength. — *Ed.*]

The DeMaw-Aurick article gives formulas for determining the overall length of the loops and for the length of the matching Q section, a quarter wavelength of 75 Ω, RG-59/U coax. The formula for the loop length is L (feet) = 1005/f (MHz). For the design frequencies I used 14.2 MHz for 20 meters and 28.5 MHz for 10 meters. After rounding off, this yields loop lengths of 70 feet 9 inches for 20 meters and 35 feet 3 inches for 10 meters. The original design is shown in Figure 1.

The Q section impedance needs to be between the loop impedance (~100 Ω) and the feed-line impedance (50 Ω). The formula for the Q section is L (feet) = 246 × V/f (MHz), where V is the relative velocity factor of the RG-59U. With the design frequency of 14.2 MHz and a velocity factor of 0.66 for polyethylene dielectric coax, the 20 meter Q section length is 11 feet 5 inches. For 28.5 MHz, the Q section length is 5 feet 8 inches.

The loops are supported at the top of the mast by a stainless steel pulley bolted to a short length of reinforced thick walled PVC. An ultraviolet resistant rope with a length twice the mast height is passed through the pulley to raise and lower the loops. The PVC is bolted to a ⅛ inch thick aluminum plate at a right angle to the mast and the plate is bolted to the mast, a scheme identical to most Yagi boom to mast arrangements. Figure 2 shows a sketch of this assembly. I had the aluminum plate made at a local sheet metal shop and the cost was quite reasonable.

The Washington coast often has some violent winter storms, so guying the mast was a requirement. I didn't like the idea of wire guys, so I decided that a UV resistant Dacron rope would be sufficient.

Materials

My location is less than a mile from the Pacific Ocean so I decided I needed high quality rust resistant wire for the loops. The Wireman (**www.thewireman.com**) offers a product called *Toughcoat Silky*, an insulated #13 AWG 19-strand 40% copper clad steel wire that fit my requirement. I decided to use a Budwig (**www.budwig.com**, also available from The Wireman) HQ-1 dipole center at each feed point. This comes with an SO-239 coax connector and I felt that would be a better way to connect the Q section coax to the loop. I soldered terminal lugs to the center conductor and outer shield of the Q section coax and to the heavy wires of the dipole center. I connected the Q section terminals to the dipole center terminals with #10 stainless steel screws and nuts. The Wireman also has a 3/16 inch UV-resistant Dacron rope with a 770 pound breaking strength that fit my requirement for the guys and the haul rope. The cost of the materials I used, including the mast plate, was less than $200.

Construction and Testing

After assembling the required materials, I decided it would be prudent to erect the mast and antenna on the ground before raising it on the roof. This proved a wise decision because I encountered some mechanical issues that I had overlooked. I started by anchoring the little A-frame tower to the ground using six 1-foot steel tent stakes. The mast consists of three 10-foot sections of steel mast from RadioShack. I bolted the aluminum plate assembly to the top section of the mast (see Figure 3), then bolted the guy supports to the mast just below the aluminum plate.

The first problem occurred when I tried to raise the mast to the top of the tower. There was no way I could do this by myself, and even enlisting the help of a neighbor proved fruitless. At that point I decided it might be a good idea to just use two of the three mast sections, reducing the mast height to 20 feet. Even this shorter length proved difficult to raise, so I pulled up the stakes and placed the tower on its side on the ground. I placed the mast in the tower and then successfully raised this assembly. After staking the tower, I used a large carpenter's level to get the mast as vertical as possible and then secured it to the tower. I staked the guy ropes at 120° intervals and secured them.

Assembling the loops was not a problem. I assembled the 20 meter loop first and connected the Q section at the feed point. After raising it, I checked the assembly with an antenna analyzer. Results were quite good. The analyzer had a reactance of only 2 Ω at 14.2 MHz and the SWR was no more than

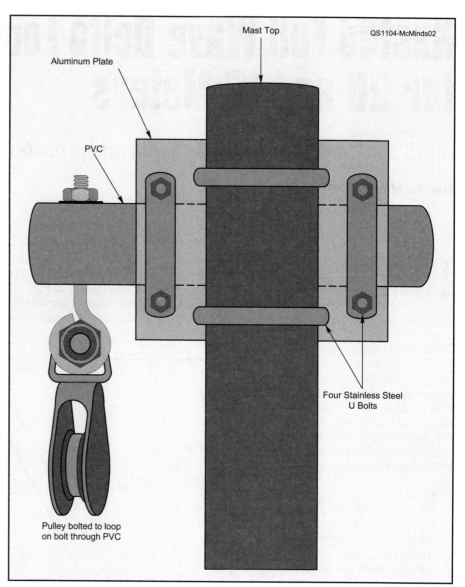

Figure 2 — Design of the mast plate and pulley assembly.

Figure 3 — Aluminum plate and pulley assembly shown bolted to the mast.

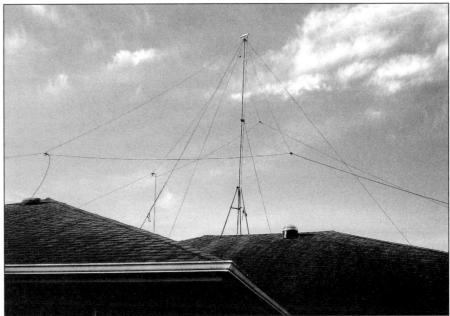

Figure 4 — Loops up!

1.8:1 at any point in the band. I obtained similar results with the 10 meter loop. Both loops were oriented so the plane of the loop was on a line of 010-190°. This placed the centers of the major lobes of the loops at about 115 and 295°, perfect for both stateside contacts and Asian DX.

The second problem occurred after I raised both loops together. With both loops taut, the amount of stress on the mast was more than the guy ropes could handle and the mast was bowed significantly toward the loops. It was obvious that I needed more support on the back side of the mast, the side opposite the loops. Fortunately I had enough Dacron rope to accomplish this and adding an additional guy just above the mid-point of the mast solved the problem.

Final Assembly

The final assembly on the roof occurred a few days later and went without any problems, thanks to the ground testing. I enlisted the help of several friends and we began by positioning the A-frame tower on the roof and aligning it to vertical. We drilled holes in the roof through the holes in the tower's footpads, then laid the tower on its side and inserted the mast with all its ropes attached. It's a good idea to coil the ropes a bit to keep them out of the way, but be sure that you don't coil them so far that you can't reach them after the mast is raised. We raised the tower and mast assembly, positioned the tower so that the holes in its footpads lined up with the holes in the roof, and bolted it securely with 3 inch lag bolts. Using my trusty GPS, I aligned the mast so that the mounting plate at its top was on the desired 010-190° line and then secured it to the tower. We positioned the guy ropes and secured them to 2 inch stainless steel screw eyes screwed into the roof. I used a stainless steel turnbuckle on each guy to aid in adjusting the tension.

Arranging the loops was easy with my friends' help. I tied the haul rope to the 20 meter loop apex insulator and raised the loop so that the apex insulator was at eye level. I tied a 3 foot piece of rope to the 20 meter loop apex insulator and then tied the other end of the rope to the 10 meter apex insulator. I raised the assembly to the top of the mast and my friends, who were holding opposite corners of the horizontal segment of the 20 meter loop (at this point the 10 meter loop was just hanging straight down and out of the way), positioned themselves so the loop was taut, and marked the spots on the roof where the eyebolt anchors should be placed. With the eyebolts in place, the support ropes at the corner apex insulators were secured and the tension was adjusted using turnbuckles.

The same procedure was used to secure the 10 meter loop. The 10 meter loop has equal segments and is slanted about 10°. Because of the narrow width of the roof, the length of the 20 meter loop horizontal segment is 15 feet 9 inches. The lengths of the other two segments are 27 feet 6 inches and the loop is slanted about 40°. I connected the Q sections to both loops' feed points and checked the loops with the antenna analyzer. The results were slightly better than the ground test. The analyzer showed a reactance of only 2 Ω at 14.2 MHz and the SWR was no more than 1.6:1 at any point in the band. The reactance at 28.5 MHz was 3 Ω and the SWR was never more than 1.7, that occurring at 28.75 MHz. I then applied roof sealant around all the screws entering the roof, connected the 50 Ω coax feed lines to the Q sections and tacked the coax down. Mission complete! Figure 4 shows the loops mounted on the roof.

Performance

The loops have been up for over a year and the performance has been all that I could ask. Although they don't compare to the five element tribander I had at my previous station, considering the low cost I'm well-pleased. I've had many stateside contacts on 20 meters and even worked Russia and Japan on 20 meter SSB with excellent reports from both. I'm anxiously awaiting a 10 meter opening to see how that loop will perform. You could use this plan with any combination of loops depending on limitations imposed by your location. So, if space and/or budget constraints are giving you trouble, consider a delta loop or two or even three. I think you'll be happy you did.

Photos by the author.

ARRL member and Amateur Extra class operator Don McMinds, K7DM, has been licensed since 1963. He has previously held calls W6EBI, WA0LGS, KB7JI, WD7X and ZF2QK. He is an avid SSB and CW County Hunter and holds USACA 656. He also has been active in the 10-X International and holds 10-X number 3779. Don earned a BSEE and MA in management from the University of Nebraska. He served 23 years in the US Air Force, retiring in 1982 as a Lieutenant Colonel.

Following his USAF service, he was an engineer at Hewlett-Packard for 17 years before retiring in 1999. While at HP he published two books on UNIX user interface software (Mastering OSF/Motif Widgets and Writing Your Own OSF/Motif Widgets). You can reach Don at 535 E Chance Ala Mer NE, Ocean Shores, WA 98569 or at k7dm@coastaccess.com.

A Simple Broadband 80 Meter Dipole

This easy to make antenna can keep you from getting stuck in one corner of this popular band.

George Prince, N6DNA

For most of my Amateur Radio life I have avoided the 80 meter band. The 80 meter coil on top of my vertical gave such little bandwidth and a dipole was just too long for my location. When solid state transceivers came on the market there was the added concern that moderate antenna standing wave ratio (SWR) would cause the final transistors to cut back power. I was electronically raised with the type 6146 final amplifier tube, but was happy to switch to solid state when the products were offered. Nevertheless, an 80 meter dipole was a dream that recently had caused me to do some investigation and antenna construction.

Can Problems be Resolved?

The biggest problem I had was the narrow bandwidth associated with the usual single wire dipole. I decided that if I did put up a wire dipole I would just cut it for the phone band to be able to work several of my ham friends who had moved to the Midwest and East Coast. Fortunately in the April 2006 issue of *QST* there was an article giving the lowdown about internal antenna tuners.[1] The article took the time to describe the problems associated with 80 meter antennas, giving wonderful graphs of frequency, power loss and SWR with a dipole antenna. Therefore I will not go into the electronic antenna details but will focus on the product and the results.

One of the bits of information deep in my old electronic brain archives was the fact that if you increase the diameter of an antenna radiator you will increase the bandwidth, or as the big boys say, decrease the sharpness of the radiator Q. I was sure there were all sorts of formulas to give me all the

[1] Notes appear on page 121.

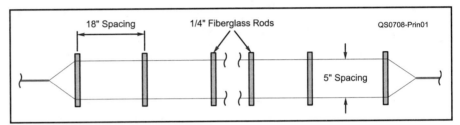

Figure 1 — Broadband 80 meter dipole, final configuration.

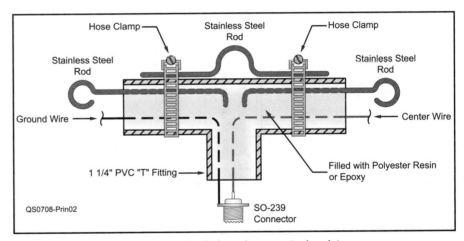

Figure 2 — Detailed view of the author's homebrew center insulator.

large radiator electronic metrics. I began to ask knowledgeable hams about the use of multiwire dipoles. I hoped two wide spaced wires would act as large diameter radiator. The answer I got was yes, but also it was explained to me that such designs were not new. Nonetheless such designs have been found to be effective and more broadband than the single wire dipole.

Making it Come Together
The Antenna Proper

I decided to use two 14 gauge enameled copper wires on each leg. I would try separating the wires, picture a ladder line, by 5 inches and see what would happen. Certainly more separation than 5 inches could be tried. I ordered enough ¼ inch diameter fiberglass solid rod to separate the wires by 5 inches with a spacer on the wire every 18 inches. I used the center frequency of the 80 meter band for the standard one wire formula to get a starting length. The result was 125 feet, or 62.5 feet for each leg. After rolling out the spool of the antenna wire, with the help of my bride, I cut all the wires and ended up with a horrible rats' nest of wire. If you decide to make this antenna,

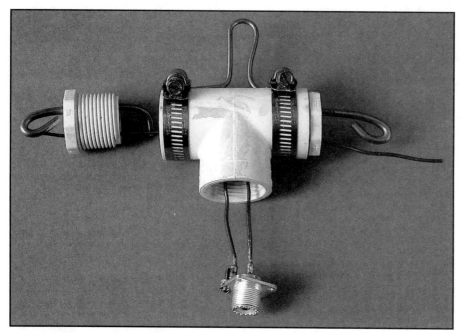

Figure 3 — The pieces of the center insulator before final assembly and sealing.

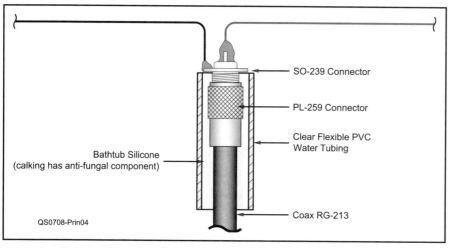

Figure 4 — Waterproof coax cable connection method.

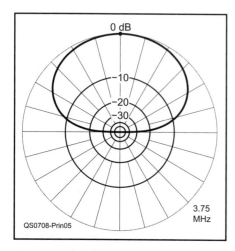

Figure 5 — *EZNEC* plot of broadside antenna elevation pattern.

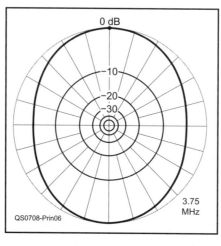

Figure 6 — *EZNEC* plot of antenna azimuth pattern at 30° elevation.

separate the long wires — don't keep them all in a cut bundle!

Spreading the Wires

I drilled each fiberglass rod in a drill press, with a holder to keep the holes aligned; then I threaded each drilled rod onto both wires of the elements. With the wires stretched I then slid the rods to the 18 inch separation and dropped epoxy on each point where the rods touched the wire. This repetitive nonsense almost made me junk the whole project, but I had hopes it would be worth the piecework. The resulting configuration is shown in Figure 1.

Center Insulator

Many varieties of antenna insulators to transition to coax are available on the market, but I chose to make mine from a 1¼ inch schedule 40 white PVC T coupling. The SO-239 female coax receptacle can be pushed into the bottom after the hot and ground wires are soldered onto the connector. I ran the electrical copper wires along the bottom of the fitting and two 10 gauge stainless steel wires along the top of the fitting, with loops on the ends that hold the antenna loop attachment of the ladder line antenna element. Details are shown in Figure 2. The plastic casting held ends of the stainless 10 gauge wire are bent to prevent coming out of the T under strain. Attaching the ladder line to the stainless 10 gauge wire loop will keep the strain off the bottom electrical lines. I then sealed the ends of the T fitting with quality duct tape around the 1 inch PVC plugs with the wire holes and carefully filled the unit with catalyzed polyester resin (epoxy can also be used).

The top center T hanger loop for the fitting was held on top of the T PVC fitting with stainless hose clamps. Sounds complicated but it's very simple and worth the effort. All electrical connections were well soldered. The ladder line ends were terminated in a short piece of stronger stranded 10 gauge copper and soldered together. The pieces ready for final assembly are shown in Figure 3.

Balun Details

My balun consisted of 10 turns of RG-213 coax, 9 inches in diameter hanging below the center T fitting. The coil is held together with plastic wire ties. I have a special way of protecting all my coax connectors that are exposed to the elements. I take a 4 inch piece of ¾ inch inside diameter by 1 inch outside diameter clear flexible PVC tubing and slide it over the PL-259 connector onto the coax before attachment. After tightening the coax fitting, I slide the tubing up over the electrical joint, and then

Table 1
Measured SWR vs Frequency

Frequency (MHz)	SWR
3.60	4.9
3.65	3.8
3.70	2.6
3.75	1.8
3.80	1.4
3.83	1.2
3.85	1.3
3.90	1.4
3.95	1.8
4.0	2.5

shoot bathtub silicon calking into the end of the clear tubing. I watch it extrude up to and past the fittings as shown in Figure 4. This makes a completely waterproof flexible fitting when hardened. It is easily removed by cutting the clear tubing with a knife. I have kept soldered wires protected in saltwater boat bilges this way for years.

Firing it Up

The dipole ends were attached to insulators and raised about 30 feet above the ground, while the center height was about 50 feet. With this construction I ran to the shack to get the SWR charted over frequency. My initial results had the center frequency almost off the bottom of the band. What to do? Well, I began cutting off 18 inch end sections of the dipole. Slowly the acceptable band began to move up to the phone band. After cutting off 10 feet of the antenna, 5 feet on each end, I ended up with the SWR values in Table 1. Unfortunately with all my trimming there may be a few inches of unequal length to the two sides, giving me an SWR that is not as low as possible. I suggest that you mark the antenna element ends with length marks so that you can trim the lengths equally.

The SWR measurements in Table 1 were obtained with an MFJ-259B SWR analyzer at the shack end of about 80 feet of Belden RG-213 coax. The radiation pattern is typical of a fairly low dipole with *EZNEC*-predicted elevation and azimuth patterns shown in Figures 5 and 6.[3]

Finally, here's why I like the antenna. I have put legal limit power to the antenna with good results. The lower broadband SWR gives any tuner more efficiency and ease when tuning to unity, but all the phone band becomes usable without a tuner and with little line loss.[2] The 10 foot shorter antenna may be important to some; nevertheless I would advise constructing the antenna longer than needed; trimming is easier than adding on to the ends. My on-the-air reports are very good. The antenna was fun and easy to make and I truly like the results. I'm on the 80 meter band now!

Acknowledgment

I wish to express my appreciation to Will Anderson, AA6DD, for his design work and ongoing advice during the construction of this antenna.

Notes
[1]J. Hallas, W1ZR, "Getting to Know Your Radio — Internal Antenna Tuners" *QST*, Apr 2006, pp 66-67.
[2]See Note 1.
[3]**www.eznec.com**.

George Prince, N6DNA, was born in Santa Monica, California in 1932 and raised on a ranch. He is a retired physician-anesthesiologist with three grown children. He first became a ham in 1961 and has held a number of calls, receiving the present one after he upgraded to an Advanced class license. His Amateur Radio pursuits have included maritime mobile operation from his 40 foot homebuilt sailboat, building vacuum tube power amplifiers, and making his own welded towers and monoband Yagi antennas. George continues to enjoy wonderful friendships he has established with fellow hams over the years. You can reach George at 600 Terry Lynn Pl, Long Beach, CA 90807 or at **gmpsr@earthlink.net**.

By Michael J. Polia, AB1AW

Shortened End-Fed Half-Wave Antenna for 80 Meters

Construct this easy-to-build shortened version of the classic end-fed half-wave radiator and enjoy one of our best "top bands."

Many of us would like to get on 80 meters, but have been discouraged due to antenna restrictions of one type of another. And, many of us do not have the room for a full size 80 meter half-wave dipole (130 feet). The classic vertical for 80 meters is also not practical due to its height and the extensive ground plane that is required. A shortened dipole may be possible, but even a half-size loaded dipole is about 65 feet and requires support of the feed line.

A random long wire is an alternative. Use of an antenna tuner with a random wire antenna, worked against a good ground or counterpoise, can be effective. To get reasonable efficiency, however, the "random wire" should be at least $1/4$ wavelength (about 65 feet for 80 meters) long. Also, if that random wire is cut to a multiple of $1/4$ wavelength, the wire impedance, as seen by the tuner, will be low. This necessitates the use of a good ground system to achieve reasonable efficiency.

A special category of wire antenna, used with an antenna tuner, is the end-fed half wave antenna, or EFHWA. This is essentially a half-wave dipole that is fed from one end, rather than from the center. The first advantage of this configuration is that a separate feed line is not required; one end of the wire is simply brought into the station and connected to the antenna tuner. The second advantage is that an EFHWA presents a relatively high impedance to the antenna tuner. This means that an extensive ground system is not required; a connection to a cold water pipe may be sufficient. Figure 1 illustrates the concept of the conventional end-fed antenna with tuner.

Shortening the EFHWA

An EFHWA for 80 meters is still a half-wave in size. We still have the problem of trying to fit it into a small suburban lot or other restricted space. We can, however, apply the theory and techniques of the classic (traditional) shortened dipole to the EFHWA to achieve a shorter antenna.

The theory and techniques for constructing a short dipole are well documented. Loading coils are the standard component added to a dipole in order to decrease its resonant frequency. The classic short dipole consists of a dipole that has two loading coils, one in each leg, as shown in Figure 2. The positions of the loading coils are typically symmetrical and dictate both the bandwidth and the resonant frequency of that antenna. For a given antenna length and coil reactance, the resonant frequency of the antenna decreases as the coils are moved toward the center of the antenna. The bandwidth also decreases as the coils are moved toward the center. If the coils are positioned at the feed point, they can be combined into one coil that has twice the inductance of one of the single coils. *The ARRL Antenna Book* contains detailed information, equations and charts for constructing a shortened dipole, including those needed for determining the values of the coil reactance and positions.[1] Once the coil reactance is determined for the desired antenna length, it is used to calculate the coil inductance for the desired operating frequency. More on this later when we calculate the coil inductance for our shortened EFHWA for 80 meters.

The classic shortened dipole is still a dipole, and is traditionally fed like a standard size

[1] *The ARRL Antenna Book*, 20th edition, pp 6-30 to 6-32. Available from your local dealer or the ARRL Bookstore. Order no. 9043. Telephone toll-free in the US 888-277-5289 or 860-594-0355, fax 860-594-0303; www.arrl.org/shop/; pubsales@arrl.org

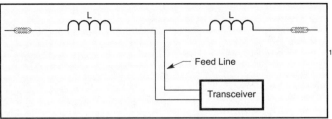

Figure 2—A half-wave dipole shortened with loading coils.

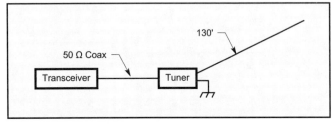

Figure 1—A traditional end-fed half-wave antenna for 80 meters fed with a transmatch or antenna tuner.

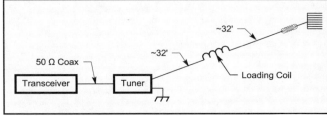

Figure 3—The end-fed half-wave antenna of Figure 1 is now shortened with a single center loading coil.

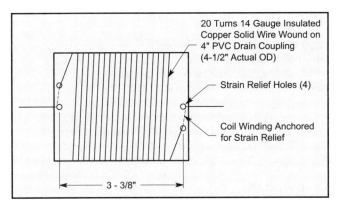

Figure 4—Coil construction for the center loaded antenna. Note the strain relief holes for wire anchor.

dipole, using coax or a balanced feed line. Just as a full size half-wave dipole can be end-fed, however, a shortened dipole can also be end-fed. This means that an equivalent end-fed, half-wave resonant 80 meter antenna can be constructed that is considerably shorter than a full size dipole. Such an antenna is constructed with a single loading coil, both for simplicity and to keep the antenna impedance at its ends equivalent to a full size end-fed half-wave dipole.

A dipole antenna, whether full-sized or shortened, can be center-fed, end-fed or fed anywhere in between. There is nothing "magic" about feeding the dipole in the center, except that it allows for an easy match to the standard low impedance (50 Ω) feed line and requires no special matching to your rig's output impedance. Any dipole can be fed off-center with the proper impedance matching between the antenna and feed line.

Off-center fed dipoles are popularly used as multiband antennas. As we move the feed point away from the center, the impedance increases until it reaches a maximum at the end of the wire. Moving the feed point to the end of a half-wave dipole results in a Zepp antenna, typically fed with a high impedance, open-wire, balanced feed line and a transmatch or antenna tuner. Finally, one end of a dipole can be fed directly by an antenna tuner (with no feed line required), resulting in an end-fed half-wave dipole.

Dipoles that are shortened using loading coils still exhibit the same feed point impedances at their centers, as well as at their ends. This means we can shorten an end-fed half-wave dipole using loading coils, in the same manner as a traditional shortened, loaded dipole, and feed it with an antenna tuner just as we would the standard end-fed antenna.

The electrical design of the shortened EFHWA is essentially the same as for a shortened dipole. Either a pair of off-center coils or a single center coil may be used. When a single center coil is used, its reactance is calculated to be twice that of one of the off-center coils. Figure 3 illustrates the concept of a single-coil shortened EFHWA with tuner. Here, the EFHWA is shortened by 50% using a single loading coil in the center, resulting in a 64 foot antenna for 80 meters.

Calculating the Antenna Size

In my implementation of this antenna, I decided to construct a half-size EFHWA for 80 meters. There was nothing magical about this length; it simply allowed the antenna to fit in my backyard. I predominantly operate CW and PSK31 on 80 meters, so I wanted an antenna with an approximate center frequency of 3600 kHz. I started by calculating the length of a standard dipole for 3600 kHz (468/3.6 MHz), or 130 feet for an 80 meter dipole. This was much too long to fit in my backyard. I needed an antenna about half of that length; that is, a total antenna length of 64 feet for operation centered at 3600 kHz. This is about 50% shorter than a full-size half-wave dipole.

The antenna would consist of two 32 foot sections with a single loading coil between the two sections. Using the chart provided in *The ARRL Antenna Book,* 20th edition (Figure 55, page 6-31), I determined that a half-size dipole with two coils located at the center (a *Dimension B, Position of Coil* of zero) required each coil to have a reactance of 500 Ω. This is equivalent to a single center coil that has a reactance (X_L) of 1000 Ω at frequency (f) of 3.6 MHz for an inductance (L) of 44 µH (where $X_L = 2\pi fL$).

To cover the phone portion of the band you will need to shorten the antenna a bit. For a center frequency of 3800 kHz, you'll need an antenna length of (468/3.8 MHz) /2 or about 61.5 feet. Two 31 foot legs will do the trick. The coil inductance drops to about 42 µH. However, this is only a difference of half a turn compared to the 44 µH coil. For practical purposes, the coil can be left at 44 µH.

Constructing the Loading Coil

I constructed the single loading coil using a 4 inch PVC drain pipe coupling and 14 gauge insulated solid copper wire. Both the 14 gauge wire and the PVC pipe coupling should be readily available at your local hardware or plumbing supply store. The outer diameter of the PVC coupling is about 4.5 inches. Twenty turns, close-wound, yield a calculated inductance of about 44 µH. I drilled a couple of holes at each end to act as a strain relief for the coil windings.

Figure 4 illustrates the coil construction. I used PVC pipe cement to cement the coil windings into place. The coil is placed between the two 32 foot legs of the antenna. Be sure to anchor it firmly. I made the legs of the antenna from an old short-wave antenna kit from RadioShack. I used the bare, stranded copper wire from that kit for the "far" leg, and the insulated lead-in for the "near" leg that entered the shack. Of course, any solid or stranded copper or copper-clad wire can be used.

Constructing the Tuner

Although nearly any tuner can be used to drive an end-fed antenna, a simple tuner consisting of a single coil and a variable capacitor is sufficient. Figure 5 shows the simple tuner I used. My tuner consists of a PVC pipe coil form for the inductor and a variable capacitor stolen from an old AM tube radio (this has a C of about 365 pF). If you don't have a suitable variable capacitor in your junk box, you can purchase one from a variety of electronic parts dealers. If you keep the transmit power under 10 W, you can even use the miniature tuning capacitor from an old portable AM radio. The coil is wound on a 5 inch length of 1 1/2 inch PVC pipe. The actual outer diameter of such a

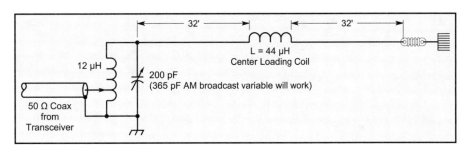

Figure 5—Although any single-wire tuner can be used, here is a simple tuner for the shortened end-fed wire antenna. The capacitor can be an AM broadcast band variable having a total C of about 365 pF.

pipe is about 1.9 inches.

I used 18 gauge solid, bare copper wire to wind the coil. The wire should be readily available at your local hardware store. I found that Ace Hardware sells 25 foot rolls of 18 gauge solid, bare copper wire…perfect for winding coils. I wound 27 turns at 6 turns per inch, to cover 4^1/$_2$ inches of the pipe. This results in a calculated coil inductance of about 12 µH. I chose this inductance because it resonates with a variable capacitor that adjusts within a range of 100 pF to 200 pF. This combination covers the entire 80 meter band.

I cemented the coil windings with hot glue to maintain even spacing between the windings (6 turns per inch). Using bare copper wire, I am able to place the coil tap at the proper point using a small alligator clip. I found that placing the tap at about 3 turns from the ground end yielded an SWR of less than 1.5:1 at 3600 kHz (with proper adjustment of the capacitor). This tap position will vary by a turn or so depending on your operating frequency and antenna installation position. Although I'm not sure of the power handling capability of this tuner, it is certainly sufficient for QRP operation. I find that I get about a 30 kHz bandwidth with a 2:1 SWR without the need to readjust the tuner setting.

Putting It Together

The antenna can be mounted in a variety of positions and does not have to be installed as a straight line radiator. As with conventional dipoles, you can install this shortened EFHWA as a sloper, an inverted V or an inverted L. The beauty of this is that you don't need to worry about the separate feed line to its center, as with a conventional dipole. I actually have the first 32 feet of the antenna running out my window, up the side of the house to the top of my brick chimney. At that point I have the coil tethered to the top of the chimney, and the second half of the antenna stretched horizontally across my yard to a tree. I brought the feed point into the shack through a window, simply closing the window down on the wire to keep it in place. Connect the feed point to the end of the tuner coil, adjust the coil tap and variable capacitor for best SWR and you are on the air! I've not tried using this antenna on other bands, but a conventional EFHWA can be made to operate on its even harmonics, so I suspect this shortened version can do the same, allowing operation on 40, 20 and 10 meters.

Michael Polia, AB1AW, was first licensed as WB1EET at age 14 in 1976. He received his Advanced class license while still in high school and earned the Amateur Extra class ticket in 2001. Mike has a BSEE from Northeastern University and an MS in Computer Science from Boston University. He has worked in various fields, including design and development of audio and radio/satellite equipment, medical and semiconductor instrumentation, and networking. Mike is currently a principal software engineer at Nortel Networks. Active on PSK31 and CW, he's interested in digital communications techniques and low power (QRP) operation. You can contact him at **ab1aw@yahoo.com**.

By Rich Wadsworth, KF6QKI

A Portable Twin-Lead 20-Meter Dipole

With its relatively low loss and no need for a tuner, this resonant portable dipole for 14.060 MHz is perfect for portable QRP.

My first attempt at a portable dipole was using 20 AWG speaker wire, with the leads simply pulled apart for the length required for a $1/2$ wavelength top and the rest used for the feed line. The simplicity of no connections, no tuner and minimal bulk was compelling. And it worked (I made contacts)!

Jim Duffey's antenna presentation at the 1999 PacifiCon QRP Symposium made me rethink that. The loss in the feed line can be substantial, especially at the higher frequencies, if the choice in feed line is not made rationally. Since a dipole's standard height is a half wavelength, I calculated those losses for 33 feet of coaxial feed line at 14 MHz. RG-174 will lose about 1.5 dB in 33 feet, RG-58 about 0.5 dB, RG-8X about 0.4 dB. RG-8 is too bulky for portable use, but has about 0.25 dB loss. For comparison, *The ARRL Antenna Book* shows No. 18 AWG zip cord (similar to my speaker wire) to have about 3.8 dB loss per 100 feet at 14 MHz, or around 1.3 dB for that 33 feet length. Note that mini-coax or zip cord has about 1 dB more loss than RG-58. Are you willing to give up that much of your QRP power and your hearing ability? I decided to limit antenna losses in my system to a half dB, which means I draw the line at RG-58 or equivalent loss.

TV Twin Lead

It is generally accepted that 300 ohm ribbon line has much less loss than RG-58. Some authors have stated that TV twin lead has similar loss as RG-58, which is acceptable to me. A coil of twin-lead is less bulky and lighter than the same length of RG-58. These qualities led me to experiment with it. One problem is that its 300 ohm impedance normally requires a tuner or 4:1 balun at the rig end.

But, since I want approximately a half wavelength of feed line anyway, I decided to experiment with the concept of making it an exact electrical half wavelength long. Any feed line will reflect the impedance of its load at points along the feed line that are multiples of a half wavelength. Since a dipole pitched as a flat-top or inverted V has an impedance of 50 to 70 ohms, a feed line that is an electrical half wave long will also measure 50 to 70 ohms at the transceiver end, eliminating the need for a tuner or 4:1 balun.

To determine the electrical length of a wire, you must adjust for the velocity factor (VF), the ratio of the speed of the signal in the wire compared to the speed of light in free space. For twin lead, it is 0.82. This means the signal will travel at 0.82 times the speed of light, so it will only go 82% as far in one cycle as one would normally compute using the formula 984/f(MHz). I put a 50 ohm dummy load on one end

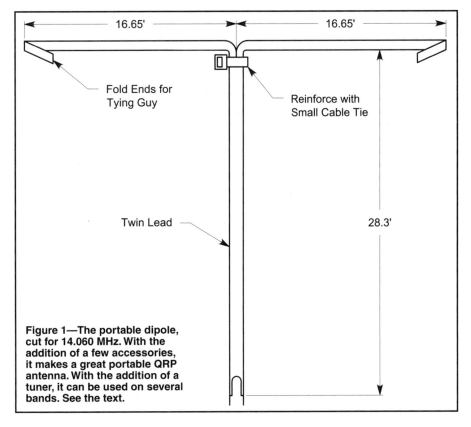

Figure 1—The portable dipole, cut for 14.060 MHz. With the addition of a few accessories, it makes a great portable QRP antenna. With the addition of a tuner, it can be used on several bands. See the text.

of a 49 ft length of twin lead and used an MFJ 259B antenna analyzer to measure the resonant frequency, which was 8.10 MHz. The 2:1 SWR bandwidth measured 7.76 to 8.47 MHz, or about 4.4% from 8.10 MHz.

The theoretical $1/2$ wavelength would be 492/8.1 MHz, or 60.7 feet, so the VF is 49/60.7=0.81, close to the 0.82 that is published. A $1/2$ wave for 14.06 MHz would therefore be 492×0.81/14.06 or 28.3 feet. I cut a piece that length, soldered a 51 ohm resistor between the leads at one end, and hoisted that end up in the air. I then measured the SWR with the 259B set for 14.060 MHz and found it to be 1:1. I used the above-measured 2:1 bandwidth variation of 4.4% to calculate that the feed line could vary in length between 27.1 and 29.5 feet for a 2:1 maximum SWR.

Now comes the fun part. With another length of twin lead, I cut the web between the wires, creating 17 ft legs, and left 28.3 feet of feed line. I hung it 30 feet high, tested, and trimmed the legs until the 259B measured 1:1 SWR. The leg length ended up at 16.75 feet. (Note: The VF determined above only applies to the feed line portion of the antenna.) There is no soldering and no special connections at the antenna feed point. I left the ends of the legs an inch longer to have something to tie to for hanging. I reinforced the antenna end of the uncut twin lead with a nylon pull tie, with another pull tie looped through it to tie a string to it for using as an inverted V. To connect the feed line to the transceiver, I used a binding post-BNC adaptor that is available from Ocean State.[1] My original intention of leaving the feed line free of a permanent connector was to allow connection to an Emtech ZM-2 balanced antenna binding post connectors. Since then I have permanently attached a short stub of RG-58 with a BNC, because I plan to either use it with my single band 20 meter Wilderness Radio SST, or with an Elecraft K1 or K2 with built-in tuner. I did this by connecting the shield to one side of the twin lead and the center conductor to the other side—no balun was used between the coax and twin lead.

After a year or so of use and further field testing, including different heights and V angles, I further trimmed the legs to a length of 16.65 feet. I found that the lowest SWR was usually obtained with the V as close to 90 degrees as I could determine visually. Also, I found that the resonant frequency (or at least the frequency at which SWR was at a minimum) is lower if the antenna is closer to the ground, and vice-versa. For example, with the top of the V at 22 feet, the lowest SWR was measured at around 13.9 MHz, and with the top of the V at 31 feet, SWR was lowest at around 14.1 MHz. In both cases, SWR at 14.060 did not exceed 1.3:1.

I used Radio Shack 22 AWG twin lead that is available in 50 ft rolls. To have no solder connections, you need at least 45 feet. When I cut the twin lead to make the legs, I just cut the "web" down the middle and didn't try to cut it out from between the wires. It helps make the whole thing roll up into a coil, and the legs don't tangle when it's unrolled, since they're a little stiff. It turned out that the entire antenna is lighter than a 25 ft roll of RG-58. This antenna can be scaled up or down for other frequencies also. An even lower loss version can be made with 20 AWG 300 ohm "window" line, though the VF of that line is different and should be measured before construction.

How High?

Wait, you say—"After all that talk about having it a half wave up, you only have it up 28 feet." A 6 or 12 ft RG-58 jumper, available with BNC connectors from RadioShack, can be used to get it higher if the right branch is available. Since impedance at the feed point is 50 to 70 ohms, 50 ohm coax can be used to extend the feed line. I have used it in the field a few times as an inverted V, at various heights and leg angles, and used an SWR meter to double-check its consistency in different situations. SWR never exceeded 1.5:1, so I feel safe leaving the tuner home. For backpacking, I leave the SWR meter home, too!

And there's a bonus: Since it has a balanced feed line, it *can* be used with little loss as a multi-band antenna, with a tuner, from 10 to 40 meters. I quote John Heyes, G3BDQ, from *Practical Wire Antennas*, page 18: "Even when the top of the doublet antenna is

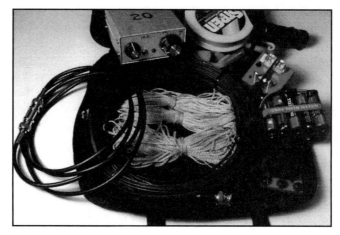

Figure 2—The author's portable station, including twin-lead dipole, 20-meter Wilderness Radio SST transceiver and support line. It all fits in the 8"×10$1/2$"×2" Compaq notebook computer case.

a quarter-wavelength long, the antenna will still be an effective radiator." Heyes used an antenna with a 30 ft top length about 25 ft off the ground on 40 meters and received consistently good reports from all Europe and even the USA (from England). It will not perform as well at 40 meters as at 20 meters, however, though 10 through 20 meters should be excellent.

Testing, Testing

To test this theory, I recently worked some of Washington State's Salmon Run contesters and worked many Washington hams and an Ohio and a Texas station on 15 and 20 meters, with the antenna up 22 feet on a tripod-mounted SD20 fishing pole, using 10 W from an Elecraft K2 from central California. The K2 tuner was used to tune the antenna on 15 meters. Signal reports were from 549 to 599. Unfortunately, this was a daytime experiment and 40 meters was limited to local traffic.

At the 2001 Freeze Your Buns Off QRP contest, it was hung at 30 feet and compared to a 66 ft doublet up 50 feet on 10, 15 and 20 meters, using a K2 S-meter. There was little if any difference. At the 2001 Flight of the Bumblebees QRP contest I compared it, at 20 meters, to a resonant wire groundplane antenna with each antenna top at 20 feet and found it to consistently outperform the groundplane. I have concluded through these informal experiments that a resonant inverted V, when raised at a height close to or exceeding a half wavelength, produces the most "bang for your buck" and that extra length or height beyond that yields diminishing returns.

A ham since 1998, Rich Wadsworth, KF6QKI, is a civil engineer in private practice as a consultant. Since earning his license, he reports, that he has become obsessed with kits and homebrewing. You can reach Rich at 320 Eureka Canyon Rd, Watsonville, CA 95076; richwads@compuserve.com.

---

[1]Ocean State Electronics, 6 Industrial Dr, Westerly RI 02891, tel 800-866-6626 or 401-596-3080; fax 401-596-3590; e-mail: ose@oselectronics.com.

By John S. Belrose, VE2CV

A Horizontal Loop for 80-Meter DX

Working DX on 80 meters doesn't necessarily require big towers or trees. This 80-meter quad loop system requires only supports of modest height—a better single-element antenna may be hard to find.

Introduction

In 1997 the author published an article on vertical full (and ground plane type half) wave loops for 80 meter DX.[1] In that article it was noted that perpendicular (horizontal) polarization is the preferred polarization, particularly at low elevation angles, since horizontally polarized waves are hardly affected by the finite conductivity of the ground in front of the antenna. An exception when vertical antennas come into their own is a vertically polarized antenna over very good ground, near the seashore or over alkaline salt flats.

A practical 80 meter horizontal dipole is, however, not an ideal antenna for DX. For optimum communications with distant stations the antenna's radiation pattern should have a null overhead, to minimize near vertical incidence sky-wave signals from atmospheric noise and interference, and a low angle lobe to maximize reception/transmission over paths to distant stations. To achieve such a pattern with a half-wave dipole it would be necessary to install the dipole a half wavelength above the ground, that is to say, at a height of 40 meters for the 80 meter band. This is impractical in many instances.

A full-wave horizontal loop for the 80 meter band at a practical height of 15 meters is a popular antenna nicknamed a "Loop Skywire" that has been in *The ARRL Antenna Book* for years. In the author's view this antenna does not have the desired radiation pattern for 80 meter DX. Aside from the fact that the direct and ground-reflected waves reinforce at an elevation angle of 90°, the loop itself has some directivity in this broadside direction. Doug DeMaw has referred to such an antenna as a "cloud warmer."

Paul Carr, N4PC proposed a solution for this problem.[2] He fed diagonally opposite corners of a square loop with equal but oppositely phased currents. For a full-wave loop this produces a null in the overhead radiation pattern, akin to the time-honored W8JK array—a pair of closely spaced dipoles fed out of phase.[3] For 80 meters N4PC used a ³⁄₄-wavelength loop, which had the desired elevation pattern, but with corner feed the azimuthal pattern is skewed compared with the loop modeled by the author.

According to the author's simulation using W7EL's *EZNEC Pro* version of the numerical electromagnetic code NEC-4D, the antenna's impedance at the input to a transmission line feeder of practical length, is not a particularly convenient value to tune and match. N4PC did not comment on this. In fact, he did not include the phasing and the feeder transmission lines in his model, and so he could not comment on the input impedance of his antenna system although he reported "no problem with tuning and matching his antenna on all bands 80 through 10 meters."

In this article the author uses numerical simulation to address the radiation characteristics and the tuning and matching

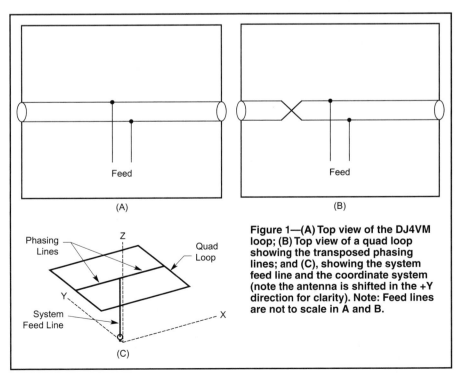

Figure 1—(A) Top view of the DJ4VM loop; (B) Top view of a quad loop showing the transposed phasing lines; and (C), showing the system feed line and the coordinate system (note the antenna is shifted in the +Y direction for clarity). Note: Feed lines are not to scale in A and B.

[1]Notes appear on page 132.

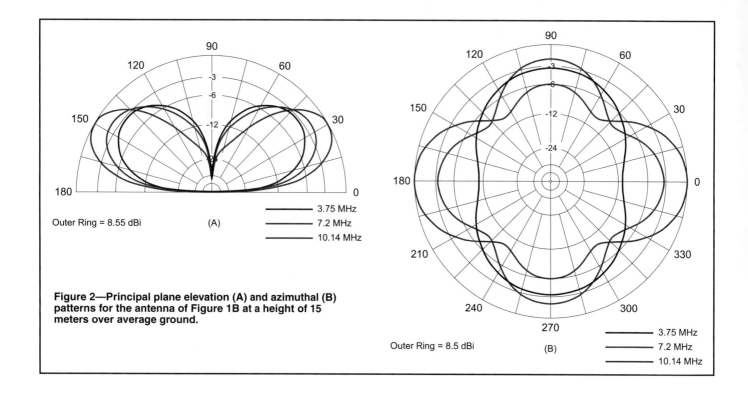

Figure 2—Principal plane elevation (A) and azimuthal (B) patterns for the antenna of Figure 1B at a height of 15 meters over average ground.

details of a symmetrical full wave quad loop designed specifically for 80 meter DX.

A Horizontal Square Loop with a W8JK-Like Radiation Pattern

W. Bolt, DJ4VM, described a multiband vertical quad loop with both of the vertical sides fed in-phase by means of a "phasing line."[4] This symmetrical feed arrangement (Figure 1A) has the advantage of ensuring a symmetrical current distribution on the loop—and hence a "clean" radiation pattern over several bands (40 meters to 10 meters).

Our interest here, however, is a horizontally polarized loop operating in "W8JK mode." Rotating the plane of his loop 90°, we now have the horizontal loop, in which the system feed line connecting at the center of the phasing lines can drop vertically at right angles to the plane of the loop (see Figure 1C). The symmetry of this loop arrangement is appealing.

The author decided to carry out a detailed numerical modeling study for this loop fed with a balanced, transposed phasing transmission line (opposite sides of the loop fed out of phase). The horizontal full wave loop, λ/4 or 20 meters on a side for 3.75 MHz, at a height of 15 meters over average ground, is numerically modeled as three separate cases:

Case 1) Out-of-phase sources placed at the centers of the sides of the loop (the sides parallel to the Y-Z plane);

Case 2) Wires are added for the conductors of a 600-Ω phasing line between the opposite sides with the source placed at the middle. (Note: The conductors for the

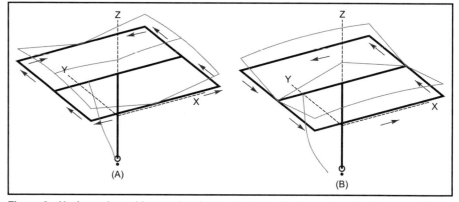

Figure 3—Horizontal quad loops showing currents on the loop wires for the case where the phasing lines provide in-phase feed (A); and out-of-phase feed (B). Note the left phasing line is the transposed feeder. The frequency is 3.75 MHz.

transmission line feeding the side of the loop in the –X direction are transposed to provide the out-of-phase feed; see Figure 1B.)

Case 3) Case 3 differs from Case 2 only in that a system feed transmission line is added, with the source on a jumper wire between the transmission line conductors at its bottom or transmitter end (Figure 1C).

All wires are no. 12 copper. The spacing for the conductors of the transmission lines is 150 mm (for an impedance $Z_o = 600$ Ω). The length of the transmission line feeder is 14 meters.

The reason for the three-case modeling sequence is to be sure that the transmission lines included in the model are performing correctly. We find that they are by computing the feedpoint impedances of the two models with different techniques. The *NEC-4D* input impedance for the Case 3 antenna at 3.75 MHz is $9.8 + j462$ Ω. For the Case 2 antenna, fed by a 600-Ω open wire transmission line 14 meters long, the input impedance is $9.9 + j464$ Ω according to *TL*, the transmission line program by N6BV and published by the ARRL.

While the source impedances are, of course, different for all three configurations, radiation patterns are substantially identical. The maximum gain is decreased slightly with the addition of the transmission lines as would be expected because of the high SWR on the transmission lines (see below). At 3.75 MHz, the gains in the principal plane (the Y-Z plane) are 6.02 dBi, 5.34 dBi and 3.93 dBi, for cases 1, 2 and 3, respectively. From this point, all discussion will be of the antenna system of Case 3 and "system impedance" will refer to the impedance at the transmitter end of the common feed line.

The principal plane radiation pattern is shown in Figure 2 at a frequency of 3.75 MHz. For interest, the pattern is also shown at 7.2 MHz, and 10.14 MHz. The calculated antenna system impedances and radiation characteristics (gain and take-off angle, ψ, are given in Table 1).

We are concerned here with the radiation pattern for 80 meter DX. Clearly the radiation patterns shown in Figure 2 are almost ideal: a deep overhead null, and a bidirectional pattern with a take-off angle (41°) that is low for the practical height (15 m) of the loop. The azimuthal pattern is also good (for an 80 meter antenna) with a front-to-side ratio about 10 dB.

Clearly, at 3.75 MHz, conductor loss in the system feeder transmission line attached to the junction of the phasing lines will be an important consideration because of the high SWR. For an open wire line 14 meters long made of no.12 wire the transmission line loss is 1.5 dB, according to NEC-4D. By using a larger diameter wire, the loss can be reduced. As an example of the benefits of using heavy-duty transmission lines, if the conductors were no. 4 copper wire, the transmission line loss would be 0.5 dB. For this calculation the spacing for the larger diameter wire is 150 mm so that Z_o is less than 600 Ω, but the characteristic impedance for this feeder is relatively unimportant. The transmission line loss at 7.2 MHz and 10.14 MHz is negligible. [While quite large, no. 4 wire is commonly used for electrical grounding. The outer shield of coaxial cable could also be used to construct an open wire line with large conductors.—*Ed.*]

Current Distribution on the Loop

To understand how the patterns for in-phase and out-of-phase feed come to be, it is interesting to look at the current distributions on the loop. Figure 3 shows the current distribution (amplitude only) and by arrows the relative phase relationship for the DJ4VM-type loop with opposite sides fed in phase, and for the same loop configured with opposite sides of the loop fed out-of-phase to radiate in "W8JK mode." Phase information is useful in determining that certain kinds of antennas are modeled correctly. For closed loops, particularly for the case with dual sources, the phase as calculated by *NEC* can be confusing.

Sudden reversals in phase may not be a cause of concern if they result from the way the wires have been defined. Positive current is defined as being from end 1 to end 2 of the wire, so if for two wires end 1 is connected to the other end 1, a 180° shift in current phase will be indicated at the junction of the wires. The actual current is continuous, as it should be, but the direction reference changes from one wire to the other. This can lead to confusion, particularly for closed loops such as our present model where in Case 1 the loop is fed in the center of two sides (two sources and no transmission lines). If the quad loop is modeled with end 1 connecting to end 2 for all wires, opposite sides will have wires defined in opposing directions. For the desired radiation pattern, the phase relationship of the sources in the model will then be 180° different from those of the actual antenna.

That is why in Figure 3 we show the relative phase relationships sorted out by the author by arrows. In the Case 1 model with two sources the wires have been defined so that with source current phases of 0° and 180° the pattern is as expected.

Table 1
Impedance at the Junction of the Phasing Lines for Out of Phase Feed (W8JK-like Mode)

Frequency (MHz)	Impedance (Ω)	Gain (dBi)	Take-off Angle (ψ)
3.75	5.5 – j 310	5.34	41°
7.2	285 + j 654	6.61	34°
10.14	73 + j 84	8.55	32°

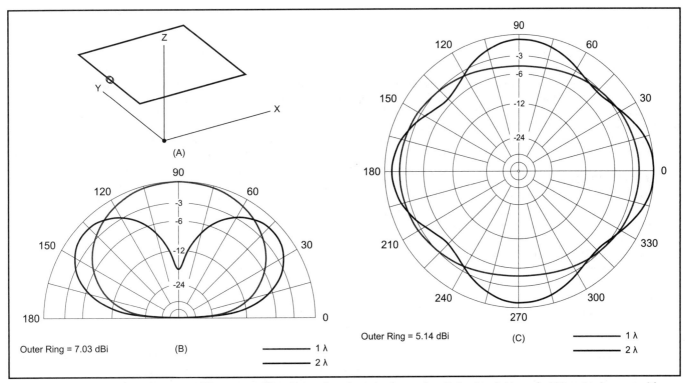

Figure 4—Elevation (B) and azimuthal (C) patterns for a 1-wavelength and a 2-wavelength horizontal loop (a 160 meter loop used for 80 meters). Note that for the 1-wavelength loop the azimuthal pattern for an elevation angle of 45° is plotted since the take-off angle is 90°.

Matching Network Capacitor Values

Let R1 = 6.8 Ω and R2 = 50 Ω (for a 50-Ω coaxial feed).

The series inductor $X_L = [R1 (R2 - R1)]^{1/2} = [6.8 (50 - 6.8)]^{1/2} = 17$ Ω

Because the system presents an inductive reactance of 343 Ω, cancel all but 17 Ω with a series capacitor of (343 – 17) = 326 Ω (130 pF at 4 kV rating). The impedance match is very sensitive to this reactance, so a variable capacitor is required.

The capacitor to ground $X_c = R2 [R1/ (R2 – R1)]^{1/2} = 50 [6.8/(50 – 6.8)]^{1/2} = 19.8$ Ω (2139 pF). This is a low voltage capacitor—approx 300 V for 1500 W at 50 Ω—and may be of fixed value.

Table 2
System Impedance

Frequency (MHz)	Impedance Ω
3.75	6.8 + j343
7.2	135 – j 37
10.14	67 – j12

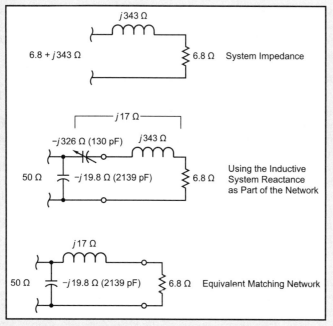

Figure A—The three steps of designing the "step-up" L-match for an inductive load.

Figure 3B shows clearly that the phases of currents in the wires parallel to the X-Z plane are out of phase (the desired W8JK mode). For in-phase feed (the DJ4VM antenna) of Figure 3A, the currents on the wires parallel to the Y-Z plane are in phase. With this arrangement we have a "cloud warmer" antenna.

A Practical Installation

For a practical installation of the loop the system impedance is an important consideration (as for any single band or multiband antenna system that depends on tuning feed line impedances). The impedances to match are given in Table 2 assuming the heavy-duty low loss transmission line (no. 4 wire spaced 150 mm, length 14 m).

A balanced Antenna System Tuning Unit (ASTU), or an unbalanced ASTU with a "common subchassis" isolated internal ground, as described in the *2002 ARRL Handbook* (pp 22.56 ff), could be used, with a 1:1 current balun between the ASTU and the transmitter. The author describes a "special ASTU" for the antenna below.

[ASTU is used as opposed to the more common ATU because the tuning performed is of the complete antenna system including the feed line, as opposed to just tuning the antenna.—*Ed.*]

We are concerned with keeping transmission lines losses low for the loop when operated on the 80 meter band (note the high inductive reactance compared with the resistive component in Table 2). Let us now consider losses in the ASTU. Power loss in ASTUs can also be an important consideration, but in this case, the power loss in the tuner can be minimized if you fabricate a "special ASTU" for this band.

The inductive component of the system reactance could be cancelled with a series capacitor, leaving a 6.8 Ω resistive impedance. The simplest network to match the low, resistive impedance to a higher value (6.8) is the L-match network, comprising a series inductor and on the transmitter side a capacitor to ground. But we do not need the series inductor because the feedpoint impedance is already inductive. Hence what we need is a series capacitor to cancel all but the necessary matching inductance and the capacitor to ground. The author described this tuning arrangement in 1953,[5] for matching center-loaded mobile whips. Great—we can build a simple and efficient ASTU for our 80 meter quad loop!

A Comparison with a "Sky Wire" Loop

Paul Reed, VE2LR, who intends to put up a 160 meter horizontal loop, brought to the author's attention an article by Richard Stroud, W9SR,[6] who has erected a 160 meter full wave horizontal or "sky wire" loop fed at a single point. He claims that his loop has "opened up a new world of DX-ing." The reader of the present article may well say, "For 80 meter DX is it worthwhile feeding the opposite sides of a loop out of phase, since I can more easily put up a skywire loop?"

The 2-wavelength perimeter loop does produce a null overhead—see Figure 4. The "skywire loop" has a gain of 5.1 dBi (take-off angle 47°) at a frequency of 3.75 MHz—compared with 4.8 dBi (take-off angle 41°) for our phased loop with a heavy-duty low loss feeder (3.8 dBi if the no. 12 feeder wires are used).

However, comparing the horizontal pattern of the 2 λ skywire loop to the out-of-phase 80 meter loop in Figure 2, the latter has a nice, clean directional pattern. For the DXer who wants to work stations in a preferred direction, 4.8 dBi directive gain with a front/side ratio of about 10 dB is an attractive antenna and the 6° lower take-off angle is well worth having. Try the loop and you will see! Increasing transmitter power can to some extent replace antenna gain, but you can only work stations that you can hear.

Comparing Vertical and Horizontal Loops

At the outset it was noted that if the ground conductivity in front of the antenna was poor, horizontal was the preferred polarization. Since the author's earlier article (Note 1) extolled the performance of vertical delta and quad loops, let us compare the performance of the horizontal quad loop with out-of-phase feed to that of a full wave delta loop on a support of the same height (15 m), for two

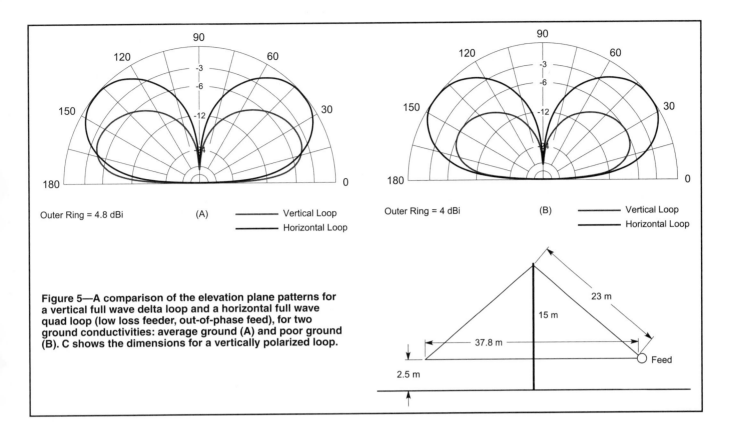

Figure 5—A comparison of the elevation plane patterns for a vertical full wave delta loop and a horizontal full wave quad loop (low loss feeder, out-of-phase feed), for two ground conductivities: average ground (A) and poor ground (B). C shows the dimensions for a vertically polarized loop.

ground conductivities: average ground (σ = 5 mS/m, ε = 13) and poor ground (σ = 1 mS/m, ε = 3). As can be clearly seen in Figure 5, for poor ground the horizontal loop wins hands down. For average ground the vertical delta loop outperforms the horizontal quad loop only for signals arriving at very low elevation angles (less than 15°).

Another consideration is background noise. The author has no side-by-side comparison of background noise for the two loop systems, vertical and horizontal, only anecdotal evidence that the noise level on a horizontal loop would be lower. Those who have used horizontal loops often report that "the residual noise level is very low," and "very seldom is the band completely dead."

A Note about Bandwidth

The antenna system bandwidth is narrow, 16 kHz (at 3.75 MHz) for a 2:1 mismatch. The operational bandwidth (estimated assuming a conjugate match) would be about 26 kHz based on the author's experience. Clearly the series capacitor should be remotely controlled.

Conclusions

While the horizontal loop antenna with opposite sides fed out of phase could be an excellent single-element for 80 meter DX, it is not recommended that it be the only 80 meter antenna for station use. An ordinary dipole is traditionally considered to be a necessary part of the antenna complement

Table 3
System Impedance Fed In-Phase

Frequency (MHz)	Impedance (Ω)
3.5	383 + j1794
3.75	5515 + j1904
4.0	863 − j1595
7.2	102 − j1094
10.14	202 + j774

for operations on the 80 meter band, since a pattern optimized for high angle sky-wave, for short to medium range paths, is required for normal operation on this band.

The horizontal loop described can, however, be arranged to provide both low and high angle radiation patterns, with additional complication. If both sides of the loop are fed in phase, then we have the desired pattern for the short to medium distance range. If both sides of the loop are fed out of phase we have the desired pattern for DX. A relay located at the center of the antenna system to switch the phase of one of the phasing lines is required to facilitate pattern selection.

This would require five supports—one for each corner and a center pole to support the phasing lines and the heavy-duty feed line. [A method to avoid the center pole would be to bring the two phasing lines directly to the ground-level system feedpoint at the center or to drop them vertically from the loop wires and then run them parallel to the ground to the center point. Doing so would alter the system feed point impedance and require changes to the matching network.—Ed.]

The ability to change patterns with the same antenna is attractive, but this requires two ASTUs because the antenna system impedance for in-phase feed is very different as shown in Table 3 (compare with Table 2).

Figure 6 shows how a remote "special ASTU" should be used for the 80 meter out-of-phase fed loop, with a coaxial cable transmission line to the "shack"; and the open wire line could be brought into the "shack" for the higher bands and for the in-phase fed loop. As an alternative, different lengths of feed line for the 80 meter in-phase fed loop could make tuning and matching more practical. This would require another transmission line relay.

Finally, if you have the room and wish to use the design for both 160 meter and 80 meter DX, make the loop twice as big (40 m on a side). This shifts concerns about keeping transmission line and ASTU losses low to the 160 meter band. The 160 meter radiation patterns will be similar to those computed for 80 meters for our "half size" loop, and the patterns for 80 meters will be similar to those computed for 40 meters.

Acknowledgments

The author works (part time) for the Communications Research Centre Canada, Ottawa, Ontario; hence computing facilities not available to the average amateur in radio are available. In particular, the author is licensed to use the *NEC-4* program.

Notes
[1]Belrose, J.S., "Loops for 80m DX," *QEX*, Aug 1997, pp 3-16.
[2]P. Carr, "The N4PC Loop," *CQ* Magazine, Dec 1990, pp 11-15.
[3]J. Kraus, "The W8JK Antenna: Recap and Update," *QST*, Jun 1982, pp 11-14.
[4]W. Boldt, "A New Multi-band Quad Antenna," *Ham Radio Magazine,* Aug 1969; see also L. A. Moxon, *HF Antennas for all Locations*, published by The Radio Society of Great Britain, 1982, pp 158 and 160.
[5]Belrose, J.S., "Short Antennas for Mobile Operation," *QST*, Sep 1953, pp 30-35, 108.
[6]Stroud, R.W., "A Large, Remote-Tuned Loop for HF DX," *CQ* Magazine, Jul 2001, pp 44-54.

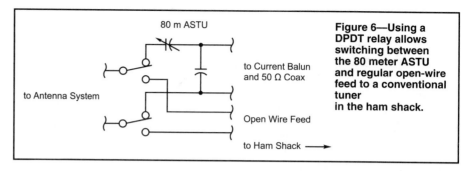

Figure 6—Using a DPDT relay allows switching between the 80 meter ASTU and regular open-wire feed to a conventional tuner in the ham shack.

John S. (Jack) Belrose received his BASc and MASc degrees in Electrical Engineering from the University of British Columbia, Vancouver, in 1950 and 1952. He joined the Radio Propagation Laboratory of the Defence Research Board, Ottawa, Ontario, in September 1951. In 1953 he was awarded an Athlone Fellowship, was accepted by St John's College, Cambridge, England and by the Cambridge University as a PhD candidate, to study with the late Mr J. A. Ratcliffe, then Head of the Radio Group, Cavendish Laboratories. He received his PhD degree from the University of Cambridge (PhD Cantab) in Radio Physics in 1958. From 1957 to present he has been with the Communications Research Centre (formerly Defence Research Telecommunications Establishment), where until recently (19 December 1998) he was Director of the Radio Sciences Branch. Currently he is working (part time) at CRC (2 days/week) devoting his time to radioscience research in the fields of antennas and propagation—a sort of transition to full retirement.

Dr Belrose was Deputy and then Chairman of the AGARD (Advisory Group for Aerospace Research and Development) Electromagnetic Propagation Panel from 1979-1983. He was a Special Rapporteur for ITU-Radiocommunication Study Group 3 concerned with LF and VLF Propagation. He is an ARRL Technical Advisor in the areas of radio communications technology, antennas and propagation; a Fellow member of the Radio Club of America and Life Senior Member of the IEEE (AP-S). He has been a licensed radio amateur since 1947 (present call sign VE2CV). You can reach the author at 17 rue de Tadoussac, Aylmer, QC J9J 1G1, Canada; **john. belrose@crc.ca**.

A Wideband Dipole for 75 and 80 Meters

Covering all the way from 3.5 to 4 MHz with one antenna takes some tricks.

Ted Armstrong, WA6RNC

On most of our MF and HF bands, a single dipole is the most basic antenna. With one exception, it can be used to cover all the usual CW, data and SSB frequencies without any tuning, if adjusted for minimum SWR at or near mid band. The exception, and the antenna designer's challenge, has always been the band from 3.5 to 4.0 MHz, which is so wide, in terms of percentage bandwidth, that many have a separate name for each end — 80 meters for the low end and 75 for the high end!

Why Not a Dipole

There have been a few designs proposed to meet the objective of a single 75/80 meter dipole in the past, but most have been proven flawed or difficult to implement.[1] The challenge is clear if we look at the SWR of a typical wire dipole tuned to mid band as shown in Figure 1. Note that with the antenna tuned to an exact match at the center of the band, we can achieve less than a 2:1 SWR over (at most) about 200 kHz. For full

[1]Notes appear on page 135.

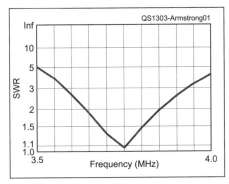

Figure 1 — Modeled 72 Ω SWR of a thin 80 meter dipole. Note the high SWR at the band edges.

band coverage we would need three separate thin dipoles.

The fraction of bandwidth to center frequency on 75/80 meters tells the story. If expressed as a percentage it is 13.3%, while for the full 10 meter band, for example, it is 5.8%, which would also be a challenge for a single antenna. My caveat about modes saves us here — on 10 meters, CW, data and SSB usage is generally in the bottom 0.5 MHz (1.8%), while FM is near the top. The two segments usually use different antenna types, often horizontal polarization for the low end and vertical for the high segment.

Similarly, 160 and 6 meters are 10 and 7.7% respectively, but they are not HF bands and also have usage divided among segments. Table 1 shows the percentage bandwidth of amateur bands from 160 meters through 70 centimeters. As indicated, 80/75 is the bandwidth challenge champ, even through our VHF and UHF bands. The other HF bands, with the caveat about 10 meters can usually fit onto a dipole, with 40 meters usually just making it to 2:1 on the edges.

Making it Work

Most of us are familiar with using over-coupled tuned transformers to make wide-band RF coupling transformers or filters. The same approach can be applied to antennas, with similar results. I investigated this approach using *EZNEC* antenna modeling software and have modeled a number of broadband antennas that work as designed over their frequency range with the SWR not

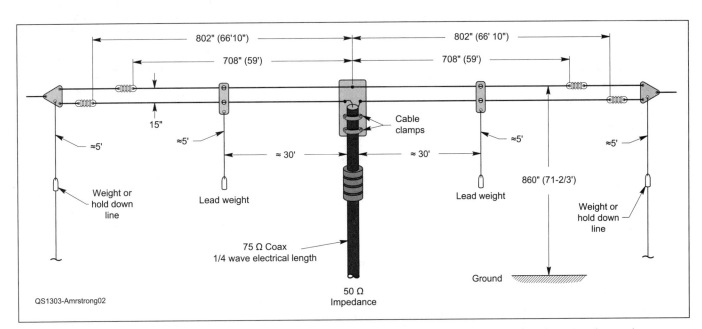

Figure 2 — Construction details and dimensions of the coupled resonator 75/80 meter antenna including ¼ wave impedance transformer of 75 Ω coax. The ¼ wave transformer should be an electrical quarter wave long, 65.6 feet in free space, 43.3 feet in standard (0.66 V_R) solid polyethylene dielectric coax. For RG-9 coaxial cable use type 43 shield beads (Fair-Rite part # 2643102402), for RG-59 use type 43 (Part # 2643540402). For Fair-Rite Products see **www.fair-rite.com**. If you have surplus 75 Ω coax and want to use it for the transmission line transformer, first measure its velocity factor and trim to a ¼ wave at 3.74 MHz. A support at the center will reduce sag.

SINGLE BAND 133

Table 1
Percentage Bandwidth of Amateur Bands

Band (meters)	Frequency Range (kHz)	Bandwidth (kHz)	Bandwidth (%)
160	1800 – 2000	200	10.5
75/80	3500 – 4000	500	13.3
60	5330.5 – 5405	74.5	1.4
40	7000 – 7300	300	4.2
30	10,100 – 10,150	150	1.5
17	18,068 – 18,168	100	0.6
15	21,000 – 21,450	450	2.1
12	24,890 – 24,990	100	0.4
10	28,000 – 29,700	1700	5.9
6	54,000 – 58,000	4000	7.7
2	144,000 – 148,000	4000	2.7
1.25	222,000 – 225,000	3000	1.3
70 cm	420,000 – 450,000	30,000	6.9

exceeding 1.5:1 across the band.[2, 3] [Note that successful *NEC* modeling of closely coupled antenna elements requires that the segment size of the coupled segments be the same and that they need to be in alignment. — *Ed.*]

There are a number of interacting parameters in the design of such an antenna. Unlike the two-band coupled resonator dipoles described in other articles, this antenna requires greater spacing than can be provided by window line. This results in a higher resonant impedance than the usual transmission line — 112 Ω in my design. Fortuitously, 112 Ω can be transformed through a ¼ wave section of 75 Ω coax to provide a good match to our usual 50 Ω systems. The resultant antenna is shown in Figure 2, while the 112 Ω SWR of the antenna itself is shown in Figure 3 and the transformed 50 Ω SWR is in Figure 4.

Validating the EZNEC Results
This horizontal antenna will not fit on a small city lot such as mine, so I needed to scale the frequency up to where it will fit and then verify that the antenna would work as predicted. The antenna would have the identical percentage band width except now it would be at a higher frequency. I scaled the frequency up to 60.5 MHz model in the built the antenna and obtained similar results to those of my larger modeled antenna. I also modeled and constructed some vertical "half antennas" fed against ground (see Figure 5) and duplicated the model results.

Putting Up the Antenna
This construction project requires lots of open space to work properly, but you will no longer have to use a tuner or multiple dipoles to cover the entire 75/80 meter band from one antenna. You can jump from the low end to the high end or anywhere in between

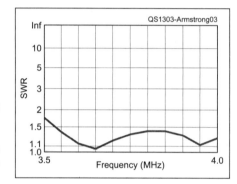

Figure 3 — Modeled 112 Ω SWR of the coupled resonator dipole of Figure 2 without quarter wave matching section.

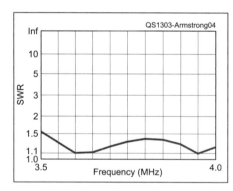

Figure 4 — Modeled 50 Ω SWR of the coupled resonator dipole of Figure 2 with the quarter wave matching section of 75 Ω Coax.

without a tuner and still have low SWR.

The design height of this antenna is 72 feet; a bit more then ¼ wavelength. At its design height and perhaps 10 feet above and below it will be less than a 1.7:1 SWR, rising to 2:1 at a height of 40 or 100 feet, all based on typical soil (conductivity of 0.005 S/m, dielectric constant of 13). Dry, sandy soil

Figure 5 — View of the 10-12 meter coupled resonator monopole, one of the smaller antennas used to validate the design process. It had a bandwidth of 17.7%

makes it look like the antenna is higher; wet soil makes it seem lower.

This broadband antenna uses two #14 AWG uninsulated antenna wires separated by 15 inches for the entire antenna length. A single spreader on each side (B in Figure 2) and the antenna end supports (C) help to maintain that separation. Don't let the wires get twisted, as that will kill the antenna's performance.

To keep the wires from getting twisted, attach a hold down nonconductive line or weights on a five foot nonconductive line to the bottom of B and C. The minimum weight of each lead weight should be

1 pound. In areas subject to heavy winds, it might be a good idea to use more weight. The center feed point is kept vertical by the weight of the transmission line transformer. That line should run as close to vertical as possible to reduce antenna currents coupled to the coax shield.

The feed point of the antenna is balanced, but the coax is unbalanced. The four ferrite shield beads on the coaxial cable help make the coax at the feed point appear more balanced and reduce the coax shield currents below the ferrites as detailed in Figure 2. Sketches of my implementation of the various support pieces are provided on the QST in Depth web page (**www.arrl.org/qst-in-depth**).

Notes
[1] One successful implementation is the four wire cage in use at W1AW. The solution presented here requires two rather than four wires, is more compact and needs a simpler support structure.
[2] J. Hallas, W1ZR, "A Folded Skeleton Sleeve Dipole for 40 and 20 Meters," QST, May 2011, pp 58-59; J. Hallas, W1ZR, "The Folded Skeleton Sleeve on Other Ham Bands," QST, Oct 2011, p 48.

[3] Several versions of EZNEC antenna modeling software are available from developer Roy Lewallen, W7EL, at **www.eznec.com**.

Amateur Extra class operator and ARRL member Ted Armstrong, WA6RNC, is a member of MARES, the Milpitas, California ARES®/RACES group and enjoys antenna modeling and experimenting. He can be reached at 721 Calero St, Milpitas, CA, 95035-4308 or at **theo_a@att.net**.

For updates to this article, see the QST Feedback page at www.arrl.org/feedback.

160 Meter Inverted Delta Loop

Work top band with an antenna not much bigger than one for 40 meters.

Charles T. Kluttz, W4TMR

160 meters has always been my favorite band, perhaps because of noise and antenna size challenges to be overcome. Over the last 40 or so years, I've used short verticals, slopers, shunt fed towers, dipoles, inverted Vs and for the last 20 years an inverted L (Γ) using 300 Ω twin lead. Because I live in a residential area my space is limited, but I am blessed with several oak trees well over 90 feet high, and have managed to get the vertical part of the Γ up 85 feet.

That Inverted L

About 10 years ago, I conducted a series of on the air tests of this twin lead Γ fed both as a single wire monopole, with both feed points tied together, and as a folded monopole, with one lead fed and the other grounded. The two configurations are shown in Figure 1. In almost every case, the folded configuration provided stronger signals in both transmit and receive. As a result the Γ was left folded and worked well. But I've never gotten over the urge to try something new from time to time.

A New Design Evolves

The original concept of this antenna was not a loop at all, but rather two Γs with their end points close together and feed points phased. This evolved through several configurations to the final form shown in Figure 2. For obvious reasons, I call this antenna an inverted delta loop although it's electrically more of a squashed monopole or skeleton conical monopole than a loop. The physical loop is supported by two oak trees and the feed point sits over a radial system originally installed for a 40 and 80 meter phased array, now used by the 160 meter Γ and an 80 meter vertical. The only reason for elevating the loop 4 feet is to provide easy access for lawn mowing

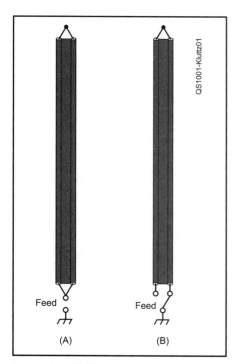

Figure 1 — At (A) a monopole made of 300 Ω twinlead. At (B) the same antenna configured as a folded monopole.

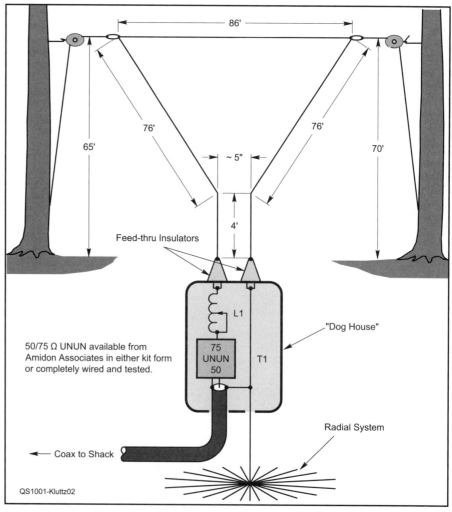

Figure 2 — The conical folded monopole I call an inverted delta loop. L1 is 17 turns, 2.5 inches in diameter, approximately 17 µH. T1 is a 50/75 Ω unun. This is available from Amidon Associates (www.amidoncorp.com) pre-assembled or in kit form.

Figure 3 — View of assembled base section.

(my wife is willing to put up with the antenna as long as I keep the grass cut!).

An *EZNEC* antenna modeling software run predicts a complex feed point impedance at 1.85 MHz of 67–j178 Ω, very close to what was measured with my MFJ-259B antenna analyzer.[1] This is easily matched using the inductor and a 50/75 Ω unbalanced to unbalanced transformer (unun). Figures 3, 4 and 5 show close-ups of the plastic food storage container used to protect the matching devices and switching relay from the weather.

[1]Several versions of *EZNEC* antenna modeling software are available from developer Roy Lewallen, W7EL, at www.eznec.com.

The ununs, inductor and relay used for antenna matching and switching are mounted on banana plugs for quick change. (The relay used to switch between one antenna and the other is not shown in the photo.)

Checking it Out

I had some concern regarding the proximity of the Γ, 80 meter vertical and 160 meter loop, but measurements of each antenna's input impedance with the antennas as shown indicated little difference from what was measured with the other antennas totally removed. *EZNEC* indicates a low angle of radiation and omnidirectional pattern that my over the air experiences seem to verify.

All that said, how well does the antenna actually work? Many comparisons between the Γ and the loop show little difference in strength within 1500 miles. Beyond that, the loop was reported stronger in almost every case. During the four months of late November 2007 through mid March 2008 I managed to work 114 DX entities in 25 CQ zones using the loop and approximately 300 W of power. To me, it's what I've pursued for a long time — a 160 meter DX antenna, only a little longer than a 40 meter dipole and requiring only a modest height.

Amateur Extra class licensee and ARRL member Charlie Kluttz, W4TMR, was first licensed in 1951 while in high school. He received a BSEE from North Carolina State University and is now retired after almost 35 years in engineering and management positions with AT&T. He enjoys contesting, especially on 160 meters, DXing on the low bands, antenna experimentation and ragchewing on 160 meters. He has earned more than 60 ARRL and CQ contest award certificates, VUCC, WAS and 160 meter WAS and DXCC. Charlie can be reached at 1100 Yorkshire Rd, Winston-Salem, NC 27106 or at w4tmr@aol.com.

Figure 4 — Close-up of assembled base section and weatherproof enclosure.

Figure 5 — View of the weatherproof plastic food enclosure containing the matching and switching components.

A Quad Loop Revisited

Call it what you like, but this design makes a good antenna for the space-limited amateur.

Floyd Koontz, WA2WVL

The antenna I am describing is known by many names depending on its shape, orientation with respect to ground and feed-point location. To some it is a delta loop, to others a three sided quad loop while others view it as a 1 λ loop. In the configuration described, with the horizontal section on top, it radiates very much like a dipole. I thus choose to view it as a shortened dipole fed at the ends. For 75 meters the total wire length is about 264 feet. The width and height vary with different installations. Figure 1 shows the configuration and Table 1 shows how the width and height are related, along with other key data.

This configuration has many advantages over a conventional center-fed dipole.

- The feed-point is near ground eliminating the hanging feed line and allowing the horizontal portion of the wire to be pulled to maximum height.
- This design works at heights of 40 to 100 feet with a feed impedance similar to, but a little higher than, the center-fed dipole.
- The width is reduced as the height increases, since the total wire length remains nearly constant. The width is down to 56% at 100 feet.
- All adjustment is at ground level without the need to lower the antenna. If a small L network is desired to obtain a perfect match, it can be mounted at eye level for easy adjustment.
- The antenna can easily be retuned from 3800 kHz to 3550 kHz with a 10 µH inductance and a relay located at ground level.
- The end-fed dipole may have reduced pickup of precipitation static since it has no open ends and can be dc grounded at all times.

Table 1
Characteristics of Loop at 3800 kHz and Retuned for 3550 kHz

		3800 kHz		3550 kHz		
Height (feet)	Width (feet)	Impedance (Ω)	Gain at 30° (dBi)	Impedance (Ω)	Gain at 30° (dBi)	Inductance (µH)
100	71.7	69+j0	5.53	55.3+j0	5.11	8.95
90	83.75	100+j0	5.09	78+j0	4.76	9.28
80	94	124.7+j0	4.69	95.7+j0	4.45	9.66
70	102.5	135.8+j0	4.38	103.5+j0	4.19	10.07
60	110	131.4+j0	4.15	100.2±j0	4.02	10.47
50	116.6	113.7+j0	4.04	87.3+j0	3.94	10.76
40	126	86.4+j0	4.10	71.5+j0	4.06	7.22

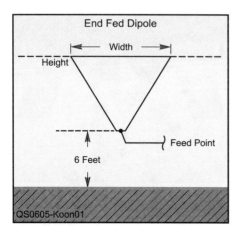

Figure 1 — Delta loop or end-fed dipole configuration.

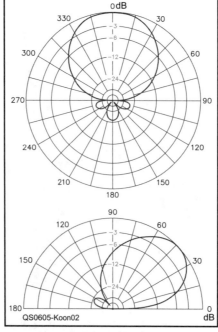

Figure 2 — Predicted performance at 3 element loop Yagi at 3800 kHz. At top, azimuth pattern at 30°. At bottom, elevation pattern at peak of main lobe.

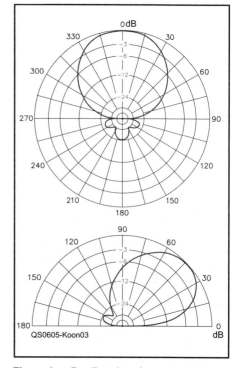

Figure 3 — Predicted performance a three element loop Yagi retuned for 3550 kHz.

Table 2
Design of Wire Beam with Delta Loop Elements
At 60 Feet and 50 Foot Element Spacing

Element	Width (feet)	Inductor (µH)
Driven element	111	10.5
Reflector	116	9.5
Director	106	11.5

Table 3
Calculated Performance of Three Element Loop Beam

Parameter	3800 kHz	3550 kHz
Impedance (Ω)	63.8 − j 0.8	47.3 − j 0.1
SWR	1.28: 1	1.06: 1
Wire Losses (dB)	0.38	0.50
Efficiency (%)	91.6	89.2
Forward Gain at 30° (dBi)	10.11	9.92
F/B (dB)	25.08	24.65
Peak Elevation (°)	41	43

- This configuration is excellent for wire beam (Yagi) designs since all elements have their feeding and tuning points near ground.

A Three Element Wire Beam

Figures 2 and 3 and Tables 2 and 3 describe a three element wire beam using end-fed dipole elements. The basic design is centered at 3800 kHz and inductors are used to retune for 3550 kHz, if desired. It could also have been designed for 3550 kHz with capacitors used to retune to 3800 kHz. Results at both frequencies are nearly identical.

The fine points of the design and construction are left to the reader.

Floyd Koontz, WA2WVL, is a retired electrical engineer with 40 years' experience designing communications systems, radio transmitters and antennas. He was first licensed in 1955 as WN9JQA and has been WA2WVL since 1961. He has written numerous QST articles about antennas over the years. An ARRL life member, he can be reached at 8430 W Park Springs Pl, Homosassa, FL 34448, or **wa2wvl@gowebco.com**.

A Suspended Quarter Wave 40 Meter Wire Vertical Monopole

You can support a monopole from the top and avoid the need for a bunch of radials.

Bob Glorioso, W1IS

The antenna described here is now in its second incarnation. The first version, thrown together to try it out, finally needed to be replaced after being up for nearly 20 years. This antenna has several unusual characteristics. First, it is a full quarter wave wire vertical. Second, the bottom and radials are 10 feet off the ground, thereby minimizing ground losses and making it a very efficient radiator. Third, the design is a bit unconventional as it has only two radials. Why? Well, you really only need two radials on any vertical to provide a balanced counterpoise and two quarter wave 40 meter radials are easier to fit into a small yard.

The catch — the radials have to be in line, 180° apart, to obtain omnidirectional coverage even if they have to be woven through the trees or brush [see the recent *QST* article by David Robbins, K7BKI, for a different approach. — *Ed.*][1] To show that you only need two radials I have included the *EZNEC* azimuth pattern even though it is a boring circle (see Figure 1). As is true for all verticals, it radiates equally badly in all directions! But don't sell a low band vertical short. This is a great DX antenna. The elevation plot (see Figure 2) shows that the take-off angle is a respectable 21°, great for DX even though the gain is not high compared to horizontal antennas. [A 40 meter horizontal dipole would have to be 90 feet above typical ground to achieve the same radiation angle. — *Ed.*]

My antenna is hanging from the limb of a pine tree about 45 feet off the ground. This leaves room for the 34 foot vertical radiator and at least 10 feet of space from the base of the antenna to the ground — plenty of room under the antenna to mow the lawn. Note that the proximity of the tree to the antenna can influence the tuning so it is best to start with longer wires and prune them to get the SWR lowest in the part of the band that you use. I spend most of my time on the lower end of the CW portion with a few trips up to as high as 7.2 MHz. Table 1 shows that I have less than 1.35:1 SWR over the part of the band I operate though my rigs are very happy without a tuner up to the high end of the band where the SWR is still less than 1.75:1.

Table 1
Measured Standing Wave Ratio (SWR) over 40 Meter Amateur Band

Frequency (MHz)	SWR
7.0	1:1
7.1	1.05:1
7.2	1.35:1
7.3	1.75:1

Construction

A dimensioned diagram of the antenna is shown in Figure 3. For the vertical radiator portion, I suggest starting with a 36 foot length of wire #14 AWG or larger. I used #12 AWG silky stranded wire available from The Wireman (**www.thewireman.com**) as item #516. I try to use #16 AWG wire or larger for my radials, so I purchased 75 feet of #14 AWG Flexweave insulated wire from The Wireman, item #542.

The most critical piece is the mount for the coax, radiator and radials. I used aluminum in my first version with an expedient strain relief for the radiator. My current antenna uses a scrap piece of double sided printed circuit board and a more respectable strain relief, an acrylic insulator (the Wireman #813 — see Figure 4).

First cut a 3 inch piece of acrylic plastic in half with a hack saw or band saw. Drill two holes to accommodate two 6-32 screws as shown in Figure 4. Next lay out the board

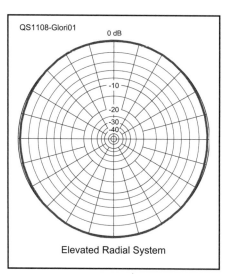

Figure 1 — 7.1 MHz azimuth plot at 21°. Note that it is omnidirectional in spite of only having two radials.

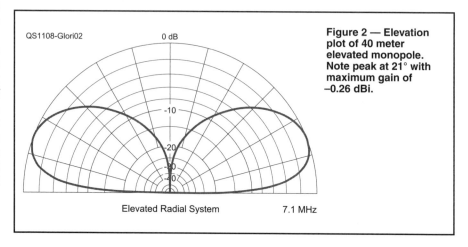

Figure 2 — Elevation plot of 40 meter elevated monopole. Note peak at 21° with maximum gain of –0.26 dBi.

---

[1]D. Robbins, K7BKI, "A Single Element Vertical Beam," *QST*, Jun 2011, pp 42-44.

to make sure you have enough room for the insulator, the coax connector and one radial screw. The other radial will be tied to the screw that holds the insulator. Make the hole for the coax connector. A punch is the easiest way but a ring of small holes and a half round file will also work as will a spade bit. Drill the holes for the insulator and one hole on the opposite side for the other radial. Mount all the parts and admire your work or panic and start over. Scrap PC board is cheap and you probably learned something anyway.

Cut the wires at least 35 feet long so you have enough wire to wrap around the insulators and some to spare for tuning. Strip about 1 inch from one end of each radial wire and tin them. Then bend the wires around the radial attach screws, one on the end of the board and the other holding the insulator, using one washer on each side of the wire and tighten. Attach insulators to the other ends as shown in Figure 5. Note the extra length for adjusting resonance

Feed the radiator wire through the hole in the insulator and wrap it around the long side of the radiator a turn or two leaving enough wire to reach the coax connector. Then solder it to the center conductor of the SO-239 coax jack. I also soldered the wrap to hold it in place. Put an insulator on the other end of the radiator.

Now get out your bow and arrow or sling shot, or warm up your arm and get a rope up 45 feet in a tree. If the radiator goes over a branch either put some shrink wrap on it or good electrical tape. I use a light cord to hold up the radials that are tied to a screw in a tree. The load on the radials is very light as trees don't move much at that height (see Figure 6).

My antenna is about 20 feet from the house so I used a short piece of RG-8X to keep the weight on the antenna down and fed that to a piece of Buryflex coax that goes under the grass and into the shack. The thinner coax and cord for the radials also keeps the antenna visibility down as it is on the street side of our house. I use a straight shovel or an edger to slit the grass and stuff the direct burial rated coax just below the turf. I have used this method to bury radi-

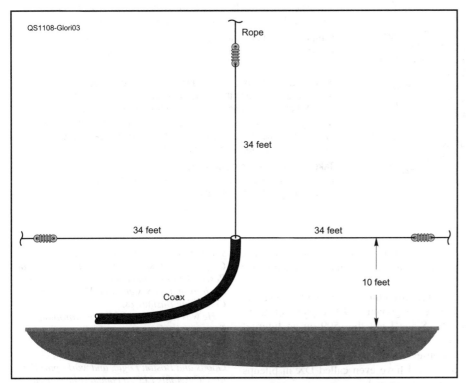

Figure 3 — Vertical monopole configuration and dimensions. (Not to scale.)

Figure 4 — Base connection point for radiator, radials and coax.

Figure 5 — Radial with extra wire for tuning — support cord is on the left.

Figure 6 — The vertical monopole suspended from my pine tree at 45 feet.

Hamspeak

Azimuth pattern — Plot of antenna radiation level as a function of azimuth angle around the antenna. Generally provided at a particular elevation angle.

Coax — Coaxial cable. Kind of unbalanced transmission line in which one conductor is a wire in the center of a dielectric with a circular cross section. The dielectric is surrounded by a tubular conductor, often made of flexible braid. In same cable types, the outer conductor is covered by a protective insulating jacket.

DX — Long distance communication — generally with stations in other countries. Often used to refer to desired countries and prefixes needed for various operating awards.

Elevation pattern — Graphical plot of the radiation intensity of an antenna at different elevation angles. For an omnidirectional antenna, the elevation pattern is the same at every azimuth angle. Other antennas will have elevation patterns that are different at each azimuth angle, so usually the plot at the most significant azimuth is shown. Elevation patterns with large signals near the horizon are generally preferred for line of site operations, such as in VHF mobile communication. Low elevation angles also provide for the longest distance communication via ionospheric propagation.

EZNEC — Antenna modeling software that provides a user friendly interface to the powerful *Numerical Electromagnetic Code* (NEC) calculating engine. Many of the antenna pattern plots used in *QST* articles are generated using *EZNEC*. Several versions of *EZNEC* antenna modeling software are available from developer Roy Lewallen, W7EL, at **www.eznec.com**.

Omnidirectional — An antenna, microphone or light source that radiates equally in all directions. In contrast to a directional source, such as a flashlight, that focuses its energy in a particular direction.

Radials — Portion of a usually vertical antenna, designed to provide an artificial ground or a connection to real ground. The multiple radials project radially from the antenna base in multiple directions. See **www.cebik.com/gp/gr.html**.

RG-8X — Coaxial cable type with 50 Ω characteristic impedance. RG-8X is of an intermediate size between RG-58 and RG-8. It has a foamed dielectric resulting in lower loss than RG-58. RG-8X can use a PL-259 plug with an adapter intended for RG-59 cable.

S-unit — Unit of measure on S-meter. Each S-unit is intended to represent a factor of 2 in input voltage at the receiver antenna terminals.

SWR — Standing wave ratio. Measure of how well a load, such as an antenna, is matched to the design impedance of a transmission line. An SWR of 1:1 indicates a perfect match. Coaxial cables, depending on length, type and frequency can often work efficiently with an SWR of 3:1, sometimes higher. Solid state transmitters frequently require an SWR of 2:1 or less for proper operation.

Takeoff angle — Angle above the ground that an antenna radiates the most power. Lower angles, near the horizon, generally are the best for long distance propagation.

---

als for my 160 Meter Inverted L and to run coax out to my K9AY receiving loop nestled in the woods opposite the 40 meter vertical.

Next tune the antenna by lengthening or shortening the radials and the radiator a few inches at a time. An antenna analyzer is very helpful for this process. All the elements should be the same length when you are finished.

Operation

This is a terrific DX antenna but is marginal for domestic contacts shorter than a few thousand miles. I also have a 130 foot dipole fed with ladder line up about 50 feet broadside toward the east and west that works well on 40 meters. DX stations from all directions are regularly stronger than an S-unit or more on the vertical and most domestic stations see the same advantage on the dipole. Independent of the orientation of the dipole, the take-off angle on the dipole is about 40°, nearly twice that of the vertical, which is why the vertical beats the dipole for DX in all directions.

I have used this antenna mostly with my Ten-Tec Argonaut 509 that puts out about 4 W. Since I got the '509 on an Internet auction site 2 years ago, I have worked 139 countries on CW and 45 on SSB using this antenna. I have even called DX in pileups and gotten through!

ARRL member Bob Glorioso, W1IS, was first licensed in 1955 as WN1EBW and later as W1EBW. After earning BSEE and MSEE degrees he earned a PhD in Computer Science. He served in the US Army as a Captain managing a small group of researchers. After leaving the military he upgraded to Amateur Extra and received his current call.

After his military service, he joined the Electrical and Computer Engineering faculty at the University of Massachusetts, Amherst. His interest in designing and building computer systems led him to the Digital Equipment Corporation, first as Manager of the Corporate Research Group and later as Vice President of the Information Systems and Management Consulting Businesses.

He was founder and CEO of Marathon Technologies Corporation, fault and disaster tolerant systems until his retirement in 2003. Currently he is on the Board of Boston Green Goods and Boston Logic, and works part time for QC Avionix LLC, a company he started with his son, Scott, K1SRG, and Russ Moore, WA1RKO, making and selling electronic devices for general aviation aircraft.

His ham radio interests are low power (QRP), mostly on CW, antennas and working ARRL Field Day with the PART club in Westford, Massachusetts. He has published several technical books, papers and articles, including ham radio articles on subjects ranging from building and modifying gear to antennas. He is also a private pilot and flies a Bonanza and a Citabria. You can reach Bob at 70 Birch Hill Rd, Stow, MA 01775-1307 or at **w1is@arrl.net**.

Surprising Results with a Low, Hidden Wire Antenna

Here's how one amateur made a stealth wire antenna system that doesn't give up much performance.

Bruce Pontius, NØADL

We live in a community that does not appreciate outdoor antennas of any kind. In addition, the houses are close together and RF interference can be a problem at neighbors' houses as well as mine. Occasional minor interference seems less objectionable to neighbors if they don't see antennas to remind them of (or alert them to) the radio operations. I have good relationships with my neighbors, but I would rather avoid RFI discussions.

The 45 foot high horizontal loop and balanced feed system described a couple of years ago in *QST*[1] would be terrific, but I don't have supports to get a loop up in the air. Forget that! Like it or not, I have to use hidden antennas except for temporary operations. In this article, I discuss my experiences with an almost unnoticeable end-fed random wire HF antenna and counterpoise system. I tend to use short transmissions on SSB and low power for digital modes, and I have had many rewarding and enjoyable contacts with this simple setup. If you're in a neighborhood that's unfriendly towards outdoor antennas, perhaps you will be encouraged to try your own stealth antenna.

"Design" of the End-Fed Random Wire Antenna

I started with a chart of relative impedance versus wire length for the HF bands. I chose a length of 92 feet, which provides a reasonable impedance for an antenna tuner on most bands. At 15 meters, the wire is nearly a multiple of $1/2\, \lambda$, presenting a very high impedance at the antenna tuner. This might also be the case at 60 and 30 meters, but these two bands are not a main goal for me. After building the antenna, I was pleasantly surprised that my MFJ-949D tuner could provide a match to the transmitter at 15 meters and does not arc or misbehave, at least at 100 W input. The antenna is about $3/8\, \lambda$ at 75 meters, and it works there, at least a little.

The next task was running the wire outside and along the roof of my house. Most of the antenna is 20 gauge insulated wire, with 18 gauge stranded bare copper to lower visibility where the wire is above the roofline and in silhouette. The wire starts at the operating location and passes through an exterior wall just above the patio roof behind the house. Then the wire runs up to the main roof, following a tortuous path over the edge of the tile roof, up to a low chimney, and then along the peak of the roof. It is lying on the tile for much of its length and in some places is held slightly above the roof where it is tied to the chimney and, further along, to a vent pipe. The last 6 feet or so of the wire, at the open end, is held off of the roof tiles by finding appropriate places to tie it. The highest spot is at the chimney, 17 feet, 9 inches above the earth.

To get the wire outside, I drilled a 5/16 inch hole through the wall from the outside and drew the wire through the wall. Be sure there are no wires or pipes where you drill! The holes were plugged with caulking material. If the wire is removed, the holes

[1]Notes appear on page 147.

can be filled and painted to match. Inside, the entry point is concealed by a china cabinet and the wire can be hidden when not in use. As indicated in the lead photo, the hidden wire antenna is barely noticeable as it exits above the patio roof and disappears over the edge of the tile roof.

I use the antenna with a portable station that takes only a few minutes to set up and put away, leaving almost no traces of a radio station. Another radio operating position, in the middle of the house, has more permanent antenna feeds for indoor antennas or for temporary VHF/UHF or satellite operations.

Developing an Effective Counterpoise

When I first tried transmitting with the random wire, there was RF all over the place, including a tingle in my fingers and nose. Adding wires to the ground lug on the antenna tuner to form a counterpoise improved things considerably. My counterpoise wires are made from insulated 20 gauge wire and tied with nylon string to furniture in adjoining rooms. The wires are 25-30 inches above the floor and close to $1/4\ \lambda$ at the frequency in use.

My first counterpoise didn't solve all the issues with stray RF. For example, on 40 meters, with only one $1/4\ \lambda$ radial, a ground fault circuit breaker in the adjacent kitchen picks up RF energy and trips. I started experimenting with the MFJ-931 Artificial Ground counterpoise tuner. With a second 40-meter counterpoise wire attached to the MFJ-931 and another '931 tuning a wire to an 8 foot ground rod just outside the wall, things are much cooler. There is no noticeable RF feedback or mischief except for the inevitable pickup in the wireless phones and audio equipment. The higher bands pose fewer ground system difficulties and do not require a tuner or a ground rod.

Figure 1 shows the system I ended up with. The transceiver is on the far right and the MFJ-949D antenna tuner is the lower box on the left. The red antenna wire goes up and to the left from the WIRE terminal on the tuner. Fixed counterpoise wires (one $1/4\ \lambda$ wire for each band in use) attach to the ground lug. More counterpoise wires, perhaps passing out through windows, might help performance but the complication does not seem worth the possible improvement.

One MFJ-931 counterpoise tuner is on the table between the transceiver and antenna tuner. The wire connected to the red terminal is approximately $1/4\ \lambda$ for the band currently in use, and I change wires and tuner settings when I change bands. Another counterpoise tuner is on top of the antenna tuner, with a wire going outside to an 8 foot ground rod. The ground rod alone

Figure 1—The station equipment setup, viewed from the back.

Figure 2—Antenna tuner settings can be recorded on a chart for faster band changes.

is used for 75 meter operation because of the difficulty in routing effective $1/4\ \lambda$ (63 foot) counterpoise wires around the house. Once the system is tuned up, bandwidth on 40 meters and up is adequate to cover most of the General class phone sections with little or no retuning. Table 1 shows the wire lengths I used for the counterpoise system. The last two columns are dimensions for a $1/4\ \lambda$ vertical antenna used for comparison testing as described later.

This setup might seem complicated but it really only takes about 12 minutes to assemble the equipment and wires from their stowed positions for a day of operating, and then only a couple of minutes to change bands. To make band changes easier, you can make a chart like the one shown in Figure 2 to preset the antenna tuner and main counterpoise tuner.

Most of the transmitter power seems to be going into the antenna. The tuner has been tested with loads simulating the wire antenna. Losses appear to be less than 1 dB on most bands, but I have not checked 80 meters. The transfer function on all bands exhibits expected changes versus frequency, demonstrating that it is not just a flat-frequency-response "dummy load" antenna and matching system.

When using two or more counterpoise tuners with RF current sensors and meters, the effects of resonance in the counterpoise wires is quite evident. For example, I tuned one counterpoise for maximum RF current while transmitting (it's tuned for minimum RF impedance—what we want is a short at the tuner). When another counterpoise wire is added, the two wires are interactive. If one is detuned from resonance, the current increases in the other and vice versa. Probably the best situation is to roughly balance the two currents, or in the case of many counterpoise wires, to cause them all to be at resonance and to equally share the RF ground currents.

On the Air with the Wire Antenna

I used a 100 W transceiver for the operating described here. Some contacts were made in 2002 and 2003, but most of my operating with this wire took place in February and March of 2004 after the sunspot cycle had continued its drop. The relatively small amount of operating time has resulted in Worked All States on 20 meters with QSL cards in hand. I'm just a few states short of Worked All States on 17 and 15 meters, and have worked all continents. A few days of operation thus far on 40 meters has yielded more than 30 states.

In only a few hours of operation during the 2004 ARRL DX Contest, I logged many stations on 10 meters and 15 meters, including all continents except Africa. My time only allowed a few contacts on 20 meters, as I concentrated on 10 and 15 while those bands were active.

The results that weekend encouraged me to try the CQ WPX contest at the end of March 2004. Again, I went for the higher bands first and logged more than 30 contacts on 10 meters and about 50 contacts on 15 meters in just a few hours of operating time. Contacts included DX stations on five continents. Running out of time, I reluctantly moved down to 20 meters and, of course, could have filled a computer log book with so many stations on the air. I was not able to make contacts through some pileups, but was quite satisfied with the percentage of successful attempts. I did listen far more than transmit. The activity on 40 meters seemed lower, at least during daytime, so I only tried for a while, logging a dozen or so in a half hour.

Comparisons with Other Antennas

The performance of the hidden wire was much better than expected, so I invested some effort in on-site comparisons with other antennas to get an estimate of just how much performance must be given up in the use of the compromise antenna and ground system. It happened that both of my next door neighbors were to be gone for two weeks at the same time, so I could put up some big antennas and blast away without breaking my cover.

First, I set up a Force 12 Sigma 5 vertical dipole for 20-10 meters in the backyard with the lower end about 2.5 feet above ground. On-the-air transmit and receive comparisons showed that the wire often

Figure 3—The 20 meter vertical antenna is about 22 feet tall, including the 5 foot wooden support post. It definitely attracts more attention than the hidden wire.

seemed to work as well or better on 20, 17 and 15 meters. I did not try 10 meters. The two antennas could be switched rapidly back and forth using the Kenwood TS-570D's two antenna ports and the front panel switch. The wire was fed through a tuner, but the Sigma 5 did not require one. I have heard of others' successful use of the Sigma 5, so I was pleased that the wire compared well with it. Therefore I decided to put in more effort to make comparisons with standard antennas.

Building a Comparison Antenna

A standard half-wave, horizontal dipole would have been most desirable for comparisons, but I don't have sufficient supports. A vertical ground plane with elevated radials seemed to be the next best standard antenna type, and it was something that I could manage in my yard.

I considered buying a good vertical antenna but didn't want to complicate the comparison with a multiband unit. I wanted to have a basic, inexpensive $1/4\ \lambda$ piece of metal for simplicity of measurements on one band at a time. Besides, I love the magic of fundamental electrical phenomena and looked forward to observing the interactions of simple vertical conductors and an elevated, tuned radial system.

The first vertical, for 20 meters, is shown

Table 1
Antenna and Radial Wire Lengths

Band (meters)	Center Freq (MHz)	Calculated $1/4\ \lambda$ (feet)	Length of Counterpoises (feet)	Vertical Radiator Length (feet)	$1/4\ \lambda$ Radial Length (feet)
75	3.925	59.6	Ground rod		
60	5.350	43.7			
40	7.265	32.2	34.0, *32.4**	32.9**	32.9
30	10.125	23.1			
20	14.290	16.4	16.2, *14.6**	16.7	17.0
17	18.140	12.9	13.4, *14.6**	13.4	13.4
15	21.375	10.9	11.5, *10.2**	13.4***	11.2
12	24.960	9.4	9.4, *7.5**		
10	28.490	8.2	8.3, *7.0**		

*The length shown in italics is for an additional counterpoise wire tuned through the MFJ-931 Artificial Ground counterpoise tuner for operation on 40-10 meters (no counterpoise wire is used on 75 meters). Also, on 40 meters and 75 meters, another MFJ-931 tunes a wire connected to an 8 foot ground rod.
**This dimension was about 10 inches too short.
***The 17 meter vertical radiator was also used for 15 meters and the antenna fed through the tuner.

Figure 4—Radials are wrapped around a hose clamp and pressed against the antenna connector. A brass strap is soldered to the connector center conductor and then bolted to the vertical radiator. Two U bolts hold the vertical radiator to the mast.

in Figure 3. The vertical radiator uses an 8 foot length of 1 inch tubing with an 8 foot length of 7/8 inch tubing telescoped inside. A 3/8 inch aluminum rod clamped to the 7/8 inch tube brings the total length to 16 feet, 9 inches. The antenna base is 5 feet above ground, mounted on a 2-inch-square wooden pole with two U bolts as shown in Figure 4. The top of the pole is guyed with four nylon ropes.

Nine 17 foot radials (seven good ones and two bent to fit my yard) were fastened at the feed point by twisting the 18 gauge stranded copper radial wires around a hose clamp as seen in Figure 4. The radials are about 5 feet above ground at the antenna base and are stretched out and tied off with nylon string to stakes (or to anything handy).

The feed point connects with straps to the vertical radiator as shown in Figure 4. One strap is fastened with a screw and nut to the bottom antenna section and the other is clamped between the pole and antenna tube. An insulator can be placed on the wood pole behind the strap if desired. The straps are soldered to the connector center pin.

Adjusting the Vertical

Before attaching all the radials, I adjusted the first four with the aid of instruments. Next I adjusted the vertical radiator for resonance at the desired frequency. Then I cut the rest of the radials to length, attached nine and again measured the antenna resonant frequency. Leaving the vertical radiator length alone at that point, I readjusted the radials to bring the antenna to resonance. This iterative process could be repeated, but results were good enough after one cycle. The final dimensions are shown in Table 1.

The signal source for these adjustments is similar to the one I described in *QEX*,[2] followed by a Motorola 2832C balanced, push-pull amplifier and a 3 dB attenuator. The power level through the precision directional couplers to the antenna can be less than 100 mW since sensitive power meters are used.

Thankfully, all this measuring must be done only once. After the antenna is adjusted, the SWR will be less than 1.4:1. The vertical can be set up anywhere and things will work properly unless large conducting objects are in close proximity.

I used similar procedures for the 17 and 15 meter versions. The 17 meter antenna used nine radials. The 15 meter antenna used all of the 17 meter radials, plus 6 more cut to the length shown and fit in between. I used the 17 meter vertical radiator length on 15 meters as well, and fed the antenna through a tuner.

For 40 meters, I added another 8 foot section of aluminum tubing at the bottom and lengthened the 3/8 inch rod to make a 33 foot vertical. This antenna was guyed at the middle with ropes. The 40 meter radials were a compromise. Three 34 foot radials fit in the yard without bending, but three additional wires required bending to fit, with two of them quite contorted.

Compromise Wire versus Full Size Vertical

I compared the vertical and the random wire on 20 meters first. An operator in the Philippines thought the vertical slightly better, but at my end, on receive, the signal-to-noise (S/N) ratio was better on the (mostly horizontal) wire. Contacts in California favored the vertical, while contacts in Idaho and Washington favored the wire, as did local Arizona contacts. A couple of stations in Texas liked the vertical a little better, while stations in the Southeastern US gave better reports on the wire. The Upper Midwest and Northeast were a toss-up.

Received signals exhibited a better S/N ratio on the wire 75% of the time or more, but often the signal strength was somewhat higher on the vertical. Ignition noise was much louder on the vertical, but it can be reduced with the noise blanker and doesn't often bother me. Sometimes the signal strength and quality advantage at both ends of the contact shifted back and forth between the wire and vertical, adding to the conclusion that the two antennas performed about the same.

On 17 meters, a fair amount of listening revealed that the wire was definitely better on receive. As on 20 meters, the S/N ratio was better on the wire. Contacts in Mexico and the Caribbean favored the wire. Stations in South America and Japan reported equal performance. During a contact with a Texas station signals shifted back and forth, with one antenna better and then the other. A station in Alabama on a vertical antenna reported better signals from the wire. In general, the southeastern US seemed about the same on either antenna, as did the Midwest and New York. This was far from a comprehensive test, but it appeared that performance was similar to 20 meters with a slight advantage going to the wire.

After listening for a while, I didn't hear anyone on 15 meters so I resorted to calling CQ. Up popped VP6MW, one of 42 residents of Pitcairn Island in the South Pacific. We had a great QSO during which signals varied widely. The wire seemed to give a better S/N signal on receive, and VP6MW reported my signals about the same on the two antennas. During operations on a net, where protocol prohibited back-and-forth transmit comparisons, the antennas seemed to work about the same.

On 40 meters, the 34 foot aluminum vertical outperformed the wire on transmit, significantly in some cases, during contacts with 20 or more stations from around the US. Most reported stronger signals with the vertical, typically at least 1 S-unit and up to 2 S-units. As on the other bands, better receive S/N ratios on the wire helped the receive performance. On the lower bands, the wire is clearly a compromise as a transmitting antenna. Nevertheless, with limited time and effort, operation on 40 meters with the wire has yielded solid contacts in more than 30 states. More counterpoise wires might help.

The Wire Works Okay, but is it Safe?

RF safety is a concern with any indoor antenna or antenna close to the house. I was able to make some measurements of the electric fields of the hidden wire and comparison vertical antennas. Using these relative voltage measurements and information and tables from the ARRL publication *RF Exposure and You*,[3] I determined that the maximum permissible exposure (MPE) would not be exceeded using 100 W on SSB and short transmission times.

I based my conclusions on the tables starting on pages 8.26 and 8.37. These tables are for ground-mounted verticals and for elevated vertical ground planes. The worst case exposure situation for the vertical antennas is when the operator is sitting right within the radials field of an elevated vertical, among the radial wires, with head and shoulders above the plane of the radials. The tables say a person could be within 11 feet of an elevated groundplane vertical antenna and be under the exposure limit, even with more than 100 W PEP of transmit power. (Duty cycle and on/off times are considered and factored in for my type of operations on SSB.)

The wire antenna slopes away from the operator, with limited counterpoise wires extending away from the operator. It was assumed to exhibit lower energy fields near the base than the vertical antennas in the tables. Also, the total energy radiated in the near field from the wire is distributed somewhat along its 92 foot length. Considerably more than 100 W of power could probably be used with the wire while remaining within the recommended MPE limits, however. Each operator is responsible for his own evaluation of his particular situation. *Note:* While the author's configuration may not exceed published limits, an antenna like this is hard to evaluate for RF safety, especially since so much of it is in proximity to people. To be safe, consider limiting power output to 50 W or less to be below the threshold at which measurements or analysis is required.—*Ed.*

Conclusions

The stealth wire works. Using an end-fed wire eliminates the need for a supported center feed, which can be difficult to do while keeping the antenna out of sight. If you have a problem with erecting a huge, high antenna, go ahead and string up this compromise. Even though it is a compromise, it is a quite effective antenna and counterpoise system—even as a portable station.

Notes
[1] K. Kleinschmidt, "A Balanced, Everyday Approach to All-Band Bliss," *QST*, Apr 2002, pp 47-50.
[2] B. Pontius, "Signal Sources," *QEX*, Nov/Dec 1999, pp 18-30. See Note 11 in this article.
[3] E. Hare, *RF Exposure and You* (Newington: 1998). Available from your local dealer, or from the ARRL Bookstore, ARRL order no. 6621. Telephone toll-free in the US 888-277-5289, or 860-594-0355, fax 860-594-0303; **www.arrl.org/shop/**; **pubsales@arrl.org**. You can also find RF exposure resources on-line at **www.arrl.org/tis/info/rfexpose.html**.

Additional Reading
The author's original, unedited article with data and pictures is available on **www.radioadv.com**.
B. Muscolino, "My Antenna is a Compromise—and It Works!" *QST*, Apr 2003, pp 59-61. This article supports the use of simple end-fed wires, but does not provide much actual same-site comparison.
K. Kleinschmidt, *Stealth Amateur Radio* (Newington: 1998). This book is devoted to operating without calling attention to yourself. It's currently out of print but may be available on-line or at hamfests.

The ARRL Web site has information on limited space antennas at **www.arrl.org/tis/info/limited.html**.

Photos by the author.

Bruce Pontius, NØADL, holds a BSEE and has been involved in the development of semiconductors and radio equipment and systems for many years. He played major roles in the development of early cellular radio equipment, digital trunking radios and narrowband data radio equipment. Bruce served as Engineering Vice President at EF Johnson Company for 15 years and worked with other companies in similar roles. He now serves as president of TRM Associates and is working in wireless communications and RFID. Bruce first got involved with Amateur Radio at age 11, building radios and test equipment with his father. He has been licensed since 1978 and enjoys operating with simple equipment and portable operation. You can reach Bruce at 15802 N 50th St, Scottsdale, AZ 85254, e-mail **bepontius@aol.com**.

By Steve Ford, WB8IMY

One Stealthy Delta

This HF antenna keeps a low visual profile while attracting plenty of attention on the air.

Loop antennas have always fascinated me. From a common-sense standpoint they seem impossible. I mean, how can you have a short circuit at the output of your transceiver and call it an antenna? I'd call it bright flash, smoke, and stream of obscenities.

But the magic we call radio is never so straightforward. Yes, a loop antenna is unquestionably a short circuit at the output of your radio—if your radio produced dc. Radio frequency energy, however, is ac and it views a loop quite differently. A loop represents an impedance load to RF. The impedance value depends on the size of the loop, the frequency of the RF and other factors, but it is most definitely *not* a short circuit.

The October 1998 *QST* carried an article of mine titled "One Stealthy Wire" in which I used a remotely tuned antenna coupler to match my radio to a random-wire antenna supported by a lonely maple tree in my back yard. If artists and musicians can go through creative "periods" when their muses suddenly decide to speak in different tongues, so can amateurs. The maple tree is still here

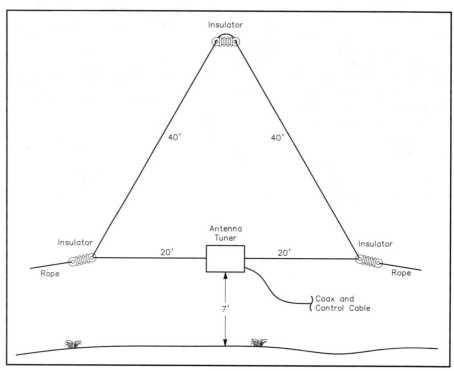

Figure 1—A diagram of the Stealthy Delta.

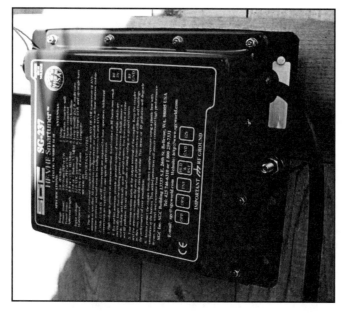

The SG-237 tuner hangs on a wood privacy fence, just behind the tree trunk.

Do you see an antenna in this picture? Probably not!

148 STEALTH

The privacy fence also acts as an anchor for one of the legs of the Stealthy Delta.

The direct-bury coax makes a discreet jaunt into the bedroom window.

and so am I, but I've abandoned my single-wire period and have embarked on the year of the loop. Or to quote Daffy Duck in the memorable cartoon, "I swear, your honor, I will never paint a malicious mustache on a work of art again… *I'm doin' beards now!*"

The Problem Remains the Same

Little else has changed in four years. I still exist on a house lot the size of a postage stamp. The local squirrels have easements written into my deed. I still have a wife who distrusts my every move and despises every antenna I attempt to create. When I wonder aloud about where I can erect my next abomination, her reply is "Cleveland."

I asked Dean Straw, N6BV, our resident ARRL antenna guru, how I could improve my situation. The exchange went something like this…

Dean: Put up a tower and a triband Yagi antenna.

Me: Do these things come with divorce documents?

Dean: How about a 100-foot dipole 50 feet above the ground?

Me: Supported by what two tastefully designed 50-foot objects?

Dean: How about a vertical loop supported by your tree?

That's when the sweatsock-filled-with-nickels-of-inspiration struck me upside the head. How about a loop not only supported by the tree, *but in the tree?*

The Stealthy Delta

A delta loop gets its classy moniker from the Greek alphabet, namely the letter *delta*, or Δ. My Stealthy Delta is a vertical wire triangle fed directly in the middle of its base (see Figure 1). For multiband HF operation the idea is to make the triangle as big as possible. It also helps to keep the base of the triangle about 7 feet or so off the ground.

For my application each side of the triangle is 40 feet in length. Remember that the wire is continuous; that's why they call it a loop. Using our wood privacy fence to hide the bottom wire, I strung the loop out 20 feet to an insulator, up into the tree (to an insulator suspended by a Nylon rope), down to another insulator on the other side of the tree and then finally back to where I began. Was it a perfect triangle? No. Was it good enough for Amateur Radio and rock n' roll? You bet.

And now that it was strung, how would I feed the Stealthy Delta? I would need an antenna tuner for multiband operation—that much was clear. With the tuner indoors I could use 450-Ω ladder line between the tuner and the feed point of the antenna. In my case, however, the ladder line would have to take a torturous route to reach the Stealthy Delta. It would have to careen through the air and directly over my wife's sacred hedges and rose bushes. That was unacceptable (to her, anyway). The alternative was to use a substantial length of buried coax, but coaxial cable is much too lossy in the face of the high SWRs that would exist between the antenna and the tuner.

If the mountain will not come to Mohamet, Mohamet must go to the mountain. Or putting it in a ham context, if the antenna will not come to the tuner without unacceptable feed line loss, the tuner must go to the antenna. Borrowing an idea from my "One Stealthy Wire" article, I invested in a new SG-237 remote automatic antenna tuner from SGC Inc (**www.sgcworld.com**). I installed the tuner at the feed point, hiding it behind the tree trunk, and ran direct-bury coax and a power cable all the way back to the station. I buried most of the wires, except for a short run up the side of the house and into the guest bedroom window.

How Does it Work?

The SG-237 is RF activated. You transmit and it finds a low SWR within a few seconds. That low SWR is achieved at the antenna. With the good-quality coax I used between the tuner and my radio, feed line loss was kept to a minimum (a little over 1 dB on 6 meters and much less on lower bands). With my Stealthy Delta the SGC tuner can find an acceptable match with an SWR less than 2:1 on any amateur frequency from 80 through 6 meters. If I had erected a somewhat larger loop, I probably could have operated the antenna on 160 meters as well.

In terms of performance, the Stealthy Delta is definitely superior to my single stealthy wire. Even on 80 meters, where it is way too short, the loop surprised me. During a recent RTTY contest I made several contacts into Europe on 80 meters, which I've never done before on RTTY from home. On 40 through 10 meters I consistently receive strong signal reports. I worked the XRØX and TI9M DXpeditions on RTTY after just a few calls and even managed to get through the pileup to work the PWØT group on 15-meter SSTV. Not bad for a wire triangle.

And best of all, the Stealthy Delta is very stealthy indeed. The tree camouflages most of the antenna. The photos that accompany this article were shot in March when the tree was bare and yet the antenna is very difficult to see. Just imagine how invisible it is when the tree is in bloom.

Will I stick with the Stealthy Delta? Certainly...for now. I can't beat the performance and convenience, but I'm sure I'll eventually think of something that will. Some day my "loop period" will give way to some other source of annoyance for my wife and child…

"I swear, honey, I will never erect another diabolical delta…*I'm doin' rhombics now!*"

You can contact the author at ARRL Headquarters, 225 Main St, Newington, CT 06111; **sford@arrl.org**.

Resources

(From the 22nd edition of the ARRL Antenna Book, Chapter 25)

Wire Antennas

25.1.1 WIRE TYPES

Solid copper wire is used for most wire antennas although the use of stranded wire is common. Solid wire is less flexible than stranded wire, but it is available "hard-drawn," which offers good tensile strength and negligible stretch. Special stranded wire with a larger-than-usual number of fine strands (such as Flex-Weave) is available for building antennas. It withstands vibration and bending in the wind better than common stranded wire and better than solid wire. Galvanized steel and aluminum wire are generally not used for antennas because of higher electrical resistance than copper. Galvanized wire also has a strong tendency to rust and making good electrical connections to aluminum wire is difficult — it cannot be directly soldered without special solder fluxes.

Solid wire is also available with and without enamel coating. Enamel coating resists oxidation and corrosion, but bare wire is far more common. Solid wire is also available with a variety of different insulating coatings, including plastics, rubbers and PVC. Unless specifically rated for outdoor use however, wire insulation, including enamel, tends to break down when exposed to the UV in sunlight. Insulation also lowers the velocity factor of wire by a few percent (see the **Transmission Lines** chapter) making it electrically longer than its physical length — this will lower the resonant frequency of an antenna compared to one made of bare wire of equivalent diameter. In addition, insulation increases wind loading without increasing strength. If enameled or insulated wire is used, care should be taken to not nick the wire when removing the coating for an electrical connection. Wire will break at a nick when flexed repeatedly, such as by wind.

"Soft-drawn" or annealed copper wire is easy to handle and obtain. Common THHN-insulated "house wire" is soft-drawn. Unfortunately, soft-drawn wire stretches considerably under load. Soft-drawn wire should only be used in applications where there will be little or no tension, or where some change in length can be tolerated. For example, the length of a horizontal antenna fed at the center with open-wire line is not critical, although a change in length may require some readjustment of an impedance matching unit. Similarly, if the wire stretches significantly, it can be re-trimmed to the desired length. Repeated cycles of stretching followed by trimming and re-tensioning will result in loss of strength and possibly in mechanical failure.

"Hard-drawn" copper wire and CCS (copper-clad steel, usually sold as the trademarked product Copperweld) wire are more difficult to handle because of their mechanical stiffness and, in the case of CCS, the tendency to have "memory" when unrolled. These types of wire are ideal for applications where high strength for a given weight is required and/or significant stretch cannot be tolerated. Care should be exercised to make sure kinks do not develop in hard-drawn and CCS wire — the wire will have a far greater tendency to break at a kink. The "memory" or tendency of CCS wire to coil up can be reduced by suspending it a few feet above ground for a few days before final use. The wire should not be recoiled before it is installed.

The electrical quality of CCS wire varies considerably. A conductivity class of 30% or higher is desirable, meaning the wire has 30% of the conductivity of copper wire of the same

Table 25-1
Copper-Wire Table

Wire Size AWG (B&S)	Dia in Mils[1]	Dia in mm	Turns per Linear Inch Enamel	Feet per Pound Bare	Ohms per 1000 ft 25°C[3]	Cont.-duty current[2,3] Single Wire in Open Air
1	289.3	7.348	—	3.947	0.1264	—
2	257.6	6.544	—	4.977	0.1593	—
3	229.4	5.827	—	6.276	0.2009	—
4	204.3	5.189	—	7.914	0.2533	—
5	181.9	4.621	—	9.980	0.3195	—
6	162.0	4.115	—	12.58	0.4028	—
7	144.3	3.665	—	15.87	0.5080	—
8	128.5	3.264	7.6	20.01	0.6405	73
9	114.4	2.906	8.6	25.23	0.8077	—
10	101.9	2.588	9.6	31.82	1.018	55
11	90.7	2.305	10.7	40.12	1.284	—
12	80.8	2.053	12.0	50.59	1.619	41
13	72.0	1.828	13.5	63.80	2.042	—
14	64.1	1.628	15.0	80.44	2.575	32
15	57.1	1.450	16.8	101.4	3.247	—
16	50.8	1.291	18.9	127.9	4.094	22
17	45.3	1.150	21.2	161.3	5.163	—
18	40.3	1.024	23.6	203.4	6.510	16
19	35.9	0.912	26.4	256.5	8.210	—
20	32.0	0.812	29.4	323.4	10.35	11
21	28.5	0.723	33.1	407.8	13.05	—
22	25.3	0.644	37.0	514.2	16.46	—
23	22.6	0.573	41.3	648.4	20.76	—
24	20.1	0.511	46.3	817.7	26.17	—
25	17.9	0.455	51.7	1031	33.00	—
26	15.9	0.405	58.0	1300	41.62	—
27	14.2	0.361	64.9	1639	52.48	—
28	12.6	0.321	72.7	2067	66.17	—
29	11.3	0.286	81.6	2607	83.44	—
30	10.0	0.255	90.5	3287	105.2	—
31	8.9	0.227	101	4145	132.7	—
32	8.0	0.202	113	5227	167.3	—
33	7.1	0.180	127	6591	211.0	—
34	6.3	0.160	143	8310	266.0	—
35	5.6	0.143	158	10480	335	—
36	5.0	0.127	175	13210	423	—
37	4.5	0.113	198	16660	533	—
38	4.0	0.101	224	21010	673	—
39	3.5	0.090	248	26500	848	—
40	3.1	0.080	282	33410	1070	—

[1]A mil is 0.001 inch.
[2]Max wire temp of 212° F and max ambient temp of 135° F.
[3]Ratings are for dc measurements and currents without skin effect.

diameter but for RF applications at HF it will have close to 100% conductivity due to skin effect. Copper cladding can be damaged by abrasion (typically at insulators) or sharp bends. Plastic insulators of sufficient strength are preferable to ceramic insulators when using CCS; they are soft in comparison and less likely to degrade the copper cladding over time. Induced defects in copper cladding eventually result in mechanical failure due to rusting of the steel core. Breaks in the copper cladding also form high resistance points to RF and will heat considerably when running high power. Heat accelerates oxidation (rusting).

25.1.2 WIRE SIZE AND TENSION

Many factors influence the choice of wire type and size (gage or gauge). Important considerations include the length of the unsupported span, the amount of sag that can be tolerated, the stability of the supports under wind pressure, the amount of wind and ice loading anticipated and whether or not a transmission line will be suspended from the span. Some sag is desirable. Removing most or all sag requires additional unnecessary tension and increases the likelihood of failure. **Table 25-1** shows the wire diameter, current-carrying capacity and resistance of various sizes of copper wire. **Table 25-2** shows the recommended maximum working tension of hard-drawn and CCS wire of various sizes. The recommended working tension is approximately 10% of the minimum guaranteed breaking strength of the wire. Together with a calculation of span sag, these two tables can be used to select the appropriate wire size for an antenna.

The National Electrical Code (see the chapter **Building Antenna Systems and Towers**) specifies minimum conductor sizes for different span-length wire antennas. For hard-drawn copper wire, the Code specifies #14 AWG wire for open (unsupported) spans less than 150 feet, and #10 AWG for longer spans. CCS, bronze or other high-strength conductors may be #14 AWG for spans less than 150 feet and #12 AWG for longer runs. Lead-in conductors (for open-wire transmission line) should be at least as large as those specified for antennas.

The RF resistance of copper wire increases as the size of the wire decreases. In most common wire antenna designs however, the antenna's radiation resistance will be much higher than the wire's RF resistance and the efficiency of the antenna will be adequate. Wire sizes as small as #30 AWG, or even smaller, have been used successfully in the construction of "invisible" antennas in areas where more conventional antennas cannot be erected. In most cases, the selection of wire for an antenna will be based primarily on the mechanical properties of the wire, since the suspension of wire from elevated supports places the wire in tension.

If the tension on a wire can be adjusted to a known value, the expected sag of the wire (**Figure 25.1**) may be determined using Table 25-2 and the nomograph of **Figure 25.2**. Alternately, sag can be adjusted to achieve a desired tension. Even though there may be no convenient method to determine the tension in pounds, calculation of the expected sag for practical working tension is often desirable. If the calculated sag is greater than allowable it may be reduced by any one or a combination of the following:

1) Providing additional supports, thereby decreasing the span
2) Increasing the tension in the wire
3) Decreasing the size (gage or gauge) of the wire

Instructions for Using the Nomograph

1) From Table 25-2, find the weight

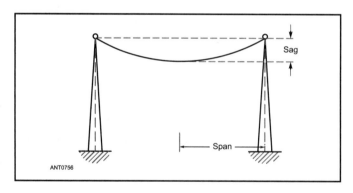

Figure 25.1 — The span and sag of a long-wire antenna.

Table 25-2
Stressed Antenna Wire

American Wire Gauge	Recommended Tension[1] (pounds)		Weight (pounds per 1000 feet)	
	Copper-clad steel[2]	Hard-drawn copper	Copper-clad steel[2]	Hard-drawn copper
4	495	214	115.8	126.0
6	310	130	72.9	79.5
8	195	84	45.5	50.0
10	120	52	28.8	31.4
12	75	32	18.1	19.8
14	50	20	11.4	12.4
16	31	13	7.1	7.8
18	19	8	4.5	4.9
20	12	5	2.8	3.1

[1] Approximately one-tenth the guaranteed breaking strength. Might be increased 50% if end supports are firm and there is no danger of ice loading.
[2] Copperweld, 40% copper

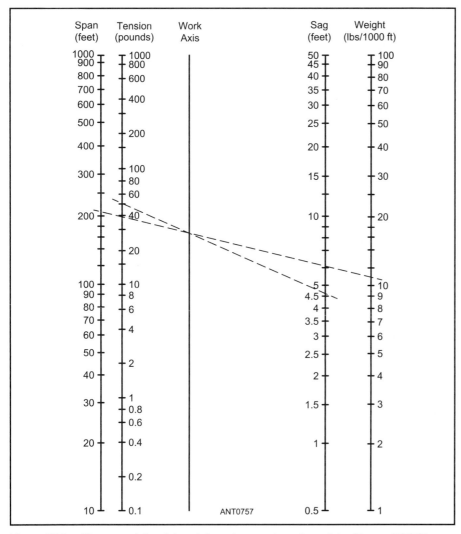

Figure 25.2 — Nomograph for determining wire sag. (*courtesy John Elengo, W1DQ*)

(pounds/1000 feet) for the particular wire size and material to be used.

2) Draw a line from the value obtained above, plotted on the weight axis, to the desired span (feet) on the span axis, Figure 25.2. Note in Figure 25.1 that the span is one half the distance between the supports.

3) Choose an operating tension in pounds, consistent with the values presented in Table 25-2 (preferably less than that recommended).

4) Draw a line from the tension value chosen (plotted on the tension axis) through the point where the work axis crosses the original line constructed in step 2, and continue this new line to the sag axis.

5) Read the sag in feet on the sag axis.
Example:
Weight = 11 pounds/1000 feet
Span = 210 feet
Tension = 50 pounds
Answer: Sag = 4.7 feet

These calculations do not take into account the weight of a feed line supported by the antenna wire.

25.1.3 WIRE SPLICING

Wire antennas should preferably be made with unbroken lengths of wire. In instances where this is not feasible, wire sections should be spliced as shown in **Figure 25.3**. Any insulation should be removed for a distance of about 6 inches from the end of each section (take care not to nick the wire). Enamel may be removed by scraping with a knife or rubbing with sandpaper until the copper underneath is bright. The turns of wire should be brought up tight around the standing part of the wire by twisting with broad-nose pliers.

The crevices formed by the wire should be completely filled by using solder that does not contain an acid-core flux. A soldering iron or gun may not be sufficient for heavy wire or in cold temperatures; use a propane or butane torch instead. The joint should be heated sufficiently so the solder flows freely into the joint when the source of heat is removed momentarily. After the joint has cooled completely, it should be wiped clean with a cloth and then sprayed generously with acrylic to prevent corrosion.

25.1.4 ANTENNA INSULATORS

To prevent loss of RF power, the antenna should be well insulated from ground, unless of course it is a shunt-fed system. This is particularly important at the outer end or ends of wire antennas, since these points are always at a comparatively high RF potential. If an antenna is to be installed indoors (in an attic, for instance) the antenna may be suspended directly from the wood rafters without additional insulation if the wood is permanently dry. Much greater care should be given to the selection of proper insulators when the antenna is located outside where it is exposed to wet weather.

Antenna insulators should be made of material that will not absorb moisture. The best insulators for antenna use are made of glass or glazed porcelain although plastic insulators are widely available and suitable for most antennas.

The length of an insulator relative to its surface area is indicative of its comparative voltage stand-off and RF

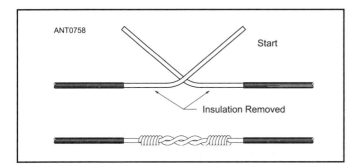

Figure 25.3 — Correct method of splicing antenna wire. Solder should be flowed into the wraps after the connection is completed. After cooling, the joint should be sprayed with acrylic to prevent oxidation and corrosion.

leakage abilities. A long thin insulator will have less leakage than a short thick insulator. Some antenna insulators are deeply ribbed to increase the surface leakage path without increasing the physical length of the insulator. Shorter insulators can be used at low-potential points, such as at the center of a dipole. If such an antenna is to be fed with open-wire line and used on several bands however, the center insulator should be the same as those used at the ends, because high RF potential may exist across the center insulator on some bands.

Insulator Stress

As with the antenna wire, the insulator must have sufficient physical strength to carry the mechanical load of the antenna without danger of breaking. Elastic line ("bungee cord" or "shock cord") or woven fishing line can provide long leakage paths and be used to provide both the end-insulator and support functions at antenna ends, subject to their ability to carry mechanical load. They are often used in antennas of the "invisible" type mentioned in the **Stealth Antennas** and **Portable Antennas** chapters. Abrasion between a woven line and a wire loop will cut through the line fairly quickly unless a fishing swivel or similar metal attachment point is used. Use of high power approaching and up to the US legal limit of 1500 W may cause sufficient leakage current to melt woven or monofilament line directly connected to a wire loop at the end of a dipole or similar antenna. A suitable antenna insulator as explained below must be used in this case.

For low-power operation with short antennas not subject to appreciable stress, almost any small plastic, glass, or glazed-porcelain insulator will do. Homemade insulators of plastic rod or sheet are usually satisfactory. Many plastics rated for outdoor use make good insulators — this includes Lucite (polycarbonate), Delrin, plexiglass, and even the high-density polyethylene (HDPE) used in cutting boards. More care is required in the selection of insulators for longer spans and higher transmitter power.

For a given material, the breaking tension of an insulator will be proportional to its cross-sectional area. It should be remembered that the wire hole at the end of the insulator decreases the effective cross-sectional area. For this reason, insulators designed to carry heavy strains are fitted with heavy metal end caps, the eyes being formed in the metal cap, rather than in the insulating material itself.

The following stress ratings of ceramic antenna insulators are typical:

- ⅝ inch square by 4 inches long — 400 pounds
- 1 inch diameter by 7 or 12 inches long — 800 pounds
- 1½ inches diameter by 8, 12 or 20 inches long, with special metal end caps — 5000 pounds

These are rated breaking tensions. The actual working tensions should be limited to not more than 25% of the breaking rating. Plastic insulators have significantly lower tension ratings.

The antenna wire should be attached to the insulators as shown in **Figure 25.4**. Care should be taken to avoid sharp angular bends in the wire when it is looped through the insulator eye. The loop should be generous enough in size that it will not bind the end of the insulator tightly. If the length of the antenna is critical, the length should be measured to the outward end of the loop, where it passes through the eye of the insulator. (See the note below about the loop area affecting the antenna's electrical length.) Soldering should be done as described earlier for the wire splice. If CCS wire is used, care should be taken to ensure insulator holes and edges are smooth. Any roughness at contact points between the wire and the insulator will cause the copper to be abraded away over time, exposing the wire's steel core and eventually leading to mechanical failure from rust. Assuming they are of sufficient size to handle the mechanical load, plastic insulators are a good choice for use with CCS wire.

Note that the large area of the loop through the insulator adds capacitance to the antenna. The larger the insulator loop, the more capacitance is created, and the greater its effect in lowering the resonant frequency of the antenna. This effect increases with operating frequency. When building a wire antenna, attach the insulators temporarily (without soldering) and adjust the resonant frequency of the antenna before soldering the insulator loop.

Strain Insulators

Strain or "egg" insulators have their holes at right angles, since they are designed to be connected as shown in **Figure 25.5**. It can be seen that this arrangement places the insulating material in compression rather than tension. An insulator connected this way can withstand very high mechanical load.

The principal attribute of strain insulators is that the wire will not fall or fail to carry load if the insulator breaks, since the two loops are interlocked. Insulator failure may go unnoticed however — strain insulators should be visually checked periodically. Because the wires are wrapped around each other, the leakage path is shorter than it would be otherwise and both leakage and capacitive end effects are higher compared to insulators where the wires are not interlinked. For this reason,

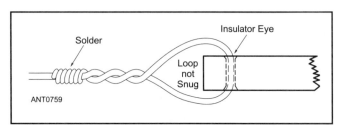

Figure 25.4 — When fastening antenna wire to an insulator, do not make the wire loop too snug. After the connection is complete, flow a non-acid core solder into the turns. When the joint has cooled completely, spray it with acrylic.

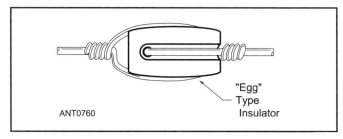

Figure 25.5 — Conventional manner of fastening wire to a strain insulator. This method decreases the leakage path and increases capacitance, as discussed in the text.

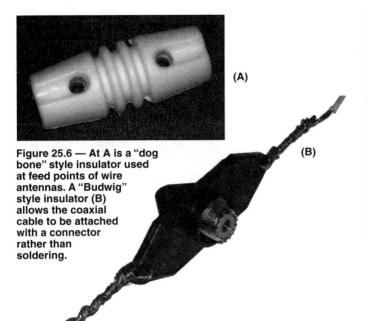

Figure 25.6 — At A is a "dog bone" style insulator used at feed points of wire antennas. A "Budwig" style insulator (B) allows the coaxial cable to be attached with a connector rather than soldering.

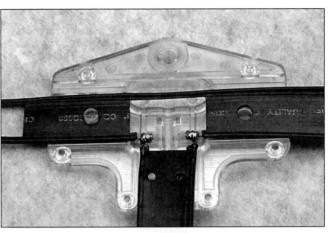

Figure 25.7 — The Ten-Tec "Acro-Bat" is made for attaching parallel-wire feed line to a wire antenna. It provides strain relief and reinforcement to the feed line to keep the conductors from breaking due to repeated flexing and bending in the wind.

strain insulators are typically confined to applications such as breaking up resonances in guy wires, where there is high mechanical load and where RF insulation is of minor importance.

Strain insulators are suitable for use at low-potential points on an antenna, such as at the center of a dipole. They may also be used at the ends of antennas used for low power operation.

Feed Point Insulators

Often referred to as "center insulators," the insulators used at the feed point of a wire antenna often have special features that help attach and support feed lines. A "dog bone" style insulator as in **Figure 25.6A** is the most common. To attach a coaxial feed line using this style of insulator, the cable's shield and center conductor are separated into "pigtails" that are soldered to the wire at each eye. The cable can be supported by looping it over the insulator and securing it with tape as shown in the figure. Note that the length of the separated shield and center conductor count as part of the antenna length — that may be significant at higher frequencies. The cable must be carefully waterproofed with a coating such as silicone sealant or Liquid Electrical Tape to prevent water from being wicked into the cable by the exposed shield. The "Budwig" style of insulator in Figure 25.6B includes an SO-239 so that the coaxial cable can be attached with a connector instead of soldered to the antenna. The PL-259 and exposed portion of the SO-239 connectors in this case should be waterproofed. This type of center insulator can be made from a PVC pipe cap or other plumbing fittings as shown later in this chapter.

Figure 25.7 shows a feed point insulator intended for use with parallel-wire feed line. The dog bone style of insulator may be used but cannot support the feed line in the same way as for coaxial cable. Parallel-wire line cannot be looped back on itself with the conductors close together. If left unsupported, the conductors of the feed line continually flex and bend in the wind which causes them to

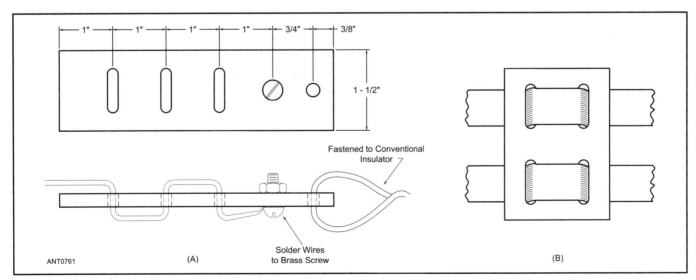

Figure 25.8 — At A, an insulator for the ends of folded dipoles, or multiple dipoles made of parallel-wire line. At B, a method of suspending one ribbon dipole from another in a multiband dipole system.

break. The tee-style of insulator in the figure captures the parallel-wire feed line and provides mechanical support, greatly reducing breakage.

Insulators for Ribbon-Line Antennas

Figure 25.8A shows the sketch of an insulator designed to be used at the ends of a folded dipole or a multiple dipole made of parallel conductor line. It should be made approximately as shown, out of insulating material about ¼ inch thick. The advantage of this arrangement is that the strain of the antenna is shared by the conductors and the plastic webbing of the line, which adds considerable strength. After soldering, the screw should be sprayed with acrylic.

Figure 25.8B shows a similar arrangement for suspending one dipole from another in a stagger-tuned dipole system. If better insulation is desired, these insulators can be wired to a conventional insulator.

Notes

Notes

Notes

Notes

Notes

Notes